THE
ROYAL BERKSHIRE
REGIMENT
(PRINCESS CHARLOTTE OF WALES'S)

THE
ROYAL BERKSHIRE
REGIMENT

(PRINCESS CHARLOTTE OF WALES'S)

BY
F. LORAINE PETRE, O.B.E.

1914—1918

The Naval & Military Press Ltd

Reproduced by kind permission of the Central Library,
Royal Military Academy, Sandhurst

Published by
The Naval & Military Press Ltd
Unit 10 Ridgewood Industrial Park,
Uckfield, East Sussex,
TN22 5QE England
Tel: +44 (0) 1825 749494
Fax: +44 (0) 1825 765701
www.naval–military-press.com
www.military-genealogy.com
www.militarymaproom.com

CONTENTS

THE ROYAL BERKSHIRE REGIMENT
1914–1918

CHAPTER XXVI

1ST BATTALION

PAGE

ALDERSHOT. DEPARTURE FOR FRANCE. THE RETREAT FROM MONS. THE AISNE. THE FIRST BATTLE OF YPRES. GIVENCHY. HULLUCH. CUINCHY. SOUCHEZ. THE SOMME. LONGUEVAL AND DELVILLE WOOD. SERRE. BOOM RAVINE. IRLES. OPPY. CAMBRAI. THE GERMAN OFFENSIVE. THE RETREAT TO THE ANCRE. THE FINAL BRITISH ADVANCE BY ERVILLERS AND ESCARMAIN. THE ARMISTICE. MARCH TO THE RHINE. NORTH PERSIA, 1919–21. BAGHDAD .

CHAPTER XXVII

2ND BATTALION

FROM INDIA. WINCHESTER. DEPARTURE FOR FRANCE. NEUVE CHAPELLE. LE BRIDOUX. THE SOMME FRONT. VERMELLES. BACK TO THE SOMME. THE ADVANCE TO THE HINDENBURG LINE. THE THIRD BATTLE OF YPRES. YPRES. THE GERMAN OFFENSIVE TOWARDS AMIENS. THE GERMAN ATTACK ON THE AISNE. THE FINAL BRITISH OFFENSIVE BY DOUAI. THE ARMISTICE. READING. THE DETACHMENT IN NORTH RUSSIA, 1919   65

CHAPTER XXVIII

3RD (SPECIAL RESERVE) BATTALION

MOBILIZATION AND EQUIPMENT OF RESERVISTS. DRAFTS. PORTSMOUTH. DUBLIN. STATISTICS. DEMOBILIZATION CENTRE   116

v

CONTENTS

CHAPTER XXIX

1ST/4TH (TERRITORIAL) BATTALION

MOBILIZATION. PORTSMOUTH. SWINDON. CHELMSFORD. ARRIVAL IN FRANCE. PLOEGSTEERT. HÉBUTERNE. POZIÈRES. THIEPVAL. ALBERT. THE SOMME. PÉRONNE. THE ADVANCE TO THE HINDENBURG LINE. ARRAS. YPRES. TRANSFERRED TO THE ITALIAN FRONT. THE ASIAGO PLATEAU. THE ASSAULT ON MONTE CATZ. THE ARMISTICE   120

CHAPTER XXX

2ND/4TH (TERRITORIAL) BATTALION

FORMATION AND SERVICE AT HOME. HITCHAM. MAIDENHEAD. NORTHAMPTON. CHELMSFORD. DEPARTURE FOR FRANCE. LAVENTIE. TRENCH RAIDS AND ATTACKS. VARENNES. THE ADVANCE TO THE HINDENBURG LINE. ARRAS. THE THIRD BATTLE OF YPRES. CAMBRAI. THE GERMAN OFFENSIVE. RETREAT FROM ST. QUENTIN. NIEPPE FOREST. THE FINAL ADVANCE. THE ARMISTICE   172

CHAPTER XXXI

5TH (SERVICE) BATTALION

FORMATION. SHORNCLIFFE. ALDERSHOT. THE BATTLE OF LOOS. GIVENCHY. THE SOMME. OVILLERS. POSIÈRES. ARRAS. CAMBRAI. BÉTHUNE. AVELUY. THE GERMAN OFFENSIVE. BEAUMONT HAMEL. THE FINAL ADVANCE BY EPÉHY. THE ARMISTICE. THE KING'S COLOUR PRESENTED. THE RETURN HOME. READING   205

CHAPTER XXXII

6TH (SERVICE) BATTALION

FORMATION. SHORNCLIFFE. COLCHESTER. SALISBURY PLAIN. THE BATTLE OF THE SOMME. MONTAUBAN. LONGUEVAL AND DELVILLE WOOD. THIEPVAL. BOOM RAVINE. IRLES. THE THIRD BATTLE OF YPRES. GLENCORSE WOOD. POELCAPPELLE. HOUTHULST FOREST. DISBANDMENT AND DISTRIBUTION   248

CHAPTER XXXIII

7TH (SERVICE) BATTALION

FORMATION. READING. SALISBURY PLAIN. WARMINSTER. ARRIVAL IN FRANCE. TRANSFERRED TO SALONIKA. THE DOIRAN-VARDAR FRONT. THE FIRST BATTLE OF DOIRAN. EAST OF DOIRAN LAKE. ON THE VARDAR. RAIDS. THE FINAL ADVANCE AND OCCUPATION OF BULGARIA. IZLIS. THE ARMISTICE. SERVICE IN THE CAUCASUS AND CONSTANTINOPLE. DEMOBILIZATION   286

CHAPTER XXXIV

8TH (SERVICE) BATTALION

FORMATION. SALISBURY PLAIN. READING. WARMINSTER. ARRIVAL IN FRANCE. THE BATTLE OF LOOS. TRENCH WARFARE. THE BATTLE OF THE SOMME. CONTALMAISON. BAZENTIN-LE-PETIT. MAMETZ. NEAR PÉRONNE. NIEUPORT AND THE COAST. POELCAPPELLE. HOUTHULST FOREST. SOUTH OF THE SOMME. THE GERMAN OFFENSIVE. THE DEFENCE OF AMIENS. THE FINAL ADVANCE. OVILLERS. TRÔNES WOOD. ST. PIERRE VAAST. EPÉHY. MORMAL FOREST. THE ARMISTICE. DISBANDMENT   318

CHAPTER XXXV

9TH (RESERVE) BATTALION

FORMATION. PORTSMOUTH. BOVINGTON CAMP. BECOMES 37TH TRAINING RESERVE BATTALION   374

10TH (LABOUR) BATTALION

FORMATION. PORTSMOUTH. PORT DUTIES AT ROUEN. REORGANIZATION   374

11TH, 12TH, 13TH (LABOUR) BATTALIONS

FORMATION. INCORPORATION IN THE LABOUR CORPS   376

1ST GARRISON BATTALION

FORMATION AND DISBANDMENT   376

CONTENTS

APPENDICES

PAGE

I	Succession of Colonels .	379
II	Sanctioned Establishments	380
III	Uniform and Equipment	388
IV	The Colours .	400
	Battle Honours . .	402
V	Old Comrades Association	406
VI	Banner for the Commemoration of the First Seven Divisions.	408
VII	Mess Plate and Furniture	409

Index   411

PLATES

	TO FACE PAGE
1ST BATTALION, 1914	1
SECOND-LIEUTENANT A. B. TURNER, V.C.	22
LANCE-CORPORAL J. WELCH, V.C.	34
2ND BATTALION, 1910 .	64
3RD BATTALION, 1913 .	116
1ST/4TH BATTALION, 1915	120
2ND/4TH BATTALION, 1915	172
5TH BATTALION, 1915 .	204
6TH BATTALION, 1915 .	248
7TH BATTALION .	286
8TH BATTALION, 1915 .	318

MAPS

	PAGE
THE YPRES SALIENT . . .	11
THE WESTERN FRONT, 1914–1918.	19
BAPAUME—ALBERT .	26
BOURLON WOOD .	39
ARRAS—BAPAUME	55
THE SOMME . .	100
THE CAMPAIGN IN ITALY	168
ITALY, N.E. .	171
ESTAIRES—BÉTHUNE	201
LA BASSÉE—LOOS	210
CAMBRAI	229
MACEDONIA (THE VARDAR FRONT)	297

THE GREAT WAR
1914—1918

INTRODUCTION

THE Royal Berkshire Regiment was represented at the front in the Great War by eight battalions, of which the 1st and 2nd were Regulars of the old Army, the 1/4th and 2/4th Territorials, and the 5th, 6th, 7th and 8th were " Service " Battalions. The Regiment was almost entirely employed on the Western Front in France and Belgium, though the 1/4th finished its war service in Italy. The only battalion which served in a " side show " was the 7th, which, after a few weeks in France learning its work, was sent off to Salonika and remained there till the end of the war, taking part in the final operations which brought Bulgaria to her knees in 1918.

In dealing with the history of a regiment with several battalions engaged, and no two of them ever in the same brigade or division together, it seems impossible to give anything like a complete history of each unit, except by treating the story of each separately, without reference to the others. In order, however, to correlate them to one another a table is attached to this note showing month by month, from the time when there began to be more than two at the front, the relative general positions of those on the Western Front.

The chapter on the 1/4th Battalion has been contributed by Mr. Cruttwell, formerly an officer in it, who has already published a more detailed history of this unit.

The War on the Western, Italian, and Greek Fronts differed widely from all previous wars and has been described rather as a siege on a gigantic scale than an ordinary war. The periods during which there was a real war of movement were few and far between.

During the long intervals between the violent episodes of open fighting, the adversaries resembled two boxers or wrestlers, each searching for an opening to attack his adversary and endeavour to bring the struggle to a bloody and decisive conclusion. Of the intervals of trench warfare it would be wearisome, and beyond our limits of space to narrate the daily events which are recorded in the War Diaries. There is a terrible sameness in the story they tell.

Life in trenches was of the same general complexion everywhere, though the degree of discomfort and danger varied from one part of the front to another. The awful wet in the waterlogged trenches of Flanders made them the worst part of the front, where reliefs had to be more frequent, because it was simply out of the question to keep men in them for the periods which were possible in a drier part, where accidents of ground surface made drainage feasible, and enabled really good trenches and dugouts to be made. There was, too, a remarkable sameness about the daily incidents. Casualties in the trenches varied from day to day. There would perhaps be several days with only a very few casualties, followed by one of more serious loss when a shell pitched in the middle of a relief in progress, or caught men seeking shelter in a dugout or a cellar.

There were other interruptions of the monotony of trench life when, instead of the daily and nightly patrols, one side or the other made a more extensive attempt to gather information by the capture of prisoners, or even to storm trenches which were dangerous or troublesome.

It is to these larger raids, and to the great battles, that we must chiefly confine our attention.

TABLE SHOWING THE RELATIVE POSITIONS OF THE SEVERAL BATTALIONS ON THE
WESTERN FRONT IN EACH MONTH FROM JUNE, 1915

All that is indicated is roughly the part of the front on which each battalion was
about the same time

Battn.	1st.	2nd.	1st/4th.	2nd/4th.	5th.	6th.	8th.
Month.	**1915**						
June	Ypres and Cuinchy	Neuve Chapelle	Ploegsteert	At home	Armentières	At home	Vermelles
July .	Givenchy	Somme	Béthune		,,	,,	Loos
August	..	Vermelles	Hébuterne		Ploegsteert	Bray-sur-Somme	Loos and Lillers
Sept. .	Hulluch		,,		,,	Albert	,,
October	Béthune				Loos	,,	
Nov. .	Cuinchy	,,			,,		
Dec. .	Annequin	Sercus		,,	Béthune		
	1916						
Jan. .	Le Touret	Estaires			Lillers	Albert	
Feb. .	Souchez					,,	
March .	..	,,				Corbie	
April .		N. of Albert				Méricourt	
May .		,,	,,	,,	,,	,,	,,
June .			Abbeville and Sailly	Laventie	Loos	Carnoy, etc.	Somme Front
July .	Longueval	Ovillers and Béthune	Pozières		Albert		Contalmaison
August	Longueval and Hébuterne	Vermelles			Pozières	Godewaerswalde	
Sept .	Serre		Thiepval		Arras	Aveluy	,,
October	..		Albert		Flers and Mametz	Courcelette	Somme, back areas
Nov .		Somme Front		Bouzincourt	East of Arras		..
Dec. .		,,		Aveluy and Varennes	..	Abbeville	Bazentin

Battn.	1st.	2nd.	1st/4th.	2nd/4th.	5th.	6th.	8th.
Month			**1917**				
Jan. .	Ovillers	Somme Front	Somme	Somme	Arras	Upper Ancre	Albert
Feb. .	Cource-lette	..		Péronne		..	S. of Pér-onne
March .	,,	Moislains	Péronne			Aveluy	,,
April .	Ancre and Bailleul	Metz en Couture	..	,,		Lumbres and Loos	
May .	Oppy	Various moves	Hermies	Arras		Arras	
June .	,,	,,	,,	,,		St. Amand	Nieuport
July .	Cambrin and Anne-quin	Ypres	Arras and Winne-zeek	Moving north		Ypres	,,
August	,,		Ypres	Ypres			Le Clipon
Sept. .	Givenchy		,,	,,	,,	,,	,,
October	Auchel		Arras	Arras	,,	,,	Ypres
Nov. .	Herzeele and Bourlon		To Italy for rest of War	,,	Villers Guis-lain	Houthulst Forest	,,
Dec. .	Lebuc-quiere			Cambrai Front	Béthune		

INTRODUCTION

Battn.	1st.	2nd.	1st/4th.	2nd/4th.	5th.	6th.	8th.

1918

Battn.	1st.	2nd.	1st/4th.	2nd/4th.	5th.	6th.	8th.
Jan.	Cambrai salient	Ypres		Near St. Quentin	Fleur-baix	Houthulst Forest	Houthulst Forest
Feb.	,,	,,		,,	,,	Disbanded	,,
March	Retreat to An-cre	Chaulnes and re-treat		Retreat towards Amiens	Aveluy		Retreat from S.E. of Amiens
April	Arras	Villers Bret-ton-neux		Albert	Albert		E. of Amiens
May		On the Aisne		Robecq	N. of Albert		
June		Near Dieppe			Bouzin-court		
July		St. Eloi			Vigna-court		
Aug. to Nov.	Final advance by Er-villers, Flesqui-ères and Escar-main	Final advance by Vimy, Douai and the Scarpe		Final advance S. of Cambrai to St. Aubert	Final advance by Car-noy, Epéhy and Vieux Condé		Final advance from Albert by Com-bles, Epéhy and Mor-mal Forest

1st BATTALION.

Aldershot, 12th August 1914.

(*Back Row, Standing*) 2nd Lt. G. Moore. Lt. A. H. Hanbury-Sparrow. 2nd Lt. J. Ransom. Lt. R. G. Perkins. Lt. C. P. Wheeler. J. H. Woods.
(*Second Row, Sitting*) Lt. and Adj. A. H. Perrott. Lt. Y. R. D. Wigan (Special Reserve, attached). Lt. P. J. Reeves. Lt. U. S. Hopkins. Lt. A. P. J. Hibbert. Lt.
E. A. B. Orr. Lt. T. V. B. Denniss. Lt. C. Fullbrook-Leggatt. Capt. B. G. Bromhead. Lt. G. H. Bishop (3rd Bn., attached). Lt. E. E. N. Burney. Lt. C. W. Frizell.
(*Front Row, Sitting*) Capt. H. H. Shott, D.S.O. Capt. L. H. Birt. Major A. Scott-Turner. Maj.-Gen. E. T. Dickson. Lt.-Col. M. D. Graham. Major D. B. Maurice,
D.S.O. Major F. F. Ready, D.S.O. Capt. T. E. Carew-Hunt. Lt. and Q.M. F. Batt. Med. Officer.
Note.—Major H. M. Finch, 2nd in command, also embarked with the Battalion.

THE ROYAL BERKSHIRE REGIMENT

CHAPTER XXVI

THE 1st BATTALION.

THE RETREAT FROM MONS. THE AISNE. THE FIRST BATTLE OF YPRES

1914

THE First Battalion was, as we know, at Aldershot when war was declared against Germany on the 4th August 1914. Orders for mobilization were received at 5.30 p.m. on that day, and the battalion was ready to start for the front on the 11th, when it was inspected by the King and Queen. The first train conveying it left Farnborough at 10.27 a.m. on the 12th, and was followed by the second at 11.39 a.m.

The officers with the battalion were the following :

Lieut.-Colonel M. D. Graham.
Major H. M. Finch.
   ,, D. B. Maurice, D.S.O.
   ,, F. F. Ready, D.S.O.
Captain T. E. C. Hunt.
   ,, B. G. Bromhead.
   ,, L. H. Birt.
   ,, H. H. Shott, D.S.O.
Lieutenant E. A. B. Orr.
   ,, U. S. Hopkins.
      C. W. Frizell.
      P. J. Reeves.
      C. St. Q. O. Fullbrook-Leggatt.
      C. P. Wheeler.
   ,, J. H. Woods.
   ,, A. A. H. Hanbury-Sparrow.

Second-Lieutenant T. V. B. Denniss.
     ,,   A. P. J. Hibbert.
     ,,   E. E. N. Burney.
Lieutenant A. H. Perrott, Adjutant.
Lieutenant and Quartermaster F. Batt.

Attached.

Major A. S. Turner,	2nd Battalion.
Second-Lieutenant J. Ransom,	,,
Lieutenant G. H. Bishop,	3rd Battalion.
Second-Lieutenant Y. R. D. Wigan,	Special Reserve.
,, G. Moore,	,,

Southampton was reached the same afternoon, and the battalion, embarking on the S.S. *Ardmore*, was at Rouen and marched to the camp de Bruyères three miles off on the 13th. Leaving Rouen by train on the 15th, it passed through Amiens, detrained at Wassigny, and marched to camp at Venerolles, where it was training till the 21st, when it marched eleven miles to billets at Landrecies. On the 22nd it marched to billets at Hargnies.

The battalion was one unit of the 6th Infantry Brigade commanded by Brigadier-General R. H. Davies, C.B. The other battalions of the brigade were the 1st King's (Liverpool Regiment), 2nd South Staffordshire Regiment and 1st King's Royal Rifle Corps.

The other brigades of the 2nd Division (commanded by Major-General C. Monro, C.B.) were the 4th (Guards) and 5th.

On the 22nd August the battalion passed the Belgian Frontier at Gognies, on the road from Maubeuge to Mons.

It was ordered to occupy a position at Villereuile-le-Sec, about five miles S.E. of Mons. The rest of the brigade were at Harmignies, Estinne, and Givry. The 1st Royal Berkshire was entrenched at 3 p.m. on the 23rd, and an hour later heavy artillery fire was heard from the direction of Mons, and German cavalry were reported towards Bray in the east. For four hours the battalion was under heavy shell fire, but, beyond this, played no part in the battle of the 23rd August. The casualties were slight—Second-Lieutenant T. V. B. Denniss and three men wounded. The ensuing night was quiet.

At 5 a.m. on the 24th orders to retire were received. No casualties were incurred, but, owing to the scattered trenches, eighty thousand rounds of rifle ammunition had to be abandoned. The Berkshire Battalion and the 1st King's Royal Rifle Corps passed back through the 2nd South Staffordshire, and took up a position at Ihy, continuing later to half a mile east of Bavai, where they arrived at 6 p.m., one company being posted to cover them.

At 3 a.m. on the 25th the battalion again stood to arms, with orders to hold on to Bavai till the rest of the brigade had cleared it on the Pont-sur-Sambre Road. Acting as rearguard of the 6th Infantry Brigade, the battalion covered the retreat as far as Pont-sur-Sambre, a march of fourteen miles. Here it passed through the 5th Brigade to billets at Maroilles, three miles east of Landrecies. About 8 p.m. "B" Company, under Major Turner, was ordered to return to the bridge on the Sambre, two miles N.W. of Maroilles, and relieve a party of the 15th Hussars which was holding it. The company was somewhat delayed by the congestion of transport, in Maroilles, and when it approached the bridge it found that it had already been captured from the Hussars. "B" Company deployed on the British side of the bridge and reconnoitred, with a view to finding a means of recapturing it. During this reconnaissance, Major Turner was taken prisoner. Meanwhile, "D" Company, under Major Maurice, with Captain Shott, Lieutenant Hanbury-Sparrow, and Lieutenant Fulbrook-Leggatt,* was ordered up to the bridge, which it reached about midnight. Lieutenant Fulbrook-Leggatt, with No. 13 Platoon, was ordered to protect the left flank, north of the Maroilles Road, "B" Company being then on the right. On this platoon a considerable rifle fire was opened by the Germans at the bridge three hundred yards away on its right flank.

The platoon was then called in to rejoin "D" on the road, and took position at the head of the company, in fours, facing the bridge. Meanwhile, Captain Shott appears to have gone forward alone to reconnoitre the position. He has never been seen or heard of since.

The position was very obscure when "D" was ordered to advance on the bridge by the road. The advance was in file, with "C," which had now come up, alongside in the same formation. The road was only about

---

* To this officer, who was recommended for the "Croix de Chevalier" for his gallantry, we are indebted for a fuller account of the action than is given in the diary.

twelve feet wide, with ditches on either side about ten feet wide and three feet deep.   Along this defile Major Finch and Major Maurice led an advance which from the first appeared to be a desperate venture.   Men began to fall at once under a fire, from the bridge along the defile, increasing in severity.   When fifty yards had been covered, the advance was checked. There was some disorder, and men sought cover by lying down on the sides of the road.   When they had been again collected, an attempt was made to continue the advance at the double.   The enemy's fire was now so heavy that very little further progress could be made.   Finally, the companies were ordered to withdraw, which they did in good order, carrying their wounded with them.   This attack by night, without proper reconnaissance, along a defile, and with tired, wet, and hungry men, was almost bound to fail with heavy loss.

The casualties were :

Officers.   Missing : Major A. S. Turner, Capt. H. H. Shott, D.S.O.
              (believed killed).
       Wounded : Lieut. Hopkins (slightly).
Other Ranks : Killed 2 ; Wounded 35 ; Missing 22.

That night the battalion bivouacked at Venerolles.   The retreat continued on the succeeding days, without any noticeable incident for the 1st Royal Berkshire, viâ Guise, Mont d'Origny and Amigny to Chauny. There the battalion temporarily took position to guard the bridge over the Oise, which was prepared for demolition.   This was on the 29th August. By the 1st September, Coucy le Château, Soissons and Baudry had been passed, and Thury was reached in the morning.   The 4th (Guards) Brigade, acting as rearguard of the 2nd Division, had fought an action against very superior numbers in the forest N.E. of Villers Cotterets, and about 1 p.m. the 5th and 6th Brigades were called back to cover their retreat.   Two companies of the 1st Royal Berkshire were deployed on either flank of a battery about a mile south of Villers Cotterets.   Here they were attacked by the pursuing Germans, whom they beat off with a loss in the battalion of one officer (not named)* and one man killed, and twenty-three other ranks wounded.   Next day the retreat continued through Panchard, where

---

* No Berkshire officer is shown on the Roll of Honour as killed on the 1st September. Probably, therefore, this was an officer attached.

the battalion had an inconvenient loss in the shape of nine hundred and twenty greatcoats, which were turned off the ambulance wagons on which they were to make room for wounded. The weather was at present very hot, but the loss would be severely felt with a drop in the temperature.

Passing through Meaux and crossing the Marne, the 1st Royal Berkshire was near St. Simeon on the left bank of the Grand Morin on the 7th September, the farthest point reached in the great retreat, the inevitable depression of which was now turned into the joy of advance. The battalion, which was now in the general-reserve of the 2nd Division, and had been reinforced up to its original strength, started its advance at 5 a.m. on the 8th, passing both the Morin streams that day and reaching La Noue. The Guards Brigade had been in action all day, but the Royal Berkshire were behind and not engaged. On the 9th the Marne was passed unopposed, at Charly-sur-Marne, by a barricaded but intact bridge.

After passing the Marne, the advance continued to Coupru.

On the 10th the battalion fought its first action since the end of the retreat. On this day the 6th Brigade acted as divisional advanced-guard, the 1st Royal Berkshire leading, with a section of Royal Horse Artillery and another of a Field Battery. At 9.15 a.m., as it approached Hautevesnes, a German column, chiefly transport, was seen moving on Chézy on the left front. The Royal Berkshire pushed forward and made good on the north side of Hautevesnes, whilst the artillery came into action S.W. of the village. At this moment a German column, evidently a rearguard, was seen marching northwards.

The battalion deployed for action against the Germans who took up a strong position in a sunken road, supported by four guns north of Brumetz. On its right was the 1st King's Royal Rifle Corps, and on its left two companies of the South Staffordshire Regiment. The advance of the battalion was directed on St. Gengoulph, and by 11 a.m. the Germans found themselves pinned to their position by the accuracy of the British fire at a range of seven hundred yards, and in danger of envelopment from the north, where the Royal Berkshire were advancing from St. Gengoulph. Under these circumstances they surrendered—four or five hundred of them. At the beginning of the action, part of the Germans had escaped by Chézy, but eventually fell into the hands of the 3rd Division. The action had established the superiority of the British rifle fire, especially of the King's Royal Rifle Corps, who bore the brunt of the fighting in the open against the enemy in the sunken road. They had the heaviest losses. The 1st Royal Berkshire lost:

Killed : Lieut. and Adjutant A. H. Perrott and 1 man.
Other Ranks : Wounded : 23.

The march to Les Crouttes on the 11th, and the passage of the Vesle on the 12th were unopposed, and on the 13th the brigade was halted at Vieil Arcy, on the southern slope of the Aisne Valley, during the construction of a pontoon bridge at Pont Arcy.

The fine weather had now broken with a heavy downpour of rain, and the loss of the greatcoats on the 2nd September was badly felt.

On the 14th the battalion, acting as vanguard of the brigade, was across the Pont Arcy pontoon bridge by 5 a.m. and moved on to Moussy on the other side of the Aisne Canal, where it found the 5th Brigade holding a line from the lime tree north of Verneuil, south-westwards to Soupir across the canal. So far, the 5th had protected the advance of the 6th Brigade, which now passed through. The advance was with two companies 1st King's Royal Rifle Corps on each flank of the Royal Berkshire, and the South Staffordshire in support. The troops were heavily shelled from the heights about Braye as they moved up the steep spurs and valleys leading up to the ridge along which runs the famous Chemin des Dames. The right flanking company, though reinforced by the South Staffordshire, could make little way. This was at a line about half-way from Moussy to Braye.

The advance was continued, under stronger artillery support, at 10.30 a.m. The Royal Berkshire moved up the valley in which is the Aisne et Oise Canal, with their left protected by two companies of the King's Royal Rifle Corps.

On their right were the King's Liverpool, and beyond them the other two King's Royal Rifle Corps companies on the Moussy spur. The centre and left of the line outstripped the right, and by noon the Berkshire Battalion was at the foot of the spur leading down east of Braye. Here, under fire from tiers of trenches in front and on the right, they were held up. The right companies of the King's Royal Rifle Corps had been repulsed by a counter attack.   They were pushed back to a line abreast of Beaune, only half a mile in front of Moussy. Here, with the assistance of the Worcestershire Regiment (5th Brigade), they were able to hold on.

The wet night which ensued was spent in digging in behind the battle outposts—" A " and " B " Companies.   The casualties of this day were :

Killed : 2nd-Lieut. R. G. B. Perkins and 1 man.

Wounded : Lieut. U. S. Hopkins, 2nd-Lieut. T. R. D. Wigan.

Other Ranks : Wounded : 37.

The position remained unchanged on the 15th.   There was heavy shelling all day, and La Metz Farm, in which were Battalion Head-quarters, was twice hit.

On the left the two companies of the Rifle Corps had joined up with the Guards Brigade, who were slowly advancing.   The casualties of this day were one man killed ; Second-Lieutenant A. P. J. Hibbert, and eight other ranks wounded.   No advance was found possible on the following days, on all of which casualties occurred from German fire.   Between the 16th and the 20th, eleven other ranks were killed and fifty-eight wounded—most of them on the 19th, when the Germans made a weak counter attack.   There were more counter attacks on the 20th and 21st, in which the Royal Berkshire, who did not get so much of them as the battalions on their flanks, lost six killed and thirty-one wounded of other ranks.

It has been stated that the 16th September 1914 marked the beginning of trench warfare on the Western Front, and between the 14th and 28th of that month there was practically no change in the general position.

On the 23rd command of the 6th Brigade passed from Brigadier-General Davies to Brigadier-General Fanshawe.   Beyond the ordinary incidents of trench warfare, there is nothing worthy of record till the 13th October, when the battalion started to join in the " Race for the Sea."   On that day it was relieved by the 239th French Infantry, went into billets at Bourg, and next day entrained at Fismes for the north.   Passing by St. Denis, Amiens, Abbeville, Boulogne, Calais, and St. Omer, it was in billets at Hazebrouck on the 17th, at Godewaerswelde on the 19th, and reached Ypres on the 20th October.

Next day the battalion marched out of Ypres north-eastwards by St. Jean to Wieltje, where the brigade was in support of the attack then being made along the Ypres-Passchendaele Road by the 5th Brigade on the north, and the 4th (Guards) Brigade on the south. The 6th Brigade was told off to support the Guards Brigade, and moved forward one and a half miles on this day to bivouac for the night. The Royal Berkshire was detached from the rest of the 6th, and placed under orders of the General-Officer-Commanding the Guards Brigade.

At 7 a.m. on the 22nd " B " Company, under Captain Lucas, was ordered to dig trenches near Zonnebeke, in rear of the right of the Guards. Captain Lucas had only joined the Regiment at the front on the 7th October, having been detained at the coast on disembarkation duty. For the short time he was with it we have the advantage of his private diary to supplement that of the battalion. His company was slightly shelled on the 23rd, but there were only three casualties. The whole battalion was reunited north of Frezenberg on the 24th.

At 9 a.m. orders were received to drive out the Germans, who had broken into the woods about Westhoek.

As this had already been done by the 5th Brigade before the arrival of the 6th, the latter was ordered to take over trenches from the 22nd Brigade. Before this was finished, orders came to attack. " B " Company, on the left, had to keep touch in that direction with a French brigade, and on its right with " D " Company, beyond which was the Liverpool Regiment. " B " was supported by " A," " D " by " C." The attack started at 3.30 p.m. and the fire which met it was generally high over the heads of the first line. The ridge running from Zonnebeke S.E. to Becelaere was reached by " B " without serious opposition. Here, as a heavy rifle fire from a hedge three hundred yards in front was encountered, the men threw themselves into the ditch of the road. " D " had been held up by fire from houses on its right, and had not advanced as fast as " B." The French, too, on the left, had been held up. When " D " came up into line, defensive flanks had to be thrown back on its right, and on the left of " B." As ill luck would have it, two burning farms in rear showed up the men on the skyline, and four officers were hit during the night (Capt. Quarry, Lieuts. Nicholson, Hanbury-Sparrow, and Second-Lieut. Warner). Attempts by the enemy to deceive the troops by sounding the British " Retire," and representing themselves as Belgians, failed ignominiously.

During the 25th the battalion's trenches were heavily shelled all day. A German battery, unlimbered, was discovered about six hundred yards to the N.E. The Germans, trying to remove it, had all their teams shot down by rifle fire from " D " Company's trenches. They then managed to man-handle five of the guns away, but suffered so severely in doing so that they left the sixth.

Meanwhile, the French on the left had come forward and were up to the line of the Becelaere-Passchendaele Road by evening.

Captain Lucas' diary tells a story of Second-Lieutenant Gross going down the road towards the left of " B." He met a truculent German officer, who had no idea the British were on the road, and promptly took him prisoner.

During the day " D " discovered a German trench at right angles to their own. Every German who tried to run away was killed, and others in the trench. Eventually the remaining fifty of the garrison surrendered.

The battalion had orders to push on as the French came up ; but, as the latter had gone too much to the right and went through the British left, the confusion which would have ensued from advancing in the midst of them was avoided by " B " holding fast. They did not succeed in getting any farther forward for the day.

On this evening Captain O. Steele, whilst reorganizing his company in its trenches, was blown to pieces by a " Black Maria."

Though the shell pitched right in the middle of and buried five men, curiously enough none was hurt in body.

During the night Sergeant Taylor and a party went out and brought in the gun which the Germans had been unable to remove.

On the 26th, when Second-Lieutenant Gross was wounded, Captain Lucas was the only officer left with " B."

On the 27th the battalion was ordered to advance and support the right of an attack by the South Staffordshire. About five hundred yards were gained, and the Royal Berkshire entrenched, with the Liverpool Regiment on its right and South Staffordshire on the left. The left of " B " and the right of the Staffordshire Regiment were in an almost impenetrable wood, and separated by two hundred yards till the gap was filled by part of " A."

On the 28th the 5th Brigade attempted an attack through the 6th, but never went beyond the trenches of the latter. " B " suffered but little this day. The trenches they had occupied were very visible to the enemy, so they dug a new one twenty yards in front and used the earth to make a parapet to the old one. On that the enemy expended most of his rifle fire, thinking the British were behind it, whilst they were lying snugly in the new one. That night the Royal Berkshire were relieved and went back to brigade reserve.

The casualties on the 24th–26th were :

Officers. Killed :   Capt. O. Steele.
     Wounded : Capt. Quarry,
          Lieuts. Nicholson, Hanbury-Sparrow,
          2nd-Lieuts. Warner, Gross.
Other Ranks :   Killed 16, Wounded 48 (and on the 26th Killed 9,
          Wounded 8).

On the 27th the losses were : Other Ranks Killed, 4, and Wounded, 23.

On the 30th, on a report (denied later) that the enemy were breaking through between the Connaught Rangers and the Highland Light Infantry, a company of the Berkshire was sent up to reinforce. All that we know of this is contained in the words of the Brigade Diary. " This company of the Berks did very good service, and, under Colonel Graham's guidance, cleared several houses on the Becelaere Road, and placed an advanced post in one."

The Battalion Diary merely records that " B " Company moved to the top of the ridge. Captain Lucas says the same.

Meanwhile, the Worcestershire Regiment and the Guards had held Gheluvelt on the 30th, but were being withdrawn on the 31st. In the evening of the 31st their flank was being turned as they withdrew. " A " and " B " Companies of the Royal Berkshire were then in Polygon Wood, under Major Finch, acting as reserve to the 1st Division. They were not aware that the evacuation of Gheluvelt had been ordered when, about 3.30 p.m. on the 31st, they were hurriedly turned out to eject some Germans who had managed to get in rear of the Guards.

The companies moved up, " B " leading. As they approached the railway line just west of Gheluvelt, they were met by a heavy fire from

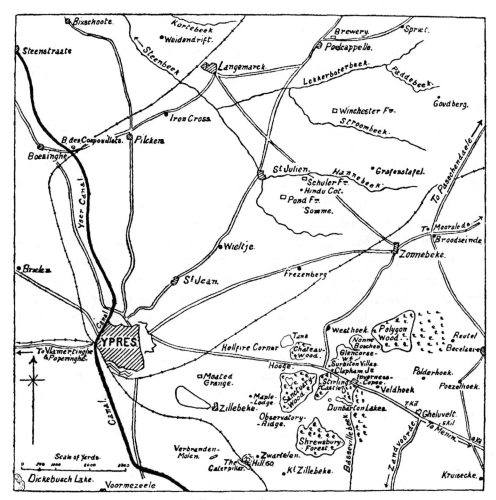

THE YPRES SALIENT

behind the embankment. This they charged and reached, but found themselves on the near side with only about one foot of cover between them and the Germans beyond, whom they could hear shouting and digging. In this position the Royal Berkshire had some casualties, including three sergeants. Captain Lucas had a bullet through his clothes which slightly grazed him.

Some of " A " were then sent round across the railway on the right, where there were no Germans, to turn the flank of those behind the embankment. They were unable to do anything in the thick wood. By midnight, when orders were received to withdraw, the Germans in front had disappeared, which was fortunate as, had they been there, within fifteen yards of the British, there must have been heavy casualties in retiring. All, including the wounded, were brought back safely.

On 1st November " D " Company joined the detachment under Major Finch as a further reinforcement from the 6th Infantry Brigade.

On the 2nd November at 8 a.m. Colonel Graham was badly wounded by a shell, and Major Finch took over command. For the events of this day we are dependent on Captain Lucas, by whom the following account is given :

It now transpired that only one weak French battalion had passed through on this front and had come to a standstill a short distance ahead.

Half " A " Company, under Second-Lieutenant Cruise, was then sent up the left of the Ypres-Menin Road, and eventually lined the road facing south near the French battalion. Shortly after, the other half-company, under Lieutenant Woods, was sent up to try and retake the trenches immediately to the left of the road, but could not get farther than the hedges of some enclosures about four hundred yards to their front. Here they remained all day.

Heavy firing was kept up, but the Germans did not press the advance further. Orders were received that at dusk, on the whistle sounding, the whole line would push forward and retake the original trenches.

On the whistle sounding, those who could be collected from " A " Company, and forty men of the Gloucestershire Regiment, all under Lieutenant Woods, advanced on the left of the road, and those of " B " Company, under Captain Lucas, on the right. Major Finch accompanied " A " Company.

By this time of the day all units were thoroughly disorganized, and these officers moved forward with odds and ends, including the French, who had attached themselves from various units. The majority of the men had little heart in the attack after their trying experiences of the day. The advance, however, appears to have taken the Germans completely by surprise, and the few men who persevered managed to recapture a considerable portion of the original trenches. Germans were seen running out of the houses in all directions, and a number were killed and a few captured. " A " and " B " Companies were now isolated. Some lengths of trench on the left of the road between " A " and " B " Companies were still occupied by Germans, and others soon began to move forward again round the right and rear of " B " Company. Captain Lucas went back to try and collect some men with whom to clear the trenches on his right. He met Brigadier-General FitzClarence (the Brigade Commander) coming up to relieve the situation with some fifty stragglers he had collected. These were handed over to Captain Lucas who pushed them forward to within a hundred yards of the trenches, where the impetus of the advance died out. He then went for further help to a farm on his right rear, which was reported to be held by the French, but found it was now held by the Germans. As further assistance was not forthcoming, he went off to find Major Finch for further instructions. Major Finch was eventually found, holding the " A " Company trenches mentioned above, with the Germans holding the continuation of them on both flanks. The time was now 9.30 p.m. and Major Finch had just received orders to withdraw to the dug-outs occupied in the morning. The companies were withdrawn without further casualties, thanks probably to the utter exhaustion of the enemy.

As for " D " Company, which was in the trench beyond those in which the Rifle Corps men had been captured, it held out splendidly all day under Second-Lieutenant Stokes, often under heavy enfilade fire. When all the companies were withdrawn after 9.30 p.m., the line was readjusted so as to run just east of Veldhoek Wood, the Royal Berkshire taking over the section immediately north of the Menin Road. There is no full list of casualties on this day in the diary, which only mentions that Major Finch, Lieutenant Frizell, and Second-Lieutenant Knott * were wounded.

* This officer (then C.S.M.) had only received a commission for good work on the 30th October. Sergt.-Major Vesey and C.S.M. Cruise had received commissions at the same time.

On the 3rd November Major Finch had to go to hospital, and command of the battalion passed to Captain Lucas, as next senior officer. The shelling was extra heavy on the 4th, and caused twenty-one casualties, including Second-Lieutenant Cruise, wounded. " C " Company, which has not been mentioned in the account of the fighting on the 2nd, was then, and still was, under the orders of the officer commanding the South Staffordshire near Broodseinde. It, with " A " and " B," returned to the 6th Infantry Brigade on the 4th.

On the 6th Second-Lieutenant Waghorn was killed by a shell. On the 7th there were two alarms of Germans breaking through, but no fighting was required of the Royal Berkshire, and nothing noticeable happened till the 12th, when the French on the left of the South Staffordshire lost some trenches and were driven back about five hundred yards, exposing the left flank of the 6th Brigade line beyond the Broodseinde to Becelaere Road, and necessitating its withdrawal in the night to a fresh line just east of that road. Second-Lieutenant Vesey was wounded on the 13th, so that all the three who had received commissions on the 30th October had now been wounded.

On the 15th the brigade was relieved by French troops and went into divisional reserve at Hooge, moving on the 17th to Ypres, and on the 18th to billets at Caestre in the back area, where the battalion remained refitting and training till the 21st December. It had had many compliments on its recent behaviour from everybody up to the Corps Commander, which culminated in the Brigadier's words, as it marched past him into Caestre, " Splendid ! just as you have always fought."

On the 22nd December the battalion left the Ypres neighbourhood for that of Béthune. Travelling by motor-'bus, it was at Béthune at midday, whence it marched to Givenchy and took over trenches in front of the village ; " A " and " B " Companies in front, " C " and " D " in reserve, where they had very little room. The mud and wetness of these trenches were a shock to the battalion, as to every other unit which entered them for the first time. Head-quarters had to be fixed in the damp and muddy foundations of a ruined farm. On the 24th Captain Wyld (3rd Wiltshire, attached) was killed in a support trench by a stray bullet.

Christmas does not seem to have been celebrated by any of the fraternization with the enemy which occurred elsewhere on the front ; on the contrary, the day was chosen for the commencement of sapping towards the German trenches by " A " Company. Next day the 1st Royal Berkshire went back into billets at Essars. Here, and at Le Choquaux, they saw out the year 1914.

GIVENCHY. HULLUCH. CUINCHY

1915

On the 4th January 1915 Captain Lucas went to England to be employed on the staff of the 87th Brigade in Gallipoli, and command of the battalion was taken by Captain C. G. Hill, D.S.O. The battalion was then at Le Touret, and next day went into the front-line trenches at Festubert, with the South Staffordshire on its left and the South Wales Borderers on its right. German shelling was very heavy, and one shell, which pitched on the Head-quarters of " C " Company, caused thirteen casualties, including Captain L. H. Birt, D.S.O., who was killed. On the 9th ten shells fell close to Battalion Head-quarters just as the adjutant was calmly playing Tosti's " Good-bye " on a piano.

Early on the 14th, just before the battalion was relieved, Lance-Corporal Bacchus, hearing some Germans working at wiring in front of the line, lined up his men silently, fired a Very pistol, and opened fire, with the result of killing eight of a German working party of twenty. The rest of the month was spent in and out of trenches near the Rue de l'Epinette, with nothing to be specially noted.

On the 1st February the Bareilly Brigade relieved the 6th which, after a period out of trenches, returned to them at Givenchy on the 15th. As the 1st Royal Berkshire were taking over on that day, the enemy burst two high explosive shells over the " Keep " which wounded Second-Lieutenant G. H. Stokes, Lieutenant and Quartermaster Boshell and five men, most of them severely. Here the battalion held the position known as the " Orchard " with posts at White House, Red House and the " Shrine." These posts were temporarily driven in by bombing on the 18th, but were regained with the aid of heavy fire opened by " C " Company.

On the 20th a minor operation was undertaken against a salient of the German trenches known as the " Duck's Bill." It must be remarked that the British and enemy lines were very close to one another in this neighbour-hood.

For this operation the 1st Royal Berkshire supplied:

(1) A storming party of Lieutenant E. E. N. Burney and thirty others.

(2) Support—Second-Lieutenant E. N. Getting and twenty men.

(3) Local reserve—Captain L. W. Bird and two platoons.

Captain C. G. Hill, D.S.O., was in general charge of operations.

At 4.50 a.m. the storming and support parties moved to the flanks so as to leave the " Duck's Bill " open to artillery bombardment, which began at 5 a.m. A quarter of an hour later they assembled opposite the extreme point of " Duck's Bill " as the bombardment lengthened range.

Lieutenant Burney, leading the stormers, reached the German trenches with trifling loss, and his men spread right and left along them, shooting, bayoneting, and bombing their occupants. Here Lieutenant Burney was badly wounded, and command of the party was taken by Sergeant Burgess, who had himself been wounded. The R.E. officer accompanying the assault could find no traces of mining operations, and at 5.40 a.m. the signal to withdraw was given. The object of the attack had been to ascertain if the enemy were mining.

The casualties in this affair were five other ranks killed, one officer (Lieut. Burney) and five other ranks wounded. The loss was chiefly from enfilade fire from the flanks. Lieutenant Burney was carried in by Private J. Penny ("B" Company), who received the D.C.M. Burney and Sergeant Burgess were recommended for reward.

After this, there is nothing to record till the 10th March, when the Royal Berkshire were at first in reserve, at the Keep, to an attack on the German trenches.

The attack began at 8.10 a.m. when the South Staffordshire Regiment on the right succeeded in reaching the enemy trench, but were unable to establish themselves there. In the centre the King's Liverpool Regiment were stopped by uncut wire, and could not reach the trench. On the left, the first line of the 1st King's Royal Rifle Corps reached the trench, but their supports were unable to get up, owing to machine-gun fire on their flanks. All three battalions had suffered heavy casualties when, at 8.35 a.m., the Berkshire men were ordered up. " A " Company (Lieut. J. H.

Woods) at once moved to Givenchy dugouts, to the aid of the South Stafford-shire, whose C.O. kept the company there.

Meanwhile, the assaulting columns had been forced back, and a renewal of the attack was postponed pending a fresh bombardment. " A " was in the trenches leading to the Mairie, half of " B " Company occupied Givenchy dugouts, and the rest of the Royal Berkshire were in reserve in their original position.

At 2.15 p.m. the second bombardment began and the Royal Berkshire were ordered to attack, if the wire had been cut, from a point N.W. of the " Duck's Bill." At 2.35 Captain Hill sent out Private Wood of " B " and another man to reconnoitre. Wood, leaving his companion half-way, went right up to the German wire, but received wounds of which he died later. Nevertheless, he managed to crawl back to his comrade, whom he sent in with a message that the wire was uncut and the German trenches strongly held. In consequence of this report the assault was put off. Private Wood's gallantry and devotion probably saved many lives and an unsuccessful attack.

A fresh attack was ordered for the 11th, to be led by " D " Company (Capt. M. C. Radford) on the left, from the neighbourhood of the " Shrine." His left to be about Observation House.

" C " (2nd-Lieut. W. G. Cox) in immediate support.

" B " (Capt. G. Belcher) local reserve.

" A " (Lieut. J. H. Woods) reserve, in Givenchy dugouts.

The morning was so foggy that the preliminary two-hours' bombardment could only begin at 9 a.m. The artillery reported having made a gap in the German wire, but, as it turned out to be only five yards wide, and the British trench from which the assault was to start had been badly damaged, the operation was postponed.

After that the battalion was in billets, at Béthune, training and keeping itself in spirits with boxing, football, etc.

On the 21st it was again in trenches at Cuinchy, where " Tofrek Day " was kept on the 22nd. There was nothing beyond the usual routine of trench warfare during the rest of March. On the 3rd April, just before 5 a.m., the battalion opened fire on the opposite German trenches and made preparations as for an attack. The object was to induce the enemy to man his trenches when a mine under them was exploded at 5.5 a.m. and did much damage. At that hour the battalion had been relieved, except the firing line, and it went to Beuvry.* When it was at Cuinchy, for the third time in this month, the line had been much thinned, in order to avoid heavy losses from German mines. There was much activity at this time in this sort of warfare, and on the 27th a German mine was located under a British one. The latter was exploded and of course fired the German one below. The resulting crater was occupied by Lieutenant Searle and ten men, but they had to retire at midnight on account of the German " minen-werfer." The crater was again occupied at 1 a.m., and before it was finally evacuated the Royal Engineers laid a mine in the bottom of it to blow up any Germans trying to occupy it. An unfortunate explosion of some bombs which were being counted on the 28th, prior to handing over the trench to a relieving battalion, caused the death of three men.

From the 29th April to the 9th May the 1st Royal Berkshire were by turns in the Cuinchy trenches, or in reserve at Béthune. On the 9th May the 2nd Division failed in an assault, and the 1st, which had just gone to Richebourg St. Vaast, returned in the evening to Richebourg l'Avoué to relieve them, and to renew the assault at 8.30 p.m.

As these trenches were quite unfamiliar to the 1st Division, it was fortunate that this assault was postponed. It was again ordered for the 10th, but again countermanded, and the battalion returned to billets at Riche-bourg St. Vaast on the 13th.

The assault was once more ordered for 11.30 p.m. on the 15th, and this time it really came off.

Major Hill's dispositions were as follows :

" C " Company (Capt. E. M. Allfrey, and 2nd-Lieuts. C. S. Searle, H. R. H. Hilliard and R. Haigh) was to lead the attack, carrying two hundred and fifty bombs.

" D " (Capt. C. W. Frizell, Lieuts. G. Gregson-Ellis, C. R. Taffs, and E. Baseden) were to pass through, on the capture of the first German trench and to take the second.

" B " (Capt. G. Belcher, Lieuts. C. W. Green and E. N. Getting, and

---

* On this day the battalion was inspected by Major-General E. T. Dickson, Colonel of the Regiment, who found it in first-rate fighting condition.

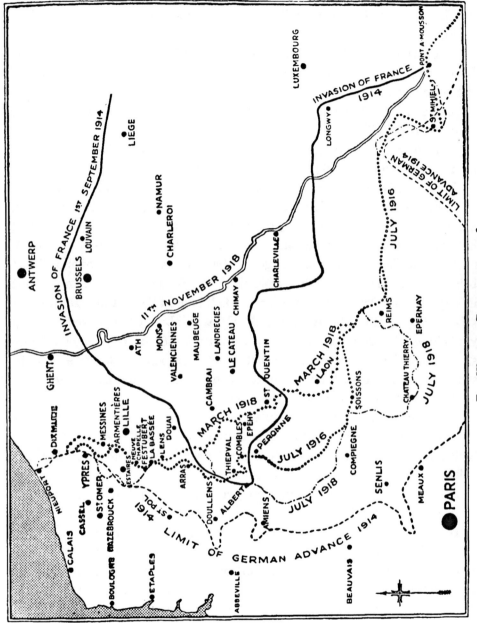

THE WESTERN FRONT, 1914-1918.

2nd-Lieut. L. H. Alison) to follow to the second trench and start consolidating.

"A" (Lieuts. W. G. Cox, 2nd-Lieuts. G. T. S. Weston, H. G. Clarke and R. D. Apps) to go as far as the first trench and consolidate the ground taken by "C."

Lieut. E. L. Jerwood, with two sections and two machine guns, to accompany "B."

The battalion was in the centre of the brigade, with the King's Liverpool on its right and 1st King's Royal Rifle Corps on its left.

The objective trenches were S. by E. of Richebourg l'Avoué, at a distance of about four hundred and fifty yards from the starting point. All companies, except "A" which was sniping the German trenches, were to get out and lie fifty yards in front of the British trenches before zero hour (11.30 p.m.).

Captain Radford was in charge of the two assaulting columns, "A" being kept in his own hands by Major Hill. By 11.15 all had moved out in single file and lay in the open, with "D" behind "C" and "B" behind "D." The night was fairly dark, and "C" were about one hundred and fifty yards forward at zero before the enemy opened on it with rifles and machine-guns. Bursting into the first trench, they bombed its defences, and in some cases were in such close contact with the enemy that they seized hold of the German rifles and shot their owners.

Meanwhile "D" had come up through a storm of fire and pushed on for the second trench, eighty yards farther on. "B," too, arrived with tools and began consolidating; it had been somewhat delayed by Captain Belcher being killed early in the advance.

At 11.45 Major Hill brought up two platoons of "A," and ordered the other two to follow.

By this time the battalions on the flanks had consolidated, but the King's Liverpool had edged too much to their right, leaving part of the trench filled with Germans whose enfilade fire caused considerable loss to the Liverpool on the right and the Royal Berkshire on the left. About two hundred of them surrendered in the morning to the Liverpool. The Berkshire casualties in this successful attack were terribly heavy:

Officers. Killed (4):   Capt. G. Belcher, M.C.
Lieuts. W. G. Cox, C. R. Taffs, H. J. Clarke.

Wounded (3) : Captain E. M. Allfrey.
Lieut. E. Baseden, 2nd-Lieut. C. S. Searle.
Missing (2) :   2nd-Lieuts. L. H. Alison, R. D. Apps.
(Both are recorded as killed.)
Other Ranks.   Killed 49 ; Wounded 290 ; Missing 75.
Total : 9 Officers, 414 Other Ranks.

After such heavy losses as these, the battalion naturally required a considerable time for refitment and the arrival and training of fresh drafts, and it went for this purpose into the back areas about Béthune and Allouagne. Its conduct in the recent attack was highly praised at inspections, both by Brigadier-General Fanshawe and by General Horne, the Corps Commander, at Grenay.   By the 2nd June it was again in trenches on the Ypres front, on the extreme British right, with French troops on its right.   Here it had nothing unusual, and on the 19th it was back at Cuinchy and reserve trenches at Cambrin.   Here it was near the 2nd and 5th Battalions Royal Berkshire. On the 26th there was a very unfortunate occurrence.   German shells were falling heavily near the mess, and the officers in it had just started to go to the cellars.   Just as they were going down the steps a shell burst close to them.   Major C. G. Hill, C.M.G., D.S.O., and Lieutenant C. W. Green were killed on the spot, and Second-Lieutenant E. K. Colbourne died of his wounds next day.   Major Hill's death was a great loss and was deeply mourned.   Captain W. L. Bird took over the command.

The brigade was taken out of the line from the 5th July till the 13th, when the battalion again found itself in trenches at Windy Corner just N.W. of Givenchy.   There was nothing out of the ordinary incidents of trench-warfare to record in July, or till the 11th August, when the accidental dropping of a detonator in the trenches, at the Brickstacks near Cuinchy, wounded five men.

On the 13th Second-Lieutenant Lacy, mining officer, was killed by the explosion of a German mine.

On the 19th the 4th (Guards) Brigade left the 2nd Division to join the newly formed Guards Division.

Mining operations on this front were as usual active, and on the 20th Captain Weston, C.-S.-M. Harrison, Sergeant Hawkes (who had been out in France since the beginning) were killed by a German mine.   The British retaliated with a counter mine which exploded a German one, badly damaged the enemy parapet, and united several small craters into one.

Again, on the 22nd, eight men were killed and twenty-four wounded.

We may pass on to the 26th September, when a Provisional Brigade (Colonel Carter's) was formed of the 1st King's Royal Rifle Corps, 1st Royal Berkshire, and 2nd Worcestershire, and attached to the 7th Division for an attack on the quarries between Hulluch and Fosse 8.

The attack, postponed from the 27th, was made at 2.30 a.m. on the 28th in bright moonlight. The Berkshire companies at that hour moved in file to the rendezvous, and formed up in company columns. They had to pass over eight hundred yards of captured German trenches, now occupied by British troops, to their objective, Fosse 8.

They were still four hundred yards from the Fosse when they were seen in the moonlight and heavily fired on. " A," " B " and " C " Companies pressed steadily on, but the fire was so heavy that they were held up when still seventy yards from the slag heap. " D " and part of " C," meanwhile, advanced and manned the British front trench.

It was at this time that Second-Lieutenant A. B. Turner started bombing down a German communication trench. Single-handed he drove its occupants before him for one hundred and fifty yards, though they were all the time throwing bombs at him. In this gallant effort he was mortally wounded, and the Victoria Cross which was awarded to him was posthumous.

The following account of his exploits was written at the time to his father (Major C. Turner, of Thatcham House, Thatcham, Berks) by Captain Frizell, who had succeeded temporarily to the command of the battalion :

" About 2 a.m. on the morning of the 28th September, we were ordered to attack a strong German position. After having got up to our objective, we had to retire about 100 yards. During the latter part of the attack your son did one of the bravest acts I have ever seen. The Germans were bombing down a communication trench on our right towards our line. Lieut. Turner, who was near there, *single-handed* bombed them back for a distance of over one hundred and fifty yards, thereby relieving the German pressure on that part. It was while he was performing this very gallant act

SECOND-LIEUTENANT A. B. TURNER, V.C.

3rd Battalion, attached to 1st Battalion.

that he received a rifle bullet in the abdomen. He was helped back to our dressing station almost at once, as it was impossible for him to stay where he was, and sent back to the collecting station on a stretcher. The next news we heard of him was that he had died at the clearing hospital at Choques near Béthune. . .   I cannot tell you how much we all miss your son. He was the soul of generosity and a very brave officer, and was loved by all of us. I have sent a full account of his very brave deed to the Brigadier, who, I know, has forwarded it on."

In another letter it is stated : " My Company-Sergeant-Major says he saw Turner do several deeds each worthy of the V.C., which honour he will probably have awarded to him."

The following is the *Gazette* notification of the circumstances under which the V.C. was awarded :

" For most conspicuous bravery on the 28th September 1915 at Fosse near Vermelles. When the regimental bombers could make no headway in Slag Alley, Lieut. Turner volunteered to lead a new attack. He pressed down the communication trench practically alone, throwing bombs incessantly with such dash and determination that he drove back the Germans about one hundred and fifty yards without a check. His action enabled the reserves to advance with very little loss, and subsequently covered the flank of his regiment in its retirement, thus averting a loss of some hundreds of men. This most gallant officer has since died of wounds received in this action."

Major Bird had been wounded, and his second-in-command, Captain Radford, D.S.O., killed. Command was taken by Captain C. W. Frizell, who was with the rear company. At this juncture Colonel Carter, commanding the Provisional Brigade, coming forward and finding the leading companies checked, ordered Captain Frizell to charge with all the men he had left. With Frizell at their head, the men made a desperate effort which carried them half-way up the slag heap. Beyond that they could not get ; for the enemy were throwing bombs down on them from the top. Forced to fall back, they retired to the front British trench one hundred and fifty yards in rear.

It was now nearly daylight and Colonel Carter decided not to attempt a renewal of the attack.

The casualties were :

Officers.   *Killed :* Capt. M. C. Radford, D.S.O.
            Died of Wounds : 2nd-Lieut. A. B. Turner, V.C.
            Wounded and Missing : Lieut. G. F. M. Hall (Killed).
            Missing : Capt. E. N. Getting.
                2nd-Lieuts. P. C. Rawson, R. A. Summers,
                J. W. V. Blazey (all now recorded as killed).
            Wounded : Major L. W. Bird.
                Capt. and Adjt. C. St. A. Fullbrook-Leggatt.
                Lieuts. E. F. Eager, D. E. Ward.
                2nd-Lieuts. R. Haigh, W. S. Mackay.
Other Ranks.   Killed 17 ; Wounded 115 ; Missing 143.
            Total : 13 Officers and 275 Other Ranks.

Captain Large, R.A.M.C., and the search parties were untiring in their efforts to bring in the wounded. Colonel Carter now went to command the 35th Brigade, his three battalions were temporarily handed over to the 22nd Brigade, and next day Captain Frizell was at Vermelles reorganizing his shattered battalion with the aid of Captain Gregson-Ellis and Second-Lieutenant Blackburn (both of whom, though sick in hospital, rejoined on hearing of the casualties) and of the reserve officers left at Vermelles.

From the 29th September the battalion was refitting and training till the 28th October, when it was again taking its turn in and out of the Cuinchy trenches, still with the 12th Division. It was in the same neighbourhood till the 23rd November, when it ceased to be under the orders of the 12th Division.

From midnight of the 15th/16th December the 1st Royal Berkshire, with the 1st King's Royal Rifle Corps and 5th King's Liverpool, was transferred to the 99th Infantry Brigade, but still remained part of the 2nd Division. The battalion was still very weak in numbers. It passed its second Christmas Day at the front in billets at Annequin, and ended the year at Bellerive.

SOUCHEZ. THE SOMME. LONGUEVAL AND DELVILLE WOOD. SERRE

1916

All January 1916 was spent by the 1st Royal Berkshire at Bellerive, or in the front near Le Touret, and there is equally nothing noticeable in February, on the 29th of which month the battalion was farther south, at

Souchez, with the French 17th Division on its right beyond the River Souchez. Here the town of Lens was clearly visible on the left front. The trenches in this low flat country were badly water-logged.

In this position the battalion remained till the last days of March, when it was at Divion in rear. April and the first three weeks of May were equally uneventful.

On the 22nd May, when the 1st Royal Berkshire were at Gouy and Servins, they were ordered to retake two trenches which had been taken from the 47th Division on the 20th, but the order was cancelled after the battalion had taken its place. The German bombardment was so heavy that it was impossible to reach the point of assembly. All preparations for the attack had again been made on the 23rd, when it was finally cancelled.

There was no more fighting till the 16th June, when a British mine was exploded on the right of the battalion front at Carency, close to Souchez. Ten minutes later there was a severe bombing fight lasting till 11 p.m. in which the Germans were repulsed. The battalion had fourteen casualties, including Second-Lieutenant Lane, seriously, and Second-Lieutenant Hannay slightly wounded.

On the 26th June a raid on the enemy front trenches was planned with a hundred men under Captain West, to start at 11.30 p.m. The scheme was to make a frontal attack in two waves with two officers and fifty-six men, whilst bombing parties on the flanks advanced simultaneously by communication trenches leading into the German trenches.

The cutting of their wire, however, had put the enemy on the alert, and, as soon as the signal for the advance was made, they opened so heavy a fire with trench mortars, machine guns, and rifles that the raiders were unable to reach their objectives. Their casualties in this failure were:

Lieutenant H. C. Thorne, missing (now recorded as killed), Second-Lieutenant Jackson wounded; four other ranks killed, and twenty-one wounded in the raiding party alone, besides eighteen more casualties in the rest of the battalion in the trenches.

The 1st July was the first day of the Somme Battle, but the 1st Royal Berkshire remained where they were till the 20th, when they entrained at Diéval, detrained at Longueau near Amiens and marched to Morlancourt, whence, on the 23rd, they moved out to bivouac in Sandpit Valley.

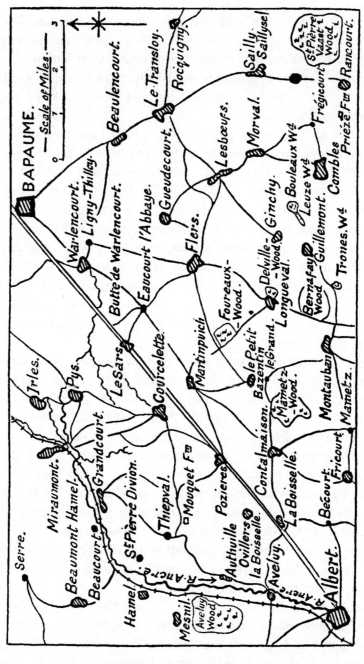

BAPAUME—ALBERT.

At 6 p.m. on the 24th they started to relieve the 1st Royal Scots Fusiliers then in Longueval and the western part of Delville Wood, with the 1st Gordon Highlanders on their left, and the 1st King's Own Scottish Borderers on their right. Three companies of the battalion were in front line ; the fourth in support. Still their fighting in the great battle was not to commence till the 27th, when there was to be a great attack on Delville Wood. At 2 a.m. on that day the battalion formed for attack on the southern edge of Delville Wood, immediately in front of South Street.

The left company, " A," under Captain Weston, was to support the 23rd Royal Fusiliers, and to be at the disposal of the officer commanding that battalion. Next to " A " came " B " (Capt. West), with " C " (Capt. Gregson-Ellis) on its right, and " D " (Lieut. Reid) covering the right flank.

The preliminary bombardment lasted from 6 a.m. till 7.10, when the battalions on either flank went forward. Two minutes later the Royal Berkshire (less " A " Company), in support of the other two battalions, started its advance in two waves. When the two leading battalions had gained two hundred yards they halted. The Royal Berkshire also halted and began digging in.

At 8.10 a.m. the advance was resumed, and the Royal Berkshire finally dug in on their objective, which was Princes Street, the ride running from west to east through the centre of the wood.

During the advance from South Street to Princes Street, the battalion had encountered considerable, but inaccurate, rifle fire, which did not do serious harm. But a machine gun, enfilading the line from the direction of Longueval on the left, seriously troubled the consolidating parties. This and another in front were silenced just as the battalion reached Princes Street.

At 9 a.m., when the battalion had dug in, the enemy opened a very accurate high-explosive-shell fire enfilading it from right to left. This lasted all day till 8 p.m., whilst the men were consolidating and suffering much from the heat and from want of water, the original supply of which in their bottles could not be replenished.

At 10.40 a.m. an officer of the King's Royal Rifle Corps came over to say that the right flank of his battalion was being bombed and required support. A dozen Berkshire bombers were sent over to help, and a pigeon

message was sent back for a fresh supply of bombs. Very fortunately
for the supply of ammunition, a dump of British S.A.A. was found fifty
yards south of Princes Street. It appeared to have been left there in one
of the earlier attacks, and overlooked by the enemy when he got back
into the southern part of the wood.

At 11.30 a fresh call for help on the right of the King's Royal Rifle
Corps was replied to with twelve more bombers. At 4 p.m. some men
of the King's Royal Rifle Corps reported that their right flank had been
slightly driven back and a Lewis gun knocked out. The remainder of
the support company was sent to help, under Second-Lieutenant R. J.
Childs, who was killed just as he reached the position. It became necessary
to send a pigeon message to Brigade Head-quarters for reinforcements,
as nearly all the supports had been used up. About 5 p.m. the enemy
shelling lessened, and from 9 p.m. till dawn on the 28th ceased entirely.
By 6.45 a.m. on the 28th the King's Royal Rifle Corps had been relieved by
a battalion of the 6th Brigade, which was to send another to relieve the
Royal Berkshire. Owing, however, to German shelling, it was not practicable to withdraw the battalion to Mine Trench till 5 p.m., and " D "
Company was so near the enemy that it had to wait till after dusk for
relief.

The battalion's casualties on these two days were :

Officers.   *Killed :*   2nd-Lieut. R. J. Childs.
            Wounded : Capt. Gregson-Ellis ; Lieut. Freeman.
            2nd-Lieuts. Moore, Parsons, Wilson.
            Missing : Lieut. J. R. Reid, 2nd-Lieut. H. J. Stidwell
            (both now recorded as killed).
Other Ranks : Killed 37 ; Wounded 182 ; Missing 37.
            Total : 8 Officers and 256 Other Ranks.

From the 29th July to the 4th August the battalion was in Mine and
Mine Support trenches and, as only about two hundred and eighty men
were left, it was reorganized in two companies, by the amalgamation of
the remains of " A " with " D " and of " B " with " C." Both these companies, reinforced by twenty men each from the transport and drums,
were in front, with the King's Royal Rifle Corps in support.

On relief, the battalion was training and refitting in back areas till the 25th August, when it moved into the Hébuterne sector in the stationary part of the British line, which had not yet advanced during the great attacks constituting the Battle of the Somme.

Here, and in the Serre sector a little farther south, it remained undisturbed till the 14th November, on which day it took part in an attack from trenches known as the "Green Line" which was in front of Vallade trench, then occupied by the battalion. Its strength was only four hundred and thirty-five other ranks, and it was assigned a broad front of eight hundred yards, with the King's Royal Rifle Corps on its right. In support of each of the outer flanks of this line were two companies of the 23rd Royal Fusiliers. It had been intended to attack in four waves, but, owing to the width of the front, it was found necessary to reduce them to two.

At 1.50 a.m. the battalion began moving forward, and at 5 a.m. formed up, with its leading wave fifty yards in front of Beaumont Trench. The two halves of the battalion were ordered to move by their outer flanks, which was held by the brigade to be justified, though it must apparently tend to create a gap between them.

As they moved across No Man's Land, there were some casualties from machine-gun fire, and the two right companies alleged that the British barrage started short and did them some harm. They had no less than one hundred and sixteen casualties amongst one hundred and fifty-nine men who left the "Green Line." With such heavy losses as these, it is hardly surprising to find the Battalion diary saying that, by the time the right half-battalion reached the German trenches, it had not enough men to cope with the enemy there. The remains worked partly towards the directing right flank, and partly leftwards to keep in touch with the left half-battalion, so that the anticipated gap formed in the centre of the right half-battalion instead of between the two halves. Only ten or fifteen men of the leading wave of the right half reached Munich Trench, their objective. These, led by Second-Lieutenants Astley and Stoneham, forced their way through the German wire and into the trench. Second-Lieutenant Stoneham and some of the men were killed. Second-Lieutenant Astley saw some Germans on the fire-step holding up their hands. Leaving two men to guard them, he went southwards along the trench in search of his comrades, but, finding none, returned to his men.

The British barrage had now lifted and Germans issuing from dug-outs commenced bombing and shooting. Astley thereupon got out of the trench, collected some twenty men of his (2nd) wave, who were twenty or thirty yards in rear, and proposed going on again. At this moment about fifty Germans with hands up emerged from Munich Trench and were handed over to the King's Royal Rifle Corps.

Not long after this many Germans got on to the fire-step and, moving down Crater Lane on the right, took the right company in flank as well as front. The position being untenable, the Berkshire men retired back into Crater Lane, which they blocked. Of the right half-battalion, the company on the right had all its officers killed, the other had three out of four wounded.

Meanwhile, the left half-battalion had moved forward with its left on Lager Alley. This having been almost obliterated and being untenable, they moved northwards on Serre Trench, which they afterwards handed over to the 14th Brigade which relieved them. This trench also was much battered, but in it were found and recaptured one officer and eleven men of the King's Liverpool, all wounded.

Of Germans, a medical officer and about thirty-five men were taken, with a trench mortar and a machine gun.

Shortly after this many men were seen moving N.E. from the German work known as the Quadrilateral, and fire was opened on them. It was stopped under the impression that they might be British, but it is certain that they were Germans evacuating the trenches, owing to the works on their south and east flanks having been taken.

Serre Trench was of great value, on account of its command. The Royal Berkshire lost cruelly. Officers, 3 killed, 3 wounded, and 1 missing. Other Ranks, 29 killed, 106 wounded, 62 missing; altogether 204 out of an initial strength of 435. Unfortunately, officers' names are not given in either the Battalion or the Brigade Diary, except in the case of Second-Lieutenant Stoneham. The only other name we can trace is that of Second-Lieutenant F. C. James.

During the 15th the left half-battalion, which had consolidated Serre Trench on the previous day, bombed along part of Munich Trench, which was in a sunken road, gained about fifty yards, and established a block with a post and a Lewis gun. From this post they fired on some Germans retreating across the open from an attack on the right. After a heavy bombardment on the 16th, the battalion was withdrawn to back areas, where it remained throughout the rest of November and December 1916, and January 1917.

BOOM RAVINE. IRLES. OPPY. CAMBRAI
1917

During the period of static warfare in 1916–1917 raids and patrolling were the main feature in the British military policy, and mention must be made of a very successful raid carried out by the 1st Battalion on the 4th February 1917 near Courcelette. A party of two officers and fifty other ranks was employed, and it is significant that its captures of prisoners exactly equalled its own numbers—two officers and fifty other ranks. The casualties of the raiders were slight, and the raid was recognized as one of the most successful of the war. The appreciation of it by the Commander-in-Chief is evidenced by the immediate grant to the officers in charge of the raid of the D.S.O. and M.C.

The battalion was still in huts at Ovillers, now well behind the British front, on the 15th February 1917, preparing for a fresh attack. On the 16th it took up battle positions at Courcelette on relieving the 5th Brigade, the whole of whose front it occupied. It was now at some distance south of the upper Ancre, and the attack of the 17th was directed on that river and Miraumont. The weather, which had been very frosty, suddenly changed to a rapid thaw and there was a good deal of difficulty in forming up. To Major Weston of the Royal Berkshire the Brigade Diary attributes the success achieved in this.

On this day the battalion was in support, and it is clear, both from the narrative, and from the fact that its casualties were small, that it was not seriously engaged. These casualties are exclusive of those from the German bombardment during the night, which were Captain N. West killed, Second-Lieutenant J. W. Jeakes wounded, one man killed, and four wounded.

The leading battalions carried the first and second objectives, though with heavy loss from the German barrage. The function of the Royal

Berkshire was mainly to carry up ammunition for them, and it was no doubt the carrying parties which suffered the casualties. At 3.30 p.m. two platoons went up to reinforce the King's Royal Rifle Corps in the captured positions. The casualties were Captain E. B. Methuen wounded, one man killed, and eleven wounded.

The leading battalions suffered very heavily, a fact which was largely due to the hour of attack having been given away by a deserter. The action was that which is called " Boom Ravine " in the History of the 18th Division.

The 99th Brigade had been so crippled that it was taken out of the line till the 10th March, when the Royal Berkshire found themselves again in front line near Irles, N.E. of Miraumont, which had been taken meanwhile.

On this day the battalion attacked and took at once the Grevillers trench.

" A " Company on the right set up a defensive flank.

One German officer and about one hundred men were taken, with three machine guns and one light trench mortar.

The casualties were :

Officers. Killed :   Lieut. Brazies.
            Wounded : 2nd-Lieuts. Layers, Denham.
Other Ranks : Killed 10, Wounded 83, Missing 1.

The Battalion Diary gives no details of the action, but the following are gathered from that of the brigade.

The attack was on a frontage of fifteen hundred yards, of which Grevillers trench covered nine hundred, and Lady's Leg trench six hundred. It lay S.W. of Loupart Wood. Zero was 5.15 a.m. and the troops were in position an hour earlier. Again, as at Miraumont, a hard frost had turned to a thaw in the night, and there was thick fog in the morning, limiting visibility to thirty yards.

Six minutes after zero the barrage lifted and the troops charged, the Royal Berkshire on the right, King's Royal Rifle Corps on the left, 22nd Royal Fusiliers in support and 23rd Royal Fusiliers (less one company with the King's Royal Rifle Corps) in reserve.

The enemy had been thoroughly cowed by the barrage and the trenches were taken at once.   Next day the battalion went back to billets at Albert, and was training there and in the neighbourhood until it marched to the Bailleul area, where, on the 25th April, it was in front line.   On this day Lieutenant A. R. D. Bacon was killed and Lieutenant Massy-Lynch wounded by shells.

On the 29th the battalion was engaged in the attack on Oppy Wood, an attempt on which by the 6th Brigade had failed on the 28th.

One company (" D ") of the Royal Berkshire had been in that attack with the King's Royal Rifle Corps and had been used up,* but what remained of it was again employed on the left of the attack on the 29th.

The 99th Brigade was now on the frontage of one thousand yards occupied on the 28th by the 6th Brigade.   On the 29th the three companies (excluding " D ") had a strength of only fifteen officers and two hundred and fifty other ranks.   The attack was to be led by it on the left, and the 22nd Royal Fusiliers, with fifty of the King's Royal Rifle Corps, on the right.   Each had to deal with a front of five hundred yards.   The 23rd Royal Fusiliers in reserve.   The German wire had not been well cut on the right half, but had been so on the Berkshire front, except on its extreme right.   The " jumping-off " trenches were very shallow and afforded little protection.

At 4 a.m. the attack went forward, with the companies in order " A," " B," " C," " D " from right to left, against Oppy Trench just in front of the wood.   " A " and " B " Companies moved on the right of the road, which was sunk about two feet and ran parallel to the line of advance, cutting the German trench at right angles.

Captain Valentine, who was with " B " Company on this day, says his men went through as though going over the top were an everyday occurrence, even though they were " loaded down like a lot of furniture removers with all the implements of war, utensils, sandbags, food, and ammunition," and notwithstanding the fact that the previous night had been nerve-shaking on account of the cries of the wounded of the last attack in front.

The German machine guns were fortunately firing high, and " B " at any rate reached the trench without heavy casualties.   Consolidation was commenced, and snipers were pushed forward into the wood, at the

---

* The Battalion Diary does not show any casualties on the 28th, apparently because " D " was under the King's Royal Rifle Corps on that day.

west corner of which they captured three machine guns, which were turned with good effect on their late owners as they retired. Many prisoners were also taken, some of whom shammed dead, till they were turned over to be searched. Many more were shot as they made for the wood.

Between 5 and 9.30 a.m. no less than five heavy counter attacks fell upon the right of the battalion. The first four were repulsed, but then bombs began to run short and " A " Company was forced inwards upon " B." Casualties were heavy, and the commanders of " A " and " B " decided to form a defensive flank along the sunken road. Here Captain Jerwood, commanding " B," was wounded in a heavy attack by the Germans, which was repulsed by rifle and Lewis-gun fire. More attacks developed against " A " and " B," which could now muster only about thirty men between them. Enemy machine guns dominated the fire of those of the Royal Berkshire, and bombs, though replenished by some German ones which had been found, had completely run out. The German store had already enabled the Berkshire men temporarily to recover lost ground.

Meanwhile, " C " and " D " on the left, to the north of the sunken road, had been driven, with the thirty or forty men still left, northwards along the trench till they joined the 5th Brigade on the left and remained with it. They took the three captured machine guns with them.

The left of the companies in the road was now exposed, and they were compelled, about noon, to retire to their starting point, where they held on.

Lieutenant Valentine went out later to verify a report that the Germans were retiring. He soon found it was very far from being true, and had to lie hidden in a shell hole till dark. Continuing his patrol then, he found the Germans occupying the trench which had been the objective, and returned home with difficulty, with the corporal and three men with him. The conduct of the battalion had been, as its commanding officer writes, beyond all praise, and the fire of its rifles and Lewis guns had devastated the ranks of the enemy, who came on regardless of losses. Towards the end, nearly all the Lewis gunners had been killed.

The casualties were :

Officers. *Killed :* 2nd-Lieut. M. A. Simon.
              Wounded and Missing : 2nd-Lieuts. H. A. Gibbs, E. C. Ready
                   (both now found to have been killed).

LANCE-CORPORAL J. WELCH, V.C.

Officers. Wounded : Capts. V. G. Stokes, E. L. Jerwood.
                              2nd-Lieuts. A. P. Aveline, G. M. Archdale.
Other Ranks : Killed 15, Wounded 89, Missing 47.
                    Total : 7 Officers and 151 Other Ranks.

For gallantry in this action the Victoria Cross was awarded to Lance-Corporal J. Welch.

The *Gazette* notification of the award of the V.C. to Lance-Corporal Welch thus describes the action for which it was granted :

" For most conspicuous bravery. On entering the enemy trench he killed one man after a severe hand-to-hand struggle. Armed only with an empty revolver, Lance-Corporal Welch then chased four of the enemy across the open, and captured them single-handed. He handled his machine gun with the utmost fearlessness, and more than once went into the open fully exposed to heavy fire at short range to search for and collect ammunition and spare parts, in order to keep his guns in action, which he succeeded in doing for over five hours, till wounded by a shell. He showed throughout the utmost valour and initiative."

On the 1st May the battalion was organized in two companies of four officers and one hundred other ranks each, and, with two similar companies of the 23rd Royal Fusiliers, formed a composite battalion which was sent up to the front at 8 p.m. It was under Lieutenant-Colonel Vernon, D.S.O. At 1 a.m. on the 3rd May these two companies were in line along a road running N.W. and an hour later moved to a taped line to the left of Oppy. The Germans seemed to know the whereabouts of it as, when Lieutenant Valentine went out to ascertain its position, there was a heavy barrage on it. He was knocked out by the barrage, and did not recover consciousness till after the attack.

The first wave of the attack advanced one hundred yards to avoid this barrage.

The Royal Berkshire attacked in two waves, with special parties told off to make strong points.

The British barrage opened at 3.5 a.m., before the troops on the flanks appeared to be quite ready. Direction was difficult to keep, and there was a general tendency to close in on the centre. The left company of the Royal Berkshire had some casualties from getting into the barrage.

The wire had been well cut and the enemy did not offer a very strong resistance. The trench was fairly strongly occupied, but there was no rifle or machine-gun fire. A good many Germans were shot as they retired over the open or by their communication trenches. During the next hour consolidation proceeded, but no blocks were made in the trench, as the Royal Berkshire were in touch with the troops on both flanks.

Bombing died down soon on the left, but on the right there was a severe bombing fight. More bombs were called for and sent up, together with a German store which had been found in the trench.

Between 5 and 5.30 a.m. men were seen getting out of the overcrowded trenches on the right and running, as if to search for a place where there was more room. Not finding it, they established themselves in shell holes behind the trench. The Berkshire companies had exhausted their supply of bombs, and had only three Lewis guns, when the enemy counter-attacked over the top in front, and along communication trenches. Coming on despite heavy casualties, the German bombers on the right were mainly responsible for driving the two companies out of the trench into the shell holes behind it, where they held on till withdrawn at night. The losses occurred chiefly in getting back out of the trench, and were caused by machine guns and snipers in Oppy.

There went into action eight officers and two hundred and ten other ranks ; at the end there remained only two officers (both slightly wounded) and ninety-four other ranks. The diary unfortunately gives no names of officers or details of casualties. Second-Lieutenant H. W. Dobbie's is the only name traceable as killed.

Nothing more of note happened in May, at the end of which month the battalion, still organized in two companies, was in reserve trenches between Arleux and Oppy.

June, too, was an uneventful month.

On the 3rd July Second-Lieutenant M. G. Roberts was killed during a relief at Cambrin. The rest of the month was spent at Annequin, the reserve area behind Cambrin. By the end of August the battalion had again risen to an effective strength of thirty-eight officers and six hundred and ninety-four other ranks, and apparently the four-company organization had been resumed. The Royal Berkshire held the right of the brigade front in the Cambrin sector, alternately with the 1st King's Royal Rifle Corps, from June till the 7th September, when it went into the right front line at Givenchy, where it remained, with the usual turns in support and reserve, till the 6th October. On that day it was withdrawn to Béthune, and next day went into billets at Auchel till the end of the month. It now had an effective strength of twenty-nine officers and eight hundred and four other ranks. It was undergoing continuous training for the coming operations of General Byng towards Cambrai, though of course no regimental officer was informed of when or where the attack was to be. By the 8th November the battalion was in billets at Herzeele, still training. On the 25th November it marched to Beaumetz-le-Cambrai. Byng's great offensive had already taken place, without the 1st Royal Berkshire being engaged, and it was now a case of defending the new salient which had been acquired. The long turn out of the main line had raised the battalion morale to a very high pitch and the men, says Lieutenant Valentine, were ready to go anywhere, whether to Italy, Ostend or Cambrai.

The events which followed in the next few days constituted the most brilliant achievement of the 1st Battalion in the war, a success which was of the most vital importance, preventing as it did the driving in of the left flank of the newly acquired Cambrai salient, and the possible cutting off of the troops at its apex.

An excellent report on the defence of the line west of Bourlon Wood was drawn up by the late Lieutenant-Colonel G. P. S. Hunt, and it is impossible to improve on it as an account of the achievement of the 1st Battalion in this great battle. Therefore, we shall content ourselves with quoting it in full, adding quotations regarding " B " Company from a statement furnished by Captain D. Valentine who commanded it on the 30th November. It will be easily understood from the plan supplied by the 1st Battalion. Colonel Hunt writes :

" The battalion came up from Beaumetz-le-Cambrai on the night of 26th/27th November in a blizzard and got very wet, with no opportunity of drying, as companies were in trenches in support of the line. Head-quarters in the Sugar Factory and Château were heavily shelled at frequent intervals.

" On the night of 28th/29th November we took over the line, and on morning of 29th ' C ' Company, on the left, participated in a small advance to straighten the line. There was a dangerous fire of machine guns and

6 N.C.O.s and men were killed, but all ranks showed marked keenness and did more than their duty, going out to bring in wounded men of the 60th Rifles who have always been our companions in the brigade.

" The line was an extended one, about 1,200 yards, and was occupied as follows :

" ' B ' Company on the right in 12 section posts which were partially connected, and had a little wire in places by the morning of the 30th.   One platoon was in reserve, dug in roughly in the bank of a slightly sunken road. Our right was some 800 yards west of Bourlon Wood.

" ' A ' Company was in the centre in a continuous trench except for two posts dug on the night of 29th/30th November to fill a gap on its right.

" ' C ' Company was on the left in the same trench, and its left was in the new trench and the posts dug during the 29th November.   There was some wire in places, and the posts were 6 feet deep and roughly fire-stepped.

" The 17th Royal Fusiliers, lent from 5th Infantry Brigade, held the line to our left astride the Hindenburg support line, and the 47th London Division held the line to our right and through Bourlon Wood.

" Half of ' D ' Company held two posts dug on the two previous nights to form a defensive flank, if necessary, on our right.

" The other half of ' D ' Company were in dugouts and shelters near the Factory.

" There were no support trenches at the time, supports being in shelters, etc., round about the Factory, which, being on the main Bapaume-Cambrai Road, was very subject to shelling.

" The line itself was behind the crest of the hill running west from Bourlon Wood and village, but on the left was on top of the hill, and farther west a good view could be obtained to the north and north-East.

" At 8.45 a.m. on the 30th November a heavy bombardment came down on Head-quarters at the Factory, and this lasted throughout the two attacks, making it extremely dangerous to approach the buildings.   At the same time our right and the 47th Division were shelled.   A message came in that the enemy had been seen assembling and deploying for attack beyond the ridge. Our guns put a heavy barrage over the ridge and on the top.

" At about 9 a.m. the Germans were seen coming over the skyline in large numbers.   We immediately opened a heavy fire with rifles and Lewis

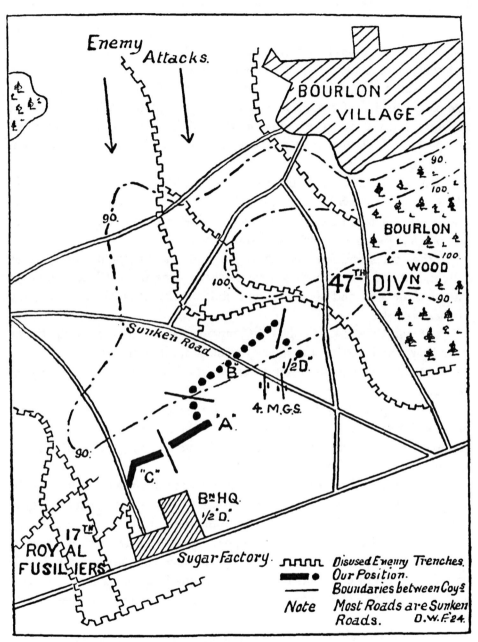

Enemy Attacks.

BOURLON VILLAGE

90.
100.

BOURLON
WOOD DIVⁿ
47ᵀᴴ
100.
90.

90.

100.

Sunken Road
½ D.
B.
4. M.G.S.
'A'
90.
"C"

Bⁿ HQ.
½ D.

17ᵀᴴ
ROYAL
FUSILIERS

Sugar Factory.

Disused Enemy Trenches.
Our Position.
Boundaries between Coyˢ
Note Most Roads are Sunken
Roads. D.W.F. 24.

BOURLON WOOD.

39

guns, assisted by 2 machine guns of the 47th Division with ' B ' Company, and inflicted enormous losses on the enemy.   The enemy, however, succeeded in forcing back some posts of the 47th Division.

" At about 10 a.m. he also succeeded in entering 3 of the left posts of ' B ' Company, some 300 Germans having attacked one platoon which stood most gallantly, but was overpowered before it could dispose of so large a number. One post of this platoon, however, under Sgt. Woollard, held its own throughout the day.

" The attack continued for three hours, and ' B ' Company's position was often critical, but every man used his arms resolutely, and finally drove the enemy off.   Those that had reached our line attempted to retire about 12.30 p.m., but were nearly all mown down.

" The attack had not come on to ' A ' and ' C ' Companies to the same extent, but the men of both companies showed the utmost keenness under the machine gun and shell fire, and undoubtedly assisted ' B ' Company to beat off the enemy.

" At one time the left of ' C ' Company was in the air, owing to the withdrawal and partial surrender of some posts on our left.

" At about 2 p.m. the enemy was again reported to be assembling for attack.

" At 2.30 p.m. the 47th Division put up the S.O.S. Signal, and the enemy was seen advancing again over the ridge.   The attack again came on ' B ' Company on both sides of the sunken road, and on the 47th Division as far as the edge of the wood.

" Left of the sunken road the enemy advanced in large numbers, but the attack was held up by our heavy fire, and that of the three machine guns on the sunken road, and it never reached our line.

" Between that and the wood the posts of the 47th Division were weak, and the Germans succeeded easily in driving them back, leaving our right in the air.   Three of our posts fell, fighting to the last, and a Lewis gun was lost with them.   The remainder succeeded in bringing the enemy to a standstill.

" All ranks behaved with the greatest spirit and determination and never gave ground.   The Lewis gunners seized every opportunity to get to better positions to kill the enemy.

" In both these attacks the Germans advanced regardless of loss. They were in full marching order with packs, and evidently thought they would break right through.

" The total casualties of the battalion were only 3 officers and 63 men, of which 46 were ' B ' Company. That company alone probably accounted for 500 Germans.

" According to Intelligence Reports, at least two German Divisions were annihilated on our Divisional Front.

" Many cases of great personal bravery were reported by Company Commanders. The Company and Battalion runners had to face the bombardment on the Factory occupied by Battalion Head-quarters, a bombardment which was admittedly very heavy and much more so than a barrage. They came through it with the utmost cheerfulness, and fortunately suffered few casualties.

" Lieut. Valentine commanded ' B ' Company with characteristic skill and coolness, and inspired confidence in all ranks.

" Capt. Pugh, M.C., commanded ' A ' Company in the centre, and his men worked under him splendidly.

" Capt. Jackson, who commanded ' C ' Company, was killed while getting to his posts on the left. His men were full of keenness.

" Half of ' D ' Company under Capt. Mousley did very good work in carrying up ammunition under heavy fire, and the other half, with 2nd-Lieut. Leach, held the posts on the right, and materially assisted in bringing the enemy to a standstill.

" All ranks were imbued with the highest sense of duty, which enabled them to do their work so well and to act up to the best traditions of the Regiment."

We now come to Lieutenant Valentine's account. After saying that dawn had passed so quietly that, between 8 and 9 a.m., he had begun to think there would be no attack that day, he writes :

" I was sitting, very sleepy, on the side of the road drinking cocoa when the nearest sentry came tumbling down from his post exclaiming with great eagerness ' S.O.S. gone up in twenty-seven different places and the Boche coming over the 'ill in thousands.' Our artillery response to the S.O.S. was immediate, and one of the quickest pieces of work I had seen. It was now that the previous weeks of training and rest told as each commander, down to the section leader, at once carried out his orders or used his initiative, and it is to this that we owe the killing of that first attack. To mention one instance of this, a young lance-corporal, just given his first stripe, in charge of a Lewis gun, at once took his gun *forward* in order to enfilade the single miserable strand of wire that we had managed to get out the night before. The damage he was able to do with his gun, which he managed to keep in action all day, was enormous. He was recommended for the D.C.M., but received the M.M. instead.

" Shelling was very heavy, but fortunately, as we had no set line of trenches, most of it was behind us, though a good deal fell near. Our rifle fire was very accurate, as the enemy had to come down toward us from the crest of the ridge, giving us an admirable target. The first wave of the attack crumpled and died. Attack after attack followed all day, in one case supported by low-flying aeroplanes, which dropped bombs and fired at us. The Lewis gun of the reserve platoon was mounted on a mound and replied to the 'planes, and in one case I am practically certain hit a 'plane at about 50 feet up. The 'plane crashed just over the ridge, but in a fight of this nature it is almost impossible to take or give credit for an event of this kind, as there are many factors that may destroy a low-flying machine.

" By this time a corporal, who had been with the battalion on and off since 1914, found a discarded machine gun and plenty of S.A.A. The quantity of S.A.A. left behind by the cavalry, who had reached this point in the first attack, was phenomenal. The corporal, who was by way of being somewhat of an expert with automatic guns, managed to get it working, and this materially assisted us.

" About midday, the platoon of my company on the left, where contact was made with ' A ' Company, was dislodged from their posts and went back a short way to other posts ; 2nd-Lieut. Palmer was wounded. On the right our posts remained intact, though the battalion on the right was suffering heavy losses and was nearly decimated.

" By this time (late afternoon) the attack had died down, and a detachment of Fusiliers were sent up to bomb out the enemy in the post vacated by our left platoon. They found that most of the enemy were dead or had retired, as my reserve platoon had previously been bombing them in an effort to dislodge the survivors. When night fell, it was found that certain other small posts had been swamped, each one dying to a man, and with a full toll of the enemy in front. The masses of German dead in front of our line must have numbered nearly 500, and, considering that the success of the action fell on the shoulders of the subordinate commanders and men, their spirit can well be judged. We were relieved at night, and went back to the dugouts where we spent the first night, a depleted exhausted crew, but elated with success. I have had the opportunity of talking with Hauptmann K. Andersen, since the war, who commanded a German company of machine gunners opposite me. He informs me that there was a good deal of mismanagement on the part of the German Staff, and that, owing to delay, the attack had to take place in broad daylight. The Germans did not extend into open order properly, as they had been informed that there were so few troops in front of them (a fact, having regard to their numbers) that they could walk over us!

" The weather was fair, occasional rain falling, though the day of the attack was fine."

How greatly the splendid defence of the 1st Royal Berkshire was appreciated by the Higher Command is shown by the following congratulatory messages :

30th Novr. 1917. From Genl. Pereira, G.O.C. 2nd Divn.

"Units of 2nd Division and 36th Divisional Artillery assisting them engaged in to-day's fighting have done magnificent work.

"Probably two German Divisions have been smashed."

2nd Decr. 1917. From Brig.-Genl. R. O. Kellett, commander 99th Infantry Brigade.

"May I thank you all very sincerely for once more having added, on the 30th November, to the laurels already won by you on many fields. The 99th Brigade has had a short but a pretty strenuous life, and in their many successes they have no page that they wish to turn down or forget, no ' regrettable incidents.'

" I am very proud of my splendid Brigade, and I am confident that all ranks will go on as they have always done in the grim determination to beat the enemy wherever we meet him, and die sooner than give back an inch of ground that we or any of our comrades in other Brigades or Divisions have gained.

"Please convey the contents of this to all ranks."

2nd December 1917.   *From Field-Marshal Sir D. Haig.*

The Army Commander has great pleasure in forwarding the following message from Field-Marshal Sir D. Haig:

"I congratulate you and the Officers and men under your command upon the successful resistance maintained by the Third Army yesterday against the powerful attacks delivered by the enemy South and West of Cambrai. In particular I desire you to convey to the General Officers commanding the 2nd, 47th and 56th Divisions, and to all ranks serving under them, my warm appreciation of their magnificent defence of the important positions entrusted to them. Though exposed throughout the day to the repeated assaults of superior forces, they beat off all attacks with the heaviest losses to the enemy, and, by their gallant and steady conduct, contributed very largely to the security of the Divisions engaged on the whole front of attack."

Perhaps an even more valuable tribute is contained in the following quotation from a précis drawn up by the General Staff of the Fourth Army:

"On the left their attack was driven off with heavy loss by machine gun, Lewis-gun, and rifle fire, but on the right the enemy forced back the Brigade on the right of the Division, and captured the three extreme right posts, the garrisons of which fell fighting to the last, and there was such a heap of German dead in and around these posts that, after the line had been restored (2nd December), it was impossible to find the bodies of our men.

"The other five posts on the right stood firm and repulsed all enemy attacks, until reinforcements restored the situation and drove the enemy back behind the Ridge.

"Too much praise cannot be given to this splendid company of the 1st R. Berks. Regt. and its commander, Lieutenant Valentine, for their valour and steadfastness in this most critical time, extending over some six hours. They met attack after attack of the enemy, who were always in vastly superior numbers, and who came on right up to them time after time, only to be mown down and retire in disorder. The casualties in this company were 46 all ranks, and a Lewis gun, but they never flinched. They claim to have killed over 500 of the enemy, and it is believed that this is no exaggeration."

For a day of such desperate fighting the Berkshire casualties may be reckoned small, especially when compared with the appalling losses incurred by the enemy.

Captain E. P. Jackson of " C " Company was killed, and Second-Lieutenants Smeaton and Palmer were wounded. Of Other Ranks 12 were killed, 25 wounded, and 21 missing, about four-fifths of these being in " B " Company.

The battalion remained in the same position on the 1st December, when the enemy shelling was comparatively slight. There was some rearrangement of companies. " C " was on the left, " A " in the centre, with " D " and " B " in support at the gunpits and quarry. " B " Company of the 23rd Royal Fusiliers, with two platoons of " D " of the same regiment, was on the right of " A " of the Royal Berkshire up to the sunken road, whilst " C " of the 23rd Royal Fusiliers took over posts beyond it.

The 2nd, 3rd, and 4th December were comparatively quiet days, and in the night of the 4th/5th the Bourlon salient was evacuated without mishap, except that the battalion, being unable to remove them, had to throw down a well some spare Lewis-gun magazines, two machine guns, and other equipment. It was in " Nissen " huts at Hermies, behind the front, till the 12th, when it again went into front line on the Canal du Nord. After a turn in rear, it was again there on the 18th/20th and then moved to O'Shea Camp near Lebucquière in the back area. Here, and again in front line, it ended the year 1917 quietly.

EXTRACT FROM THE GENERAL STAFF PAMPHLET.
" THE STORY OF A GREAT FIGHT."

A Proud Day for Englishmen.

The story of the subsequent fighting on the BOURLON-MŒUVRES front is one so brimful of heroism that it deserves its place in English history for all time. The most determined attacks of four German divisions, with three other German divisions in support, were utterly crushed by the unconquerable resistance of the three British divisions in line. The 30th November, 1917, will be a proud day in the lives of all those splendid British soldiers who, by their single-hearted devotion to duty, prevented what would have become a serious situation had they given way.

Good Work by Small Posts.

The garrisons of three posts on the front of the 2nd Division (1st Bn. Royal Berkshire Regiment) fell fighting to the last man and when the line at this point was restored, such a heap of German dead lay in and around the posts, that it was impossible to find the bodies of our men.

In this locality, five other posts, also held by the 1st Bn. Royal Berkshire Regiment, repulsed all the enemy's attacks and maintained themselves until our reinforcements had restored the situation. These posts showed the utmost valour and steadfastness in a most critical period, extending over some six hours. The enemy made attack after attack, always in vastly superior numbers, and time after time came right up to our posts, only to be mown down by our fire and driven back in disorder. The casualties of these posts were 46 of all ranks. They claimed to have killed over 500 of the enemy.

The story of the gallant fight against odds put up by the garrisons of these posts, both those who survived and those who died valiantly, constitutes one of the many examples furnished by the fighting of this day of the supreme importance of the resistance that can be afforded by small parties of determined men, who know how to use their weapons and are resolved to use them to the last.

The Effect of Our Rifle Fire.

Accurate rifle shooting played a large part in the repulse of the enemy's attacks. Hundreds of men actually killed Germans, and there are instances of one cleaning and loading a rifle for a comrade who was picking off Germans. When an attack had been beaten off, men cleaned their rifles and collected small-arm ammunition to be ready for the attack.

EXTRACT FROM A DESPATCH BY FIELD-MARSHAL SIR DOUGLAS HAIG, DATED 20TH FEBRUARY 1918.

" After a heavy preliminary bombardment and covered by an artillery barrage, the enemy's infantry advanced shortly after 9 a.m. in dense waves, in the manner of his attacks in the first battle of YPRES. In the course of the morning and after-noon no less than five principal attacks were made in this area, and on one portion of the attack as many as eleven waves of German Infantry advanced successively to the assault. On the whole of this front a resolute endeavour was made to break down by sheer weight of numbers the defence of the London Territorials and other English battalions holding this sector.

Early in the afternoon large masses of the enemy again attacked west of BOURLON WOOD and, although beaten off with great loss at most points, succeeded in overwhelming three of a line of posts held by the 1st Bn. Royal Berkshire Regiment, on the right of the 2nd Division. Though repeatedly attacked by vastly superior numbers the remainder of these posts stood firm, and when, two days later, the three posts which had been overpowered were regained, such a heap of German dead lay in and around them that the bodies of our men were hidden.

All accounts go to show that the enemy's losses in the whole of his constantly repeated attacks on this sector of the battle front were enormous.

The greatest credit is due to troops at MASNIÈRES, BOURLON and MŒUVRES for the very gallant service performed by them on this day. But for their steady courage, and staunchness in defence, the success gained by the enemy on the right of our battle front might have had serious consequences."

THE GERMAN OFFENSIVE. THE RETREAT TO THE ANCRE.
THE FINAL BRITISH ADVANCE BY ERVILLERS AND ESCARMAIN.

1918

On the 3rd January the 1st Royal Berkshire were in front line, expecting to be relieved that night. At 4.30 p.m. the enemy suddenly opened a heavy bombardment and commenced an attack on the front and right of the battalion in numerous parties of about thirty men each. Two unprotected sentry posts had to be withdrawn behind the wire to save them from being surrounded. The enemy occupied these posts in force and began consolidating. Meanwhile, the relief was in progress, and by 10 p.m. all the battalion was out of the trenches, except two platoons of " B " and Battalion Headquarters.

At 10.30 p.m. Brigade orders were received to evacuate three support posts. It was stated that the British artillery would fire for half an hour, after which strong officers' patrols were to be sent out to recover the posts which had been lost earlier. The bombardment, from 12.25 to 12.55 a.m., was rather feeble and none too accurate, and when patrols went out under Second-Lieutenant Grimes on the west, and Lieutenant Hudson on the east of the canal, they came under machine-gun fire. The night was moonlit, and it was impossible to approach the posts unseen, as on both sides thick belts of old German wire had to be passed in single file. Under orders from Brigade, the patrols returned, after losing two killed and five wounded. Nothing more of note occurred in January, or in the first half of February.

On the 15th February the battalion was in front line near Villers Plouich, to the right of their position in January.

On the 18th a daylight patrol, under Second-Lieutenant Reynolds and Sergeant Jenkins, reached an enemy dugout on Partridge Road and shot the sentry. The patrol was driven off after some fighting, in which at least two more Germans were accounted for, but no identifications were obtained. Lance-Corporal Davy was killed.

At 11 p.m. on the 19th a strong patrol, under Second-Lieutenant Lord, ransacked the gunpits where the enemy had been working. A lighted brazier and other signs of recent occupation were found, but nothing to identify units. There were no casualties and no prisoners.

Second-Lieutenant Wright was wounded on this day by a German " pineapple " falling in the entrance of " B " Company's Head-quarters.

Though there is little mention of it in the Battalion Diary, that of the Brigade shows that on this day an unsuccessful attempt was made on a barricade erected by the enemy on a road, which practically neutralized the efforts of parties approaching from the north. A bombardment by four light trench mortars was a failure, owing to the guns all jamming. The enemy, who held their position with machine guns and bombs, wounded seven of their assailants, and two or three more were missing. The rest of February calls for no remark. On the 6th March the battalion was in front line at La Vacquerie, when Second-Lieutenant J. A. Grimes, M.C., was badly gassed and died next day. He was gassed whilst trying to rescue a man who had been buried by a shell. Second-Lieutenants Beer and Foster, and twenty-nine other ranks were also gassed, though not fatally.

German gas shelling was very bad at this time and on the 11th a bombardment, lasting three and a half hours, with mustard gas caused very heavy casualties.

Eleven officers suffered from it : Major C. Nugent, Captains M. C. Dempsey, R. M. Porritt (Medical Officer), Lieutenant J. W. Johnson. Second-Lieutenants W. Leach, E. E. Kirby, A. J. Harris, J. Titley, A. S. Durham, T. M. Gower and W. S. Winstanley. Also two hundred and fifty-seven other ranks. Few of these cases would have been bad enough for evacuation to England, but for the necessity of clearing the hospitals in France in the ensuing fighting.

On the 21st March the battalion was in Corps reserve at Manancourt, when, at 5 a.m., the order to stand by was received on the opening of the great enemy offensive on the Somme. The day passed for the 1st Royal Berkshire in uncertainty, listening to the sound of guns on all sides of the salient. On the 22nd they were still waiting, ready to move at once, and disturbed by many rumours. The transport was ordered back north-west-wards to Le Mesnil en Arrouaise. Intermittent shelling began, and at 10.45

the battalion was ordered to stand by ready to defend Manancourt.

On the 23rd the shelling increased. There was no news, and the general uneasiness increased. The 5th and 6th Brigades had moved northwards, and the 99th was left at the disposal of the 5th Army commander.

At 9.30 a.m. Captain Pugh with " A " Company, and Lieutenant Valentine with " B," were moved forward to Equancourt to reinforce the line. Their orders, says Lieutenant Valentine, were very indefinite.

" As we progressed down the road," he writes, " it became clear that a big break had taken place. Huts, camps, wagon parks, and even horse lines were deserted and abandoned, whilst various bodies of troops moved about in apparently aimless fashion. We had little difficulty in finding the front line. It came to meet us, and in green open fields we just lay down and started to throw up a light cover of earth. Large enemy forces commenced to assemble in front, supported by guns of all calibres which, with the utmost bravery (and confidence), came into action just behind the enemy's skirmishers.

" Our two companies hung on, but the supporting troops left and right commenced to move back. Our position became untenable, as the enemy was supported by all arms, artillery, planes, mortars, machine guns, etc., and we had no support of any sort. A field-gun battery just behind had fired all their ammunition and gone galloping off. After conferring with a colonel of the London Division, who were on our left, we decided to retire to higher ground, and endeavour to effect contact left and right, and form a line. Under a tornado of fire from the enemy, we made our way up a gradual hill and over the ridge. Here we found that the other troops there had left and gone farther back to an improvised line, so we made after them, a much depleted two companies. We finally found Brigade Head-quarters and received orders to trek back, as we were too weak to make an efficient force."

The survivors of these two companies eventually joined the transport at Rocquigny, after retiring through Ytres and Bus. We now return to Battalion Head-quarters and " C " and " D " Companies. At noon they moved eastwards to the railway. They were scarcely in position there when the advancing enemy appeared, and they had to retire, fighting a rearguard action, by the cemetery (where Captain Mousley was wounded) to Léchelle Wood. Here the battalion suffered a heavy loss by the death of Lieut.-

Colonel G. P. S. Hunt, who was killed as he was rallying all the troops within reach.*

The retreat reached the line Le Mesnil en Arrouaise-Rocquigny where the remnants of this part of the battalion attached themselves to troops of the 47th Division, under Lieut.-Colonel Dawes, and spent the night there. The transport was forced by the enemy advance through Manancourt, soon after noon, to leave Le Mesnil and fall back for the night to a point south of Le Transloy. Here Captain Pugh, M.C., took command of the battalion. Early in the morning of the 24th, Head-quarters with " C " and " D " Companies, were involved in a heavy fight in front and on both flanks, and were forced back through Gueudecourt to Le Sars. The transport had been sent, by Brigade orders, through Le Transloy, Les Bœufs, and Longueval to Flers, and on subsequent days went right back to Léalvillers.

As for " A " and " B " Companies, they had moved up from Flers to Gueudecourt where, with the 23rd Royal Fusiliers, they held the village till 4 p.m. They were then relieved and moved back to a sunken road between Eaucourt-l'Abbaye and Ligny Tilloy. It was here that they were rejoined by " C " and " D " Companies. The four companies held six hundred yards of line facing east, with the 23rd Royal Fusiliers on their right, and the 10th Duke of Cornwall's Light Infantry on their left. Here the night was passed with as much rest as could be obtained in the intense cold. At Gueudecourt Brigadier-General Barnett-Barker and his Staff-Captain E. J. Bell, M.C., had been killed by one shell. At dawn on the 25th March the line was fiercely attacked, especially on the left, where the troops, after vain efforts to reorganize them and control the fire, were forced back, and the whole line, after resting for two hours, had to retire, which was done without much confusion, and with a stout resistance put up wherever opportunity offered. This was especially the case at Le Sars and the high ground west of it. Here the units became more and more scattered, and the Berkshire companies lost touch with Battalion Head-quarters.

The retirement continued slowly as far as the high ground between Pys and Courcelette, which was found to be held by units of the 5th Brigade. Through this line the companies passed back to the Ancre at Beaucourt.

---

* Lieut.-Colonel Hunt was recommended for a posthumous V.C. The recommendation went as far as Army Head-quarters, but was not approved.

Battalion Head-quarters and twenty other ranks, meanwhile, had joined the 1st King's Royal Rifle Corps and moved back to Miraumont. There orders were received to return to the Pys line and reinforce the troops there, but before reaching it the battalion was ordered back through Grandcourt to the high ridge W. of the Ancre near Beaucourt.

Here the brigade was reorganized and supplied with food and S.A.A. Another very cold night was passed at this place. During the day two hundred men from the 6th Somerset Light Infantry were posted to the battalion as reinforcements. These men were absorbed into a composite battalion under the command of Major Smith of the 1st King's Royal Rifle Corps and put into line near Auchonvillers where they were in action.

At dawn on the 26th, the battalion, with other units of the brigade, moved back to the old British line near Beaumont Hamel and took over two hundred yards of trenches, which they held all day without close contact with the enemy, though they were under machine-gun and rifle as well as artillery fire. They had, at last, begun to feel that they had reached a line of resistance where they were backed by artillery behind them. In the afternoon the New Zealanders began to come up, and at 10.30 p.m. the battalion went to Mailly Maillet, where they had a quiet night and, notwithstanding the cold in the open, a good rest.

During the 27th they moved to billets at Forceville. The two hundred men of the Somerset Light Infantry rejoined their own regiment, but the Berkshire still had enough men to be useful, though on the 28th they only sufficed for reorganization in two companies. Before this was completed, the battalion was ordered to supply two companies of one hundred and thirty men each, as part of the composite battalion in which the whole of the 99th Brigade was being organized. These were hurriedly made up—" C " under Lieutenant Astley and " D " under Lieutenant Crosbie—and moved into a position under Aveluy Wood, north of Martinsart. The rest of the battalion went to Léalvillers, where the first line transport was established.

During the succeeding night the composite battalion, on being relieved, went to Engelbelmer.

On the 30th another composite battalion of the 2nd Division was formed, to which Second-Lieutenants H. J. Odell and G. H. Herring of the 1st Royal Berkshire were attached. On the 31st there was yet another change of organization.   The original composite battalion now ceased to exist, and formed two units (*a*) the 23rd Royal Fusiliers and 1st King's Royal Rifle Corps under Lieut.-Colonel Winter, (*b*) the 1st Royal Berkshire under Major R. J. Brett* and 2nd Oxfordshire and Buckinghamshire Light Infantry. These two battalions were known as the CIN and CERT Battalions respectively.   As soon as the 2nd Division was relieved, the normal formation was resumed.

The casualties of the battalion between the 21st and 27th March are not shown in detail, but the Brigade Diary gives them approximately as—

Officers : Killed 1, Wounded 3.
Other Ranks : Killed 19, Wounded 83, Missing 62.

Names of officers are not given, but we know that the officer killed was Lieut.-Colonel Hunt.

April, as the Battalion Diary says, was not an " exhilarating " month for the battalion.   At the beginning it had scarcely two hundred old hands left. Numerous reinforcements from other units raised them to a ration strength of twenty-eight officers and seven hundred and forty-nine other ranks at the end of the month, but the reinforcements, which arrived whilst the battalion was in the throes of changing sectors, were all young and inexperienced soldiers, and there was great difficulty in getting them sorted out into the companies before the battalion was again in the line on the 14th April.

The section of the line to which the battalion had been transferred, when it took over from the Grenadier Guards on the 14th April, was about Boiry St. Martin, some six miles south of Arras.   In this neighbourhood it was in and out of trenches for the rest of April.   The casualties of this month were small—one officer (Lieutenant Shipston) and ten other ranks wounded. This employment continued without any special feature till the 13th May when the battalion, then in reserve at Lanerlière, began to have platoons of American Infantry attached to it for training.

Much progress in training the young drafts was made in May, and the brigade was inspected by the Corps-Commander on the 23rd.

On the 1st June there was a heavy bombardment, by which Captain E. D. D'O. Astley and one man were killed, and eight men wounded.

---

* Major Brett succeeded Colonel Hunt in permanent command of the battalion and eventually brought the cadre home.

On the 28th a patrol of " B " Company, under Second-Lieutenant Murray, returning from a reconnaissance, encountered a patrol of about twenty-five Germans near the British line, who fled when bombed but left behind nothing to identify them. Apparently there were no casualties in the British party.

There was a bad epidemic of influenza when the battalion was in brigade reserve near Monchy in the early days of July.

On the 16th practice began for an important raid in the near future. It came off on the 23rd, and was directed against the German trenches about Ablainzeville. The raiders consisted of two hundred and three other ranks with six officers, and was commanded by Captain Stokes, M.C. The Battalion Diary gives no details, but says it was very successful, bringing in five prisoners, and having killed about fifty Germans, in addition to those killed by the barrage.

The casualties on the British side were: Second-Lieutenant F. S. Boshell killed, and Second-Lieutenant Bysh wounded; of other ranks thirty-one wounded, most of them slightly.

The raid started at 12.30 a.m. and all was over by 2 a.m.

On the 5th August the battalion was in front near Ayette, on the 13th in support behind Douchy, but did not take part in a raid by the King's Royal Rifle Corps and Liverpool Regiment on the 14th.

Orders were received on the 18th for the brigade to attack in the early morning of the 21st, with the 1st Royal Berkshire and 23rd Royal Fusiliers leading, and the King's Royal Rifle Corps in support. The battalion was in position at 1.30 a.m. on that day, with orders for " B " and " D " Companies to take the first objective.

" A " and " C " would then pass through them and capture the second. The attack was to be supported by six tanks. The final British offensive had already begun some time before in other parts, and the battle of the 8th August, which Ludendorff has described as the fateful day, had been fought and won. On the front where the battalion now was the advance from the line on which the great enemy offensive of March had been stabilized only began on the 21st August.

At 4.55 a.m. the attack began, in a mist which made it very difficult to keep direction. The tanks especially were soon in difficulties and could give very little help. Nevertheless, all the objectives were gained with very little resistance, except from isolated machine guns. The 3rd Division now passed through to attack Courcelles.

On the 22nd the 99th was relieved by the 76th Brigade, and withdrawn to what was known as the Purple Line, with orders to be prepared to carry out an attack on Ervillers, east of Courcelles, next morning. At 5 a.m. the 1st Royal Berkshire marched by platoons from Quesnoy Farm to the Ayette-Bucquoy Road, which it crossed at 7 a.m. Here the final details of the attack on Ervillers were settled.

At 10 a.m. the battalion moved under shell fire to the assembly positions, and at 11 a.m. the attack began through the German barrage. As the advance progressed there were some casualties, including the Rev. C. K. Bell, C.F., and Lieutenant W. L. Humbley, both killed. All objectives were carried without very serious opposition from the German infantry, who surrendered freely as the British came on. Meanwhile, the 5th Brigade, on the right, had failed to carry Béhagnies and throughout the day the 99th Brigade, in Ervillers, was much troubled by artillery and machine-gun fire from the ridge N.E. of Béhagnies.

The final disposition of the battalion was, " A " in a sunken road beyond Ervillers ; " C " and " D " in the Ervillers-Bee Wood trench ; " B " with Battalion Head-quarters, behind. The South Staffordshire were holding the eastern edge of Ervillers.

At 10 a.m. on the 24th, when the disposition was the same, orders were received to attack the heights N. of Mory, beyond the infant stream of the Sensée which flows below the eastern side of Ervillers, and to get into touch with the Guards Division holding the Mory " Switch." The 1st King's Royal Rifle Corps were to support and assist this attack, as well as the tanks. No attack on the troublesome ridge N.E. of Béhagnies was to be made, so it was to be masked by a smoke screen. If opportunity offered, the cavalry were to pass through and turn southwards from the east side of Mory. At the same time, an attack was to be made south of Sapig-nies, which itself lay south of Béhagnies. The latter position would thus be turned on both flanks. The attack, originally fixed for 12.30 p.m., was postponed till 3.30.

At 2.45 the Royal Berkshire moved off, by platoons at intervals of one

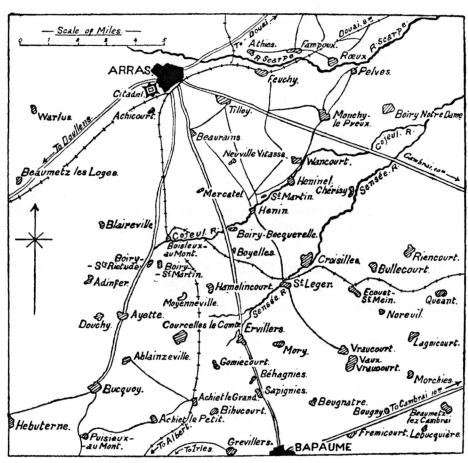

ARRAS—BAPAUME.

hundred yards to its jumping off position, keeping in the valley north of Ervillers. Having arrived there, they halted for twelve minutes before advancing again. As they moved on they found themselves still heavily fired on by machine guns on the Béhagnies ridge on their right, whilst their left was harassed by another machine gun in that direction. As the right and some tanks worked up, the whole line resumed its advance and ended up in a sunken road in touch with the Guards Division in Mory " Switch." The machine-gun fire from Béhagnies Ridge still continued till dusk. A large number of prisoners was taken, representing five different regiments, and heavy casualties were inflicted on the enemy by the infantry and tanks.

In the Berkshire Battalion there were no officer casualties. In other ranks there were sixty or eighty, mostly from machine guns. The cavalry had duly moved up, but the machine guns prevented their getting through. The movement of the battalion was so rapid that no list could be made of captured material.

The weather was still very hot, but supply arrangements worked well, and there was no shortage of food or water during the day. At night the battalion was relieved by one from the 187th Brigade, and went back to Ayette.

The casualties in the period 21st/24th August were:

Officers. *Killed:* Lieut. W. L. Humbley and the Revd. C. H. Bell.
      Wounded: Capt. Lord, M.C., M.M.; Lieut. Baldwin;
            2nd-Lieuts. Bush, Cumming, and Thorby.
Other Ranks: Killed 24; Wounded 196; Missing 7; to Hospital
            (gassed) 35.

The rest of August and the first two days of September were passed in the neighbourhood of Ayette, and on the 3rd the battalion was again near Mory, in reserve for an attack on the high ground between Morchies and Lagnicourt. The 23rd Royal Fusiliers and 1st King's Royal Rifle Corps, in front, took all objectives with very little opposition, and without calling on the Royal Berkshire, which bivouacked near Vaux Wood. Command of the 99th Brigade was assumed on this day by Brigadier-General A. E. McNamara, C.M.G., D.S.O., who, at 9.15 p.m., gave orders for the battalion to move next morning a short distance forward. The 4th was spent at

Lagnicourt, a move being made in the evening to relieve the 2/5th South Staffordshire at Hermies and Demicourt, west of the Canal du Nord and south of the Bapaume-Cambrai Road. Here they remained on the 5th/6th, and at 5.30 a.m. on the 7th parties of " A " and " B " Companies, under Second-Lieutenants Allson and Kirby, went out to establish posts on the west bank of the canal, in which they were completely successful, taking nine prisoners and one machine gun. Second-Lieutenant Kirby was wounded, one man killed, and three wounded.

At 10 a.m. a counter attack on these posts was repulsed, but a more serious one took place at 4 p.m., supported by a barrage of heavy artillery and trench mortars. This resulted in the loss of the newly established posts.

The casualties of the whole day were : Second-Lieutenants Kirby and Allson wounded. Other Ranks, 5 killed, 19 wounded and 15 missing.

From the 8th to the 16th the battalion was in support at Beaumetz ; then in Corps reserve at Mory till the 27th, when it moved up again to trenches west and east of the Canal du Nord. The British had taken Ribécourt ; but Graincourt, two and a half miles N. by W. of it, was still in the enemy's hands. The left of the battalion required protection, so an outpost line was set up. " C " and " D " Companies were in front, " B " in support and " A " in reserve. Much annoyance was experienced from an enemy machine-gun nest which, though surrounded, still held out till it was captured, with one hundred prisoners, by the Guards.

An attack was to be made on the 28th September, and at 2 a.m. the Royal Berkshire started for the assembly point, which was reached at 3.15 a.m. The route was very difficult, as the night was very dark and Flesquières, through which it passed, was encumbered by debris of all sorts.

At 4.45 the attack started, with " A " Company on the right supported by " D," and " B " supported by " C " on the left. By 5.30 a.m. the first objective, Graincourt trench, had been taken with slight opposition. By 9.15 a.m. the battalion was holding the west bank of the St. Quentin Canal, a result with which the Brigadier was much pleased when he visited Battalion Head-quarters at Noyelles soon after noon. " A " and " B " Companies were then in front line, with " C " and " D " in trenches at Noyelles, heavily shelled.

That night orders were received for the attack and passage of the canal at 5 a.m. on the 29th. The 17th Royal Fusiliers were already across when, at 4.30 a.m., news was received that they had been strongly counter attacked but were still holding on on the east bank. The advance at 5 a.m. was led by " A " crossing the only bridge still standing, which was destroyed by the enemy's artillery immediately afterwards. The company was hard pressed on the east bank when " D " was ordered to reinforce it, " B " remaining on the west bank, maintaining thence a superiority of fire which greatly assisted the attack. " C " was in dugouts at Noyelles as Battalion Reserve.

Owing to the destruction of the bridges, it was only later in the day that " B " could cross.

At 1.30 p.m. " C " was ordered to relieve a company of the 1st King's Royal Rifle Corps which had crossed and was attacking the " Green Line " and Range Wood. But Second-Lieutenant Gould, who had carried out a reconnaissance in this direction, reported that Range Wood had already been taken at 2.25, and British troops were beyond it. All objectives had been carried when, at 5 p.m., the battalion was organized in depth. At 8 p.m. it was in position to meet a counter attack which appeared to be indicated by the heavy bombardment. However, there were no signs of the enemy massing and the battalion was relieved.

The casualties in the operations between the 27th and 30th September had been three officers wounded (names not stated), 17 other ranks killed, 83 wounded, and 18 missing.

On the 1st October the 1st Royal Berkshire was at Nine Wood (Bois des Neuf) behind Noyelles till orders were received, on the 7th, to attack next day. The battalion was in rear of the 23rd Royal Fusiliers and 1st King's Royal Rifle Corps when they advanced at 4.30 a.m. As they approached a sunken road, they came under the fire of some Germans who, after surrendering, had started fighting again. These were soon disposed of, and the first objective, which had already been taken by the leading battalions, was reached. Here it was found that the 3rd Division on the right had lost direction and moved to its left across the front of the 99th Brigade. When the Royal Berkshire passed through it to the second objective they found no troops on their right, owing to this movement which had brought what should have been on their right in rear of them.

" B " Company was in touch with the 1st King's Royal Rifle Corps, but was about five hundred yards from " C " on its right.   Consequently, as Forenville, south-east of Cambrai, was approached, " C " and " D " Companies on the right came under intense machine-gun fire from both flanks, and were unable to get beyond the main road short of it.

Soon after 8 a.m. five German tanks forced the 3rd Division back to the first objective, and commenced working along it.

One tank, moving north from Seranvillers on the right rear, was driven back by the British machine-gun fire, and some more, operating near Niergnies on the left, appeared to be out of action.   At 8.30, in consequence of this threat, " C " and " D " Companies were ordered back to the first objective.   These two companies, now only about eighty strong, got back under heavy machine-gun fire from both flanks.   The battalion was then reorganized, with " A " and " B " holding the front objective, and " C " and " D " five hundred yards in rear.

At 1 p.m. orders were received for an attack on Florenville, which was at first fixed for 4.30.   The King's Royal Rifle Corps on the left, with two companies of Royal Berkshire and two platoons of the 23rd Royal Fusiliers on the right, were to advance on Florenville, whilst the 3rd Division captured Seranvillers to the south.   As it appeared that the latter attack had already commenced, the main attack was put forward to 3 p.m.

" A " and " B " Companies advanced under heavy machine-gun fire from Seranvillers, which the 3rd Division had failed to take.   For some time little progress could be made.   When, however, Seranvillers was at last taken by the 3rd Division, the 23rd Royal Fusiliers were able to pass through and take Florenville about 6 p.m.

Early next morning the division was automatically relieved by the passage through it of the Guards to continue the advance.

The Berkshire casualties in this action were :

Officers.   Killed : Lieut. C. C. Hedges, M.C., 2nd-Lieut. E. Saville.
          Died of Wounds : 2nd-Lieut. W. Tomey.
          Wounded : 2nd-Lieuts. C. H. Banner, K. B. Catchpole.
Other Ranks : Killed 16 ; Wounded 86 ; Missing 12 ; Gassed 4.

The battalion was reorganized at Flesquières, where the Brigade Commander addressed and complimented it on its action.

On the 16th October it was at Wambaix. By the 23rd the battalion had followed the general advance in this part of the front as far as Vertain, some thirteen miles east of Cambrai, where it received orders to relieve the 2nd Highland Light Infantry and to attack next morning at 4 a.m., with the 23rd Royal Fusiliers on its right and the 9th Northumberland Fusiliers on the left. Assembly positions were reached by 11.45 p.m., with " A " Company, supported by " B," on the right, and " C " on the left, with " D " in reserve. The first obstacle to the advance was the Ecaillon stream, which was found to be much deeper than was supposed, reaching to the waists of the men. Then, as they breasted the rise beyond it, severe machine-gun fire was met. Nevertheless, the Royal Berkshire, and the 23rd Royal Fusiliers on their right, pressed forward for a total distance of some four thousand yards, passing over two streams and a difficult country, and remaining in touch with one another. On the left, however, the Northumberland Fusiliers had not been so successful, and consequently, the left flank of the Royal Berkshire was exposed to a depth of two thousand five hundred yards. This necessitated the formation, by " C " and " D " Companies, of a defensive flank facing N.W. This defensive flank was continued towards the S.W. by the 1st King's Royal Rifle Corps. In the advance three hundred prisoners and ten machine guns had already been captured.

The enemy counter-attacked at 1.45 p.m., but failed to make any progress, or to shake the British line.

A patrol, sent out at 1 a.m. on the 25th, found the enemy holding, with machine-gun posts, the railway from Valenciennes to Avesnes.

At 9.30 a.m. it was reported that the 3rd Division was holding the Bellevue Farm on the right, and the battalion was ordered to place posts on the railway, which was done and touch obtained with troops on both flanks. Later, the posts were moved forward to the stream beyond. In the evening " A " and " B " Companies were between the railway and the stream, with " C " and " D " behind the railway. Here they were relieved by the 1st King's Royal Rifle Corps in the early morning of the 26th, when the battalion moved to the east side of Bermerain.

The casualties in this operation were :

Officers. Wounded : Capt. E. L. Jerwood, M.C.,
                     2nd-Lieuts. H. J. Odell, H. Stout, J. Gould, D.C.M.
  Other Ranks : Killed 10 ; Wounded 66 ; Missing 7.

The casualties for the whole of October were 2 officers killed and 10 wounded. Of other ranks 46 were killed, 268 wounded, and 16 missing. At the end of the month, when the battalion was at Escarmain, its ration strength had fallen to 32 officers and 492 men. It had fought its last fight in the European War, for, after spending the first days of November at Escarmain and St. Hilaire, it was at the former on the eventful morning of the 11th when hostilities ceased.

Of the march to the Rhine after the Armistice, there is nothing to be said. The principal stages were Maubeuge, passed on the 19th, Charleroi on the 26th November.

At the end of December 1918, the 1st Battalion was at Arnoldsweiller, midway between Aix-la-Chapelle and Cologne.

North Persia

1919–21

We had intended not to carry the history of the 1st Battalion beyond the year 1918 ; but it has been suggested that some account of its operations in Northern Persia should be added, and the following has been drawn up by Captain M. C. Dempsey and is here given with only slight verbal alterations :

On 29th April 1919 the battalion, under the command of Captain (Brevet-Major) R. J. Brett, arrived at Chiseldon to reform after the war, and prepare for foreign service in the autumn. On 16th June it moved to Chatham, where it remained until it embarked at Gravesend on 18th September under the command of Major (Brevet-Lieut.-Colonel) W. B. Thornton, D.S.O., *en route* for Iraq.

After spending ten days at Karachi the battalion reached Basra on 28th October, and Nasiriyeh, a small town on the Euphrates, on 15th November. On 19th December, in consequence of minor trouble on the Upper Euphrates, the battalion was moved to Hillah—near the ruins of ancient Babylon— where it remained until, in the latter half of April 1920, it moved to Karind. Lieut.-Colonel (Brevet-Colonel) A. Mudge, C.M.G., had taken over command of the battalion on 15th March.

The village of Karind, situated at a height of some five thousand feet above sea-level, is fifty-two miles by road over the Persian border, and some hundred and forty miles north-east of Baghdad.

The country round Karind village had been chosen as the hill station to which British troops in Iraq could be sent to escape the extreme heat of the summer, and a large camp was erected there. It should be remembered that, with the exception of a small line in the extreme north-west corner of the country, and a few miles in the extreme south-east, Persia is entirely devoid of railways. On the journey from Baghdad to Karind the railway ended at Quaraitu, which place served as railhead to the battalion for the next twelve months, for the greater part of the time at a distance of some four hundred and fifty miles.

The troops in Northern Persia at this time consisted of the 36th Indian Mixed Brigade of :

Four Battalions (1 British, 3 Indian).
Guides Cavalry.
" A " Battery Royal Horse Artillery.
One Pack Battery.

The Head-quarters of the Brigade were at Kasvin, where the reserve was, and the remainder of the force was disposed between that town and Enzeli on the Caspian Sea, which was also occupied.

In consequence of the Bolshevik landing at Enzeli, the battalion left Karind for Kasvin on 25th May in two echelons. The distance to be covered was three hundred and twenty miles. Battalion Head-quarters, " B " and " D " Companies, moving in motor-lorries, arrived at Kasvin on 30th May—" A " and " C " Companies, marching, covered the distance in twenty-four days, arriving at Kasvin on 18th June. The Band, married families, and various details, together with the battalion baggage, remained at Karind.

On arrival at Kasvin the battalion came under the orders of Brigadier-General H. F. Bateman-Champain, commanding the 36th Indian Mixed Brigade.

The battalion occupied tents on the northern outskirts of Kasvin until, on 6th August, it, in conjunction with the 1st Battalion Royal Irish Fusiliers, and the 2nd Battalion York and Lancaster Regiment, occupied an outpost

position west and north of Kasvin, at a distance of from three to four miles
from the town, to prevent a further advance on the part of the Bolsheviks,
who at one time advanced as far as Kuhin—twenty-two miles from Kasvin
—driving the Persian Cossacks before them.

On 31st July " A " and " C " Companies had moved out to the Kuhin
area to help the retirement of the two Indian battalions from their position
there. On completion of this duty they returned to Kasvin.

The battalion occupied this position until 20th August, when, in consequence of a rapid Bolshevik withdrawal towards Enzeli, it returned to
camp at Kasvin. There it remained until, on 27th October, in consequence
of the collapse of the Persian Cossacks and subsequent advance of the
Bolsheviks, it moved in Ford vans and lorries to Gangah (82 miles from
Kasvin and 60 miles from Enzeli). There, with the 2nd Gurkha Rifles,
" A " Battery R.H.A., and one Squadron Guides Cavalry, it remained for
the winter. Lieut.-Colonel (Brevet-Colonel) S. G. Francis, D.S.O., was now
commanding the battalion. The small Persian village of Gangah, situated
on the Safed Rud, consisted of only a few mud-huts—ill-adapted for a Persian winter with its heavy snowfalls, frost, and gales. Rations were short
throughout the winter, as the passes which had to be crossed on the way
from railhead were frequently blocked with snow, and weeks would elapse
without the arrival of a mail. Despite these conditions, the health of
the battalion did not suffer greatly.

The force at Gangah was in touch with the Bolsheviks throughout
the winter, and various patrol encounters and raids took place. Major-
General Sir Edmund Ironside was now commanding the 36th Indian Mixed
Brigade.

The most important of these raids was carried out on 18th November,
when the battalion, in conjunction with the remaining troops of the small
force at Gangah, advanced some seven miles into the territory occupied
by the Bolsheviks, driving them back without serious difficulty, and remaining out until 27th November, when it returned to Gangah. The chief
share of the work fell to " C " Company, who met with some resistance in
crossing a small river—the Tariq Rud—on the 19th when two men were
wounded, the only casualties in the battalion.

The battalion had no further encounters with the Bolsheviks during the winter, though one or two small raids were carried out in the hills around Gangah against Persian brigands in Bolshevik pay.

From 24th January 1921 until the battalion left Gangah one company was kept at Manjil, eleven miles from Gangah on the only road to Kasvin. There was a bridge over the Safed Rud at Manjil.

On 9th April the battalion left Gangah for Kasvin, which it reached on the 16th, after a difficult march due to the amount of water in the various mountain streams which had to be crossed, and the fact that in many places the only existing road had been washed away.

The battalion remained at Kasvin for six days, and on 22nd April commenced its three hundred and seventy-eight miles' march to railhead at Quaraitu. The march was completed in twenty-seven days (including four halt days) an average of over sixteen miles a day actual marching. On 22nd May the battalion left Persia and entrained for Baghdad.

2nd BATTALION.
Meerut, India, Autumn 1910.

(*Back*) 2nd Lt. L. M. Handley. 2nd Lt. A. D. Gordon. 2nd Lt. C. H. Dent.
(*Middle*) Lt. H. S. Lickman. Lt. A. G. F. Isaac. Capt. G. P. S. Hunt. Lt. M. C. Radford. Capt. A. J. Fraser. Lt. C. L. Waters. Lt. L. W. Bird. Capt. W. B. Thornton. Lt. G. W. P. Dawes.
(*Front*) Capt. O. Steele. Major J. G. R. Walsh. Major E. Feetham. Lt.-Col. R. N. Gamble. Major G. H. Arbuthnot. Capt. A. G. E. Bingley. Capt. F. H. Moore.
(*On Ground*) 2nd Lt. C. Nugent. Lt. A. H. Mankelow.

CHAPTER XXVII

THE 2nd BATTALION.

From India to France. Neuve Chapelle. Le Bridoux

1914-1915

ON the date of the Declaration of War against Germany, the 2nd Battalion was still at Jhansi. On the 24th August 1914 it was warned to be in readiness to embark at an early date for England, and on the 4th September it moved from barracks into a rest camp, proceeding the same evening by two trains to Bombay, which it reached, after spending five days at Deolali on the way, on the 14th September. Going straight on board the transport *Dongola*, it awaited the formation of the convoy with which it sailed on the 20th.

The four-company organization, which had been adopted in April for training only, was brought into full operation at Deolali during the halt there. The convoy with which was the *Dongola* comprised forty-five troopships, was escorted by four warships and three armed auxiliary cruisers, and was organized in three divisions, the *Dongola* leading " B " Division.

The Indian Ocean was crossed without any interruption by the *Emden*, which was then still raiding in the Middle East. After safely passing the Red Sea and the Suez Canal, the guard of the convoy was taken over by the French Navy. A good many ships had now left it for other destinations, and it was still further reduced at Malta, whence the rest went on to Gibraltar. There the *Dongola* was berthed alongside the *Somali*, a transport carrying the 2nd Rifle Brigade, a battalion with which the 2nd Royal Berkshire was destined to be in close association throughout the war. There was some delay at Gibraltar, partially caused by news of an armed enemy raider, which was duly captured and brought in by British destroyers.

The *Dongola* and *Somali* then proceeded without escort till, off Ushant, wireless instructions were received to proceed to Liverpool, at which port the battalion disembarked on the 22nd October 1914, and was joined by ten officers and one hundred and ninety-two other ranks.

From Liverpool the battalion went by rail, on the 22nd, to Hursley Park Camp, Winchester, where it arrived next day. Here it was engaged in mobilizing as a unit of the 25th Infantry Brigade, 8th Division. The other battalions of the brigade then were the 2nd Rifle Brigade, 2nd Lincolnshire Regiment, and 1st Royal Irish Rifles. The 13th London Regiment was attached on the 12th November. The brigade was commanded by Brigadier-General A. Lowry-Cole, C.B., D.S.O. The 8th Division comprised the 23rd, 24th, and 25th Infantry Brigades and was commanded by Major-General F. Davies. It formed part of the 4th Corps commanded by Lieutenant-General Sir H. S. Rawlinson. On the 4th November the battalion marched to Southampton and embarked on the *Kingstonian* for Havre, where it landed next day with a strength of thirty officers and nine hundred and seventy-eight other ranks. The officers were :

Lieutenant-Colonel E. Feetham, Commanding.

Major J. G. R. Walsh.

Captain A. G. Macdonald, Officer Commanding " A " Company.

,,　　W. B. Thornton,　　　　,,　　　　" C "　　　,,

,　　G. P. S. Hunt,　　　　　　　　　　" D "

,　　A. E. F. Harris,　　　　　　　　　　" B "

,　　G. H. Sawyer.

,,　　A. J. Fraser.

,,　　T. R. Aldworth,　　Adjutant.

Lieutenant M. C. Radford.

..　　　R. G. C. Moody-Ward.

　　　　C. Nugent.

　　　　D. A. MacGregor.

　　　　A. D. Gordon,　　Machine-gun Officer.

　　　　E. F. Eagar.

　　　　W. A. Guest-Williams.

　　　　G. C. O. Mackwood.

Lieutenant G. G. Hodgson.
      ,,   A. H. Saunders,   Transport Officer.
Second-Lieutenant G. F. Gregory.
      ,,   H. R. W. Wood.
Captain and Quartermaster H. S. Lickman.

Attached.

Captain A. P. O'Connor,	R.A.M.C. (Medical Officer).
,, G. R. Wyld,	3rd Wiltshire Regiment.
,, L. W. Kentish,	5th Royal Fusiliers.
Second-Lieutenant N. West,	1st Royal Berkshire.

Second-Lieutenant
  ,,   A. G. L. Owen
        R. Crowley
        A. B. Raynes } Royal Sussex Regiment.
  ,,   G. S. Middlemiss

Having completed mobilization, the battalion entrained, on the 9th November, for Strazeele, where it arrived next day and was billeted with the 8th Division about Merville.

The situation in this direction at this time was that the great German effort to break the Allied line at Ypres had failed, and the troops were already settling down for the winter to the miserable and often monotonous trench warfare which was generally to characterize the war on the Western Front right on till the victorious advance in the latter half of 1918.

On the 14th November the 2nd Royal Berkshire, with the rest of the 8th Division, marched by Estaires to the front-line trenches at Fauquissart, in which it relieved the 1st East Surrey Regiment. This line faced south-west along the Rue du Bois, and the right of the 25th Brigade was about one and a quarter miles north by east of Neuve Chapelle. The brigade covered a front of about two miles. For the next month the battalion was in occupation of these trenches, being relieved every third day by one of the supporting battalions. The system of reliefs was for two battalions of the brigade to occupy the trenches, whilst the other two were in Brigade reserve. When in Brigade reserve, the position was at Laventie, about two miles behind Fauquissart, except for three days (7th–9th December), when it was farther back at Estaires. Throughout, the battalion which worked with the 2nd Royal Berkshire was the 2nd Rifle Brigade. No Man's Land varied in breadth, the nearest distance of the British from the German trenches being about forty yards.

The British trenches were in very low-lying ground, where constant pumping was necessary to keep them more or less clear of water. Even then, they were utterly miserable.

By the end of November, when the weather was mild, many men were suffering from so-called frostbite of the feet, which was afterwards known as " trench feet." There was incessant work at improving trenches, which was mostly carried out by the battalions occupying them, though those in reserve had constantly to supply working parties to assist. The battalion was of course constantly under fire, and casualties in varying numbers were of daily occurrence. The total amounted to eight men killed and twenty-three wounded.

The first reinforcements (seventy-eight men) joined on the 8th of December.

From the 14th to the 20th December the battalion was in trenches at Rue Bacquerot, where it relieved the 2nd Devonshire Regiment on the former date, and was relieved by the 2nd Scottish Rifles on the latter. Casualties continued as usual, and most days saw a certain number sent to hospital owing to the severe trials of conditions in the trenches. The trenches occupied by the 2nd Royal Berkshire and 2nd Rifle Brigade were on the left of the brigade front, those on their right being held by the Lincolnshire and Royal Irish Rifles. On the left of the Berkshire trenches were two companies of the London Regiment. One battalion of the brigade, in turn, was always in Corps reserve at Estaires. The 23rd Brigade was on the left, the 7th Division on the right of the 25th Brigade, but the positions varied from time to time in the brigade. An attack on the 18th December by the 23rd Brigade captured some German advanced trenches which were again lost. In this the 2nd Royal Berkshire was not engaged, though the brigade was ordered to demonstrate. On the 21st December the battalion returned to their former job and system of reliefs at Fauquissart. In their front, as in other places in the line, there was on the first Christmas Day of the war an informal truce between the opposing troops, some of whom met and conversed in No Man's Land, until this was prohibited about 11 a.m. on Christmas Day.

The Germans, after their manner, protested against the repair of British wire whilst continuing to repair their own, against which the British of course protested in turn.

Work at improving the trenches went on steadily and continuously, and there was constant bombing with the primitive hand-grenades and trench-mortars, which had not yet been replaced by Mills grenades and Stokes mortars.

During the last days of 1914, and the early part of January 1915, water in the fire trenches rendered them untenable. By this time a serviceable breastwork with shelters had been constructed above ground-level, at the cost of some increase in the daily casualty list, and *points d'appui* in rear of it were being prepared. The battalion continued taking its turn with the 2nd Rifle Brigade in these trenches during January and February 1915. The weather varied; it was cold and snowy in the latter part of January. Second-Lieutenant R. Crowley was wounded on the 16th January, Major J. G. R. Walsh on the 22nd, Captain G. P. S. Hunt on the 10th February, Lieutenant H. R. W. Wood on the 12th.

On the 1st March 1915, on the 8th Division being relieved by the 7th, the battalion went into billets at Laventie, and next day marched north-westwards to billets at Riez Bailleul, where it remained till the 9th, when it marched to take part in the attack on Neuve Chapelle. So far, the casualties in the battalion since its landing in France had been :

Officers : Wounded 6.
Other Ranks : Killed or Died of Wounds 46; Wounded 110.

Having marched during the night of the 8th/9th March, the battalion took position in the trenches astride the road leading south-east from Rue Tilleloy to Neuve Chapelle.

At 7.30 a.m. on the 10th March the battalion was disposed for attack, with two companies in front of the breastwork and two in rear of it, astride of Chimney Crescent Road. At 8.5 the advance started in four lines on a front between one hundred and fifty and two hundred yards. During the bombardment preceding the advance, the battalion suffered somewhat severely from " shorts " of the British artillery, Colonel Feetham's report stating that one shell alone buried twelve or fifteen men, who were only extricated after the advance, some dead and others badly wounded.

The German front-line trenches were carried with little opposition, and the first objective line was reached and made good. Here the battalion set to work to fortify itself. The German trenches to the right were blocked by a party under Lieutenant A. D. Gordon, who was severely wounded by a German who had already surrendered. Casualties from " shorts " continued till the first objective was reached.

At 9.30 a.m. the 2nd Rifle Brigade passed through the 2nd Royal Berkshire, which was still under a heavy enemy fire and lost, amongst other casualties, Captain and Adjutant T. R. Aldworth, and Lieutenant A. H. Saunders, both killed.

The other officer casualties on this day were :

Killed : Lieut. A. B. Raynes (3rd Royal Sussex, attached).
Wounded : Capt. A. E. F. Harris.
          Lieuts. C. Nugent, A. D. Gordon, E. F. Eagar, T. V. B. Dennis.
          2nd-Lieut. J. A. Cahill.

In this position the battalion remained during the night of the 10th/11th, and the day of the 11th. The officer casualties on the 11th were Captain A. J. Fraser and Lieutenant J. Ransom wounded. At 3.45 a.m. on the 12th the battalion was ordered forward to the eastern edge of Neuve Chapelle to support a projected attack by the 2nd Rifle Brigade. This attack was postponed, and the 2nd Royal Berkshire were sent back to their former position. They were again brought forward, at 9.45, to support the attack which was then fixed for 10 a.m. It was again postponed till midday, and finally cancelled. The battalion remained in support till 5.15 a.m., when the 2nd Rifle Brigade attempted to advance, but found the ground so open, and under such heavy enemy fire, that the attack had to be abandoned. The 2nd Royal Berkshire continued throughout the night of the 12th/13th on the eastern side of Neuve Chapelle. Its losses on the 12th in officers were heavy, considering there was no regular attack.

Killed : 2nd-Lieut. R. G. R. Hogen.
Wounded : Capts. W. B. Thornton, R. G. T. Moody-Ward.
          2nd-Lieut. J. W. Hillyard.

The losses in other ranks are not separately stated for the 11th and 12th.

At dawn on the 13th the battalion went back to its position of the 11th, but returned again at dusk to relieve the Rifle Brigade east of Neuve Chapelle where, during the night, the breastwork was much improved.   On the morning of the 14th Colonel Feetham, on appointment to command the 24th Brigade, handed over the battalion to Lieutenant D. A. MacGregor.   All day on the 14th there was heavy German shelling, but the casualties were less, owing to the improved cover.   In the period 10th to 15th March the casualties in other ranks, in addition to the officers named above, had been :

Killed or Died of Wounds 75 ; Wounded 220 ; Missing 17.

All the missing were believed to have been killed, as the nature of the operations was not such that any of them were likely to have been taken prisoners.

On the 16th March the battalion was relieved in the front trenches and sent back to four hundred yards west of Neuve Chapelle.   On the 18th, leaving behind to support the 2nd Rifle Brigade " C " and " D " Companies, the rest of the battalion went into billets at Croix Barbée.   Colonel Feetham had returned to command of the battalion on the 17th.

After relieving the 2nd Rifle Brigade in the Neuve Chapelle trenches for two days, the 2nd Royal Berkshire were relieved by the 1st Gloucestershire on the 23rd, and marched to billets at Bac St. Maur.   Second-Lieutenant M. D. Colbourne was wounded on the 21st March, and Captain P. A. K. Townshend next day.

The total casualties up to the 31st March since landing in France were :

Officers :   Killed 4.
            Wounded 17.
Other Ranks :   Killed or Died of Wounds 110.
            Wounded 340.
            Missing 27.

From Bac St. Maur the battalion marched, on the 1st April, to billets at Croix Blanche, where it was inspected and its turn out highly approved by Major-General E. T. Dickson, Colonel of the Regiment.   On the 2nd April Lieut.-Colonel Feetham made over command of the battalion, on his own appointment to command the 1/1st Staffordshire Brigade, to Major R. P. Harvey, who had joined the 2nd Battalion on the 21st March.   From the 5th to the 12th April the battalion occupied, alternately with the 2nd Lincoln-shire, billets at Croix Blanche and trenches near Rue Petillon.   On the latter date it returned to Bac St. Maur to billets in divisional reserve.   Next day it went into Brigade reserve billets near Fleurbaix, where it was inspected by the Brigade-Commander, and on the 16th it and other units which had been engaged at Neuve Chapelle, were inspected and addressed by the Commander-in-Chief, Sir J. French.

The only officer casualty in April was Second-Lieutenant A. G. Bourchier, accidentally wounded on the 12th.   On the 14th Major R. P. Harvey and Captain and Adjutant D. A. MacGregor proceeded to Neuve Chapelle and there read the burial service over the battlefield where so many Berkshire men had died.

On the 28th and 29th the 7th Division took over the lines of the Meerut Division, and was relieved of a corresponding part of its own front by the 8th.

After a turn of three days in the trenches at Bois Grenier, the battalion was at Fleurbaix again, at Bac St. Maur, and Laventie, and on the 30th April relieved the 2nd Rifle Brigade in its old trenches at Fauquissart.   On the 4th May at Laventie, Major H. M. Finch, D.S.O., assumed command of the battalion, which returned next day to Bac St. Maur and remained there till the 8th May.

During the period 16th March to 8th May 1915 the casualties had been :

Officers : Killed 1, Wounded 3.
Other Ranks : Killed or Died of Wounds 11.
        Wounded 25.

On the 8th May at 11 p.m. the battalion moved to assembly trenches for the attack on the German position.   At 5 a.m. on the 9th May the breast-work was occupied by the 2nd Rifle Brigade, with " C " and " D " Companies of the 2nd Royal Berkshire in support, and " A " and " B " in reserve in trenches behind it.

From 5 to 5.40 a.m. an intensive bombardment was poured upon the German trenches.   As it lifted, the Rifle Brigade left the breastwork to face a tremendous rifle and machine-gun fire.   The orders for the attack had required " C " and " D " Companies to move up to the breastwork as the Rifle Brigade left it.   What happened seems so curious and suspicious as

regards the origin of some orders * that it seems best to give the words of
the report written by Captain Nugent who was in command of the battalion
at the end of the action : " ' D ' Company advanced to the breastwork and
found some of the 2nd Rifle Brigade still there.   Those that had succeeded
in getting out of the breastwork were lying immediately in front of it, the
only cover offered them being some vegetation about ten inches in height.
The front fire trench was seen to be full of men.   ' D ' Company advanced
over the breastwork in the ordered formation.   They found the old fire
trench full of men belonging to the 2nd Rifle Brigade, 1st Irish Rifles, and
of the battalion.   These stated that an order had been passed along not to
advance farther, but from what source this order emanated it was impossible
to ascertain.   The Officer-Commanding ' D ' Company then collected these
details, and, together with those of the company under his immediate command, ordered them to advance in two rushes to the enemy's trench, the first
rush to extend to about half the distance.   On completion of the first rush
some men of the Irish Rifles and Rifle Brigade came rushing back shouting
' Retire at the double.'   The Officer-Commanding ' D ' Company ascertained
by whom the order was given, and, considering it to be a retirement in earnest,
ordered his men to crawl back to the trench and sap.   He then withdrew his
men to the breastwork in order to reorganize and to clear the old trench and
sap, so that the men still in front would be able to drop into them on retirement.

" Shortly afterwards orders were received by the Officer-Commanding
' D ' Company to collect and reorganize all men of the battalion still in the
breastwork.   These were ' B ' Company less two sections, ' A ' Company less
six sections, and two sections of ' D ' Company.

" ' C ' Company's experience was much the same as that of ' D ' Company.
It had advanced beyond the breastwork when an order was passed from the
Brigade-Commander ' No further advance.'   A few minutes later another
order ' Advance to the first German trench ' was passed.   The company
prepared to carry out this last order when a group of men came rushing back
shouting ' Retire at the double.'   These men were ordered to halt and lie
down with the company.   By whom either of these orders was issued is

---

* That is as to whether they did not emanate from disguised Germans, or Germans
speaking perfect English.

unknown. Shortly afterwards the survivors of this company received orders to withdraw to the breastwork, which they did. ' B ' Company advanced in rear of ' D ' Company, but only two sections passed beyond the breastwork, the remainder having been ordered to remain in the breastwork by the Officer-Commanding the company, who was afterwards wounded. The survivors of the two sections retired to the breastwork when the order to withdraw was given.

" The first two lines of ' A ' Company, under Captain D. A. MacGregor, passed over the breastwork and moved forward towards the German trench, carrying some of ' C ' Company with them. It appears probable that some of them succeeded in entering the enemy line, as it was afterwards ascertained that Captain MacGregor was wounded and taken prisoner. At 11.10 a.m. orders were received from Brigade Head-quarters to reinforce the troops who had succeeded in reaching the German breastwork. This was to be accomplished by passing down a sap made by the 13th (Kensington) Battalion, The London Regiment, and from there crawling forward man by man across open ground to a mine crater, then to rush the German parapet. The ground to be covered was beaten by machine-gun and rifle fire.

" This movement commenced about 12.30 p.m., but when about half-way to the crater, the 13th Kensingtons on the left, and the 2nd Lincolnshire in front, retired with a rush towards our breastwork. They had evidently received an order so to do from an officer of the 2nd Scottish Rifles (this order was afterwards verified by the officer who gave it). As it appeared to be a general retirement, the Officer-Commanding the battalion ordered it back to our breastwork. Orders were then received from Brigade Head-quarters to stay the movement of reinforcing and the battalion remained in the breastwork prolonging the left of the Scottish Rifles."

The casualties in this confused and disastrous attack were very heavy.

Officers. *Killed* (7) : Lieut.-Colonel H. M. Finch, D.S.O.
Major R. P. Harvey.
Captain and Adjutant R. G. T. Moody-Ward.
Lieuts. C. G. Watson, L. E. M. Atkinson.
2nd-Lieuts. J. Druitt, A. G. Bourchier.
Officers : *Wounded* (5) : 2nd-Lieuts. N. West, W. Aldworth, L. A. Paterson, W. R. Wacher, D. G. L. Bridge.

Officers. Missing (6) *:* Capt. D. A. MacGregor.

                     Lieuts. G. G. Hodgson, E. L. Lipscombe.

                     2nd-Lieuts. R. E. Cunliffe, M. Day, T. Watkins.

                     (All of these were killed except Capt. MacGregor.)

Other Ranks : Killed or Died of Wounds 52.

                  Wounded 185.

                  Missing 39.

Total casualties : 18 Officers and 276 Other Ranks.

At 12.45 a.m. on the 10th May the battalion was ordered back to Croix Blanche, where it assembled about 2.30 a.m.

After this costly action of the 7th May the command was held at first by Captain C. Nugent, the senior surviving officer, who on the 17th gave place to Captain G. P. S. Hunt. Returning to its billets at Bac St. Maur, the battalion was busy reorganizing till, on the 16th May, it moved to Estaires.

The month from the 25th May to the 25th June was spent in occupying trenches at Neuve Chapelle for six days at a time alternately with the 2nd Lincolnshire Regiment. The system at this time was to have one battalion in the front trenches, and the reserve battalion distributed with two companies in close support and two in billets at Laventie. On the 25th June, the brigade having been relieved by the Jullundur (Indian) Brigade, the 2nd Royal Berkshire went into billets near Sailly. The trenches occupied by them in June were in front of the road leading south-east from the Rue Tilleloy to Neuve Chapelle, at the end nearest the Rue Tilleloy.

After this there followed a long period, from the 26th June to the 23rd September, during which the 2nd Royal Berkshire and the 2nd Lincolnshire Battalions worked in conjunction defending the trenches at Bois Grenier. During it the battalion had two tours of Divisional reserve in billets at Bac St. Maur, one from the 9th to the 14th July, and the other from the 17th to the 31st August. The latter was the longest respite from the front-line work so far enjoyed. The tours of front-line service varied from three to six days. It was at this period that the work of the battalion snipers was facilitated and improved by the introduction of rifles with telescopic sights.

On the 29th July Second-Lieutenant G. G. Paine was wounded whilst observing with his field glasses, which were smashed by the bullet which wounded him. Next day Second-Lieutenant B. Russell, with a patrol, crept out through the grass in daylight and brought in two German iron wire posts of a new pattern. Going out again at night, he threw grenades into an occupied German listening post, and, after some firing, returned safely.

On the 31st July Captain N. B. Challenor was killed whilst observing with a telescope, and the bullet which killed him also wounded Lieutenant C. W. Battye.

During August half a company of cyclists and a considerable number of the King's Royal Rifle Corps were attached to the battalion for instruction. It met with the approval of Lieut.-General Sir W. Pulteney, commanding the 3rd Army Corps when he inspected it on the 23rd August, Of officers Second-Lieutenant F. H. Way was killed on the 11th September, Second-Lieutenant W. C. Adams wounded on the 12th.

The total casualties among other ranks between the 10th May and the 24th September were:

Killed or Died of Wounds 26.
Wounded 172.

On the latter date the 2nd Royal Berkshire went into the trenches near Bois Grenier at night, and took positions ready for the attack to be made next day on the German position. In this attack the battalion was under the command of Lieut.-Colonel G. P. S. Hunt, whose report on it is used in the following account.

The British trenches facing, in the neighbourhood of Le Bridoux, nearly south, formed a re-entrant semicircle of about one thousand yards diameter from the salient on the Bois Grenier–Le Bridoux Road on the left to the Well Farm salient on the right. The opposing German trenches ran more or less straight from points somewhat over one hundred yards in front of the two salients. From the back of the British re-entrant to the German line was over five hundred yards, but there were old fire trenches within the semicircle in which troops could assemble with a very much smaller distance to pass to the enemy trench. In these the 2nd Royal Berkshire assembled, with the 2nd Rifle Brigade on their right, and the 2nd Lincolnshire on their left. The three assaulting companies of the battalion were in the order "A," "B," "C" from right to left. There had been heavy bombardment of the German trenches for three days and much of the wire had been cut. The three companies were to assault each with two platoons in front line and the other two one hundred yards behind them ; bombing parties were told off from each company.

The attack started at 4.30 a.m. " A " Company, whether from the wire being imperfectly cut in their front, or from their exposure to view by an enemy searchlight, or from the greater readiness of the Germans in this part, failed to get into the enemy's front trench with more than a few men, who were not strong enough to hold on. The losses of the company were heavy ; Captain W. A. Guest-Williams was killed on the parapet, Lieutenant Vesey badly wounded, and Second-Lieutenant R. L. H. Simmons with the right bombing party was also killed. " B " Company in the centre was more successful in breaking into the German trench, where however it found itself separated from " A " on its right by a gap across which Captain Sawyer immediately began to attack towards the right. The German work known as the Lozenge was also cleared by bombers. The bombers on the left of this company missed the communication trench which they were intended to follow, and got into the Lozenge on their right. " C " Company on the left also got into the German front trench and bayoneted or drove out its defenders, but the left platoon suffered rather heavily from a machine gun. Lieutenant G. F. G. Gregory was killed leading his bombing party on the left which came into touch with the Lincolnshire, who had also got into the front trench. It had been very dark still when the assault was launched, many German dugouts were overrun, and their occupants fired from them on the rear of the troops who had passed.

The fight now developed into one mainly of bombs in the front trench which, as we know, had not been taken on the front of " A " Company, and there was much shelling, which caused loss to " D " Company in reserve in the assembly trench on the cinder track from which the others had started. The bomb fight swayed backwards and forwards as each side alternately was short of or well supplied with bombs. The long gap between " B " Company and the Rifle Brigade was never cleared, owing to the failure of " A " to get into the German trench. No one on the Berkshire front was successful in getting into the German second-line trench.

About noon " B " and " C " Companies found their outer flanks exposed by the falling back of the troops there. About 1 p.m. the Lincolnshire on the left found themselves unable to hold the enemy, and their withdrawal necessitated that of the Royal Berkshire. The casualties in retiring to the British line were not nearly so heavy as those in the advance. They amounted in all to :

Officers. *Killed* (7) : Capts. R. W. L. Oke, W. A. Guest-Williams.
Lieuts. R. H. G. Trotter, G. F. G. Gregory,
J. Vesey, M.C.
2nd-Lieuts. R. L. H. Simmons, B. Russell.
Wounded: Capt. G. H. Sawyer.
Lieut. G. E. Hawkins.
2nd-Lieuts. G. W. Lindley, H. T. R. Merrick.
Other Ranks : Killed or Died of Wounds 124.
Wounded 201.
Missing 60.

The losses would perhaps have been even heavier but for the existence of some deep ditches which facilitated the bringing forward of the men, though in the case of a party of " A " Company a ditch in front of the enemy's parapet was fatal. The men were bombed in it, especially when crowded up trying to rush the parapet.

The 25th Brigade was relieved by the 24th at 11 p.m. on the same day.

During the period from the 26th September to the 21st November the battalion, and the rest of the 8th Division, continued to occupy the trenches in the neighbourhood of Bois Grenier, but, thanks to the arrival from England of many new formations for service in the front line, it was possible to reduce the extent of front held by the division, and so to allow each unit a longer time in Divisional reserve at Bac St. Maur, and Brigade reserve at Fleurbaix. Between the 9th and the 22nd October the battalion was amalgamated temporarily with the 8th York and Lancaster Regiment, eight platoons of the latter being attached to the 2nd Berkshire and vice versâ.

On the 24th October there was a change in the constitution of the 25th Brigade. The 2nd Lincolnshire Regiment and 2nd Rifle Brigade left it for the 70th Infantry Brigade, from which it received in exchange the 11th Sherwood Foresters and 8th King's Own Yorkshire Light Infantry. This exchange was, however, reversed on the 9th November. On the 22nd November the battalion marched with the brigade viâ Vieux Berquin to the

1st Army Reserve Area about Sercus, where it settled down in huts, and later in billets, for a long period of relief from trench work, and to vigorous training in all branches.   This was varied, between the 20th and 23rd December, by a tour of divisional manœuvres.   On the former date Lieut.-Colonel G. P. S. Hunt, having been appointed to the command of an infantry brigade, was replaced in command of the battalion by Major A. M. Holdsworth.

On this second Christmas Day of the war there was no repetition of the informal truce of 1914, but a dinner was provided for the men of the battalion from Regimental funds.

The year 1915 was finished at Sercus.   During all the period spent in the 1st Army Reserve Area the battalion was busy training and replacing its recent losses.   It was accommodated sometimes in huts, and sometimes in billets.

THE SOMME FRONT.   OVILLERS.   VERMELLES.   BACK TO THE SOMME.

1916

On the 9th January 1916 the battalion again returned to the trenches, marching on that day to Estaires, and on the next relieving the 12th King's Liverpool Regiment in the trenches near Croix Maréchal, and, on being relieved there on the 14th by the 2nd Lincolnshire Regiment, it went back to Brigade reserve billets at Fleurbaix, about one mile north-west of Croix Maréchal.

From the 15th January to the 27th March the battalion, working with the 2nd Lincolnshire, was defending the trenches near Croix Blanche, with the usual intervals in Brigade and Divisional reserve.

So far the battalion and the 8th Division had been almost continuously in the area west of Lille, a low damp country in which the state of the trenches in wet weather was a constant misery for the troops condemned to them.   It was now about to move to a less waterlogged and flat country in the area of the future Somme Battle.   On the 28th March it marched to Lestrem, where it entrained, and at 1 a.m. on the 29th detrained at Longueau near Amiens, and marched to Flesselles.   There it halted till the 4th April, when it moved on to St. Gratien, and next day to billets in Divisional reserve at Millencourt.   From the 8th April it was defending various sectors of the area held by the 8th Division to the east of the River Ancre, north of Albert, extending from La Boisselle on the right to Aveluy Wood on the left. Its tours of Divisional reserve were either at Millencourt or Henencourt Wood. At the latter place athletic sports were held.

There was a raid by the enemy on the 1st Irish Rifles on the right of the 2nd Royal Berkshire which reacted on the latter. Lieutenant E. M. Medlicott and one man were killed and three wounded. During this tour the officer casualties were:

> *Killed :* Capt. A. J. Bowles, 2nd-Lieut. H. Davies (both on 10th April).
> 2nd-Lieut. E. M. Medlicott (11th April).
> *Wounded :* Capt. S. H. Hugo (19th April).
> Lieut. A. J. G. Goodall (21st May).
> 2nd-Lieut. R. Fidler (8th May).

The 30th June 1916 was the eve of the commencement of the Battle of the Somme, and during the night of the 30th June–1st July the battalion left Long Valley Camp, where it then was, to take up assembly positions for the battle of the 1st, in which its objective was the village of Ovillers, north of La Boisselle. On the right of the 2nd Royal Berkshire was the 2nd Devonshire, on the left the 2nd Lincolnshire Regiment. These three were the leading battalions of the 25th Brigade ; the 1st Irish Rifles were in support, and the 2nd Rifle Brigade in reserve. During the night of the 30th June–1st July the front and support trenches were shelled by the enemy. At 6.35 a.m. on the 1st July the British barrage opened, and at 7.30 the attacking troops went forward. During the barrage it was necessary to send out parties to open passages in the British wire, which had not been sufficiently cut.

The moment the attack started the battalion encountered a terrific rifle and machine-gun fire from the German trenches in front of Ovillers, which effectually prevented the waves reaching the enemy line. A small group on the left of the Royal Berkshire did succeed in getting into it, but was eventually bombed out again. By 7.45 both the Officer-Commanding (Lieut.-Colonel Holdsworth) and the Second-in-Command were wounded, in the sap on the left front of the advance, and the former handed over command to Second-Lieutenant C. Mollet (acting adjutant), who at the end of the action was the senior officer fit for duty, and wrote a brief account of it. He says that by 7.45 the British parapet was swept by such a storm of rifle and machine-gun bullets that exit from it was impossible. The Germans had put down a barrage on the front line since 6.35 a.m.

No news was received from the neighbouring battalions, which were evidently, as shown by their casualty lists, suffering at least as heavily as the Royal Berkshire. By 9 a.m. the Royal Berkshire could muster but two and a half platoons. They had gone into action with a strength of twenty-four officers and eight hundred other ranks. So terrible had their losses been that, by 9 a.m., they had left only four officers and three hundred and eighty-six other ranks. They had lost 53 per cent., the Lincolnshire had lost 62 per cent., the Irish Rifles 64 per cent., and even the Rifle Brigade, in reserve, lost 18 per cent. Before this war it used to be said that no troops could stand a loss of over 25 per cent. of their numbers, and that figure only applied to the very best. With losses such as had been suffered, it was plainly impossible to attempt a renewal of the attack, and the brigade remained in its old lines till night, when it withdrew, on relief by the 37th Infantry Brigade, to bivouacs in Long Valley. Even before this it had been necessary to withdraw the shattered battalions of the front and support lines and replace them (about 3 p.m.) by the less badly mauled 2nd Rifle Brigade. The casualties on this terrible day in the 2nd Royal Berkshire were as follows :

Officers. *Killed* (4) : Capt. R. C. Lewis, M.C.
       Lieuts. A. J. G. Goodall, O. G. Payne.
       2nd-Lieut. S. F. Schneider.
  Died of Wounds : Lieut.-Colonel A. M. Holdsworth.
  Wounded (7) : Major G. H. Sawyer, D.S.O.
       Captains R. Haye and J. A. Cahill.
       Lieut. W. G. Adams.
       2nd-Lieuts. W. S. Mackay, R. G. Green,
       W. Gale.
  Missing (8) : Capt. H. T. Rowley.
       Lieut. B. S. Robinson.
       2nd-Lieuts. H. Godfrey, B. H. Belcher,
       J. V. R. Owen, F. G. Shirreff, H. Heming,
       S. H. Bedford.
 Total Officer casualties 20.

Other Ranks : Killed or Died of Wounds 73.
                 Wounded 251.
                 Missing 93.
Total All Ranks 437.

After the disastrous losses of the 1st July it was necessary for the battalion to spend the period from the 2nd July to the 21st in reorganizing. It marched on the 2nd from Long Valley Camp near Albert to Dernancourt, and reached Ailly-sur-Somme by rail on the 3rd. It was now moving northwards, with the division, to a new area. Moving partly by march and partly by rail, it reached billets at Béthune on the 14th July.

On the 4th command of the battalion had been assumed by Major (T/Lieut.-Colonel) R. Haig, D.S.O., from the 6th Battalion Rifle Brigade. On the 21st the battalion marched to Divisional reserve billets at La Bourse, preparatory to going again into the trenches in the 8th Divisional area near Vermelles, five or six miles south-east of Béthune. When in Brigade reserve at this time trenches, not billets, were occupied. In this area the battalion remained till the 9th October 1916, during which period it was only twice in Divisional reserve, from the 7th to the 14th August at Sailly-la-Bourse, and from the 1st to the 8th September at Fouquières. Second-Lieutenant E. M. Webster was killed on the 1st August, Captain S. H. Hugo during a heavy bombardment and raid by the Germans on the 21st. For a week from the 4th September Lieut.-Colonel Haig was in command of the 25th Brigade, his place being taken during his absence by Major A. A. H. Hanbury-Sparrow, D.S.O.

On the 24th September a party of the battalion carried out a night raid on the German trenches, with the object of obtaining information as to the strength of defences, units defending them, their numbers, etc. The party was divided into three sections. The right party (A), under Second-Lieutenant V. R. Humphreys, consisted of fourteen other ranks ; the left (B), of similar strength, was under Second-Lieutenant R. C. Slade-Baker ; and the covering party (C), under Captain D. E. Ward, the officer-in-charge of the whole operation, comprised ten other ranks. A and B parties were to enter the trench at a distance of twenty yards from one another and clear it outwards, whilst C was to support them, when in the trench, by attacking their opponents from above it, and by repelling counter-attacks. The artillery was to bombard the German support and communication trenches for twenty minutes after zero hour, and trench-mortars were to co-operate on the flanks. The raiders, who were to start from as close as possible to the Germans, were to spend ten minutes in the trench. Signals to be by reed horn blown by the Officer-Commanding raiders. The men, who were armed with bombs, truncheons, etc., and, in the case of C, with rifles, had their faces blackened to render them less conspicuous.

The attack started at 9.15 p.m. Unfortunately the " Bangalore Torpedo," intended for the demolition of the German wire, failed to explode. Nevertheless, both A and B parties reached the trench, though much hampered by wire. There a fierce bomb fight was engaged in with the Germans, who had taken shelter behind the parados and threw their bombs from there. After five minutes of this fighting, the raiders were obliged to retire to their own lines. Though no prisoners could be taken, owing to the position taken up by the Germans, a good deal of useful information as to trenches and other defences, strength of defenders, and other matters was obtained.

The casualties were :

Officers. *Killed :* 2nd-Lieut. V. R. Humphreys.
            Wounded : Captain D. E. Ward, 2nd-Lieut. R. C. Slade-Baker.
Other Ranks : Killed or Died of Wounds 3, Wounded 6.

On the 10th October the battalion, being relieved in trenches by the 6th Leicestershire Regiment, marched to billets at Nœux les Mines. It was now bound for the Somme area again and, proceeding partly by march, partly by rail, and partly by motor-bus, it reached Citadel Camp at Doullens on the 16th October. Thence it moved, on the 19th, to Brigade reserve in trenches in the support line. The 8th Division had now been transferred from the Xth to the XIVth Corps. On the 22nd the battalion went forward to close support trenches behind the 2nd Lincolnshire Regiment, which it was to support in an attack next day at Zenith trench. It had three companies in Lark, Spider, and Fly trenches.

The attack, which had been fixed for 9.30 a.m., was postponed till 2.30 p.m. In front line the 2nd Lincolnshire was on the right, 2nd Rifle Brigade on the left. As the leading troops advanced, the Royal Berkshire moved up into the trenches vacated by the 2nd Lincolnshire, " C " and " B " Companies leading, followed by " A " and " D." This advance was attended by heavy casualties from German artillery fire. Just after 3 p.m. " C " and " B " Companies were ordered to reinforce the Lincolnshire, who were meeting with very strong opposition. At 4.15 " A " Company was ordered to support the Rifle Brigade in the first objective, and then to attack Zenith trench from the N.W. flank. At the same time " B " Company was ordered, if opportunity offered, to attack Zenith trench from the front. Ten minutes later " C " was ordered to co-operate with " A " and " B." Presently it was ascertained that the 2nd Lincolnshire had failed to reach the first objective, owing to the strong reinforcement of the defenders of Zenith trench. The projected capture of that trench had failed, and at 8 p.m., after the attackers had retired to their starting point, orders were received for a fresh attack at 3.50 a.m. by the Royal Berkshire on the right and Royal Irish Rifles on the left. It was decided that each battalion should attack with one company in first line, and one in second line twenty-five yards behind it. This attack also failed, owing to heavy machine-gun and rifle fire from Zenith trench, and at 4.30 a.m. on the 24th October the battalion was ordered back to its original position. It remained in close support trenches till the night of the 27th October, when it was moved into Brigade reserve in trenches farther back.

The casualties during these days were :

Officers. *Killed* (5) : Capt. M. H. Hissey.
Lieuts. E. Baseden, F. A. J. Oddie.
2nd-Lieuts. C. W. Griesbach, W. C. Hales.
Wounded (7) : Major A. G. Macdonald, D.S.O.,
Capt. E. C. Griffen.
2nd-Lieuts. J. C. L. Davies, E. A. Lloyd, B. K. Berry, W. J. Robinson, Rev. W. Elwell, C.F. (attached).
Other Ranks : Killed or Died of Wounds 50.
Wounded 143.
Missing 10.

On the 28th October the battalion was withdrawn from Brigade reserve, and, from the 29th October to the 2nd November, was at Citadel Camp. From the 3rd to the 7th November it was in billets at Méaulte. On the

8th it went into Divisional reserve at Briqueterie and on the 9th again returned to the front line, where it relieved the 1st Worcestershire Regiment in the left sub-section. Here it remained till the 11th, when it went into Brigade reserve, but returned to its recent position for the 14th and 15th.

Between the 10th and 15th the casualties in the ranks were very heavy, being : Killed 15, wounded 75 (56 of them gassed ; two died later of wounds). Lieutenant W. D. Lennard was wounded on the 11th, Lieutenant G. H. Carter and Second-Lieutenant W. A. Bartman on the 12th, the former dying of his wounds. On the same day Lieutenant W. E. Howse was gassed (not fatally), on the 14th Lieutenant W. H. Flint was wounded. These heavy casualties appear to have been the result of a gas-shell bombardment. The Brigade Diary notes that gas shells were specially numerous on Hog's Back Trench, where the battalion was at the time.

Being relieved on the 16th, the battalion was back near Méaulte on the 17th and 18th, after which it moved by rail to billets at Métigny.

Here it remained from the 20th November to the 27th December, busy reorganizing and training after the heavy losses on the Somme Front. Here, and at various camps in the back areas, the names of which and the dates on which they were occupied it is not necessary to give, the battalion continued training and recouping till the 27th January 1917, when it returned to front-line trenches at Rancourt.

ADVANCE TO THE HINDENBURG LINE. THE THIRD BATTLE OF YPRES.

1917

At Rancourt the battalion continued taking its turn in the trenches in what appears to have been a fairly quiet time. It went into Brigade Reserve from the 8th to 10th February, and then proceeded to G.H.Q. Reserve, where it remained till the 21st, when it marched to Bray-sur-Somme to trenches. On the 28th February it was at Linger Camp Curlu. It went up to Brigade support on the 2nd March, and into front line that night. Captain R. W. Wood and three men were wounded, and one man was killed on this date. In the night of the 3rd/4th March the battalion " side-slipped " to the left to take up battle positions, and on the morning of the 4th it was engaged in a big attack which had been carefully practised in rest billets on a model of the trenches.   The attack was on Pallas trench, which ran south, from a point opposite the S.W. corner of Moislains Wood (which itself was S.E. of St. Pierre Vaast Wood) in the direction of Moislains.

It was very dark still when the men left the trenches, following the barrage.   The slope of the hill in that direction caused the first wave and its " moppers-up " to bear a little too much to the left.   The support company, thanks to Captain Scobell having taken a compass bearing, moved quite straight.   The first wave passed over Pallas trench, and, whilst this was being mopped up, the second wave reached it and passed on to join the first, which was now well past Fritz trench, the next trench parallel to Pallas. It had been so damaged by the British artillery that the wave following the barrage, still in darkness, had failed to recognize it.   There was no resistance in either Pallas or Fritz trenches.   Some of the men even got into Bremen trench, the next beyond Fritz.   When the mistake was discovered, they retired to Fritz trench and consolidated their position there.   About 4 p.m. on the 4th, the support company in Pallas trench was so heavily bombarded that it could only muster twelve men under Lieutenant Cahill.   He was reinforced by two platoons of the Rifle Brigade, and a Lewis gun from the Irish Rifles.   During the day the Germans made several attempts to counter-attack, which were all repulsed.   One, at about 4 a.m. on the 5th, was more successful, and about three hundred yards of trench were lost on the right of the battalion.   The platoon sent up to assist there, under Lieutenant Parsons, reached Fritz trench to the left of the place intended, and there Parsons was killed.   Captain Hanbury-Sparrow, whose gallantry was highly praised by Colonel Haig, was wounded for the second time in the German counter-attack.

A counter-attack by bombing down Fritz trench was now organized by Captain Cahill and Lieutenant Prest.   It is a little difficult to follow in detail Colonel Haig's account of the different fights between Germans and British between Pallas and Fritz trenches during the 5th, but it appears that the Royal Berkshire were still holding a new trench between these two in the night of the 5th/6th when, at 3.50 a.m. on the latter date, their relief by the Royal Irish Rifles was completed, and they retired to Curlu on the Somme.

The casualties in these two days of heavy fighting were :

Officers. *Killed* (2) : Lieut. G. N. Parsons ; 2nd-Lieut. J. A. Neaton.
    Wounded (6) : Capts. A. A. H. Hanbury-Sparrow, D.S.O.,
       W. B. Scobell.
       Lieut. B. Haye.
       2nd-Lieuts. H. S. Gunson, P. D. Harrison,
       E. G. Faulkner-Smith.
Other Ranks : Killed or Died of Wounds 63.
      Wounded 170.
      Missing 16.

At Curlu, on the 6th in the afternoon, the battalion was inspected by the General-Officer-Commanding XVth Corps, who read a message of congratulation from the Commander-in-Chief.

From the 8th to the 10th the battalion was in Brigade reserve in Junction Wood. On being relieved by the 2nd Lincolnshire Regiment, it proceeded to the front line in Fritz trench till the 13th, and then had two days in Brigade support at Lock Barracks and Bouchavesnes. On the 16th March its disposition was, " C " and " D " Companies in front in Fritz trench, with advanced posts in Bremen and German Wood trenches, " B " in support in Pallas trench, and " A " in reserve in the old British fire trench.

The German retreat to the Hindenburg Line had now begun.

On the 17th, as it was ascertained that the enemy had evacuated his trenches, " B " Company was sent forward to hold an outpost line on the Canal du Nord east of Moislains, the main line of defence still being Fritz trench. Here the battalion was relieved, on the 19th, and went back to Junction Wood till the 23rd. On the 24th it advanced again to relieve various battalions which had pushed forward as the Germans evacuated more trenches. It was out of the front line during the day of the 26th, but returned the same evening to relieve the 2nd Lincolnshire in the main line of defence.

On the morning of the 30th an attack was made on the village of Sorel-le-Grand. This turned out to be a bloodless operation. Six patrols, each of twelve men and a N.C.O., were told off from " A " and " C " Companies, with one officer from each. The rest of these companies were in support, and the other two in reserve. When the patrols entered the village, towards 5 a.m, they found the German rearguard was gone. By 7 a.m. an outpost line had been set up east of the village. There were no casualties; indeed, the casualties of the whole period 6th March to 3rd April only amounted to six other ranks killed or died of wounds, and nine wounded.

The night of the 30th April/1st May was spent in front line about Fins, and on the latter date the battalion was in the main line of defence, Murlu-Equancourt. The Germans at this time were nearly at the end of their retirement to the Hindenburg Line. On the 2nd April the battalion replaced the 2nd Lincolnshire in the outpost line.

On the 4th April it was engaged in an attack on Metz-en-Coûture, with Gouzeaucourt Wood as its objective. It was in co-operation with the 20th Division. The attack was finally arranged for 2.15 p.m., having had to be postponed on account of snow rendering the work of the artillery difficult. At the prescribed hour the battalion moved off in line, with the 20th Division on its left. About 3.30 p.m. the right company reported that it was held up by rifle fire in front of the enemy's wire, and was digging in. The support company reported to the same effect. Colonel Haig then ordered the right company to try and work round the flank. At 3.50 another message reported the enemy being reinforced and about to counter-attack the Berkshire right. To meet this, " C " Company was sent up from reserve, its place being taken by a company of the 2nd Lincolnshire. Ten minutes later Colonel Haig ordered the left company to try and get round under cover of the hill on his left. Soon after this, Metz-en-Coûture was taken by the 20th Division, and, as there was now a considerable gap between its right and the left of the Berkshire, the 2nd Lincolnshire were ordered to send one company to fill it. With this reinforcement on his left, Colonel Haig ordered " A " Company, under Captain Cahill, round to the left to try and get into Gouzeaucourt Wood from the west. By 9 p.m. " A " Company reported having entered the wood which its patrols were searching.

At dawn on the 5th April the battalion found itself in the wood, in contact with the 20th Division on its left, and the Rifle Brigade on its right. The difficulties of the attack were considerable in the snow, and Colonel Haig does not consider his casualty list excessive under the circumstances. It was:

Officers: (names not stated) Wounded 3.
Other Ranks: Killed or Died of Wounds 23; Wounded 22.

A curiously large proportion of killed to wounded.

At the end of his report Colonel Haig adds a tribute to the good work of his patrols, sent out on the night before the attack under Lieutenants Hinde and Curtis. " These officers," he writes, " remained out about eighteen hours in close touch with the enemy, and when the enemy did retire shot down ten of them."

When the battalion was relieved, on the night of the 5th/6th April, it went back to Fins, and next day to Gouzeaucourt and Murlu, whence, on the 15th, it went to Brigade reserve at Hendecourt, and next day took over the outpost line from Gauche Wood to the road to Gonnelieu. Two companies were in front, one in support and one in reserve.

On the 18th the battalion co-operated with the 23rd Brigade in an attack on Villers-Guislains. The scheme of the attack was for the 23rd Brigade to attack the village, the final capture of which was expected to be completed about an hour after zero. The 25th, on the left of the 23rd, was to co-operate during that hour by firing heavily on all machine-gun positions likely to inter-fere with the attack, which was from south to north. The function of the 2nd Royal Berkshire was to send out strong patrols to dig in at fixed points, to bomb down a trench leading from Quentin Mill to Villers-Guislains, and to block it if there was strong opposition ; also to supply " mopping up " parties to deal with occupied dugouts, and to keep up a heavy rifle and Lewis-gun fire. All this was done ; the details need not be gone into, as they are only to be understood with a complete trench map. The battalion had no serious fighting, and its casualties for the day were only three men wounded. It was relieved by the 2nd Lincolnshire at 10.15 p.m.

After the capture of Villers-Guislains the battalion was in billets at Hendecourt till the 21st, when it supplied two companies to support the attack of the 2nd Lincolnshire Regiment on Gonnelieu. That village was taken with little opposition, and the supporting companies of the 2nd Royal Berkshire had no casualties. From the 22nd April till the 14th May the battalion took its turn alternately in the outpost and support lines, and then returned on relief to billets at Sorel-le-Grand. From the 15th May till the 5th July it had a good deal of moving about, but, as it was never in the front line, we will not give details, which would be of little interest. The moves were sometimes by march, sometimes by rail, and eventually " A," " B," and " C " Companies relieved the 1st Worcestershire at Ypres, whilst " D " was detached to the 171st Tunnelling Company, Royal Engineers.   Next day the three companies relieved the 2nd East Lancashire in the front trenches of the right sub-section of the 8th Division's front ; one company each was in front, support, and reserve till the 9th, when the battalion was rejoined by " D " at Dominion Camp.   " B " and one platoon of " C " were left behind in line to carry out a raid planned for the 10th.

In over three months, from the 4th April to the 9th July, the casualties had been only two other ranks killed and seventeen wounded.

The raid above alluded to was duly carried out, by the detachment left behind, in the night of the 10th/11th July.

The strength of the party was one hundred and sixty-eight all ranks ; the platoon of " C " had been added to " B " on account of the presumed strength of the enemy's position.   Zero hour was 1 a.m. on the 11th July. A quarter of an hour earlier the raiders were ready in Kingsway.   As the barrage began punctually at zero, the company pressed rapidly forward, reaching the German front without casualties, except from the British barrage, into which some sections pushed on too rapidly.   Of the company 50 per cent. had never been in action before and therefore lacked experience. The second objective was reached in fourteen minutes.   When the first trench was passed it was so dark that it was difficult to recognize the entrances to dugouts, and some of these were passed by unbombed.

In consequence of this, some Germans lurking in one of them came out with a machine gun and brought it into action after the raid had passed. This gun and its team were knocked out by Sergeant Sturgess.   The Germans put up a good fight everywhere ; only one prisoner was taken, and he, thanks to the intelligent self-restraint of Private Bowden, at whom the German had fired.   Bowden, realizing the importance of prisoners for identification purposes, restrained his natural inclination to bayonet the man, who held up his hands as soon as he had fired.*   In one case two Germans, pretending to surrender, threw bombs, and were of course killed.   Many strongly held dugouts were bombed, and there must have been numerous casualties in them.   Independently of these, it was estimated that thirty of the enemy had been killed in hand-to-hand fights.

* Bowden was awarded a parchment certificate for this.

The Berkshire casualties were :

Officers (names not given) : Wounded 2.

                                    Wounded and Missing 1.

Other Ranks : Killed or Died of Wounds 3.

                   Wounded 35.

                   Missing 2.

The raiding party rejoined on the 11th, and went with the battalion to Ouderdom, and afterwards to Rebecques and Tournehem for training, which lasted till the 24th. It then returned to Dominion Camp, and on the 29th to Swan Château. On the 30th it was at Halfway House, ready for the coming attack from Ypres towards the east and north-east. The first positions in front of the 8th Division were to be attacked by the 23rd and 24th Brigades, with the 53rd Brigade (18th Division) on their right, and the 45th Brigade (15th Division) on their left.

The 25th Brigade was not to attack till 6½ hours after zero, when it would advance with the 2nd Royal Berkshire in reserve, and the other three battalions in front line. The Berkshire Battalion was to assemble just west of Halfway House at 4 hours after zero. As the front line advanced at zero plus 6 hours 28 minutes the battalion would follow, throwing out patrols to connect with the brigades on either flank.

When the battalion moved punctually from west of Halfway House there was not much shelling, but it had to bear to its left as far as the Menin Road to avoid the 5·9" barrage which the Germans were putting down on their old fire trench. When the battalion, having re-formed here, moved on Château Wood it encountered severe shelling, and had some casualties. Being somewhat scattered, it was again formed beyond the wood. A short way beyond this it was found that the 53rd Brigade was somewhat behind, and the 2nd Royal Berkshire formed a defensive flank which commanded the ground as far as Glencorse Wood, the enemy's machine guns in which were giving much trouble and causing many casualties.

The advance was then ordered by the General-Officer-Commanding, to stop for the present, as the 15th Division was held up.

At 11.5 a.m. the battalion was ordered to reinforce the right of the 2nd Lincolnshire. Two companies and Head-quarters were now in reserve, the other two divided between the defensive flank and the 2nd Lincolnshire. The 15th Division was still hung up in Glencorse Wood.

Soon after noon a counter-attack was launched against the 2nd Lincoln-shire, and at 12.30 the Berkshire was ordered to withdraw as far as three hundred yards east of Ziel House and prepare to receive a counter-attack. A surprise bomb attack, at 2 p.m. on the left, caused some confusion and retirement, but the troops rallied and recovered the lost ground.   At 3.3 p.m. Brigade orders directed the battalion to consolidate and hold on at all costs.

At this time the 2nd Lincolnshire, on the left of the 2nd Royal Berkshire, was not up to the line, and was unable to straighten the line on account of heavy machine-gun fire on its left.   At 4.30 " C " Company in front line had to be reinforced by half of " A," and at 8 p.m. orders from the Brigade required a company to be sent to reinforce the Rifle Brigade on the railway to the left.   At 8.40 the Berkshire were informed that, though the rest of the 25th Brigade was to be relieved by the 24th, they were to remain with the 24th.   The commander of the 24th Brigade sent them to occupy the position now vacated by the 2nd Lincolnshire.   Here " C " was on the right, " D " on the left, and, later in the night, " B " returned from the Rifle Brigade which it had supported since 8 p.m.

The 2nd Lincolnshire was not completely relieved by the Royal Berkshire till 4 a.m. on the 1st August, as the weather was very bad and the going very heavy.   At 11.45 a.m. on the 1st the battalion was informed that it would be relieved by the Loyal North Lancashire, but, owing to the heavy going and the German shelling with heavy stuff for six hours after noon, it was not till 6 p.m. that the relief was complete.   The sections moved off as they were relieved, and were directed to Pioneer Camp, whence they were sent on to Winnipeg Camp.   Most of the battalion arrived there that night, but some stragglers only reported there the next morning.   The Battalion Diary says it was " not seriously engaged," but the tale of casualties was hardly light.

Officers.   Died of Wounds : 2nd-Lieut. J. C. Lee.
    Wounded :   Lieut.-Colonel R. Haig, D.S.O.
           2nd-Lieuts. W. C. Snelling, N. D. Bayley.
Other Ranks :   Killed or Died of Wounds 26.
     Wounded 107.
     Missing 15.

After this action the 2nd Royal Berkshire went back to the Steenworde training area, returning to the front on the 13th August. " A " and " C " Companies went to the Esplanade, Ypres, " B " and " D " to Bellewarde Ridge, and on the 15th the whole battalion moved to Westhoek Ridge to assembly positions for the attack on the next day.

The first objective was the road leading south-east from Zonnebeke along Glasgow spur, the second parallel to it just east of the village, and the final objective was as far beyond the second as the second was beyond the first.

The Berkshire Battalion was to lead on a front of three companies (" A," " B," " C "), each in two waves of half-companies, with " D " " mopping up," as far as Zonnebeke Redoubt, after which it would become the reserve company. When the first wave had taken the Iron Cross Redoubt, the second would pass through.

It was 4 a.m. on the 16th when the battalion was formed up on tapes. At 4.45 the advance commenced, and little difficulty was experienced in getting forward beyond the marshy bed of the Hannebeke where the battalion was re-formed. About fifty prisoners had been taken so far. It now appeared that the troops on the right had not advanced as fast, and " C " Company on the right was deputed to guard this flank as " A " and " B " went forward. After this the battalion was under a heavy machine-gun enfilading fire from Nonne Boschen and Polygon Woods on its right flank. The greater part of Iron Cross Redoubt and the defences north of it were captured, with another fifty prisoners. The right had suffered severely and was now held up, and the Irish Rifles on the left were not up with the left company which, under Captain Cahill, had got in places on to the green line, still far behind the first objective. A line of small posts was now formed, but, owing to casualties and heavy fire from the right flank, and even the right rear, the line was now very weak. This line was on the crest north of Polygon Wood. At 10.30 a.m. a strong counter-attack was launched by the Germans from the E.S.E. and against the front. Exactly what happened in this is unknown, but the result was that the line was driven back to the west of the Hannebeke, where the battalion had assembled in the early morning. The German attack stopped at the Iron Cross Redoubt, but the losses of the Royal Berkshire had been so heavy that Lieut.-Colonel Hanbury-Sparrow's report says that there were only left four officers (one wounded) and about one hundred men.   The units were much mixed up, and this figure probably represents the number available for formation.

At 3 p.m. another German attack developed from the south-east and from Nonne Boschen Wood and Zonnebeke Redoubt.   The attack progressed slowly in face of the British heavy artillery now firing, but by 5.30 p.m. it was within six hundred yards of the brigade front.   Owing to shortage of ammunition, firing by the British had to be much limited.   At this juncture the division on the right retired in some disorder, exposing the right of the 8th, whilst the left had already been left in the air, owing to the retirement of troops on that side.   There were now only sixty Berkshire and twenty Lincolnshire men available to form a defensive flank, on the right facing west, to cover the retirement which had to be made.   No further German attacks took place and the battalion, on being relieved by the 2nd Northamptonshire, went into reserve on Bellewaarde Ridge. It was reorganized as soon as possible in four platoons, the strongest of which was about thirty men.   The fighting strength of the battalion was now only three officers and one hundred and fifteen other ranks.   It had behaved very well, but had lost terribly.   In the first retirement a considerable number of wounded, including at least one officer, had to be left behind to fall into the enemy's hands.   The battalion claims to have brought down at least one German aeroplane by rifle fire.

The casualties on this day were :

Officers. Killed   (2) : Capts. J. A. Cahill, M.C., H. E. Howse.
            Wounded (7) : Capts. J. B. M. Young, E. G. Hales.
                    2nd-Lieuts. W. A. Grove, E. W. H. Cabespine,
                        M. W. West, W. J. Phillips, H. A. V. Wait.
            Missing (5) : 2nd-Lieuts. S. M. Loundan, A. E. Mills,
                        E. L. Thompson, A. E. Berry, G. R. Threlfall.
                        (The last three were afterwards reported as
                        prisoners-of-war and 2nd-Lieut. Mills as killed.)
Other Ranks : Killed or Died of Wounds 24.
            Wounded 223.
            Missing 120.
Total : Officers 14 ; Other Ranks 367.

From Bellewaarde Ridge, on the 19th August, the battalion proceeded by bus to Caestre for training, where it remained till the 26th.   Next day it moved to the II Anzac Corps area, where it was in camp in Divisional reserve at Canteen Corner till the 10th September. On the 11th, when it again moved into front-line trenches, and later into support, it was reorganized on the basis of two companies—" A-B " commanded by Captain J. A. Lowe, and " C-D " under Captain H. H. Flint, M.C. Nothing notable occurred till the 27th September, when the 24th Brigade relieved the 25th, and the battalion went into Divisional reserve at Menegate Camp, where it remained till the 12th October, when the 24th and 25th Brigades again changed places, the 25th going to the left sub-section of the 8th Division front.

On the 20th October one platoon of " D " Company raided the enemy's trenches. A patrol sent out at 7 p.m. found a gap of six yards width in the German wire, and heard a working party about one hundred yards to the north. The strength of the raiders, sent out at 3.55 a.m., was one officer and thirty-five other ranks and they were divided into three parties—" A," " B," and " C." The objectives were the infliction of loss and capture of prisoners. On entering the German trench " A " was to move northwards along it, " C " southwards, and " D " eastwards along a communication trench.

Starting with the barrage, the party reached the German wire, and found a line of shell holes connected up by covered passages. These were in front of thick wire, but no enemy was found in them. The party then passed through the six-yard gap, and entered into the German front-line trench, which they found empty. After a ten minutes' search, which discovered nothing of any use for identification, the party returned without any casualties. They had not been fired on, though the Germans in the support trenches sent up flares. The front trench had been very badly damaged by the British artillery. Nothing else of note occurred during October. On the 31st the battalion returned to Divisional reserve at Menegate, where it remained till the 11th November.

On the 12th the 25th Brigade was relieved by the 18th Australian Brigade, and the battalion went into the La Motte area for training. On the 16th the 8th Division relieved the 3rd Canadian Division in the left sector of the Canadian Corps front towards Bellevue, north-east of Passchendaele, and most of the rest of the month was spent in Ridge Camp. On the 22nd

Lieut.-Colonel Hanbury-Sparrow, having been badly gassed on the 19th, had to give over the command of the battalion to Lieut.-Colonel C. R. H. Stirling, M.C., of the 2nd Scottish Rifles.

Besides Colonel Hanbury-Sparrow, the casualties in this period had been :

Officers.   Killed : Lieut. M. S. Carswell (17th September) ;
Lieut. R. L. Hope-Lumley (11th October).
Wounded : Major H. P. Allaway, M.C., Captain J. A. Lowe, Lieut. A. F. R. Browne, M.C.
(All on the 19th November.)
Other Ranks : Killed or Died of Wounds 24.
Wounded 94.
Missing 1.

On the 1st December the 25th Brigade was in line on the right front of the VIIIth Corps, with orders to attack next day in conjunction with the IInd Corps on its right.   The brigade was to attack on a three-battalion front, with the 2nd Royal Berkshire on the right, 2nd Lincolnshire in the centre, and 2nd Rifle Brigade on the left ; Royal Irish Rifles in reserve.   The front was a little north of Passchendaele, at the extreme eastern limit of the British advance in 1917 in this direction, and the object was a line running from N.W. to S.E., passing one hundred and fifty yards west of Wrath Farm to a point about two hundred yards north of Exert Farm, where it curved back towards the south-west.   The left boundary of the battalion's area was a line directed N.E. towards Wrath Farm.   The assault was to be in three waves.   The formation was " B " Company on the left, half of " D " on the right, " C " and the rest of " D " to form a defensive flank on the right in the later part of the advance, and " A " to act as reserve.

The attack was to be carried out at night, and the battalion was formed up as soon as it was quite dark.   " A " lost its way in the dark, and did not reach its reserve position till 9 p.m.   Others were also in difficulties in the marshy ground, which had to be passed on duck-boards, which had in places been destroyed.   It was not till 11.30 p.m. that the battalion could be manœuvred into its proper stations for the attack, and it had already lost some men from shelling.   At 1.55 a.m. on the 2nd December " B " and " D " Companies were led forward by Colonel Stirling.   The 2nd Lincoln-shire were in touch on the left.   For the first three minutes the movement was unobserved by the enemy, as the moon was hidden by clouds. Then he began sending up signals, and opened a heavy but ill-directed and not very damaging fire. The Lincolnshire now bore off too much to their left, and it was found impossible to keep the left of " B " Company in touch with them. At 2.4 a.m. the German barrage fell heavily on the road in rear, and on the reserve and support platoons of " B " Company, and the Head-quarters of the company was blown up. Meanwhile, a platoon each of " B " and " D " had made its way into the Southern redoubt and were engaged in bayonet and bomb fighting, with many casualties on both sides. They lacked support, owing to the left of " B " having been moved to the left to try and keep touch with the Lincolnshire. The remnant of these platoons was finally forced back to the S.W. corner of the redoubt, where they dug in. The rest of " B " Company, on the left, had gained the trenches connecting the Northern and Southern redoubts, killed many Germans, and captured three machine guns. This party was led by Second-Lieutenants Upton and Tremellen. On the right " C " Company, under Second-Lieutenant Smith, had formed a defensive flank as directed, but had had much fighting to get into touch with " D." It captured an officer, thirty men, and one machine gun. Beyond these points, which were considerably short of the objective, the battalion seems never to have pushed forward, and it had some difficulty in holding on where it was during the day. The operation was by no means a complete success, and its failure is attributed by Colonel Stirling to want of depth in his centre, due to the easing off to keep in touch on the left.

The casualties were :

Officers. *Killed :*   Lieut. S. H. Troup.
         Wounded : 2nd-Lieuts. W. A. Grove, H. E. E. Osborne,
                   C. E. Morris.
         Missing :   2nd-Lieuts. H. A. V. Wait, F. Giddings (both now
                   recorded as killed).
Other Ranks : Killed or Died of Wounds 35.
             Wounded 83.
             Missing 33.
             Total 151.

After the action of the 2nd December the battalion was sent by rail to Boirdinghem and was training in the Moringhem area from the 4th till the 25th, the fourth Christmas Day of the war.

On the 26th it marched to the Wieltje area, and on the 30th relieved the 24th Brigade in the line about Bellevue.

YPRES. THE GERMAN OFFENSIVE TOWARDS AMIENS. THE GERMAN ATTACK ON THE AISNE. THE FINAL BRITISH OFFENSIVE BY DOUAI.

1918

The 25th Brigade was relieved by the 23rd on the 3rd January 1918, and the battalion went by rail to Warrington Camp in the Branhoek area. Here, and in the Wieltje-St. Jean area, it remained till the 25th again relieved the 23rd Brigade in the front trenches. It seems unnecessary to detail the various posts of the battalion in this neighbourhood down to the 21st March, 1918, sometimes in line, and sometimes in the different reserve areas. Nothing of special note, outside the usual routine of winter trench warfare, occurred.

In the period from the 3rd December 1917 till the 21st March 1918 the casualties were :

Officers. Killed :   2nd-Lieut. W. V. Knowles (3rd December 1917).
          Wounded : 2nd-Lieut. W. A. Upton, D.S.O. (31st December).
                  2nd-Lieut. R. W. Griffiths (6th March 1918).
Other Ranks : Killed or Died of Wounds 15.
          Wounded 69.
          Missing 3.

The 21st March 1918 was the first day of the great German spring offensive towards Amiens against the 5th British Army, and on the 22nd the 8th Division was sent to the Amiens-St. Quentin Road, on the extreme British right, to help in stemming the flowing tide of German victory. The 2nd Royal Berkshire entrained on the 22nd at Arques, detrained at Guillancourt, and marched to camp at Chaulnes, which the Germans had not yet reached.

Here the diary of the battalion unfortunately fails us ; for it gives no detailed account of its movements from the 24th to the 31st March, the most critical period of the great offensive. The only entry in the Battalion Diary for these days is to the effect that it "took part" in operations. We can hardly be surprised at this, looking to the terrible strain and fighting of this period and the enormous losses of the battalion in action.

We have only been able to gather a rather sketchy outline of its action from the Brigade Diary.

At midnight on the 22nd the brigade received orders to move up by omnibus to the left bank of the Somme, between Roncy-le-Grand on the right and Pargny, about two miles downstream. Here it would be facing east. The 2nd Royal Berkshire was on the right, the 2nd Rifle Brigade on the left. The move to the river was under heavy shell fire to relieve the 50th Division which, having been heavily engaged, was now passing back westwards through the 8th. Meanwhile, the enemy had advanced to the right bank, forcing back over the river such troops as were still on that side. The first orders placed all three battalions * in front line, but the Berkshire were, by later orders, drawn back into reserve. At the close of the day the 2nd Lincolnshire and the 2nd Rifle Brigade were holding the bank, whilst the 2nd Royal Berkshire had two companies at Morchain and two at Monk's Quarry.

At dawn on the 24th the Germans attacked, passing the river at Pargny, Béthencourt and Fontaine-lez-Pargny by rafts, and by trees felled across the stream. They were at once attacked by all troops in front line, and eventually the brigade reserve (2nd Royal Berkshire) was thrown in. An obstinate defence was put up at Monk's Quarry on the right and other places.

In this hotly contested battle Lieut.-Colonels Paton of the Rifle Brigade and Stirling of the Royal Berkshire were both dangerously wounded. By 2 p.m. the brigade was holding trenches astride the Morchain-Pertain Road, and west of Potte.

At 10 p.m. orders were received for the brigade to attack next morning from in front of Licourt, in conjunction with the 24th Brigade and the French 24th Division. The attack was to be by the 2nd Royal Berkshire on the right, and the 2nd Rifle Brigade on the left, each battalion being led by a composite company one hundred and sixty strong. The attack of the 24th Brigade and the French division failed to mature, and the enemy attacked at 6.15 a.m. Owing to the British troops having been moved northwards to Licourt for the attack, in order to clear the front of the French division, the enemy found the front only thinly held, with a dangerous gap on the right of the brigade.

* Brigades had recently been reduced from four to three battalions.

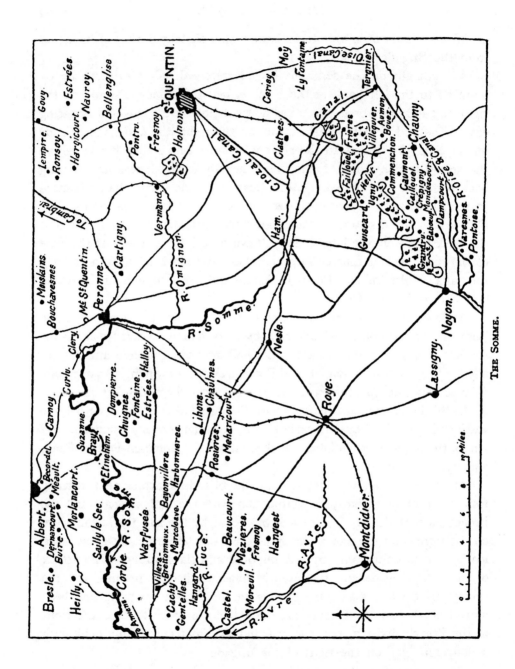

THE SOMME.

At 10.15 the brigade was just south of Morchain preparing to fall back, as the troops on both flanks had already done so. A force of about five thousand Germans had entered Dreslincourt at 9 a.m. in right rear of the brigade, and strong parties were pushing northwards. The brigade had no troops in hand, and its casualties were terribly heavy. At 3.15 p.m. it was back at Omiecourt, and the enemy had occupied the western edge of Pertain, and was advancing twelve hundred yards on the right flank of the brigade.

There is no further record for the 25th March, but the retreat seems to have continued slowly ; for at 7.30 a.m. on the 26th the 25th Brigade was just west of Lihons, about four miles behind Omiecourt. At 8.30 it was reorganized, with orders to be ready to move at ten minutes' notice.

At 10.55 the Royal Berkshire was on the railway south of Lihons, on the line Lihons-Méharicourt, with the 1st Sherwood Foresters on its right. The 23rd and 24th Brigades had been withdrawn clear to Lihons at 2 p.m., and at 4.30 p.m. the 25th began its retirement, which ended in its assembly at 6 p.m. west of Rosières en Santerre. On this line the 8th Division was ordered to hold to the last. The German pressure had apparently slackened somewhat, and the night was fairly quiet.

At 8.30 a.m. on the 27th the fighting strength of the 2nd Royal Berkshire was reduced to nine officers and one hundred and sixty-eight other ranks, and the other battalions of the brigade were even weaker. At 9.15 some troops of the 8th Division which were still east of Rosières fell back, but were again carried forward by the General-Officer-Commanding 25th Brigade and strengthened by the 2nd Rifle Brigade. At the same time the Royal Berkshire were ordered southwards to replace the 2nd Rifle Brigade behind the right front of the division. At 1 p.m. the retirement of the division on its left resulted in exposure of the left flank of the 8th Division. From this time till 8 p.m. a series of counter attacks northwards was carried out by portions of many units, including the 2nd Royal Berkshire. Men were thrown in from different brigades, transport lines, and every available source. At 6 p.m. the troops to the left of Rosières station were placed under the command of Brigadier-General Grogan of the 23rd, those to the right under Brigadier-General Haig commanding the 24th Brigade. The 25th Brigade was commanded by Brigadier-General Coffin, V.C.

At this time there were serious reports of the enemy massing for attack.

At 7.30 p.m. the line had been established through Rosières station north-westwards to Harbonnières cemetery, and the 50th Division was ordered to relieve the 8th in it.

The withdrawal of the 25th Brigade commenced about 9 a.m. on the 28th March, and by noon it was in Divisional reserve.

At 3 p.m. it was ordered to retire to Moreuil, where it was assembled, the 2nd Royal Berkshire being still in reserve.

On the 29th, after being ordered back to Jumel and again forward to Moreuil, the brigade was posted astride of the road leading N.E. from Moreuil, facing E.S.E. and with orders, if forced back, to retire northwards fighting rearguard actions. They appear to have had no fighting on this day, and at 11 p.m. they were ordered to the high ground north of the wood which they had held during the day. The Germans had been found earlier in the day occupying the wood E.S.E. of Moreuil. On the 30th at 1 a.m. a French regiment was found about three-quarters of a mile from the brigade position. Its commandant proposed crossing the Avre, by the bridge at Castel, to the left bank. By agreement with the 20th Division, the 25th Brigade was to move to Castel and hold the bridge there; but when it was reached, about 6.30 a.m., it was found that the French were in sufficient strength to hold it. The brigade, therefore, followed the rest of the 8th Division to Rouvrel, S.W. of Castel. Here they had some food and rest on the Dommartin Road north of the village, and then crossed the Noye stream to Cottenchy, where they were well behind the farthest point of the German advance.

At 12.45 the brigade was ordered back to Rouvrel to protect the right flank of the 24th Brigade, and took position south-east of the village on the south side of a wood, where they were placed temporarily under the General-Officer-Commanding 24th Brigade, their own G.O.C. being then at Divisional Head-quarters.

At 5 p.m. they were sent across the Avre at Castel to support the 23rd and 24th Brigades which were relieving the 24th Division. The morning of the 31st March was fairly quiet. The 2nd Royal Berkshire were in Castel, supported by the 2nd East Lancashire on the railway.

At 2.30 came news of the line being broken, and the 25th Brigade, as reserve of the 8th Division, was ordered to restore the situation. The Royal Berkshire and East Lancashire were ordered to assemble on the railway west of Castel, and at 3.14 orders issued for the counter-attack. It was to be commanded by Major Griffin of the Berkshire, who had under him also three companies of the East Lancashire with machine guns.

It was in the Moreuil Wood that the breach had been made, and the objective was an outlying copse on the north-west of that wood opposite the Castel Bridge. The attack was completely successful and Major Griffin occupied a line running from S.W. to N.E., passing between the copse and the main wood. But in front of him there was higher ground held by the enemy in the wood, which he reported rendered his position dangerous, and, as his men were very wet and weary, he asked to be relieved when darkness should render this feasible. At 7.45 p.m. the 23rd Brigade was ordered to relieve him, but the operation could not be completed till the early hours of the 1st April.

For the period 22nd/31st March officer casualties can be given for each day, but those of other ranks are only given in mass. The casualties were :

Officers.

22nd March. *Wounded :* 2nd-Lieut. H. Bromhall.

23rd March. *Wounded :* 2nd-Lieut. H. G. Rew, Captain J. A. Lowe, 2nd-Lieuts. B. Mountjoy, J. C. Murray, L. Smelt, Capt. S. L. Rozelaar.

24th March. *Killed :* 2nd-Lieut. J. F. House.
Died of Wounds : Lieut.-Col. C. R. H. Stirling, D.S.O., M.C.
Wounded : 2nd-Lieuts. T. P. Latchford, A. V. Raper, F. C. Parsons, H. T. L. Wooster.
Missing : 2nd-Lieut. R. C. Hurry.

25th March. *Wounded :* 2nd-Lieuts. A. B. Jeffries, E. G. Smallcombe, L. Tremellen.
Missing : Capt. H. A. Curtis.
2nd-Lieuts. T. D. Burne, A. E. Farmer.

26th March. Nil.

27th March. *Wounded :* Capt. W. H. Glenister.

28th March. *Wounded :* Capt. H. H. Flint, M.C., 2nd-Lieut. J. E. Pettit.

29th March. Nil.

30th March. Nil.

31st March.   *Killed :* 2nd-Lieut. L. C. Wells.
                Wounded : 2nd-Lieuts. W. A. Applegate, G. W. Mant,
                    M.C., A. D. Wiltshire, J. B. M. Young, M.C.
Total : Killed 2, Died of Wounds 1.
         Wounded 21.
         Missing 4.
         Total 28.
Other Ranks for whole period—
    Killed or Died of Wounds 35.
    Wounded 182 ; Missing 88.
    Total 305.

On the 1st April the battalion was relieved by French troops and proceeded to billets at Cottenchy, whence it proceeded by stages to Le Quesnoy, where it was busy reorganizing and receiving reinforcements from the 5th till the 11th April. The battalion was in back areas and had no casualties up to the 19th April. On the 20th it relieved the 54th Australian Battalion in the defences N.E. of Villers Bretonneux, and became the centre attack battalion there. This was the extreme point in the advance on Amiens reached by the Germans.

The Battalion Diary makes little mention of what happened on the 24th, but the Brigade Diary gives further particulars. On that day the German offensive was renewed north and south of Villers Bretonneux.

At 7.30 a.m. the Royal Berkshire reported that the enemy was in the aerodrome on the main road. The attack there had fallen upon the 2nd Rifle Brigade, the right company of which had given way, but the centre had held on. One company of the Berkshire was ordered to counter-attack the western " hangar " of the aerodrome, in order to establish connexion between the centre company of the Rifle Brigade and the reserve about Villers Bretonneux. The company moved out, but found that the enemy was in complete possession of Villers Bretonneux, and the attack was impracticable. By 10 a.m. the enemy was in the western outskirts of the village, and at 10.50 the 2nd Royal Berkshire was ordered to attack from the north, aiming at the eastern edge of the village. This attack also being found impossible, the battalion formed a line north of the village, facing south, whilst the Australians and other troops faced Villers Bretonneux on the west.

A counter-attack in the night, by the 18th Division and two Australian Brigades, resulted in the village being practically surrounded by the morning of the 25th.

In the attack on that day the 2nd Royal Berkshire came under orders of the 15th Australian Brigade attacking from the north and west. At 8.50 a.m. it was reported that the Germans had machine guns on the railway to the west of the village and the 2nd Royal Berkshire was sent to deal with them. After this it was engaged in " mopping up " the village. During these operations the battalion captured about three hundred prisoners, and many machine guns and trench-mortars. About sixty were taken by them and the Durham Light Infantry. After noon these two battalions were ordered to leave one company each to complete " mopping up," the rest to organize defences against the enemy on the east and north-east of the village.

The casualties of the 24th and 25th were :

Officers.
24th. *Died of Wounds :* 2nd-Lieut. S. B. Cooper.
      Wounded : 2nd-Lieut. A. A. Davison.
25th. *Killed :* 2nd-Lieut. H. A. Mossman, M.C.
      Died of Wounds : 2nd-Lieut. K. E. Moore.
      Wounded : 2nd-Lieuts. E. T. R. Hoare, J. Breakell, W. Vaughan,
            M.M., C. A. Jones, J. L. Carter, A. S. Knight, M.C.
Other Ranks for the two days :
  Killed or Died of Wounds 66.
  Wounded 183 ; Missing 8.
  Total 257.

The battalion remained at Villers Bretonneux on the 26th, and next day went back out of the line, on relief, to billets at Glisy. From the 27th April to the 5th May, when it moved into the IXth Corps area, the 25th Brigade was at various places out of the line, at Glisy and near Hallencourt. The 8th Division was now about to be sent for a supposed rest cure into the French area, where the front from Soissons to Rheims was to be held by four British and four French divisions only. The 25th Brigade went, on the 5th May, by rail from Saleux near Amiens to Fère en Tardenois. Remaining near there till the 9th, it marched on the 10th and was attached to the VIth French Army at Courlandon.

Next day it marched to Ventelay, and on the 12th it relieved the 358th French Infantry in the right sector of the front of the French 71st Division. The 2nd Royal Berkshire took the place of the 4th Battalion of the 358th French between the 27th April and the 26th May at Guyencourt, a short way south of Pontavert on the Aisne.

On the 20th May it was relieved by the 2nd Rifle Brigade, and on the 24th relieved the 2nd East Lancashire in the right sub-sector of the brigade front. There had been no casualties.

On the 27th May the Germans commenced their offensive against the Aisne which carried them to the Marne once more, the nearest point to Paris which they had reached since their defeat in the First Battle of the Marne in September 1914. Again for this offensive the Battalion Diary, as in March, gives no details beyond saying it took part in the operations, and we have to seek information in the diaries of the 25th Brigade and the 8th Division. The position of the 25th Brigade in the early morning of the 27th May was just north of the Aisne, on its right bank, in the angle between the river and the high road Laon-Rheims. The 2nd Royal Berkshire was in front line towards La Ville-aux-Bois.

In support was the 2nd Rifle Brigade, with the 2nd East Lancashire in reserve near the right bank of the river. Brigade Head-quarters were on the left of the reserve.

The German attack burst with great fury on the whole front of the brigade, carrying everything before it. The barrage on the trenches, and heavy shelling of the back areas commenced at 1 a.m. At 4.5 a.m. the German infantry attack commenced, supported by tanks, and covered by a smoke screen. Within an hour the redoubt line had been penetrated on the left, and even Brigade Head-quarters were involved in the fighting. The Brigade Commander passed to the left bank of the Aisne at Gernicourt to organize defences along that bank. On the left of the 25th was the 24th Brigade. At 6.35 a.m. a pigeon message from the Head-quarters 2nd Royal Berkshire reached the Divisional Head-quarters saying that Lieut.-Colonel Griffin, Captain Clare, and the rest of the Head-quarters were surrounded, but were holding out to the last in the hope of being relieved. They were apparently north of the river and they never could be relieved.

In a message, the hour of which is not decipherable, the 25th Brigade notified the division that it had been forced across the river and had blown up the bridges.

At 2.30 p.m. the 8th Division could no longer hold the line of the river, and a new line was set up from Bouffiguereux on the right through Roncy and Concevreux to Maizy. The position at this time was as follows :

Parts of the wood of Gernicourt, on the right front of the line, were still held by remnants of the 22nd Durham Light Infantry, 1st Sherwood Foresters, the 25th Brigade, and a French territorial battalion. The South Lancashire was between Bouffiguereux and Roncy, with the Cheshire on their left at Concevreux. The remains of the 23rd and 24th Brigades were mixed up with these battalions, and the Borderers were in close support at Roncy. The whole of these troops were placed under the General-Officer-Commanding 75th Division behind Roncy, who was to hold this line to the last, and to arrange as far as possible to withdraw the remains of the 8th Division at night into support. All the 8th Division artillery and the French batteries had been reported captured or out of action before the earlier position had been lost.

The Brigadier, Brigade Major, and Signal Officer, and Captain Lowe (attached) of the 25th Brigade were casualties, the two former missing, the others wounded. The 74th Brigade (50th Division) held the line from Concevreux to Maizy, the 25th Division was on the right.

The result of the day's fighting was that the centre and left of the IXth British Corps had been forced back to a position between the Aisne and the Vesle facing west and north-west, whence on the succeeding days it was driven across the Vesle, and gradually south-eastwards between the Vesle and the Ardre.

We have to deal with the casualties as in the case of the March offensive, that is, giving dates for officers, but not for other ranks.

The casualties were :

> *Officers :*
> 27th May. *Killed :* 2nd-Lieuts. W. F. G. Joseph, J. C. Gunn.
> *Wounded :* 2nd-Lieuts. J. W. Pavey, E. H. Horncastle, W. H. C. Rooke.

No dates are given for the missing, but they probably nearly all belonged to the 27th. They were :

Lieut.-Colonel J. A. A. Griffin, D.S.O., Capt. A. D. Clare, M.C., Lieuts. H. G. Senior, E. S. Haighton, O. Wild, R. V. Gilliat, R. A. M. J. de C. McDonnell, 2nd-Lieuts. F. H. Miller,* H. G. Nicholls, D.C.M.,* C. D. Williams, W. A. Upton, R. B. Haddow, G. L. Gold, H. E. Flight, G. S. Halley, J. M. Bennett, W. Vaughan, M.M., Captain R. Whittaker, Captain C. M. Fowler (R.A.M.C. attached).

Other Ranks : Killed or Died of Wounds 2.
Wounded 51 ; Missing 653.
Total : 24 Officers and 706 Other Ranks.

The number of missing is indicative of the nature of the battle, for it is evident that a large proportion of these must have been killed or wounded whom it was impossible to bring back. Many, too, no doubt were surrounded and cut off like the Head-quarters of the battalion.

On the 31st May the 8th Division was withdrawn from the line to Nanteuil. Its fighting strength on this day, after the losses since the 27th, was only seven officers and one hundred and twenty other ranks. It was ordered to report to the Head-quarters of the 74th Infantry Brigade at Nappe, and then to form, with other remnants of the 8th Division, one battalion to be called the 1/8th Composite Battalion, which moved into reserve in the Bois de Courton. On the 2nd it moved into close support at the Neuville-Chaumuz Road, and on the same day a 2/8th Composite Battalion was formed from troops at battalion transport lines, such as drummers and newly arrived reinforcements. To this battalion the 2nd Royal Berkshire contributed two officers and fifty other ranks. The 1/8th Composite Battalion remained in close support, the 2/8th in reserve till the 8th June, when both were called up to hold the line till the 11th. On the 12th the Composite Battalion was withdrawn from the front and was broken up, its components going back to their original battalions.

Next day the 8th Division was re-transferred to the British Army, and the 2nd Royal Berkshire reached Fère Champenoise where it entrained in the afternoon, passed by Paris, detrained next day at Longpré-les-Corps-Saints, and marched to Merlessart, far from the front towards Dieppe. Here, and at other places in the distant back areas the battalion was engaged in reorganizing and training till the 14th July, when the 8th Division was transferred from the XXIInd to the IVth Corps. During the earlier days

* Afterwards reported killed.

of July there were regimental and brigade sports, and a divisional horse show.* The battalion was still training till the 19th, when it proceeded by rail from Feuquières to Pernes and marched to camp at Bois d'Ohlair. On the 22nd the 8th Division replaced the 52nd in the right sector of the 8th Corps front, the 25th Brigade being at Mont St. Eloi, N.W. of Arras. The 2nd Royal Berkshire remained here without any fighting till the 5th August, when it moved by lorries to Neuville St. Vaast. Thence it crossed the Vimy Ridge to relieve the 2nd West Yorkshire. The passage of the ridge had to be made two men at a time, with thirty-five yards' interval between each pair. On the 27th August the battalion moved into the Bailleul sector, relieving the 7th Argyll and Sutherland Highlanders.

Here it had in front line " B " Company on the right, and " D " on the left, with " C " in support, and " A " in reserve.

On the 28th it was known that the enemy was retreating on this front and orders issued for pursuit next day. The two leading companies were " B " and " D."

During the advance on the 29th the following casualties occurred :

Officers. Killed : Lieut. A. J. Carlisle.
           Wounded : Lieut. A. G. C. Rice,
                      2nd-Lieuts. L. Smith, J. W. Shepherd.
Other Ranks : Killed or Died of Wounds 7.
                Wounded 26 ; Missing 8.

The advance on this date was not an extensive one. It commenced at 2.30 p.m. and reached Canada trench, with outposts in trenches farther on, but no full account of it is to be found in the diary of the battalion.

Being relieved on the 1st September, the battalion went into Ecurie Wood Camp till the 9th, when it relieved the 2nd East Lancashire in the right sub-sector of the brigade sector.

At 9.30 p.m. on the 15th the enemy raided the right post at the junction of Wibble and Want trenches. The battalion's casualties were : Other ranks, one killed, one wounded, and five missing.

There was no important change of position till the 21st September

---

* The battalion was replenished from many different sources ; but it is said to have been extraordinary how these complete strangers at once identified themselves with the Regiment and transferred their allegiance to it.

when, at night, the battalion pushed forward about six hundred yards, but was partly driven back on the following morning by an attack on its right flank.   The following account of operations on this and the following night is based on the report of Lieut.-Colonel A. G. F. Isaac, now commanding the battalion.   The attack by the 25th Brigade was to be made with the 2nd Royal Berkshire on the right, 2nd East Lancashire on the left, whilst the 2nd Rifle Brigade was in reserve on the line at present held.

At zero (11 p.m.) the British barrage began and the attacking troops followed it.   The German barrage started four minutes later, less heavy than had been expected.   No other opposition was met with till the objective was reached, after an advance of seven hundred yards, but one trench was heavily shelled as it was occupied by " B," the supporting company. The advance was led by " A " and " C," " D " remaining behind in reserve. About 5 a.m. on the 22nd " A " Company, on the right, reported that the 49th Division on its right was falling back from Square Wood, and thus exposing " A's " right flank.   On the left " A " was in touch with " C " and was facing Hollow Copse, which lay N.E. of Square Wood.   The consequence of this exposure of " A's " right was that the 2nd Royal Berkshire's front had to fall back as far as Gavrelle support trench.

On the 22nd orders were given for another attempt to gain the objectives of the previous night, and at midnight the attack started, covered by a barrage.   On this occasion " A " and " D " companies led.   The enemy showed little or no fight, and were brought out of their dugouts and marched to the rear.

By 2 a.m. on the 23rd all objectives had been reached and consolidation commenced.   There were no signs of a counter-attack, but a patrol pushed out under Sergeant Mead came upon a dozen of the enemy, of whom it killed three and captured three.   Altogether two officers and forty-seven other ranks were taken, besides five machine guns and an automatic rifle. The Berkshire casualties were :

Officers.   *Killed :* 2nd-Lieut. F. M. Finch.
         Wounded : 2nd-Lieut. A. A. Bryant.
         Missing : 2nd-Lieuts. G. A. N. Boston, P. H. Burch, S. H.
                  Oswell.
Other Ranks : Killed 8, Wounded 31, Missing 5.

The battalion left the front line on the 24th September, and was training till the 1st October. There was an inspection by the Divisional commander on the 30th September, and a presentation of medals.

On the 2nd October the 2nd Royal Berkshire returned to the front line in the left sector of the brigade front. The enemy was then believed to be retiring, but a patrol found this was not correct.

In the night of the 5th/6th October "C" Company attacked Hollow Copse, with a view to clearing it of the enemy and consolidating a position on its eastern side. The copse was just beyond the trenches captured on the night of the 22nd/23rd September. The attack commenced at 9.30 p.m. behind a rather weak barrage. "C" Company was chiefly engaged against the western edge of the copse, with one platoon under Lieutenant Gosling pushing out to the right on the S.E. corner. This platoon reached a point within twenty-five yards of the S.E. corner, whilst two others found themselves obliged to dig in eighty yards short of the west side. Lieutenant Gosling was thus somewhat isolated, and had to be extricated from his position by the fourth platoon. The attack made no further progress in the face of a strong machine-gun defence in the copse, and about 2 a.m. the troops were ordered back to their starting point. The casualties had been slight : three men killed, and four wounded.

The attack on Hollow Copse was renewed in the early morning of the 7th October.

"D" Company led in the attack on this occasion, starting at 5.5 a.m. Ten minutes later one platoon had worked up the north side of the copse, and established itself on the eastern edge.

By 5.45 the whole copse, up to its eastern edge, had been carried, a few prisoners had been made, and the rest of the defenders driven out. Some further advance was made by "D" Company before it was relieved, at 3 p.m., by the 2nd Rifle Brigade, and sent back to support.

The attack was continued by "A" and "C" Companies, but it would be impossible to explain all the details of fighting given in the report without an elaborate trench map. The report summarizes the day thus : "As a result of the day's operations, Hollow Copse was captured. The total length of approximately 3,500 yards of hostile trench was cleared of the enemy. Two officers and forty-four other ranks were captured, and three heavy machine guns taken. Our approximate casualties amount to one officer * and three other ranks killed, and fourteen other ranks wounded."

The Germans were now in full retreat towards Douai, and the pursuit continued during the days following the 7th October without serious fighting.

The Quéant-Drocourt German line was occupied on the 11th, and the railway beyond it made good. The 2nd Royal Berkshire appear to have had no fighting, though the Brigade Diary mentions that the 23rd Brigade attacked the Quéant-Drocourt line on the night of the 11th about Vitry. In the night of the 11th/12th the battalion was at Esquerchin and Petit Cuiney close to Douai, which was in flames. The enemy shelled Esquerchin heavily that night. During the night of the 13th/14th much patrolling was done to gain information as to the enemy's withdrawal. The patrol of "C" Company under Second-Lieutenant A. J. Eastman was unfortunately surrounded by the enemy, and Eastman and four other ranks were reported missing. On the 14th the enemy's resistance appeared to be stiffening, and there was much shelling, including gas shells. The forward area held by the battalion received much of this from 3 to 7 p.m. The shelling was less heavy during the ensuing night. Next night the battalion was relieved by the 2nd Rifle Brigade.

The casualty list shows that there was no serious fighting between the 9th and the 15th October.

One officer (2nd-Lieut. Eastman) was missing, 3 other ranks were killed, and 13 wounded.

After the 15th October the advance along the River Scarpe progressed steadily without fighting. At Tilloy on the 3rd November the battalion gave an entertainment to the children of the village, which was followed by a speech by the Mayor to the children and the battalion.

St. Amand was reached on the 9th November and at Pommerœuil, on the 11th, the Armistice ending the Great War was announced.

The casualties between the 7th October and 11th November had been :

Officers. Killed : Lieut. J. C. Maurice (7th October).
    Wounded : 2nd-Lieut. J. W. Cusden (7th October).
    Missing : 2nd-Lieut. A. J. Eastman (14th October).
Other Ranks : Killed 8 ; Wounded 29 ; Missing 4.

* 2nd-Lieut. Maurice, " D " Company, killed by a sniper in the Fresnes-Rouvroy trenches.

By the end of December 1918 the battalion had reached Enghien, and demobilization began on the 2nd January 1919. After this it was at Ath till the 3rd May when, at cadre strength, it entrained for Dunkirk, embarked there for Southampton, and reached Reading on the 17th May. On arrival at Reading the cadre and band were formed up outside the railway station, and received an address of welcome from the Lord-Lieutenant of Berkshire. Proceeding to the Town Hall, another address was received from the Mayor and Corporation. Light refreshments were provided, and then the cadre and band marched through the principal streets of Reading to the Depot Barracks, receiving an enthusiastic reception on the way.

THE DETACHMENT IN NORTH RUSSIA

1919

In the case of the 1st Battalion Royal Berkshire Regiment some account of the expedition to North Persia has been given. For the same reason we add the following notes on the operation of a detachment of the 2nd Battalion in North Russia against the Bolsheviks. A composite battalion, the 1st Oxfordshire and Buckinghamshire Light Infantry, was composed of four companies of which " A " was a company of the Oxfordshire and Buckinghamshire, " B " one of the Royal Warwickshire, " C " one of the Devonshire, and " D " one of the 2nd Royal Berkshire.

This composite battalion, and one of the Hampshire Regiment commanded by Lieut.-Colonel Sherwood Kelly, V.C., together with a Trench Mortar Battery commanded by Captain J. L. Carr of the Royal Berkshire Regiment, formed a Relief Brigade for General Ironside's Force in March 1919. The brigade was commanded by Brigadier-General Grogan, V.C.

It assembled at Aldershot and proceeded to Crowborough Camp. The Royal Berkshire detachment was commanded by Major Macdonald, D.S.O., with Lieutenant P. H. Hight as second-in-command. The platoon commanders were Lieutenants W. S. Mackay, Denis de Vitré, A. H. Denham, and Second-Lieutenant Paines.

After about three weeks' training and equipment at Crowborough, the Force was inspected by Lord Rawlinson prior to embarkation. It embarked at Southampton on the S.S. *Tzar* and reached Archangel in about a week.

There it met with a great reception.   The brigade, with a Volunteer Brigade and the Slovak-British Legion, was inspected by and marched past General Ironside.   The Hampshire Battalion started first in barges up the river Dwina, and was followed next day by the composite battalion.   On arrival at Beresink on the left bank of the Dwina, Lieutenant W. S. Mackay, with his platoon of the Royal Berkshire, was left to guard the advanced base.

The rest of the battalion proceeded to relieve the Royal Scots at Koslova and Mala Beresink on the River Vaga, a tributary of the left bank of the Dwina.   This was about two hundred and fifty miles south of Archangel, and the journey had taken two days.   Here the right company was on the left bank of the Vaga and the left company on the opposite bank.   The whole country which was the scene of operations was flat, marshy, and covered by pine forests.   The whole area is unpassable in summer, except in a few strips on the banks of the rivers.   The rivers overflow during the early summer thaw.   By midsummer the rivers are so low that barges and other craft frequently ground.   All houses outside Archangel were of wood, of which also all defensive block-houses were constructed.   The temperature in the hottest part of the summer was above the English average for the season, and mosquitoes were extremely troublesome.   Of course, in this high latitude, there was a short period during which the sun never set.

During the first two weeks a small attack was made by the Oxfordshire and Buckinghamshire company, in which its commander was wounded. The Royal Berkshire company, " D," then relieved the right company in front and sent out several patrols at night.   Lieutenant Denham made two reconnaissances with his platoon, with the object of locating the line of the Bolshevik forces and a machine-gun nest which had been giving trouble.   In the second of these a lance-corporal was wounded.

When five weeks had passed here, the enemy raided Oust Vaga where the reserve company was stationed in rear of the front line.   The attack was driven off by the Devonshire company, Captain Carr's Trench Mortar Battery, and the patients in hospital.

There was also a revolt of the Slovak-British Legion.   One company of this was commanded by Lieutenant G. F. R. Bland of the Royal Berkshire, who was murdered, as well as nine other British and Russian officers.

Captain Barrett of the Royal Berkshire, commanding another of the mutinous companies, escaped and was awarded the M.C.

In July " D " Company (Royal Berkshire) was withdrawn. Number 14 Platoon (Lieut. Denis de Vitré) took over the guard of the advanced base at Beresink from Lieutenant Mackay's Platoon, and the other three platoons returned to Archangel.

Thence they were sent towards Onega to guard against a possible attack by the enemy on the right flank of the main force during its withdrawal. The three platoons held a series of posts near Tabari, but, beyond sending out patrols, they had no adventures ; for the enemy was never within one hundred miles of them.

On the 25th September they were back at Archangel, as well as the rest of the force, including Lieutenant Denis de Vitré's Platoon from Beresink.

On the 27th September, just before the White Sea was frozen over, Archangel was evacuated under the direction of Lord Rawlinson. The evacuation being completed without mishap, the force returned home.

The whole expedition is described by an officer as a " glorious picnic " in which there was practically no fighting.

CHAPTER XXVIII

THE 3rd (SPECIAL RESERVE) BATTALION

AT the time of the Declaration of War in August 1914 the Depot of the Royal Berkshire Regiment and the Head-quarters of the 3rd Battalion were at the Barracks, Reading.

At this time the Depot was commanded by Major F. W. Foley, D.S.O., and the 3rd Battalion by Lieut.-Colonel F. G. Barker. The Adjutant was Captain A. M. Holdsworth.

Colonel Foley went shortly afterwards to raise the 5th Battalion Royal Berkshire Regiment, with which he served in France till he was wounded in December 1915.

The first duties of the Depot and the 3rd Battalion Staff on the order for mobilization were the calling up, clothing, and equipment of all army reservists of the Regiment. About eighteen hundred were called up, of whom five hundred and forty were despatched to complete the 1st Battalion at Aldershot. The calling up was completed between the 4th and the 8th August 1914.

The remaining one thousand two hundred and sixty reservists proceeded to Cosham with the 3rd Battalion, which had been mobilized on the 8th August and sent to Cosham, and on to Fort Purbrook with a strength of about five hundred and fifty men. At Fort Purbrook the battalion formed part of the Portsmouth Reserve Infantry Brigade. The other units of this brigade were the 3rd Battalion Oxfordshire and Buckinghamshire Light Infantry, 3rd Highland Light Infantry, and 3rd Leicestershire Regiment.

The quarters of the Royal Berkshire Battalion were changed, on the 27th October 1914, from Fort Purbrook to Victoria Barracks, Portsmouth, where it remained with the same brigade till the 12th November 1917, when it was transferred to Portobello Barracks, Dublin.

116

3rd BATTALION.
Perham Down 1913.

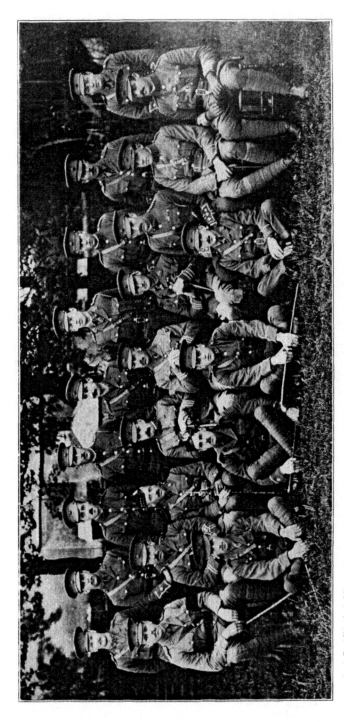

(*Back Row*) Medical Officer. Lt. C. V. Bennett. Lt. A. G. Pearson. Capt. G. W. Hopton. Capt. R. P. Harvey. Lt. H. M. Martineau. Lt. G. Searles. Capt. A. P. Strange. Lt. G. H. Bishop.

(*Second Row*) Capt. St. J. S. Quarry. Capt. A. M. Holdsworth. Maj. H. J. Stone (attached). Maj. F. W. Foley. Lt.-Col. F. G. Barker. Maj. P. W. North. Capt. O. Steele. Capt. C. Challenor. Capt. G. W. Morris.

(*Front Row*) Lt. E. B. Methven. Lt. Grant (attached). Lt. O. B. Challenor. Lt. A. G. F. Isaac.

In 1914 the following officers served in addition to the above:—Lts. R. H. Peters and G. Belcher (leave 1913). 2nd Lts. C. W. Green, E. N. Getting, R. W. J. S., R. G. R. Hogan, M. P. McNamara.

In March of that year Major P. W. North, then Acting Lieut.-Colonel commanding 20th Durham Light Infantry, was appointed to command the 3rd Royal Berkshire, on the retirement of Lieut.-Colonel F. G. Barker, who was awarded the C.B.E. in recognition of his services with the battalion during many years, as narrated in the First Volume of this History. At his own request, Colonel North was permitted to continue on active service instead of returning to England to command the 3rd Royal Berkshire. The actual command was therefore taken over temporarily by Lieut.-Colonel F. W. Foley, D.S.O., and it was not till December 1918, after the Armistice, that Colonel North took over the command from him to carry out the troublesome job of demobilization.

During the War 21,605 men passed through the 3rd Battalion, besides officers.

Of these 21,605 other ranks, 13,533 were trained and despatched in drafts to the Expeditionary Force. Deducting these, and also 1,062 still serving with the battalion on the date of its final disembodiment, there remain in round figures 7,000 to be accounted for. These were non-effective for various reasons ; transfers, discharges, deaths, desertions and demobilizations, spread fairly evenly in small numbers over the whole period of the war.

The average strength of the battalion was about 1,600. Of course fluctuations of the total were occasionally considerable ; as, for instance, on the 1st September 1916, when there was a sudden influx of 590 from the disembodied 9th Battalion, or at periods when numbers were reduced by specially large drafts.

Of the total of 21,605 it is estimated that only about 4,000 joined as untrained recruits. The rest were men who served with the Expeditionary Force from one to five times.

Most of the Regiment's new men joined from the 9th Battalion during its existence from November 1914 till September 1916. After that they went from the Training Reserve Battalions to the Expeditionary Force. In April 1918, however, the 3rd Battalion Royal Berkshire received about eight hundred new men direct. That was just after the great German offensive of March.

Colonel North has kindly furnished an account of the final period of the

3rd Battalion's existence, after he took over command from Colonel Foley in Dublin in December 1918.

Officers and men from all battalions of the Royal Berkshire Regiment were sent to the 3rd Battalion for demobilization, including returned prisoners-of-war, who had suffered many hardships.

Demobilization was bound to be a troublesome business, hampered by feelings of discontent at real or fancied grievances in its conduct.

The regulations for demobilization were complicated and difficult for the men to understand. Many, especially those who had had most of the fighting, thought they were not getting fair treatment. There was a sense of grievance on the part of the men who had been to the front against those who had been at the base or in England. Perhaps the worst difficulty of all was over the " pivotal men " who were supposed to be employers of labour who would provide work for others. They were mostly men who had only been taken at the end of the war, and it is not surprising that others who had borne the heat and burden of the day were inclined to regard them as a class who were getting out early under false pretences.

Certainly there were cases where the term " pivotal " was misapplied and these, when brought to his notice, Colonel North reported to superior authorities. Further to prevent discontent, which was sure not to be discouraged in a city like Dublin in 1918, Colonel North issued a short and simply worded notice, drafted by Captain Mant, giving a clear explanation of the regulations as applicable to the battalion, such as the most ignorant could understand. Moreover, his " Demobilization Office " was always ready to explain difficulties to any man referring personally to it.

The men soon came to understand that, as far as their battalion was concerned, the rules were to be fairly carried out, without favouritism.

Colonel Foley had instituted an excellent system of messing and the men were always well fed. They were also provided with plenty of amusement in the shape of football, boxing, cross-country running, etc., for the fit. The wounded or sick, who could not join in these, looked on till they were sufficiently recovered to have their time occupied with ceremonial parades, musketry training, and an occasional battalion parade with a picnic dinner in the Phœnix Park.

There were occasional rounds up of Sinn Feiners, which the men enjoyed, and in which fortunately there were no casualties.

Colonel North's difficulties in demobilization were perhaps not very different from those of other commanding-officers in a similar position ; but he was very successful in overcoming them and keeping the battalion contented and efficient to the end.

Of the 1,062 men left on the 5th September 1919, when the battalion was disembodied, 1,040 were made over to the 2nd Battalion, and 22 to the Depot.

The officers' plate was put in the hands of trustees, on terms suggested by the Earl of Abingdon, Honorary-Colonel of the Battalion. The various regimental funds were also settled in terms which have been published in the " China Dragon " at the end of 1923.

CHAPTER XXIX

THE 1st/4th (TERRITORIAL) BATTALION

By
C. R. M. F. CRUTTWELL, Fellow of Hertford College, Oxford.
Formerly Captain 1st/4th Royal Berkshire Regiment.

THE 4th Battalion at the outbreak of war had nearly a complete establishment both of officers and men, and had attained a high level of efficiency, thanks to the devoted labours of Colonel O. Pearce-Serocold, who had commanded it for ten years. It had gone into camp at Marlow on the 2nd August for the annual fifteen-days' training; but the men had scarcely settled into their tents before they were brought back to Reading and dispersed very early the next morning. Excitement and expectation were in the air, and many of those from distant parts of the county remained at their respective armouries until the order for mobilization was at last received at 7.20 p.m. on the evening of the 4th August. The news was spread through the night by the police and volunteers on motors and cycles, until by 2 p.m. on the 5th the complete battalion was reassembled in Reading. After stores had been drawn and medical inspection completed, twenty-eight officers and eight hundred men left that evening for their prearranged war-station at Portsmouth, while two officers and sixty-five men remained at Reading to receive the transport from the removal depot. Three days of trench-digging on Portsdown Hill were succeeded by a move to Swindon, where the whole division was assembled under the command of Major-General Sir R. Heath. Here on the 14th a pressing invitation to volunteer immediately for foreign service was received from the War Office. At this time the Regular Army had not yet been engaged, the formation of new units had scarcely begun, and the character of the war was barely envisaged. Many therefore most naturally asked why

120

1/4th BATTALION.

Chelmsford 1914–15.

(*Back Row*) 2nd Lt. F. R. K. Hine. 2nd Lt. J. H. Goolden. Lt. S. Boyle. Lt. G. H. W. Cruttwell. 2nd Lt. D. J. Ward.
(*Second Row*) 2nd Lt. C. T. Kaunhoven. 2nd Lt. E. P. Carter. Lt. G. Moore. 2nd Lt. C. R. N. Cruttwell. 2nd Lt. G. S. Field. Lt. R. W. P. Palmer. Capt. F. A. Willink. Lt. W. L. E. Gordon. 2nd Lt. G. M. Gathorne-Hardy. 2nd Lt. C. D. R. Sharpe. 2nd Lt. O. W. Heffer.
(*Sitting*) Capt. W. E. N. Blandy. Capt. H. V. H. Thorne. Capt. G. A. Battcock. Capt. and Adjt. G. M. Sharpe. Col. P. O. Serocold. Major F. R. Hodges. Capt. J. L. Aldworth. Capt. C. A. L. Lewis. Capt. E. S. Holcroft.
(*On Ground*) Lt. O. B. Challenor. Lt. and Q.M. J. Payne. Lt. S. J. N. Auld. 2nd Lt. R. Lund. 2nd Lt. A. C. Hughes. Lt. K. D. Bean (R.A.M.C.). 2nd Lt. L. E. Ridley. 2nd Lt. H. M. W. Wells.

those who had taken the trouble in peace time to prepare amidst widespread indifference for the defence of the country should be the first called upon to extend their statutory engagements when an emergency arose. Nevertheless within three days more than two-thirds of the men and practically all the officers responded.   On the 16th August a new move was made to Dunstable, where four days were spent amongst the rounded chalk downs, before a hot and dusty march of seventy miles carried the battalion to its final destination at Chelmsford.   They rested during the four nights of the journey at Stevenage, Hoddesdon, Waltham Abbey, and Fyfield, being received everywhere with great kindness and enthusiasm in billets.   Chelmsford became for seven months the Head-quarters of the 48th Division, which was responsible for the outer defences of London on the east.   During this period the battalion was itself stationed in the western half of the town, except from the 24th September to the 16th October, when it occupied three adjacent villages, Broomfield and Great and Little Waltham.   The relations between the town and the inhabitants were excellent throughout and many abiding friendships were made.   The landowners and farmers made the troops free of the land, and training was carried out uninterruptedly through a fine autumn and a wet winter.   In September the battalion changed its title to the 1/4th owing to the formation of a second-line unit.   It also lost for duty with the New Armies the permanent sergeant-instructors, one of whom had been attached to each of the eight companies ; but was most fortunate in retaining its Regular Adjutant, Captain G. M. Sharpe, and Regimental-Sergeant-Major Hanney, who was afterwards to gain distinction as a Captain in the 1st Battalion.   In December the double-company formation was adopted.   The two Head-quarter companies from Reading formed the new " A " Company under Major Hedges, while Captain G. A. Battcock commanded " B " Company, composed of the men from Wallingford, Wantage and Newbury, Captain Lewis " C " Company from Windsor and Maidenhead, and Captain H. U. H. Thorne " D " Company from Abingdon and Wokingham.

Many memories will remain of these laborious months, when all ranks were very keen and eager, sparing no effort to make themselves ready for the time of testing ; of Company training in the park at Hylands, fights on Galleywood Common, route marches up the long slope of Danbury Hill, journeys along the Colchester Road to Boreham Range, in the darkness of a winter day, the day's firing and the return after dusk, of long hours spent in guarding the great Marconi Station in rain, snow and mist.   Embarkation orders were unexpectedly long in coming.   The 2nd London Division left England in February, the North Midland early in March 1915, before the battalion entrained amidst crowded streets on the evening of the 30th March and sailed from Folkestone in the packet-boat *Onward*.

Submarines were as yet an embryo menace in the Channel.   With one destroyer as escort the boat crossed rapidly and peacefully through a calm and clear night.   In the camp known as the Blue Base, high on the hill above Boulogne, the men with one blanket apiece endured a bitter frost in tents and awoke to driving snow.   That evening they entrained at Pont de Briques, and travelling slowly through the night arrived at Cassel at daybreak.   The road ran over that steep hill on which the town is built, and the rising sun displayed the vast panorama of the level Flemish plain broken to the north-eastward by the bold outline of the Mont des Cats.   Here too they heard for the first time the faint pulsing of the distant guns.   Billets were provided at Winnezeele, a straggling village of outlying farms, close to the Belgian frontier.   On the 2nd April, Lieut.-General Sir H. Smith-Dorrien, then commanding the 2nd Army, inspected the 145th Brigade, consisting of 1/4th Royal Berkshire, 1/5th Gloucestershire, 1/4th Oxfordshire and Buckinghamshire Light Infantry, and the 1/1st Buckinghamshire Battalion.   Sir Horace was exceedingly optimistic in his address to officers and N.C.O.s : he expressed his confidence that we could break the German line, whenever we liked, and that the fall of Budapest, and the forcing of the Dardanelles were only a matter of weeks.

Flêtre, a village on the great paved road to Lille, three miles W. of Bailleul, was the next halting-place, which bore many marks of the successful attack by the 4th Division on the 14th October 1914.   Thence the march was resumed on the 7th April through Bailleul, then intact of war, to Romarin, a small village just within Belgium, two miles north of the Armentières Road. It was three miles behind the firing line and the crackle of rifle fire was plainly audible.   Here the battalion received its preliminary instruction in trench warfare from the 10th Brigade of the 4th Division, the four companies being distributed during their forty-eight hours' tour between the 1st Royal

Warwickshire, 2nd Seaforth Highlanders, 1st Royal Irish, Royal Dublin Fusiliers, and 7th Argyll and Sutherland Highlanders (T.F.).   No casualties were sustained, and much was learnt from the good comradeship and helpfulness of this regular brigade.   During the four days subsequently spent at Steenwerck a Rugger match was played at Pont de Nieppe between the 4th and 48th Divisions.   The latter side, which was victorious, was captained by the famous England three-quarter, Lieutenant Ronald Poulton-Palmer of the 1/4th Royal Berkshire, who here played his last game.   On the 15th April the battalion took over its own line for the first time from the 2nd Hampshire at Le Gheer on the east face of Ploegsteert Wood.   Defended mainly by detached posts, and strong points in ruined houses, with such suggestive names as First and Second German Houses, this sector was reminiscent rather of outposts than of orthodox trench warfare.   The wood was bright with spring, scarcely touched by shell fire, and the enemy entirely inactive.   After forty-eight hours in this pleasant spot the battalion returned to Romarin ; their march being accompanied by the roar of mines, artillery and concentrated rifle and machine-gun fire, which heralded the sudden outbreak of the battle of Hill 60 just before sunset on the 17th April.   The relief of the 4th Division was now complete ; they marched back to Bailleul, leaving behind them a great board to state that " Plugstreet " Wood had been taken by them in October 1914, and handed over intact to the 48th Division.

The line held by the division during the next two months was wholly within Belgian territory, with a frontage of nearly five thousand yards, which stretched from a point about five hundred yards south-east of Wulverghem on the north to just south of Le Gheer.   The 143rd Brigade were on the left, 145th in the centre, and 144th on the right.   The Royal Berkshire were on the left of the 145th, and worked on a self-relieving system by which two companies spent alternate periods of four days in the trenches and in local reserve. They held a frontage of seven hundred yards, forming an abrupt curve in the low ground between the wood and the River Douve.   On the left the famous hill of Messines scarred with tier upon tier of trenches peered into our positions, and though barely two hundred feet above sea-level loomed like a mountain among the mole-heaps of Flanders.   The trenches in this muddy area were in reality sandbag breastworks offering a tempting target to and a poor protection against shell fire.   The organization of the line was also, as judged by later standards, extremely incomplete.   No support line existed, the only rearward defences being a collection of breastworks and strong points within the wood ; though a reserve line was dug within the next six weeks through Romarin and Neuve-Église.   On the right of the battalion sector no communication trench existed, but reliefs could be carried out by day under shelter of the sharp bluff known as Prowse Point, which concealed movement from anything but aerial observation.   On the left a communication trench existed, but was practically useless, as it led up the exposed forward slope to some reserve breastworks near the Messines Road, barely shoulder high, and themselves unconnected with the security of the wood.   Hence on this side reliefs, rations and stores had to be brought up by night over bullet-swept ground.   The security of life was therefore unusually dependent on the activity of the enemy, but both his infantry and gunners were in general unenterprising.   The Saxons in the trenches opposite lived up to their mild reputation : they contented themselves with a little sniping, and an occasional burst of fire on working-parties, one of which killed the well-beloved Poulton-Palmer on the night of the 4th May.   He was the first officer to fall, and was buried by the Bishop of Pretoria (Dr. Furse) in the Battalion Cemetery on the west edge of Plugstreet Wood, by the side of the Messines Road.

The artillery also left the sector alone, which was the more fortunate, as our field guns were at the time confined to a ration of one shell per gun per day, and had not at present received any stock of high explosive.   The Warwick Brigade, on the left, indeed suffered somewhat severely from enfilade fire: but the enemy's activity was mainly directed against the many scattered farm-houses, the village of Ploegsteert, and the Château de la Hutte.   This last building, surrounded by a lovely garden, was on the top of Hill 63 facing Messines, and formed an admirable observation post looking away to the busy chimneys of Lille, Roubaix and Tourcoing and the limitless eastward plain.   Neither were any gas attacks directed against the division, though the wind blew steadily for weeks from the N.E. out of a clear sky. The energy of the enemy was wholly directed on the Second Battle of Ypres, which raged incessantly a few miles to the north, where the sky was illuminated each night by the blazing city.   Few events broke the even calm of the two months' trench life in which the battalion suffered no more than thirty casualties. An elaborate demonstration was arranged on the 9th May, when the Battles of Souchez and Festubert started farther south, the main items of which were long bursts of rapid fire, and the exhibition of trench bridges " obviously concealed," to quote the Divisional orders. Similar devices for deceiving the enemy were ordered when a mine was exploded opposite the Oxfordshire Light Infantry. A green rocket was sent up : and a half-company spent several hours marching up and down the corduroy paths of the wood to simulate the arrival of reinforcements while their rifles were ostentatiously exhibited in the fire-trench to suggest that the garrison was at double strength !

Much useful work was done by patrols, whose opportunities in the long grass and standing rye between the lines were numerous. Lieutenant G. M. Gathorne-Hardy on one occasion stayed out from noon till 4 p.m. mapping the ground, and examining the German wire and defences. He received the M.C. and his faithful follower, Sergeant Westall, the D.C.M. for this exploit.

Life in the trenches, in the bright spring weather, was accordingly very pleasant. The flimsy shelters, boarded and lined with fresh straw, were very comfortable ; each section cooked its food in little ovens made of a biscuit-tin built round with clay. The officers' mess had a kitchen-range from Anton's Farm, a ruined building within the trench-line, and a large room where six persons could eat at once.

Life in reserve was almost entirely spent in the great wood, which was then regarded as the chief show place of the British front, and to which came many journalists and distinguished visitors. In those days it was scarcely touched by shells ; and as it stretched over one and a half miles, and reached in places a depth of fourteen hundred yards, its dense timber easily afforded a secure habitation for parts of two brigades. The 4th Division had spent much labour and ingenuity upon it. It was everywhere intersected with corduroy paths, which defeated the mud and enabled rations and stores to be brought up easily in the worst weather. The centre of the wood was named Piccadilly Circus, whence many of these paths radiated : Regent Street and the Strand were the two great lateral highways ; while Bunhill Row preserved the name of the London Rifle Brigade. The local reserves lived either under canvas or in log-huts erected during the winter by the various regiments who had carved or painted their devices outside. Battalion Head-quarters with one company lived at the Piggeries on the western outskirts of the wood, where the enormous bricked and covered sties, completed only a month before the outbreak of war, easily accommodated two hundred men.

Life in reserve was more strenuous than in the trenches. The defences were exceedingly incomplete ; the firing-line was not even continuous when the division arrived. A great gap some four hundred yards wide had to be protected by breastworks, known as the Grouse-Butts. Although the enemy was within two hundred yards, he never made the faintest attempt to interfere with this work, or to destroy it by shell fire. The men were more-over kept exceedingly short of sleep. The line was held at this time very thinly, as all available troops were engaged either at Ypres or Festubert. Accordingly reserves were not allowed to sleep in the wood, but were kept by night in the support breastworks, which had to be manned after dusk and evacuated before dawn. As these trenches were too narrow to enable a man to lie down, when carrying his equipment, he was naturally unable to get much rest ; and by the beginning of June lack of sleep was beginning to have a serious effect upon the fitness of the men.

The villages immediately behind the line were, in these early days, full of civilians who led a very profitable and not abnormal existence. Ploegsteert, though badly battered and shelled every afternoon at 3.30, preserved much animation : the men marched periodically to Nieppe to have hot baths in the enormous brewery vats ; at Armentières, only two miles behind the line, every kind of luxury could be obtained, and two variety performances, the " Follies " and " Frivolities," were on view in the evenings.

In the first week of June the battalion enjoyed a welcome rest of four days in huts at Korte Pyp, a grassy plateau near Neuve-Église. Aerial observa-tion was little feared in those days, as the camp was pitched without any concealment in an open field only two miles from the enemy. Here Major-General Sir R. Fanshawe, the new G.O.C., made his first inspection of the troops whom he was to command for the ensuing three years. The next tour of duty was partly in unfamiliar trenches, as the line held was now of a total length of fourteen hundred and fifty yards, extending northward over the Messines Road to a bridge over the Douve. A week passed quietly in these Warwick lines, in spite of their bad reputation. The 5th Battalion, which had recently come to France with the 12th Division, was entertained for instruction, and there were many meetings of Berkshire friends. This new division was to relieve the 48th on the 24th June, when the battalion marched away to Bailleul and spent the night there in preparation for a move southwards.

The battalion marched south for three days, gradually edging away from the firing line, spending its nights at Vieux Berquin, with Bavarian graves dotted all about its apple orchards, and Gonnehem, a singularly pleasant village at the edge of the Artois coal-fields. Its final destination was Lapugnoy, a large industrial village on the St. Pol railway, five miles west of Béthune, lying in a valley overlooked on either side by densely wooded hills. Seventeen days were comfortably spent here in Corps reserve, with alternations of drill, route marches and wood fighting. Visits were paid to Béthune, the Head-quarters of the Guards Brigade, then a gracious little city with its Grand Place and cathedral untouched by war. This area was then the meeting-place of the British and French armies ; and from Lapugnoy you could see on the road the Indians, returning to the trenches in motor-buses ; and on the railway interminable trains conveying multitudes of Zouaves, Algerians and Negroes in open trucks to the furnace of Souchez.

On the 11th July the 1st and 1/4th Berkshire Battalions spent the day together at Fouquières-lès-Béthune, one of those rare meetings in war which afford such intense pleasure. Next day a fresh move was made into the mining district to a miserable hamlet called Houchin near Nœux-les-Mines, where three days were spent in great discomfort bivouacking under pouring rain and wind in an open rye-field. Each day working-parties went to Sailly-Labourse facing Loos, and looked with curiosity at a grotesque iron structure with two towers, the celebrated " Tower Bridge," which was taken by the British attack of the 25th September. On the fourth day (16th July) the men had as usual marched eight miles and dug for four hours ; at 9 p.m. they started off in pouring rain on an all-night march of fifteen miles towards Lillers. After a dismal journey with frequent checks, as the brigade transport in front stuck in the mud, after the guides had twice lost their way in the inky darkness, they arrived at dawn in Lières, a tiny remote village in a fold of the chalk, full of cherry trees, and after resting there a day proceeded to La Berguette station near Lillers. Here they

entrained for Doullens, to become part of the 3rd Army (commanded by
Sir C. Monro) and to take over a part of the French line.   After leaving
Doullens, they marched up the Authie Valley between chalk downs strangely
like those of their own home county, and bivouacked in another great wood,
that of Marieux.   The ground was littered with empty petrol tins, the legacy
of the French aerodrome, below in the orchards two batteries of long French
155's were packing up ; an enormous country house close by, called Mon
Plaisir, was being prepared for the Head-quarters of the 7th Corps.   The
roads were covered with the impedimenta of two armies.   Another stage in
the adventure of war was beginning : the romantic or terrifying ignorance
of the future was again sharply emphasized.   But nothing very exciting
happened.

The battalion moved up towards the line in a leisurely way ; it halted a
few days at Bayencourt, a stinking little village full of flies and harlots,
before relieving the French at Hébuterne.   The 5th Gloucestershire and 4th
Oxfordshire were the first in the trenches, whom the French Territorials
received with enthusiasm, putting fresh flowers in all the dugouts and
writing up greetings on the walls.   Captain G. H. W. Cruttwell took half
" B " Company into Hébuterne to exchange guards before the main relief
took place.   After dining with the officers he was given, as a farewell present,
the best mattress in the village.   The relief was completed on the night of
the 22nd July and Hébuterne with the trench line immediately in front of it
became the home of the battalion for the next eleven months.   It was a good-
sized village of perhaps one thousand inhabitants, about ten miles S. of
Arras, on no highway, but the converging point of many small roads ; it lay
in a shallow pocket of the rolling chalk downs and was surrounded on every
side by orchards of the bitter cider apple.   Almost every house was a one-
storied farm of three or four rooms with considerable outbuildings of mud and
plaster, and extensive cellars, capable in close billets of holding one or two
platoons.   Though a good deal broken up, with perhaps a dozen intact
houses, it contained at least three thousand troops, including the Brigadier
and (generally) three battalion-commanders.   On our arrival we found to
our surprise a few civilians still clinging to their homes, including a Garde
Champêtre and an aged woman.   They were cleared out at once as the centre
of the village was only six hundred yards from the line.   The flight of the

remainder of the inhabitants in the previous October had been precipitate, for all articles of furniture from beds to crockery had been abandoned. On one wall the fugitives had scrawled up an appeal to the soldiers to take care of their newly weaned calf. The village was screened from direct observation by the enemy, who shelled it but little until 1916, and probably failed to realize how extensively it was used for billets. It had been turned by the French into a very formidable centre of resistance, and much ingenuity and labour had been spent on its defences. The northern half beyond the pond and the green formed a " keep " or large redoubt with a permanent garrison of a battalion, which was to be held at all costs even if the enemy broke through the village and cut it off. The eastern approaches of the village had further been defended by two lines admirably sited in the orchards, the inner of which was connected by communication trenches with the village cellars.

The fire-trenches themselves were little more than a quarter of a mile from the village, but were situated on a forward slope looking down upon the enemy, who lay in a depression with his rearward defences writ large in chalk on the opposite hill, and visible in all their detail for nearly three thousand yards. Two great pivots of the German system closed the view, on the left the Wood of Gommecourt, on the right Serre Village, both destined twice to resist attack next year in the Somme Battles. As the organization in depth was so complete, our front line was thinly held, and the battalion was often responsible for more than a mile of trenches. The soil, unlike that of Flanders, invited digging, so that there was no need of breastwork. The French had constructed quantities of large dugouts sometimes capable of holding twenty-five men and calculated to resist the impact of a 5·9 shell. Those occupied by officers had been comfortably furnished with mattresses, chairs and tables from the village. The approaches to the line had also been secured by numerous communication trenches (there were seven in the battalion area) eight or nine feet deep, with direct access to the village cellars.

The placid routine of what was called " peace-warfare " with its limited risk therefore continued throughout the summer. Danger from snipers was less than at Plugstreet, as the trenches were from four hundred and fifty to nine hundred yards apart. The French gunners, who remained for a month, while our batteries were registering, had obtained a complete mastery over the enemy. After their departure he became more active and inflicted a certain number of casualties by intermittent fire on the trenches ; one lucky shell in particular destroyed half a platoon of " A " Company, as they were halting on their way to the trenches in a dangerous and conspicuous supporting point known as the Brickfields. More than a month was spent continuously at Hébuterne, where the same self-relieving system was practised, before the brigade was withdrawn into Divisional reserve. Rest billets were provided at Authie, in which the Berkshires and 4th Gloucestershire of the 144th Brigade spent alternate periods of twelve days during the next four months. It was seven miles behind the line, was never shelled or bombed, and probably provided the best and pleasantest billets within the Divisional area. It lay athwart a trout stream, in a deep beech-covered valley ; the woods of which were speedily denuded to form hurdles and revetments for the Corps line, General Snow's pet project, for which he was inclined to starve the fighting trenches.

On the 7th September, General Monro, the G.O.C. 3rd Army, inspected the battalion. It is perhaps worth while to record his opinion as expressed in a speech taken down at the time.

> " After hearing what your Divisional-General has said of you, I expected to see a very fine body of men on parade to-day, and I can assure you—I say so straight out—that I am not in the very least disappointed—your bearing as well as your order and steadiness in the ranks, and the way in which you put your equipment on all go to show that you know the right thing and prove the high standard which you set before you. I am well acquainted with your 1st Battalion, and have served with them in this present war. They have lived up to the high traditions which attach to the Regiment, and to the good name which they have won in the past. You are proud to belong to such a regiment ; you have already reached a high standard, and I hope and believe that you will continue to retain it. I hear from your Divisional-Commander that you have conscientiously carried out all the work allotted to you. In the sentry-line your vigilance has been beyond all criticism. You have done good work in all that pertains to the work of the trenches, digging and so on. Moreover, your conduct in the village and in billets has been uniformly good."

During this period rumour began to be active. Few secrets have been worse kept than that of the offensive of the 25th September. Leave was stopped indefinitely a fortnight before the battle began. It was therefore in an atmosphere of intense expectancy that a return was made to the trenches on the 17th September. The relief was effected by day, as the great communication trench nearly two miles long had now been constructed from Sailly-au-Bois over the slope of the hill into Hébuterne.

Symptoms of the attack were not long in showing themselves. The bombardment " from the Vosges to the Sea " of which the German communiqués spoke, started on the 21st. The artillery in the Hébuterne sector had not been reinforced, but they did their best, firing about five thousand rounds during the next three days on the enemy trenches and communications. Early on the morning of the 23rd, a flight of twenty-one aeroplanes, an unprecedented spectacle in those early days, passed over Hébuterne to bomb the station of Valenciennes. On the 24th it became generally known that in certain contingent circumstances, carefully kept secret, the 145th Brigade would attack between Gommecourt Wood and the Puisieux Road, with the Berks and Bucks as the assaulting battalions. On that day therefore the divisional artillery cut three narrow lanes in the German wire, which was promptly repaired under cover of darkness. Saturday the 25th broke wet and misty. The only unusual feature observed that morning was a herd of cows and harvesting men dimly seen near Puisieux, scarcely a mile from our lines. The noise of battle was, however, loud in the immediate north, where three or four miles away the French IXth Corps were fruitlessly attacking Ransart. Streams of messages kept arriving, to tell first of the initial British victory at Loos, then of the impressive totals of guns and prisoners captured by the French in Champagne. The men were in high spirits, and believed that they were about to share in a general advance; " B " Company had a sweepstake as to who would capture the first German prisoner. Though later messages spoke only of violent counter-attacks and of ground lost, it did indeed seem as if a general attack was projected for the 26th. All the last preparations were feverishly pushed through during the night. New dumps were dug, and filled immediately with all the requisites of an assault, tools, sandbags, trench bridges and flags for marking out positions in the captured line; and new maps were issued to come into use at midnight. Both sides were very excited and restless, and the night was alive with rapid fire, shouts and cheers. Early next morning a British aeroplane flying very low over the German trenches proved them to be thick with men by attracting a heavy fire. But an optimistic message from the 3rd Army saying that " in view of the great Allied successes both north and south it is possible that the Germans may evacuate their trenches, in which case you must be prepared to slip quietly into them at a moment's notice," was more than discounted by another line which read " work may now be resumed as usual in the trenches." The great scheme had failed, and it was the turn of the enemy to be jubilant. Well acquainted with our plan of attack, he kept calling from Gommecourt through a megaphone, " Come on, Bucks! Come on, Berks! The Royal Berks will lead the attack." The turmoil of the last few days was now succeeded by a complete calm in which scarcely a gun spoke.

The inactivity was continued throughout most of October ; for with the falling of autumn came thick white mists, during which it was impossible to discern the hostile lines for days on end. Patrols wandered about in the daytime, sometimes killing the hares, which abounded in the thick high grass, and by night explored the saps and wire of the enemy. On one occasion a party was challenged in a dense fog, and a brisk fight ensued with bombs, revolvers, and rifles. The patrol withdrew safely after inflicting damage and suffering none—one man who lost his party remained in No-Man's Land for eight hours until sunrise showed him his bearings and he crept safely into a sap. Private A. Gibbs, a huge stout-hearted man from Wokingham, greatly distinguished himself in this encounter.

No casualties were suffered in these patrols until the 14th December, when a party from " A " Company were ambushed in a sunken road between the lines, losing one killed and three wounded. The dead man was recovered by Captain Blandy, who was led to the spot by Lance-Corporal Clayton, who had been severely wounded in the affray. He afterwards obtained a commission and was killed on the Somme. Not long afterwards Captain Goolden and Corporal V. H. Taylor retaliated by shooting two Germans of the 169th Regiment near their own wire.

The autumn calm was broken by a violent bombardment on the 16th/17th October from the heavy guns of what was called the Bavarian travelling circus. Most of " D " Company's trenches were destroyed, but thanks to the solidity of the dugouts there were no serious casualties. The 1/4th Oxfordshire on the right near Serre Hill were still more heavily assailed, and had their first experience of lachrymatory shells. The enemy with some enterprise suddenly opened fire upon us at point-blank range with two field guns, which galloped into Gommecourt Park and unlimbered in full view. Lieutenant Coombes of the Buckinghamshire Battalion gallantly got a machine gun into the open and silenced them with oblique fire. An infantry attack was believed to be imminent, as aeroplanes reported gas cylinders along the enemy's line between Gommecourt and Serre. The whole trench garrison therefore stood to arms throughout the night, repairing the trenches and the wire, but there was no sequel to the bombardment.

The winter was cold, with much snow, frost and rain. The 48th Division remained in the line throughout its course, and indeed until spring was far spent. It is said to be the longest spell allotted to any division throughout the war without a rest in Corps and Army reserve. The wastage in the battalion was naturally considerable, though casualties remained light ; but after a year in France, it had lost one-third of its officers and about four hundred N.C.O.s and men. Drafts on the other hand were very slow in coming, and by the 1st March 1916 only amounted to one hundred and three men. Many changes occurred in the commands during the winter, which may be summarized here. Colonel Serocold left on the 14th February 1916. He had served with the battalion for thirty-two years, and had commanded it for eleven and a half. All Berkshire people know of the affection and respect with which he was regarded. Those whom he commanded alone can fully appreciate the debt owed to his training and personal example. He was succeeded by Lieut.-Colonel R. J. Clarke, C.M.G., D.S.O., from Abingdon. The Regular Adjutant, Captain G. M. Sharpe, a most lovable personality ideally suited for his position, had already left in October and was soon to command the 1st Battalion. He was succeeded by Lieutenant L. E. Ridley, who was killed in the August battles round Pozières. The commanders of " A " and " D " Companies, Major F. R. Hedges and Captain H. U. H. Thorne, went home through sickness at the end of 1915. Captain Thorne afterwards won distinction in command of the 12th Royal Scots, and was killed in the Battle of Arras, 9th April 1917, leading the first wave of assault

" in the old chivalrous way," as his brigadier wrote. Their places were filled by Captains W. E. H. Blandy and R. G. Attride. The R.-S.-M. Hanney left amidst general regret to take a commission, and his place was taken by R. A. Hogarth, C.-S.-M. of " A " Company, a very efficient successor.

The winter months were hard, as the reduced battalion, with companies of a fighting strength of only ninety to one hundred and ten men, held the same frontage (about fourteen hundred yards) under far more trying conditions. It is true that companies from New Army Divisions were constantly arriving for instruction, but during the few days of their visit they could not relieve the garrison of any of its burden. On the contrary, work and responsibility, especially for officers and N.C.O.s, was considerably increased.

The trenches whose sides had remained unrevetted owing to the lack of hurdles, began to fall in as early as November. After a storm or a thaw, liquid mud reaching as high as the thighs made movement almost impossible. Sump-hole covers floated away, and a man might be plunged in the darkness into water up to his neck. Many of the saps were blocked, and at one time it became necessary temporarily to abandon a portion of the front line. Most of the dugouts, too, finally collapsed, in at least one instance killing several of their occupants. The plight of the shelterless men was often extremely wretched. They lived in water and liquid mud, which mingled with their food and with the fabric of their clothing. However, thigh boots gradually arrived in sufficient numbers, and did much to prevent trench feet ; whale oil was rubbed in, and adequate arrangements for drying and hot baths were organized by the R.A.M.C. in the village. Moreover, it was found possible to hold the line more thinly ; so that during the normal eight days' stay at Hébuterne no one (except the machine gunners) spent more than forty-eight hours in the front-line trenches. But in February the battalion had a very exacting time with twenty-five days in the trenches and only four in reserve. During this month also fighting activity began to increase. Large numbers of 9- and 8-inch howitzers had gradually been accumulated by both sides. Hébuterne began to experience organized bombardment : several thousand shells were directed against it on consecutive days. Thus cases of shell-shock were for the first time seen. About this time Company-Sergeant-Major Lawrence of " B " Company was blown to pieces. He was a fine type of the Berkshire countryman from near Newbury ; though nearly forty-five years old, he made light of every hardship, always cheerful, encouraging others and devoted to duty.

It must not be considered, however, that war was without its relaxations. An excellent Christmas dinner was provided at Authie, when each man received two plum-puddings, a tin of cigarettes, a packet of cigars, chocolate, socks, a shirt and muffler provided by various funds. The Division organized a football cup, two travelling variety entertainments, and Major Barron of the R.A.S.C., a travelling cinematograph. Thus the winter passed slowly into a reluctant spring. Spring brought many signs of the imminent offensive. The forward villages such as Sailly, Courcelles and Bayencourt were completely cleared of their civilian population. Two 15-inch howitzers appeared amidst the wild daffodils in the orchards of Sailly ; gun-pits and enormous dugouts were constructed in Hébuterne. Numbers of light railways supplemented the single line which had supplied the 48th and 4th Divisions ; troops grew thick upon the ground, the 56th Division appeared upon the left and the 31st on the right, so that in May the divisional front scarcely exceeded that held by one battalion during the winter. The 4th Army had now been formed, of which the 48th Division was on the left in the 10th Corps. Commanding Officers and Adjutants attended divisional conferences two or three times a week ; while parties were constantly detailed to witness demonstrations of gas, smoke and flame-throwers. Finally drafts received during March renewed the strength of the battalion to eight hundred and seventy-four men. Early in April a new assaulting trench of about ten hundred yards was dug by the 145th Brigade, in order to strengthen out the line and to lessen by four hundred yards the distance from the enemy. The task was completed in a single night by the Oxfords and Gloucesters, who worked for six hours with the Berks lying out in front as a covering party. Though the enemy was only two hundred and fifty yards away and the moon shone intermittently the work was unmolested and apparently undetected, so that the night cost the brigade no more than fifteen casualties. Next morning a German aeroplane flew low over the new growth taking photographs, and a heavy bombardment ensued which was repeated for some days, but as the trench was tenanted only by night little damage was inflicted.

On the 8th May after a welcome refreshment at Authie the battalion took over from the 4th Oxfordshire what was called " G " Sector on the extreme right of the brigade.   This tour was destined to be memorable.   The ground was difficult and unfamiliar : it had been the scene of a fierce battle in June 1915 for the possession of Touvent Farm and the outskirts of Serre, and was everywhere cut up by old trenches and shell holes, still littered with bones and skulls.   Communications were bad, as all rations and supplies had to be brought from Hébuterne through communication trenches one and a half miles long and in bad repair.   The front line was no more satisfactory : it formed a sharp salient projecting towards Serre, held by disconnected posts, ill-defended, close to the enemy, and joined to the support line by only two communicators, one at either end of the salient.   So vague and difficult of identification was this area that Captain Cruttwell almost walked into the German lines while trying to establish contact with " D " Company on his left, and was greeted with a shower of rifle grenades.

The first week, however, in this dreary spot passed uneventfully without casualties.   But on the 15th the usual shelling seemed more methodical and to suggest registration on every point of tactical importance.   The two anxious company commanders were therefore relieved when at midnight a violent bombardment was opened upon the 56th Division on the left.   But as soon as the guns of the 48th Division had been securely switched off on to a false target in response to the S.O.S., the enemy showed his real hand.   All his batteries were directed with extreme violence against the Berkshire front.

It was now 12.30 a.m. on the morning of the 16th May ; the raid had begun.   " B " Company held the right or south side of the salient with two platoons in seven detached posts on a frontage of six hundred yards.   Two sections with a Lewis gun were in the supervision trench fifty yards in rear, and the remainder in local reserve four hundred yards farther back.   Captain G. H. W. Cruttwell had his head-quarters in a strong point called Pimlico, eight hundred yards from the front line, where he disposed of a platoon of " A " Company, which was reinforced by two platoons of " C " Company returning from a working party.   The dispositions of " D " Company, which stretched back on the left from the point of the salient, were almost precisely similar.   The plan of the bombardment, which was a masterpiece of method, was as follows : From 12.30–1 a.m. the whole of the front and supervision line was heavily bombarded, but the extreme violence of fire was directed against the front of " B " Company.   At 1 a.m. after a red rocket was shot up, the fire lifted upon the support and reserve lines, and deluged all tactical points.   At Pimlico, in particular, 5·9 shells were thrown at the rate of one hundred per minute, enveloping it in a dense fog of smoke and fumes, and destroying nearly half of the supporting platoon of " A " Company.   All lateral communications were simultaneously encased in a frame of fire.   The hostile infantry now entered " B " Company, overpowering and destroying the right-hand post of nine men.   One party moved to the right along the supervision trench, but were finally checked by the coolness of Lance-Corporal Cooke and his Lewis-gun team.   The remainder of the Germans, thus protected behind, wheeled to their right and attacked the other six posts from their immediate rear.   The remnant was in sore straits ; their defences were blown to pieces, their rifles were broken or buried, their bombs scattered ; they themselves had been shaken or buried and were left defenceless.   A survivor tells how the Germans appeared behind them, ordered them in English to mount the parapet or they would be shot.   Then Private Chapman tackled an officer with his fists and was shot down fighting bravely.   However, a few edged away to the right where Lieutenant Ward organized twelve survivors in Post 1, where they resisted stoutly in intact defences, and withdrew safely into the deep communication trench.   Sergeant Holloway, a stout soldier from Abingdon, remained with a few men in the post, who faced to front and rear and drove off the enemy until a party of the 13th West Yorkshire (31st Division) was moved to the left and secured the situation. Meanwhile the supporting platoon had been organized for defence four hundred yards back by Lieutenant Field, who remained with his men though severely wounded, and touch was regained with Company Head-quarters by Lieutenant Gathorne-Hardy, who volunteered to come up with his usual disregard of danger.

The turn of " D " Company came at 1.40 a.m., but the infantry attack was not pressed, probably because the enemy had already obtained the prisoners needed for identification.   The occupants of the three right-hand posts had been killed or buried, but five men were saved from No. 1 by the patient courage of Private Appleby, who dug them out one after another, while Captain Boyle and Sergeant Pitman extricated Lance-Corporal Sargeant and a few comrades from the No. 3, shooting meanwhile a German who appeared on the parapet.   As soon as Corporal Sargeant was free he collected bombs, and found an immediate target in a party of Germans who were hauling off two wounded prisoners.   Posts 4 and 5 on the left remained intact and full of fight.   Singing as they fired, " Pack up your troubles in your old kit bag, and smile, smile, smile," they held off the enemy who could be dimly seen, distinguished by white armlets, filing through their wire and forming up in three lines.   This sector was speedily secured by a reinforcement of twenty men under Sergeant V. H. Taylor ; they had been summoned by Corporal Page, a gallant Wokingham man, who volunteered to go back through the fiery curtain of the barrage and escaped unhurt.

The bombardment continued unabated until the first light of dawn, and then ceased abruptly.   Movement was dangerous in the ruined trenches, especially as the enemy fired showers of rifle grenades at every gap and caused several casualties.   But the wounded were all evacuated by 10 a.m., though it sometimes took four hours to get the stretcher from the front line to the village dressing-station.   The losses amounted to 98, of whom 18 were killed and 29 missing (most of the latter being reported prisoners-of-war).   " B " Company was the weaker by sixty men, or half its fighting strength.   Captain Boyle was awarded the M.C. for the successful defence of his sector, and Corporal Sargeant the Military Medal.   Thus the battalion came through its first serious test and was not found wanting : the Divisional and Corps Commanders both sent their praise of the endurance, discipline and fighting spirit shown on that night.   On the 17th May the division was withdrawn into Army reserve.

The brigade route-marched from Couin to Beauval on the 18th, where a fortnight was spent in excellent billets.   The time was occupied with route-marches, grouping practices at the range, and platoon and company training. It was remarkable with what a keen pleasure the men turned to drill and small company schemes after the monotonous months of trench warfare. A splendid compliment was paid to " D " Company by the Corps Commander, Sir A. Hunter Weston, who met them one day on the march.   Stopping their commander, Captain Attride, he said that he had never seen a finer body of men in France ; that he was proud of them, as they had every right to be proud of themselves for their conduct on the night of the 16th.

On the 31st the brigade moved to the St. Riquier training area near

Abbeville, which was alive with troops of every arm busily rehearsing the Somme Battles. The Berkshires were billeted in the villages of Maison Roland and Gapennes successively, in both of which the attitude of the civil population showed a quickly overcome hostility. Ten strenuous days were spent in the progressive training of the battalion, brigade and division. Reveillé was at 4 a.m. and work usually lasted from 6 till 1 p.m., while the nights were twice begun with brigade attacks and finished in bivouac. But the men enjoyed their time; they grew hard for battle with supple limbs and the indescribable thrill of physical hardness. Their afternoons were spent in cricket and football, and their evenings in all the greedily enjoyed delights of normal civilian life.

On the 10th June the battalion set its face again eastward, and after two long and dusty marches was back in a filthy bivouac at Sailly. The whole countryside bore witness that the time was at hand. The villages were full of camps and dumps; on the bare slope E. of Sailly the guns were ranged tier upon tier. The trenches also were filled with as ardent an activity; here were parties digging new shelters and Stokes-gun emplacements, there were fatigues bringing up gas cylinders, smoke-candles and all the diverse paraphernalia of the modern offensive, while the enemy's artillery incessantly harassed these suspected activities.

The 24th found the battalion back at Couin, where they were to stay until the fateful 1st July. The damp, ill-ventilated and crowded huts were responsible for a good many cases of sore throat and rheumatism. But there was little time to be sick, while all the final preparations for the great attack were being perfected. Blue hearts, the distinguishing mark of the Berkshires, were sewn on to the back of the steel-helmet cover and tin triangles fixed to the haversack, which was worn on the back in fighting order. It is of interest to preserve the detail of the equipment with which the men went into battle. Two sandbags were tucked in front of the belt; one Mills bomb was in each of the bottom pockets of the tunic; fifty extra rounds of ammunition were slung in a bandolier over the right shoulder. Each man carried in his haversack one iron ration, cardigan waistcoat, soft cap and pair of socks; the waterproof sheet was folded and strapped on outside and the mess-tin fastened to the lowest buckle of the haversack. Every other man carried a pick or shovel slung, and the Brigade with a fatherly solicitude advised all ranks to carry a pipe, matches and tobacco. The great bombardment had begun on the 25th, and night after night watchers on the hill of Couin, four miles behind the lines, saw with exultation and confident expectation the great shells picking out the enemy's line with fire.

On the 1st July the 48th Division was in Corps reserve and took no part in the battle, except the 5th and 6th Warwickshire, who fought with great bravery in Serre, though suffering terrible losses, which included both their commanding-officers. The rest of the division was concentrated round Mailly-Mallet, which was reached about 1 p.m. after innumerable checks in the encumbered roads. On the way detachments of Indian cavalry were passed resting their horses by Bus. The remainder of that day was spent in bivouac in an open field, close to which a 15-inch howitzer fired intermittently. No shells, however, fell near, though the place was only three miles west of Beaumont Hamel, where the 29th Division was so furiously engaged. In the morning the news had come of the capture of Gommecourt Cemetery and of Serre, and the disappointment was exceedingly bitter when at nightfall it was announced that the VIIIth Corps was everywhere back in their old front line.

Next morning the 145th Brigade received orders to attack over unknown country early on the 3rd, their objective being the north side of Thiepval beyond the Ancre brook. Attempts made during the day by the Brigadier and commanding-officers to get forward and pick up the lie of the land were frustrated by the dense clouds of smoke and dust. The brigade moved up therefore during the night to Mesnil one mile behind the lines very much in the dark, assailed during their march by lachrymatory gas, whose curious sweet scent was smelt by many for the first time. The company commanders went forward to the trenches to get what information they might. On their right loomed a great black mass, and they debated whether it was a hill or a cloud. Suddenly an array of lights and the flicker of rifle fire revealed it as the steep slopes of Thiepval. Just as " A " Company was filing into the trenches Lieutenant Hughes brought a rumour, speedily confirmed, that the attack was cancelled. The battalion retraced its steps and bivouacked at Mailly-Mallet. The men who had moved out in high spirits were greatly cast down, but it is certain that but few would have survived an improvised attack against a position of such dominating strength, which was yet to resist assault for nearly three months.   Next day guns and limbers moved in great streams towards the south, a sure indication that our energies were being concentrated on widening the gap already made.

The battalion returned to Couin and thence on the 8th July to the monotony of the trenches, where the general depression was increased by torrents of rain, and the spectacle of the dead of the 31st and 56th Divisions lying out in heaps unburied.   A show of activity was maintained in this disturbed area, another assaulting trench was dug to continue that already described for seven hundred yards in a southerly direction, and a few casualties were sustained in the bright moonlight.   Much work was required on the damaged trenches, which were handed over in good repair to the 5th Gloucestershire on the 12th July.   Next day one hundred men went over to see the 5th Battalion in the Bois de Warnimont.   Thirteen months had passed since they received their first trench instruction from the 1/4th ; they had now been reduced to a tiny remnant after their attack on Ovillers, and had lost every officer except their C.O.   On the 14th a fleet of motor-'buses carried the 145th Brigade southward to the Ovillers-La-Boiselle sector ; and the battalion was lodged in the crowded village of Senlis.

The great attack of that day had bitten into the third German line between Longueval and Bazentin-le-Petit on a front of some three miles. The principal British efforts for the next six weeks were therefore directed towards getting more elbow-room on either flank.   The position on the north was particularly cramped, as the Prussian Guards had resisted with desperate bravery in Ovillers until the 11th, while the whole sector was overlooked and enfiladed by Thiepval Hill.   Consequently progress, though steady, was slow and dearly bought.   At this time the British line skirted the southern orchards of Pozières, and thence ran westward just north of Ovillers to return in a sharp backward curve to the old front line at Authuille. The attack was timed for the 23rd July, so that ample time was available for studying the ground.   The first impression of complete devastation was profound : a board stating " This is La Boiselle " indicated a confusion of chasms and mounds from which the very brick dust had been blown away. Battalion Head-quarters remained here in a solid and elaborate German dugout.   Two platoons of " B " Company held the short front line just west of Pozières.   The guns were unceasingly active and men remarked that what was called " a lull " would in the old days have been considered a heavy bombardment, while road junctions and assembly points were frequently deluged with gas shells.

On the night of the 21st, Lieutenant Downs explored with a patrol the south-west corner of Pozières in spite of the nervous alertness of the enemy, and was specially thanked by the Anzacs on the right for the value of his information.

On the 22nd, detailed orders for the attack were issued. The battalion was to support the 4th Oxfordshire. Their jumping-off ground was an irregular line called Sickle trench curving towards the enemy some five hundred yards south-west of Pozières ; their objective was the enemy's front line, some three hundred yards away, which consisted of a similarly curved trench bulging out towards the south, and a strong point connected with the east corner of the trench by a sap, one hundred and fifty yards long, which was destined to enfilade the attackers in No-Man's Land. The Oxfordshire Light Infantry attacked at dawn and entered the enemy's trench, but were immediately squeezed into the protruding centre. Meanwhile " B " Company (Captain Aldworth) and " C " Company (Captain Lewis) were waiting in the twilight on a tape just in front of Sickle trench some two hundred and fifty yards away. No certain information could be gained, only the contradictory stories of wounded men trickling back, but two runners sent forward to reconnoitre reported that the position was critical.

It was now 3.55 a.m. (summer-time), the day was coming and the hostile barrage grew more intense. Captain Aldworth therefore took the responsibility of ordering both companies forward to support the Oxfords. For this prompt decision, which undoubtedly secured the success of the whole operation, and for his personal bravery Captain Aldworth was awarded the M.C. The companies arrived in the trench after some loss from shell fire, which killed Second-Lieutenant Clayton on the left. During the advance " B " Company was split in two, Nos. 5 and 8 Platoons being divided by "C" Company from Nos. 6 and 7, who entered towards the left with Captain Aldworth. The position was still precarious as two battalions were crowded in the centre of the trench in a space of perhaps three hundred and fifty yards. It was necessary at once to clear and hold the flanks. Lieutenant Downs drove the enemy out of the strong point on the right, advanced up to the heavily wired German second line which ran through the outskirts of Pozières, and, though repelled, barricaded and secured the right-hand limit of the objective (point 81). In the fierce hand-to-hand fighting, eleven Germans were killed and two captured. Meanwhile the strong point on the left (point 11) was attacked on two sides. One party of " B " Company, under Captain Aldworth, who bayoneted a German himself, and Lieutenant Tripp advanced up the trench with bomb and bayonet ; another party headed by Lieutenant Wakeford jumped out of the trench and ran over the open to the disputed point. Thus threatened the enemy gave way and the left limit of the objective was also secured. Lieutenant Wakeford was shot dead at the moment when he was climbing into the trench. Half an hour later (6.30 a.m.) a company of the Bucks with fixed bayonets appeared over the brow of the hill from Ovillers on the immediate left. Moving in perfect order and with great fire they drove the enemy out of his trenches in complete confusion ; and many of those who escaped the Bucks, were destroyed by enfilade fire from the machine guns of " C " Company. Both flanks were now thoroughly safe, as the Anzacs had seized the whole of the ruins of Pozières, and could be seen during the morning imperturbably lighting fires to fry their bacon on the captured ground. Thus the attacking battalions were now free to sort themselves out. The junction with the Bucks was fixed at point 11, " C " Company held the left, " B " Company the centre, and the Oxfords the right of the captured trench.

The morning passed quietly, the men had their breakfasts, and put the trenches in a sound state of defence, receiving a constant supply of material from parties of " D " Company excellently organized by Captain Attride. During the afternoon the enemy shelled the positions with great violence. More than 50 per cent. of " B " Company, whose trenches were the most damaged, were put out of action, and many of the carriers from " D " Company were also hit. Private C. J. Sadler from Wokingham, a company stretcher-bearer, dressed them all and put them in shell-holes until nightfall. While performing these brave actions, which gained him the D.C.M., three of his ribs were broken by a shell. The violence of the shelling seemed to herald a counter-attack, which the greatly reduced forces would have found it hard to repel. It was therefore with great satisfaction that the battalion found itself relieved at 10.30 p.m. by the 5th Warwickshire, and was able to get some

rest in the old German line south of Ovillers.   But the rest was short, as by
1.30 p.m. next day they were back in the trenches, holding the line which
the Bucks had just captured some four hundred yards long, spanning the
top of the narrow valley down to Ovillers.

Two hundred yards from the left of this line a German strong point
remained, which being on higher ground could enfilade the whole of the
captured trenches.   " D " Company was accordingly ordered to attack it at
1.50 a.m. on the 25th.   Arrangements were made direct with the artillery
through Major Todd, the forward liaison officer.   These worked admirably,
as the batteries concerned gave a five-minutes' intensive bombardment in the
darkness with the greatest apparent accuracy.   But the hopes raised were
unfulfilled ; the Germans replied at once with a destructive artillery and
machine-gun fire, which caused many casualties and made it impossible to
develop the attack.   As all chance of surprise had gone, the Commanding
Officer refused Captain Attride's request to renew the attempt.   The enemy
was indeed in great strength and made a counter-attack with bombs upon
Nos. 13 and 14 Platoons at 5.15 a.m.   Headed by Second-Lieutenants Taylor
and Cooke, the men retained their positions with a hot fire of rifle grenades.
During this fight C.-S.-M. Rider, who had just joined the battalion, had the
first opportunity of showing that combination of bravery and capacity which
was to earn him the M.C.   That evening the 5th Gloucestershire relieved the
battalion, who were withdrawn to bivouac near Albert.   Their losses were
moderate, if judged by the standards of the late war.   They amounted to
two hundred and thirty or about 35 per cent. of the numbers actually engaged.
Of these only twenty-seven, a singularly low proportion, were killed.   Three
officers were among the latter number, Second-Lieutenants Wakeford,
Clayton, and Teed.   The battalion had been fortunate in its first offensive
action and merited the praise bestowed by the Divisional and Corps Commanders.

They needed a respite from fighting ; for though losses were practically
made good by a succession of drafts, time was needed to assimilate them into
the companies.   Conscription had come into force in the spring, and as
voluntary supplies had fallen very low, the average length of service among
the new-comers was no more than three months.   Their knowledge of the
rifle was often imperfect and of the bomb nil, while their marching powers

needed serious testing. The companies also which had suffered in an unequal degree from the battle required much rearrangement, and many N.C.O.s had to be created and familiarized with their work. Ten pleasant midsummer days were spent at Cramont, and devoted entirely to company training. Each man during this period threw at least two live bombs, a practice which proved of the greatest value in August fighting. On the 9th August steps were retraced over crowded roads in a three-day march to Bouzincourt, where the cellars used as refuge against the constant long-range bombardment were found to be full, and a bivouac was chosen outside the village.

The sector of attack was to be exactly the same as before, and such were the difficulties of the uphill advance that our line was only half a mile farther east. On the night of the 12th, however, the 5th Royal Berkshire taking the enemy by surprise, had won an important success by seizing Ridge Trench at the crest of the slope with a long view northward and eastward. This was actually accomplished at the cost of three casualties ; and they were relieved next morning without incident by three platoons of the 4th Oxfordshire, to whom the 4th Royal Berkshire remained in support in the dugouts round Ovillers. While waiting comfortably here they were called upon within twenty-four hours to face their hardest ordeal since landing in France. The first hint of trouble came at 9.30 p.m., when the Oxfords sent a message that the enemy were trying to bomb them out of the trench. An hour later Lieutenant Garside was sent forward with Nos. 1 and 2 Platoons to supply bombs. It was intended that the Oxfords should undertake the counter-attack themselves, and " D " Company was also put under Colonel Bartlett's command with a further store of bombs at 12.30 a.m. Colonel Clarke realized that the situation was becoming more serious, and though assured that no further help would be needed, ordered the two remaining companies to be in instant readiness. Captain Lewis accordingly brought " C " Company into the communication trench leading to the Oxfords Head-quarters, which were in the line captured by the Bucks on the 23rd July. Here they waited after bombs and bandoliers had been served out. After two hours had passed in uncertainty, Colonel Clarke received an unexpected request from Colonel Bartlett that he should himself undertake the counter-attack. This he naturally refused : the Oxfords knew the ground, which his men had never seen, were on the spot and had already one and a half Berkshire companies. The Brigadier, however, found that the Oxfords were not in a position to take the action required, and making a virtue of necessity ordered Colonel Clarke to do so with all possible speed.

It was now 3 a.m., and as the Oxfords estimated that one and a half hours were required for the battalion to get into its assaulting position, the attack was fixed for 4.45 a.m. with a preceding barrage of seven minutes' duration. " C " Company and the remaining two platoons of " A " therefore hurried forward with all speed, and reached the point of assembly (the point 18 of 23rd July) at 4.15 a.m. Here Captain Pickford of the Oxfordshire Light Infantry supplied the disastrous information that another hour would be needed to get into position instead of the half-hour previously estimated. Colonel Clarke at once went to make the necessary alteration with the artillery ; and the companies doubled forward with " C " leading. Haste was most necessary, for the day was breaking, and the trenches were battered. The enemy showered shrapnel upon the men, who crouched as they ran. When Captain Blandy of " A " Company reached the head of the communication trench it was broad daylight and his watch already stood at 5.10 a.m. His two remaining platoons were waiting in the fire trench very weary, for they had been carrying all night. The company turned right-handed and entered an empty and ruinous stretch of trench. A man looked over and exclaimed, " There are our boys going over on the right." These were " C " and " D " Companies. At this moment an officer of the Oxfordshire came along and tried to straighten things out, but he lacked detailed orders, or the knowledge where the flanks of the companies should rest. Moreover, there was no barrage.

But the three companies went on their way most bravely to almost certain failure and death. As they tried to cross the two hundred and fifty yards of open ground, the Germans, profiting from the absence of shell fire, stood up in their trenches aiming deliberately and accurately at the advancing lines. Short rushes from shell-hole to shell-hole proved so costly that few if any of the men managed to get within one hundred yards of the enemy. Captain Attride was wounded in the body and Captain Lewis in the thigh, and hardly an officer was left. No bravery or determination on earth could turn failure into success. On their right flank was a half-finished communication trench linking up the British line with Ridge Trench, and so the survivors edged into this poor shelter. Captain Lewis reached it with his orderly's help and though grievously wounded was brought into safety. Captain Attride was shot dead through the head as he was being hoisted into the place of refuge. He was a fine natural soldier, who had commanded " D " Company for nine months with great tact and ability, and the best of comrades. Captain Blandy was shot through the face and partially blinded, as he stood out of the way of a wounded man in the bottom of the trench. Some men still lay out in shell-holes unable to move, for the enemy picked off everything that stirred. Suddenly a British aeroplane appeared sounding its horn, for whose information Sergeant Page lit some flares, which he had with him. The pilot, a good friend in necessity, instantly flew back, and signalled to the artillery. The 9·2's opened quickly upon the Germans, who withdrew their heads and enabled the survivors to reach safety. The casualties were naturally heavy. Of officers there were also killed Lieutenant O'Hara (1st East Surrey, attached), Second-Lieutenant Beasley (whose little son afterwards received from the King's hand, at Reading, the Military Medal which his father had won), and Second-Lieutenant Bartram, while Second-Lieutenant Taylor was wounded. He lay out for forty-eight hours tended with wonderful devotion by Sergeant Westall, who was given a bar to his D.C.M. This sergeant, the bravest of the brave, was taken prisoner next autumn when serving with the 2/4th near Arras. He was last seen in a shell-hole during a daylight patrol, laughing at the Germans who were firing rifle-grenades at him, but afterwards returned safely from captivity. Casualties among other ranks amounted to one hundred and forty, including fifty-nine killed and missing. Failure is often more heroic than success, and these loyal men fought and died with great honour.

A converging attack was now started against Thiepval, that stubborn fortress which was to hold out until the 27th September. The 48th Division having gained the Pozières Ridge began to encircle it from the S.E., while steady pressure was maintained on the west from the old front line beyond the Ancre. On the 18th August the 143rd Brigade attacked on a line one thousand yards north of Ovillers, their right flank being secured by a bombing attack of " B " Company, 4th Royal Berkshire. The operation which started at 5 p.m. was completely successful ; Captain Aldworth handled his men with skill, and captured twenty-seven prisoners with a machine gun, besides driving many of the enemy into the hands of the Warwicks. The fighting went on till midnight with fierceness and confusion, attack and counter-attack succeeding each other as fresh supplies of bombs were brought up, but " B " Company, whose men threw splendidly, held their ground. Here Lieutenant Ridley was killed at the head of his bombers. Captains Cruttwell (O.C. " D " Company) and Lacy, Lieutenants Wix and Smith (3rd East Surrey, attached) were wounded, and of other ranks nine were killed and thirty-six wounded.

The battalion, whose fighting strength was now less than five hundred, was to take a last successful share in the Somme fighting before being withdrawn.

The division had now arrived at a point midway between Ovillers and Thiepval. A line of tattered stumps on the skyline, ten hundred yards away and one hundred and seventy feet above them, were the orchards which marked the southern outskirts of the village. A deep and narrow valley stood between them and the hill, across which the enemy had established a line of trenches curving towards Ovillers. The whole of the division was engaged in this attack, with the 145th Brigade in the centre, and the 143rd and 144th on the right and left respectively. The two assaulting battalions of the 145th were from left to right the 5th Gloucestershire and 4th Royal Berkshire, each having a frontage of about three hundred yards. The trench to be attacked by the battalion ran back from the point of the salient in the valley (point 79) athwart the eastward slope of the hill. A splendid barrage was furnished by the artillery, more than fifty guns firing with signal accuracy over the front of the battalion. " C " Company on the right moved up close behind it, and seized their objectives without difficulty from the defenders, who were buried in the ruinous trenches. Though the 8th Royal Warwickshire on their right were unable to join hands, the flank was secured by a strong point dug with the aid of the 5th Royal Sussex, the Pioneer Battalion of the Brigade, and held until relief without a counter-attack but under heavy shelling.

On the left the opposition was more lively, for point 79 was the key of the German position, and both the trench and a collection of dugouts hard by had been scarcely touched by our heavy guns. Three platoons of " A " Company moved against it, one up an old communication trench, and the other two along the open on either side. The enemy showed great spirit, standing on his parapet to fire and throw bombs at the attackers, in spite of the heavy execution inflicted by the cross-fire of Lewis guns from the British trenches. But the attack finally broke through the disputed point. For this success much credit must be given to Lance-Corporal Rixon of Reading, who was in charge of the first bombing party in the communication trench. Leaping on to the parapet, he directed the fire of his bombers, and escaped unhurt by a singular good fortune. He was afterwards rewarded with the Military Medal. The Germans could not retire under cover, as the flank trenches were already occupied by the British ; and as they ran back along the naked valley they presented a target which was not neglected. Ten only were taken alive, but their dead lay thick upon the ground. " A " Company had by now lost its officers, but there was no lack of direction or control, thanks to Sergeant White, an old Territorial of many years' standing. He organized the captured position, inspired the men to work, and kept them steady throughout the night under a rain of shells, thus well earning the D.C.M.

The attack had been well planned and was cheaply executed. Thirty-one men were killed or missing, and fifty wounded (including Second-Lieutenants Garside and Buck). The men were particularly pleased and proud of a success won over the 5th Grenadier Battalion of the Prussian Guard, who had just been sent to Thiepval after a commendatory speech from the Kaiser, which, as often, failed to ensure good fortune. Next day the battalion was relieved by the 74th Brigade and returned to bivouac in Bouzincourt. The 48th Division, every unit of which had been engaged at least three times, was to enjoy a hard-earned rest.

The Army-Commander wrote of it that it had " fully maintained the best traditions of British infantry. Its record shows a high sense of discipline and honour in all ranks." General Jacob, commanding the IInd Corps, added that " results have exceeded expectation. Your record in the recent operations is first rate . . . you have all done nobly."

Many places now harboured the battalion, which spent only forty-eight hours in the trenches opposite Beaumont Hamel during the next seven weeks.

First they stayed at Bus, that shady village with the white château where General Fanshawe so long kept his Divisional Head-quarters, then at Beauval and Candas, a new village whose inhabitants with a singular naïveness imagined that the blue hearts, which the men wore as distinguishing badges, marked a dangerous brand of storm-troops and expressed their intention to have the hearts of their enemies. So strong were they in their mistaken conviction that they locked their doors and refused an entry, until matters were explained by the interpreter. Finally for the first ten days of that wettest of Octobers they lived in Sombrin, nine miles S.W. of Arras, where no better billets awaited the officers than an alternative between barns and dripping unboarded tents. During all this time drafts arrived in both men and officers, the latter coming from a variety of regiments, 5th Norfolk, 4th Northamptonshire, 4th Royal Sussex and 10th Middlesex. There came also a gratifying harvest of decorations won during July and August, culminating in the award of the D.S.O. to the commanding-officer, who had gained the implicit confidence of all ranks by his careful study of their comfort and thorough grasp of every detail of organization. On the 10th October they drew near the line again, spending some days at Souastre, the village on the hill overlooking the splintered wood of Gommecourt. Here they found the liveliest activity prevailing; for the Battle of the Ancre had been planned to begin on the 14th October, though bad weather caused repeated postponements for a month. Working-parties descended to Hébuterne every day to pursue mining operations under the direction of the sappers; two strenuous days in the trenches cost sixteen casualties.

However, no prolonged effort was expected of the battalion which moved back again and spent the rest of October in various billets round Beauval. Captain Aldworth now left to attend the Senior Officers' Course at Aldershot. He left " B " Company in a high state of efficiency. The men were much gratified by the promotion to commissioned-ranks of the following N.C.O.s for bravery and good conduct in the field : Sergeants Wickens, Ross, Turner, Rogers, Cawley and Crust. The two last named were to win Military Crosses, and to command " B " and " A " Companies in Italy.

On the 31st October the brigade marched eastward and settled at Millencourt, the village on the western hill looking down upon Albert. The great battle had now died down, but the winter was to bring in its train wet and cold, an enemy more insidious and more trying to morale and endurance. A move was soon made forward into the great featureless waste for the possession of which more than a million men had been killed or wounded. For more than seven miles east of Albert the eye could pick out no natural landmark beyond a few broken sticks, once trees. The surface of that evil country, churned up and scooped out by innumerable shells, was literally a sea of mud ; where water had collected in the hollows it was deeply stained with green and yellow, the result of gas and fumes. No buildings were available for the great army spread about this area, and but few dugouts ; the vast majority of all ranks lived out in rough shelters or under the imperfect protection of sodden tents. As, moreover, the artillery still maintained the characteristic activity of battle areas, the few roads and paths available for communication and transport were heavily shelled, especially through the hours of darkness. The hardships, therefore, greatly exceeded anything yet experienced. For example, when the battalion took over from the 11th Argyll and Sutherland Highlanders at the so-called Lozenge Wood in pouring rain, they found a camp which consisted only of one bivouac sheet per platoon with eight tents for officers ; while a complete absence of material prevented any attempt at improvement. In the trenches neither reserve nor support lines afforded any shelter, while the front trench was considered to be in good condition if the liquid mud at the bottom did not exceed a foot in depth. Further, no hot rations could be brought up, as the cookers were compelled to remain behind the ridge at Martinpuich, more than two miles away ; and the " Tommy's Cookers " which were served out to each section were useless in the absence of any shelter against the mud and rain. These were dangerous trenches, the left of which was isolated by a gap of three hundred yards from the next battalion. The enemy were here standing on their last line before Bapaume on the slope rising towards Loupart Wood. The pivot of their defence was the Butte of Warlencourt, an ancient burial-place, which rose steeply some fifty feet above the surrounding country, which had hitherto defied capture. Six or seven casualties were the price of every day in the trenches, which when augmented by cases of trench-foot proved quite a severe drain on companies still much below full strength. There was more sickness than at any other time in the war, partly due to the fact that there was no rest, comfort or security behind the lines. The men were never withdrawn to billets and missed for months the sight of a civilian population.

Few incidents broke the monotonous interchange between camp and trench. Early in December, Second-Lieutenant Crawley, who had been given twenty men to be used only on patrol work, successfully dispersed a German working-party near Destremont Farm, killing thirty and sustaining no loss. On the other hand, the Head-quarters of " A " and " C " Companies were destroyed by shells on the 8th/9th December, and twelve casualties were suffered. The greatest inconvenience in occupying captured trenches was perhaps the accurate knowledge which the enemy possessed of the site of the few remaining dugouts, which he made continual targets. On the 14th December the battalion, now reduced to five hundred and forty of all ranks, moved to Bécourt Camp near La Boiselle. Here the men kept Christmas as well as might be, but without the festivities of the previous year at Authie. They had lost during this year of heavy fighting seven hundred and seventy-nine men (exclusive of sickness). Only four officers now remained of those who had come out in March 1915 : Colonel Clarke, Captains Goolden and Challoner and Lieutenant Payne the Quartermaster. M. Hénaut, the interpreter, remained on until the departure for Italy next autumn, always willing, cheerful, and helpful, a universal friend.

By this time the battalion had largely lost its exclusive Berkshire character, which had knit it together in a cohesion of local pride.

A welcome move to the back areas followed Christmas ; first to Bresle, W. of Albert, where the brigade was inspected by the new Corps-Commander, Sir W. P. Pulteney ; then by train to Citerne, a quiet comfortable village intact of war, south of the Somme. Here from the 9th–28th January, the severity of the cold, which was exceptional throughout this winter, was mitigated in billets. There was much to be done in the way of training, as the new platoon organization had come into force. Its object was to create a self-contained unit of specialists, with the four sections divided into rifle-men, Lewis-gunners, bombers and rifle-bombers. This higher degree of specialization threw a greater strain upon the intelligence of the average soldier, and upon the responsibilities of platoon and section-commanders ; its full realization was indeed found impossible in 1917, as no adequate time for training proved available.

On the 28th the train brought the battalion back to Hamel, whence they moved to Cappy, high on the southern bank of the Somme, overlooking its great loops and frozen marshes.   Houses and barns were, curiously enough, available as billets, though the village was only two thousand yards behind the old French line of the 1st July, and there were also some great Adrian Huts built by the French, which accommodated a company apiece.   The frost was now at its height ; night after night the thermometer marked 20 or more degrees of frost ; the water froze solidly in the buckets while transported to the trenches, and, as fuel was scarce, the hardships were great. But there were compensations, for the hardness of the trenches made all digging impossible.   On the 16th February a thaw set in, and the low country was enveloped in mist for many days, during which the enemy was able to perfect in secret the plans for his great retirement.   March came in with a return of frost and snow, but the front was gradually waking into life.   The Germans persisted in masking their withdrawal by a lively activity ; and though the Allied Commanders had not penetrated their design, the partial retreats round Bapaume led to unusual curiosity as to the immediate future. Consequently raids for purposes of identification became frequent ; and one was successfully carried out by the Royal Berkshire on the night of the 7th/8th March without any loss.   The portion of trench to be entered was shut off by a " box-barrage," which encased it in a frame of shells on both flanks and in the rear.   Three parties of eight each, under the command of Second-Lieutenant Hampshire entered without difficulty ; but as all the birds had flown beyond the limits of the barrage, they were compelled to make another attempt at 2.45 a.m.   This time they found a small dugout, which when bombed yielded two prisoners, who were carried off safely under a hot but inaccurate fire.   They proved to belong to King Constantine's Own 88th Infantry Regiment, and were distinguished by a Crown with the letter K beneath on their shoulder-straps.   The Divisional-General, who was delighted with this successful operation, obtained for Lieutenant Hampshire the M.C., and for Sergeant A. C. Evans, Corporal H. Hart, Lance-Corporals J. Mazey and G. W. Hutchings the M.M.

The results of the weary and bloody months of the Somme Battles now became manifest ; for the enemy began his general retreat on the 17th/18th March.   The 48th Division was in the forefront of the retreat south of the

Somme. The 1/7th Royal Warwickshire Regiment were the first British troops to enter Peronne, and the flag which they hoisted on the ruined towers is now preserved in the Imperial War Museum. The battalion was in reserve at Cappy practising advance guards, for open warfare had become a present reality. There was a new excitement in the operation orders of the 20th, which began : " The Battalion will move to Peronne at 11 a.m." For the first time since they went abroad men could move unmolested over enemy country. There was a delusive touch of spring in the air, and hopes ran high as the mire and clay were exchanged for the green country beyond. They found Peronne, which had survived so many battles and sieges in the past lying utterly waste. Though the French gunners had spared the place, the Germans had devoted it to utter destruction : in the streets were all manner of débris, including furniture and children's toys, and in the suburbs all the fruit trees had been felled.

Next morning they marched south-east along the Cologne brook, which was crossed at Doignt. Everywhere the pioneers were busily repairing the roads ; the great craters at the cross-ways were being filled up, the tall poplar trees which had been felled were being dragged out of the way. From Flamicourt and Tincourt the liberated inhabitants streamed out to meet the troops ; the Germans had destroyed their homes, and their faces, from which, as the War Diary records, " all life and hope seemed to have departed," were eloquent of the last thirty months' misery. The enemy pursued his way backwards with deliberation ; the heaps of metal lying abandoned in the village streets being almost the only indication of undesired haste. The 5th Cavalry Division rode past the infantry on the 24th, but the limits of his retreat were soon clear and his rearguards offered a more determined resistance as they approached the outposts of the Hindenburg Line.

By the beginning of April the 145th Brigade was round Villers-Faucon in support to the remainder of the division, which was fighting forwards beyond Epéhy. On the 4th, it was ordered forward to take the three small villages of Ronssoy, Basse Boulogne, and Lempire, which clustered together at the head of a valley, with an undulating hill to the east. Snow fell throughout the day and obscured the attempts of the company officer to see the lie of the land. The battalion moved forwards from Villers-Faucon in a dense cold mist at 2 a.m. through narrow snow-clogged lanes, but arrived punctually at 4 a.m. at the rendezvous, Templeux Wood, where touch was obtained to right and left with the 8th Warwickshire and 4th Oxfordshire. The companies deployed silently east of the Wood, each having a frontage of two hundred yards, and a depth of six waves in two lines, divided by a distance of fifty and twenty-five yards respectively ; a formation suitable to semi-open warfare where no elaborate defences were expected. They had to cover sixteen hundred yards before reaching Ronssoy, between it and them were a number of small coppices, linked up with small lanes and ditches, among which the enemy's outposts were believed to cover the village by a line drawn from north-west to south-east six hundred yards in front of it. The morning was ideal for surprise unless the mist confused direction, and therefore no barrage was provided unless called for by signal rockets.

The fortunes of the three attacking companies were as follows—" B " Company advancing on the right was within two hundred yards assailed by enfilade fire from a slag-heap, which was quickly encircled and captured by a platoon working in co-operation with the Warwicks. Eight hundred yards farther on they found the German outpost position wired and well manned ; signals to the artillery brought a barrage, which enabled the position to be easily rushed. Their task was now accomplished, and facing S.E. of Ronssoy they formed a defensive flank, and enabled the main attack to proceed in safety. " A " Company, therefore, under Captain Challenor pushed on in the centre, broke through the German wire, swept across the eastern outskirts of the village and seized the cemetery beyond. Here they divided ; one platoon joined hands with the 7th Gloucestershire who were by now in possession of Lempire and Basse Boulogne, two hamlets just N.E. of Ronssoy. The remainder prolonged " B " Company's defensive flank along a bank two hundred yards S.E. of the village. This was a fine advance of one and a half miles over unknown country, the leadership of Captain Challenor was extremely good, and the successful division of forces immediately after the assault, when confusion is most apt to occur, merits especial praise. He was awarded the M.C. within a few days. Sergeant Millican of Reading should also be remembered ; for when his platoon-commander was killed at the entrance to the village he instantly took charge and led his men with distinction. To " D " Company fell the lion's share of the fighting and of the booty. Approaching unawares in the first light of dawn to the southern entrance of the village, they overpowered two posts, killing every man and capturing two machine guns. Neglecting an open flank—for the Oxfords were held up in Ronssoy Wood—they burst into the village. Here was the wildest confusion. No attack was expected in the stormy weather, and the enemy were just sitting down to breakfast in their dugouts and cellars. The snow showed up figures running confusedly about the streets; at a corner a feld-webel was shouting and beckoning to his men to fall in. The men, wild with excitement, hunted them through the streets and cellars, making a great slaughter. The place was littered with dead bodies; the Commander of No. 16 Platoon, Lieutenant Rogers, killed eight single-handed. The fugitives ran in disorder up the hill, flinging their packs behind them. Captain James (who was also to be rewarded with an M.C.) collected his men, and wheeled to the east of the village to exploit success. Through the mist a field battery appeared one thousand yards away limbering up and galloping over the ridge into Hargicourt. Unfortunately, by some mistake our barrage descended on the eastern exits of the village, causing several casualties and preventing further progress. After securing an outpost line, the men turned to the task of clearing up Ronssoy. The victors ate their enemies' breakfast of soup, coffee and sausages; they collected hundreds of unopened letters just distributed by a morning mail, they examined the equipment and packs, in which everything was brand-new, for the Germans had just received a fresh outfit on returning from Russia. All were wonderfully excited and high-spirited, and have always declared since that it was the best fight in the war; while General Fanshawe, who as usual was not far behind, said on arrival that he had not seen a better day's work since he had been in France.

The enemy attempted no counter-stroke beyond ineffective shelling; every now and then Uhlan patrols—the first the men had seen—appeared on the skyline; and some scouts from " C " Company who managed to look into Hargicourt saw parties digging feverishly at new defences. The casualties in officers were somewhat heavy, as they had led and directed their commands gallantly over a long stretch of difficult unfamiliar country. Four were killed—Second-Lieutenants Garside, Heppell, Hunt and Bostock, and two wounded, Captain James and Lieutenant Rogers. Other ranks escaped very lightly with nine killed and thirty-nine wounded.

When the battalion returned after a rest at Hamel to this sector on the

13th April the Battle of Arras had begun, but the enemy though heavily defeated in the north was still able by persistent delaying actions to prevent the British from getting to grips with the Hindenburg Line. Our advance had gone no farther than two thousand yards east of Ronssoy, still below the crest of Hargicourt Hill, which was guarded by the key position of Guillemont Farm. This was given as the objective of the battalion in a combined Divisional advance on the night of the 14th. The attack was a failure, or rather was arrested before development. The night was pitch dark, wet snow fell continuously, and without firing lights it was impossible to see five yards. " C " and " D " Companies began to form up for the assault at 11.30 p.m. ; their password, " Wilson," celebrated the entry of the United States into the war. Before they moved off an enemy patrol on the right flank noticed them and reported to the artillery, who directed a heavy fire against them, causing thirty casualties. As the men were so cold that they could scarcely hold, much less fire, their rifles, the Brigade ordered the attack off and refused to allow its renewal that night. General Fanshawe generously said that " if it had been possible to reach the objective the battalion would have done so." The farm was to fall to the 144th Brigade on the 24th April. The rôle of the two Berkshire Companies, " A " and " B," engaged in support on the right was not wholly satisfactory. They lost touch with the other brigade and darkness ended before they had developed their orders ; but they sustained no more than ten casualties. Next day they took over the whole of the captured ground to hold defensively after a long and arduous relief. They were relieved on the 29th and returned to Villers-Faucon to enjoy a fortnight's rest in the warmth of a tardy spring. Reinforcements brought their strength up to seven hundred, but the quality and physique of the men was not beyond criticism : for of the first thirty-five who arrived, five wore trusses, and three suffered from malformations of the foot.

By the beginning of May the great attempt to burst through the German lines, which had aroused such high hopes, had definitely failed. The centre of gravity shifted to the extreme north, where preparations on a vast scale were beginning for the Third Battle of Ypres. Accordingly in the south where the division remained a period of so-called inactivity set in. On the 12th May the battalion, temporarily under Major Aldworth's command as the C.O. was Acting-Brigadier, moved into the XVth Corps Area at Combles, after a personal farewell from the old Corps-Commander, who addressed the 145th Brigade on the march and expressed his regret at losing such gallant and well-behaved troops.   They traversed the centre of the Somme waste, still inconceivably desolate, to Beulencourt two miles south of Bapaume, and re-entered the line in front of Hermies on the 15th relieving the 9th Sherwood Foresters ; these were the northern trenches from which the great surprise attack against Cambrai was launched on the 20th November. Before them was ranged the vast fortress of the Hindenburg Line, which took advantage of every undulation in the ground, while the British defences on the contrary were no more as yet than a series of detached outposts and strong points each garrisoned by a platoon.   The Berkshire line extended over two thousand three hundred yards, and when taken over required such elementary protection as a belt of continuous wire.   The wide and ill-defined No-Man's Land, sometimes one thousand yards in extent, contained many tactical features such as farms or clumps of trees, but though constantly patrolled provoked no combats.   One small raid which was attempted against the battalion was promptly crushed by the good leadership of Sergeant Garrett, an intelligent young soldier from Wokingham, who obtained the Military Medal.   No more than fifteen casualties were suffered during these six weeks, but among them was Captain Down, an able and considerate officer, who was killed after a service of fifteen months with the battalion.

On the 30th June this interlude came to an end with a rest at Bailleulval, a village six miles S.W. of Arras.   Here every sign suggested that a share was soon to be taken in the offensive.   Constant drafts brought the total strength to nine hundred and thirty, the highest figure yet reached since embarkation. Three weeks were spent in an arduous preparation, many attacks were practised over the old trenches in the front of the village, the Brigadier tested the capacity of each officer to use his compass, and the Divisional-General carried off the senior officers for staff-rides.   On the 21st July all doubts were resolved when the battalion entrained at Mondicourt for Flanders.   They passed through their old resting places, Marles and Lapugnoy, past Lillers and Hazebrouck, teeming centres of activity, detrained at Godeswaersvelde at 10.45 p.m., and marched wearily to Houtkerque, where they billeted at dawn.   It was next door to Winnezeele, their first sojourn in Flanders.   The journey had lasted twenty hours, and the distance covered was at least seventy miles, though only forty-three in a direct line. Such are the necessities of transport in war.

The prolonged and terrible struggle now about to begin was the last attempt to break through in the west on the old plan. It was believed that the immense collection of guns, ammunition, railway material and every kind of transport would prove irresistible, that the bombardment prolonged with unparalleled intensity over many days would open to the attacking troops the Flemish coast with the submarine bases then at the height of their most dangerous activity. These expectations were doomed to disappointment. For continuous trench lines which could be smashed to atoms, the Germans substituted an organization of great depth, where machine-gun nests and pill-boxes were almost indistinguishable from the muddy sea which surrounded them. As the foremost zone was lightly held, the attackers after an initial success found their energies almost exhausted by their labours in the mire, and the main resistance still spread indefinitely before them. Many a pill-box, which required for its destruction the direct impact of a 9·2 shell, escaped intact, though the soil all round was torn to pieces. Moreover the staff-work of General Gough's 5th Army was thoroughly bad, as far as the 48th Division was concerned. Impossible objectives were given the troops, with inadequate reserves. Artillery support was at times insufficient, and once at least the attack was contingent on the aid of tanks, but was persisted with in spite of their absence. Finally, as is well known, the incredible weather made victory impossible. The great storm which raged throughout the initial attack of the 31st July was the harbinger of a month's almost unprecedented rain. Terrible as was the last month of the Somme Battles, all the events now to be described were fought under far worse conditions. Except for a few pill-boxes, no shelter was available for the troops ; the corduroy paths, sole means of communication over the bottomless mud, were gassed and shelled day and night. The artillery placed almost wheel to wheel in the morass sunk deeper and deeper, and could not extricate themselves for days from the storm of shells. Even the light railways, on which their supplies depended, sank themselves from lack of solid foundation. Finally, far behind, junctions, dumps and rest-camps were attacked by long-range fire and bombs with an as yet unequalled persistency. Nevertheless, as General Ludendorff admits, the stubborn spirit of the British soldier tested and shook the German defence to the uttermost. The 31st brought the battalion no excitement. They moved up slowly to the battle during the unexpected lull, and relieved the 188th Brigade on the 5th August, S. of St. Julien. Here in the sodden country on either side of the foul Steenbeck brook, water stood everywhere, it blotted out the trenches and flooded the pill-boxes. After four days of incessant shelling they crawled back through a violent thunderstorm to Dambre Camp, west of Ypres, after suffering losses of eleven killed and thirty-one wounded. Here for a week they practised sedulously for the new attack of the 16th, a large-scale model of the ground being available for the inspection of officers and N.C.O.s at Divisional Head-quarters. On the 15th they marched by slow stages, with a hot meal at evening, to St. Julien. Next morning, at 4.45 a.m., the British barrage thundered out its awful salute to the dawn. Men advanced against the enemy on a front of twenty-five miles ; the second act of this great drama had begun.

The attack as a whole was a complete failure, though the French pro-gressed on the left towards Houthulst Forest and the 23rd Division took Langemarck. In the centre the progress of the 48th Division was infinitesimal. They were faced by fresh troops, who fought bravely in their defensive labyrinth ; the promised tanks were unavailable and the weight of troops was far too weak for the ambitious objectives assigned to them. The task allotted to the battalion proved disappointing ; as Brigade reserve it was intended to sweep through the assaulting battalions to the final objec-tive. But its actual rôle was reduced to hanging about almost stationary under heavy shell fire sometimes moving slightly to either flank to fill up gaps against threatened counter-attacks.

The brigade started to the assault from the eastern bank of the Steenbeck on a frontage of twelve hundred yards. It was expected to advance a good mile without supports through the mud, everywhere ankle deep, and to take three fortified lines on its way. It was faced by the 7th Bavarian Regiment, part of a good division, the 5th Bavarian, which had just come into line and was fully prepared, for the enemy's barrage descended within three minutes of the commencement of our own. It was therefore not surprising that except in one place no impression was made even upon the first of the three lines, that of the Langemarck Road. The battle swayed about the pill-boxes, disused gunpits and fortified farms, which studded the country. Each pill-box in particular had to be taken by a distinct operation, the best method being a rush by bombers, who crept up and threw their missiles through the loop-holes, which meanwhile were silenced by concentrated machine-gun fire. One of these structures, which was surrounded by water and approachable only by a narrow causeway, defied capture throughout the day.

The four Berkshire Companies had varying experiences in the battle. " A " Company on the right was heavily hit at zero hour by the barrage, which killed Captain Tripp (3rd East Surrey) and wounded the only other officer, Second-Lieutenant Brooke. Second-Lieutenant Buck then took over and maintained a defensive line in touch with the Ulster Division some two hundred yards in front of the jumping-off ground, and repelled two attempts of the enemy to thrust forward small parties through gaps in the line. " B " Company also experienced great difficulty in getting through the moving barrage. Captain Norrish, their commander, walked up and down looking for a gap, and finally led his men through a rift near the north-east corner of St. Julien. This company spent the day in support to " A " and without getting to grips with the enemy lost forty men. " C " Company alone had some small share of fighting. At 7 a.m. they encircled and took Hillock Farm which was holding up the advance of the Bucks, killing fifty of the garrison and capturing a few survivors. During the morning the Buckinghamshire pushed bravely and laboriously up to the Green Line on the Langemarck Road, and bit into two hundred yards of it, with both flanks in the air. " C " Company after losing all its officers provided some protection in a defensive left flank by clearing the enemy (who yielded six prisoners) from some gunpits about five hundred yards N.N.E. of St. Julien. This was accomplished under the leadership of C.-S.-M. Heath, who received the M.C. The losses of this company amounted to at least fifty men. " D " Company had the lightest trial, for they did not cross the brook until the barrage had slackened at 5.15 a.m., and throughout the day they remained in support to the Buckinghamshire Battalion near the eastern bank, losing about thirty men. The total casualties, which were the lightest in the brigade, amounted to 35 killed and 138 wounded (including 5 officers) or about one-third of the battle strength.

The battalion had a short respite from battle, but was brought back to attack the same ground on the 27th August. For although no renewal of the general assault was found practicable until the 20th September, it was deemed necessary, as a preliminary, to seize the low ridge of Gravenstal, which rises sixty feet above the Steenbeck, and gave the enemy eyes to see our preparations as far as Ypres. The same objectives were assigned, though the 145th Brigade was this time in reserve to the other two. On the right of the 48th was the 61st, or second-line Territorial Division ; their first co-operation on the battle-field was not fortunate, for both were unable to make headway and lost heavily. The plan of attack, which lacked all imagination, shook general confidence in the 5th Army Staff. The same impossible advance was expected without the aid of tanks, though by now the water lay knee-deep in the valley. Men struggling forward could be seen hoisting one another out of the glutinous mud which had engulfed them to the middle. To crown all, the attack started at the singular hour of 1.55 p.m. All the final preparations were open to the enemy's eye, and throughout the afternoon his machine guns played with deadly effect on the reserves crowding up the narrow tracks. The only success achieved was the seizure by the 144th Brigade of five hundred yards of the Green Line between Springfield and Keerselare Cross Roads. The Berkshires were not engaged, but took over at nightfall from the Warwick Brigade, who had exhausted themselves in fruitless attacks on the right of the Divisional front. Further attempts next day by the 1/4th Oxfordshire to extend our occupation of the Green Line proved unavailing, for the combatants were entirely exhausted. On the night of the 28th the battalion was relieved by two companies of the 2/10th London Regiment, thus half a battalion held defensively the whole attacking front of a brigade. The losses this time amounted to 11 killed, including Captain Norrish (10th Middlesex, attached) and 51 wounded.

Withdrawn to Dambre Camp and then to St. Jan Ter Beezen, the battalion was pursued with long-range shelling and night bombing, but moved far to the rear on the 16th September to Audenfort near Calais, where the inhabitants, sheltered from the realities of war, proved at first far from friendly. During the musketry training which occupied most of the time, " A " Company had the satisfaction of beating all the other companies of the division in a practice fired under the eyes of the G.O.C.

A final return was made on the 27th September to the same blighted region, now enveloped with the dense mists of autumn. The tide of war had flowed forward for more than a mile since the great attack of the 20th, and the British troops were pursuing their bloody way beyond the eastern slopes of the Gravenstal Ridge. On the 4th October the 143rd Brigade advanced some fifteen hundred yards, with the 145th in support. For the next three days the Royal Berkshire moved about uneasily behind the front lines, changing their bivouac every night, continuously soaked by the rain which again fell pitilessly. On the 7th they crawled through the trackless mire, plentifully besprinkled with gas by the way, to the front lines. In twenty-four hours the 7th Worcestershire took over after a long and arduous relief, which was complicated by the killing or burying *en route* of nearly all the guides sent back to direct them. Next day the familiar rôle of Divisional reserve was allotted to the battalion while the 144th were being shattered in another fruitless attack. That night motor-lorries took the exhausted men back to Dambre Camp. Their losses were not heavy—16 killed and 68 wounded—but they had enjoyed no real sleep for five nights, and all agreed that the hardships they had experienced far exceeded all others in the war. Thus ended their intermittent share for seventy days in that tremendous and ill-conducted battle, which had cost them in all over four hundred men.

Hence they moved south by rail and settled until the end of October in huts at Villars-au-Bois north-west of Arras, making the acquaintance of the 2nd Canadian Division. Adequate drafts arrived of both officers and men, the former mainly from the 3rd Wiltshire Regiment, the latter from the Motor Transport, who, though ignorant of infantry work, became very good soldiers. From the 2nd–10th November they occupied the trenches in front of Vimy Ridge, which looked into the ruined mining town of Lens, a sector which had been admirably organized by the Canadians. They were thanked by the 31st Division for co-operating in a daylight raid on the 8th. The help took the form of emitting smoke-clouds and of manipulating life-sized dummies to represent raiders issuing from the trenches, who, as desired, drew the enemy's fire on their wooden bodies.

Here they suffered their last casualties, three wounded, on French soil. For while they rested from the trenches at Savy and Villars Brutin, where the

Scarpe rises, while they were speculating on the evening of the 21st November about their chances of being thrown into the new dramatic Cambrai Battle, they received orders to entrain for Italy.

The Italians had suffered on the 25th October the frightful disaster of Caporetto, and, driven back to the Piave in headlong rout with the loss of two hundred and fifty thousand prisoners and a third of their artillery, they were now making praiseworthy efforts to hold the line of the river. To stiffen their backs and to give them the needed time for reorganization it was determined to send out British and French troops, of whom the 48th Division were one of the first-fruits. The Berkshires made the journey in two trains commanded by Colonel Clarke and Major Aldworth respectively, which travelled by different routes after leaving Troyes. The itinerary of this war-time journey is interesting. Colonel Clarke's train arrived at Dijon in the evening of the 23rd after twenty-six hours' travelling, passed Lyons at daybreak, but failed to reach Avignon until 2 a.m. on the 25th. It was already twelve hours late, and lost further time through an accident at Toulon where crowds of excited southerners waved and cheered by the way. At 8.10 a.m. on the 26th the frontier was passed at Ventimiglia, and Savona reached at nightfall. Small welcome was given in this part of Italy to her deliverers, where the unpopularity of war was patent. The journey of the 27th led past Pavia to Cremona, where the men stretched their legs during a sixteen-hour halt by marching through the city with bands playing. The confusion on the Italian railways was such that the detraining station of Saletto, east of Mantua, was not reached until the morning of the 29th November. Thence they marched through Noventa, where the Italian Veterinary Corps were trying to nurse back into condition the horses and mules which the retreat had grievously tried, to the Château of Colonel Cabely, an Italian nobleman killed at Gorizia, where the men lay down with one blanket on the chilly magnificence of bare marble floors.

Major Aldworth's train ran more rapidly over the Mount Cenis, which it crossed at midnight on the 24th. The men marvelled at the great snow mountains during the descent towards Turin, which it reached at noon. Here the Italians provided a rousing welcome, their ladies offering the soldiers chocolate, cigarettes and little silk flags. The journey was continued circuitously viâ Milan to Pavia, and thence through Mantua to Nogaro, which received the men in billets by 9 p.m. on the 27th November. Arrangements for the comfort of the troops in either train were good.   Hot drinks were available at least twice a day, and were often supplemented by the zeal of the Red Cross ladies.

The lot had fallen in a fair ground for the battalion. The Italians reorganized themselves and held their own line, so that the 48th Division (in General Haking's XIth Corps) remained for long in Army reserve.   The two halves of the battalion reunited and settled on the 15th December at S. Croce Bigolina, which lies east of the Brenta, midway between Padua and the Asiago Plateau.   Here they spent Christmas in great happiness and festivity, spending £50 sent by the County Association.   The New Year brought a hard bright frost which froze the running streams ; work was light and the men throve greatly.   They were inspected by General Plumer the Commander-in-Chief and by General Haking, whose genial intercourse with individuals was greatly appreciated.   The departure on the 24th January to Paviola was amidst mutual regret ; the admirable parish priest, who had heartily promoted good relations, sent a parting message to commend " the honourable and chivalrous relations " between the women and the troops.   " A " and " C " Companies now spent February at the Convent di Praglia near Padua to work at the Central School of General Head-quarters. On the 27th the battalion at last returned to the line, taking over part of the Montello area from the 2nd Queen's (7th Division).   The experience was not arduous, for in reserve the narrow wooded dells of the long hill afforded a secure harbour-age, and even in the front line the danger was very small.   A series of disconnected posts, every other with a Lewis gun, looked across that capricious shingly mountain stream to an inactive and silent enemy.   For the weary and disillusioned Austrians had no intention of provoking the British.   A fortnight therefore in this area cost no more than one killed and one wounded. On the 14th March the Italians relieved the battalion, which marched west-ward for many days till it settled at Valle in the hill country near Vicenza. Here the Commanding-Officer left to command the newly formed Machine Gun Battalion.   He had led the men through all their serious fighting with great organizing and administrative ability.   He kept a strict discipline, but never worried the men about trifles.   He was succeeded by Lieut.-

Colonel Lloyd Baker of the Buckinghamshire Battalion, an officer of great charm, tact and kindness, who had served earlier as Staff-Captain to the 145th Brigade. Men and pack-ponies were now constantly exercised in hill climbing, which led to the belief, quickly fulfilled, that they were destined for the mountains. On the 23rd April they climbed the hills to Granezza in showers of snow and hail, and billeted there four thousand five hundred feet above sea-level as the Brigade reserve behind the British lines on the Asiago Plateau, where they were destined to remain until the final triumph in October.

The trenches, which were blasted out of solid rock on the forward slope of the hill, afforded a magnificent panorama. The eye looked down in the foreground to the Asiago Plateau, where the villages, dotted about in the vast No-Man's Land, still showed a regular and habitable outline ; beyond rose a regular line of pine-covered mountains towering into the snowy cloud-capped bastions of the Alps. May was spent in the front line, but only brought as casualties three wounded. Such was the calm that officers slept in pyjamas in the front-line trenches. Second-Lieutenant Stott of " D " Company earned the M.C. and the Italian Silver Medal for Valour by a successful raid with two platoons, which captured an elderly Hungarian of the 24th Honved Regiment, who tripped into a shell-hole while seeking to escape. On the 22nd May they returned to the gorgeous summer of the plains at Cornedo, where they welcomed sun-helmets and suits of drill. Here they prepared for an attack, which was to begin on the 16th June. But the Austrians, goaded by their German masters, at last awoke out of sleep and forestalled us by twenty-four hours with their last ambitious offensive. After a short intensive bombardment with shell and gas the enemy advanced at day-break against the 23rd and 48th Divisions. They thrust with energy and initial success against the latter, whose front line was seriously depleted by influenza. They drove a deep wedge between the Oxfordshire and the 5th Gloucestershire and advanced more than ten hundred yards, over-running most of the guns which had been brought forward in anticipation of our attack. But cramped together in a blind and difficult country and exposed to cross-fire from either flank, their progress was soon arrested. The Berkshires, who were in Brigade reserve, joined hands during the day with the two assaulted battalions, and " D " Company with the Oxfords suffered some loss, including their commander Captain C. Buck, the only officer killed during the Italian year.

Very early next morning " C " Company with a platoon of " A " advanced to our old front line, meeting with only a shadow of resistance and capturing sixty prisoners. When patrols were thrust forward into No Man's Land the Austrian disorganization was manifest. The division recovered all their guns, took more than ten hundred prisoners with eight abandoned mountain guns. The battalion lost only five killed and thirteen wounded. Thus ignominiously ended the great Austrian attack.

A long rest followed in the plains until the 10th August, during which the division lost its devoted and inspiring General, Sir R. Fanshawe, who returned home. The next sojourn in the trenches was not without its incidents, though the unhappy Austrians had now re-sunk into a spiritless passivity. Great patrol activity was shown ; for example, a party under Second-Lieutenant Crawford shot five Austrians on the 15th August, who were foolish enough when challenged to stand outlined against the evening sky ; next day further damage was inflicted by Lieutenant Baxton with his bombers. On the 26th August an ambitious raid was made by all four companies against the enemy's trenches on either side of Asiago. The area to be attacked was bombarded for thirty minutes and then enclosed in a box-barrage. The men traversed the wide No-Man's Land undiscovered in the darkness and mist. " C " Company entered the trenches on the right, seized fifty prisoners, and, according to programme formed a defensive flank. " B " Company then took possession of the weakly held trenches covering Asiago town, capturing six prisoners. " A " Company then passed through them to explore the southern houses of the town, but most of them lost direction through getting mixed up with the Bucks on the left, and only one platoon encountered an enemy who showed some fight in cellars and dug-outs.

" D " Company then extended the exploration and drove the Austrians headlong through Asiago. The withdrawal, though encumbered by nearly one hundred prisoners, took place with surprising ease, even systematic shell fire being absent. Seventy-seven casualties were suffered in this well-planned operation, including five killed and missing. The success brought Captain Cawley, who was wounded, the M.C. and Italian Silver Medal, and C.-S.-M. Alder received the same decoration with the D.C.M.

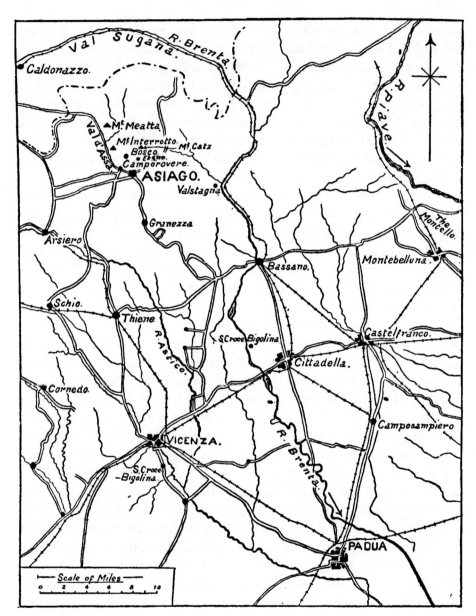

THE CAMPAIGN IN ITALY.

September and most of October passed uneventfully for the battalion, which was now commanded by Colonel Whitehead. The last stage had now arrived, the Central Powers were crumbling to pieces, Turkey and Bulgaria had gone, but the Italians preferred to wait until the 25th October before launching their blow at the dissolving fabric of the Austrian Empire.

The attack in the mountains was contingent on an allied success on Brenta and Piave, and was therefore delayed until the 29th, when the Austrians were flying towards the Tagliamento. On that day, patrols of " C " Company, finding that the enemy had abandoned his front line, pushed through Asiago, a silent town, and advanced to the northern limits of the valley, where they found French patrols exploring Ebene, and met with machine-gun fire from a hillock six hundred yards away. The Austrians had everywhere withdrawn to their Winterstellung or Winter line along the slopes of the mountains, which barred ingress to the side valleys leading up to their great lateral artery, the Val Sugana. During that night, therefore, " B " Company was sent forward to test the strength of the resistance there encountered. They occupied the villages at the foot of the mountains, but found the enemy in force before them. Here and there they extracted stray prisoners ; and one party of seventeen from Bosco, who foolishly refused to move when machine-gun fire was opened on their escort from Monte Catz, were punished by the death of sixteen of their number. On the 31st " A " Company after a similar exploration still found a powerful resistance before them. Thus the dramatic swiftness of the overthrow to follow next day was quite unexpected. That night the Corps ordered a general attack at dawn, which Major Battcock, who was acting as intelligence officer, organized with his admirable energy and thoroughness. At 5.35 a.m. "C" and "D" Companies from right to left assaulted Monte Catz, the key to the whole position, advancing in two lines with a screen of skirmishers. " C " dashed opposition aside and seized the summit by 7.30 with sixty-five prisoners, while " D," reinforced by " B," after a sharp fight, cleared the machine-gun nests on the south-west slopes. Elsewhere things had gone less well. The Austrians warded off the 144th Brigade from Monte Interrotto and passing to the offensive had even thrown them back beyond the uttermost villages of the plain, Camporovere and Bosco. Thus the whole success of the Berkshires was endangered, though " A " Company, maintained in reserve at Asiago, kept connexion between the two brigades. Further, the commander of " D " Company acting upon a false rumour of instructions withdrew from the slopes of Monte Catz, leaving " C " practically isolated upon the summit. This company, however, learning that on the right the Bucks and beyond them the French were fully victorious, advanced with ardour and determination past the Sichestal trench, the last organized defence of the Austrians. The blow was decisive (as Lord Cavan's despatch states), and the booty already considerable, for the battalion took that day four hundred and eighty prisoners and thirty guns and destroyed many more. Next day the Winterstellung crumbled to pieces.

The division held the Val d'Assa and marched up rapidly towards the vital Val Sugana.

The rout of the Austrians was pitiable and almost unparallelled in war. Famished and hopeless, a military ruin and a political wreck, they fled head-long into the mountains or surrendered in vast embarrassing hordes. Every track was filled with swarms of unarmed men, keeping as a rag of self-respect the determination not to become prisoners of the Italians. A corps-commander and three divisional-generals were among the spoils of the division. On the 2nd November a few devoted men kept alive here and there a spark of resistance; for example, a company of the Oxfords drove one hundred Austrians from Mount Meatta after a sharp fight. During the day a regiment of red-capped Bosnians surrendered to the battalion, who, unlike the majority, preserved discipline, and grounded their arms smartly at the command of their officers.

On the 3rd the enemy's confusion was, if possible, increased by the mistaken idea that the Armistice had come into force. The division unmolested, though encumbered by prisoners and booty, advanced inexorably. That night the advanced guards penetrated the Val Sugana, while the Royal Berkshire lodged at Caldonazza just south of the entrance, where a vast park of ordnance and two hundred guns lay abandoned. Next morning news arrived that the Armistice had been signed and was to take effect from 3 p.m. Until that hour the weary troops pressed up the valley, still taking vast quantities of prisoners, then they halted.

The war ended for the Berkshires in the village of Vigalzano. They had covered thirty-five miles in sixty hours over rough mountain tracks.   Not a man had fallen out.   They had lost in their last triumphant battle 17 killed and 23 wounded.   The full tale of their individual captures is not recorded, but the division carried away 22,000 men and 600 guns.   Thus their warfare was accomplished and their deliverance achieved.

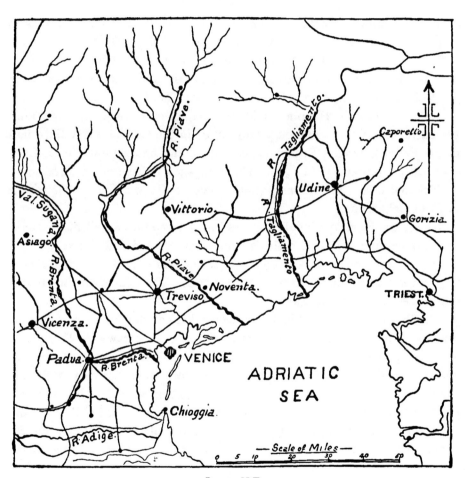

ITALY N.E.

CHAPTER XXX

THE 2nd/4th (TERRITORIAL) BATTALION

FORMATION AND SERVICE AT HOME.

1914–15

THE following notes on the early days of the Battalion have been supplied by Colonel Lionel Hanbury, C.M.G., D.S.O. The 2/4th Royal Berkshire Regiment was formed early in September 1914 by the Berkshire Territorial Force Association under the Presidency of J. H. Benyon, Esq., Lord-Lieutenant of the County.

Colonel Lionel H. Hanbury, V.D., was requested to raise and command the battalion. Colonel Hanbury had served in the 1st Volunteer Battalion of the Royal Berkshire Regiment since 1886, and had commanded it from 1907 till his retirement in 1909. He re-engaged in September 1914.

The first billets and training ground were on his own Farm at Hitcham in Buckinghamshire.

The Home Farm and buildings were transformed into excellent quarters, the men sleeping in lofts and sheds which were floored and closed in.

A good cook-house was erected and water laid on. The men fed in a large covered shed, and a canteen was organized. The Village Reading Room was placed at their disposal.

The War Office was unable to supply anything at this time, and all camp equipment had to be improvised, bought locally, or borrowed. The public was very generous in providing blankets ; and palliasses were made by the village women out of canvas supplied. The men were, however, well fed, and the quarters were good, and they much regretted when they had to leave Hitcham. The only officers at the commencement were the C.O., Captain C. Bartram who was appointed Adjutant, Lieutenants W. Whittaker and R. Lund. The men were recruited all over Berkshire, and, after being sworn

172

2/4th BATTALION.
Chelmsford 1915.

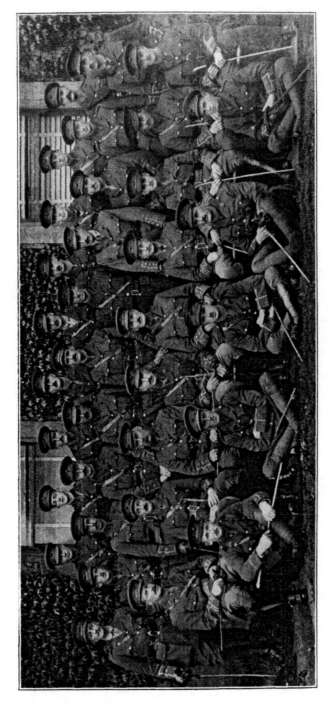

(*Back Row*) 2nd Lt. R. Holland. 2nd Lt. T. C. Keble. 2nd Lt. G. S. R. Webb. 2nd Lt. J. H. Skene. Lt. J. A. Reeves. 2nd Lt. W. O. Down. 2nd Lt. G. A. Brooke. Lt. O. J. Dowson. Lt. and Q.M. C. G. H. Smith.

(*Second Row*) 2nd Lt. E. O. Lambart. 2nd Lt. N. G. Hunt. 2nd Lt. H. J. Gale. Lt. H. C. Meysey-Thompson. Lt. G. T. Simonds. Lt. F. W. Dilke. 2nd Lt. J. F. Duff. Capt. A. N. Palmer. 2nd Lt. G. H. Hawkes. Lt. R. V. C. Freeth. Lieut. F. M. J. White.

(*Sitting*) Capt. E. P. Lucas. Capt. J. C. Hammond. Capt. T. Shields. Major J. H. Simonds. Lt.-Col. M. Wheeler. Major C. Bartram. Capt. R. Whittaker. Capt. C. J. D. Cave. Capt. F. L. Hadden.

(*On Ground*) 2nd Lt. M. D. Walker. 2nd Lt. C. E. Brooke. 2nd Lt. R. G. Imray. 2nd Lt. A. Bartram. 2nd Lt. A. A. Austen-Leigh.

in at Reading, were sent in batches to Hitcham. The officers were quartered under canvas with a mess in the stables. The training was carried on under great difficulties, as there were no regular instructors, and nearly all the officers had only recently joined. Uniform for the men was provided by the County Association as soon as possible, but at this time both clothing and boots were difficult to procure. Sergt.-Major Butler was now sent from the 1/4th Battalion and proved to be of the greatest assistance, and was not only respected and obeyed but also loved by all the officers and men.

Early in November the battalion moved to Maidenhead, where fourteen empty houses, a theatre, skating rink, and the drill-hall were all secured for their accommodation. This system worked very well, as about fifty men were billeted in each house and were well under control. They were nearly all clothed in khaki and light equipment, and three hundred rifles were secured for their instruction. Some drafts of men who were not passed fit for general service, and some who did not volunteer for service abroad, were sent from the 1/4th Battalion at Chelmsford, and in exchange some two hundred were sent from Maidenhead to fill up the 4th Battalion. Training was by this time going ahead, and a good deal of route-marching, musketry and drill was got through.

The battalion numbered nearly one thousand. At this period (December 1914) severe floods took place at Maidenhead and the lower part of the town was inundated. The skating-rink had to be abandoned, and all communication east of the town was cut off. A good drum and bugle band was formed which was much appreciated by the men. On Christmas Day a very good dinner was provided by the townspeople and, as leave was only allowed to a small percentage, it was thoroughly enjoyed.

The first war duty performed by the battalion was having to find a guard for prisoners-of-war at Holyport. When the first guard arrived at about 10 p.m., the camp was in a very unprepared state, and any determined prisoner could easily have escaped. There were thirteen prisoners already there, the first Germans who had arrived. This camp afterwards became one of the Officers' Prisoners-of-War Camps.

Early in February 1915 the battalion was ordered to Northampton to join the division (2nd South Midland) which was now formed under the Marquess of Salisbury ; Colonel Ludlow, C.B., commanding the brigade to which the 2/4th Berkshire were posted. The men were billeted in North-ampton, and found good quarters with the bootmakers who form the bulk of the population there.

An excellent disused school was secured as Battalion Head-quarters and the training was now progressive and well arranged. Musketry was carried on both on miniature and full-sized ranges. Japanese rifles were issued to the division, pending issue of British service rifles. They were very good weapons and were afterwards sent to Russia. In April the division moved to Chelmsford to take the place of the 1st South Midland Division, which had left for the Front.

Here again the men were billeted and were rationed by the A.S.C. During the sojourn at Chelmsford, the battalion was sent to Epping to dig trenches for the defence of London, and also to piquet roads in Essex, as spies in motor-cars were now on the road, and were using signals for aero-planes. A scratch transport was formed under Lieutenant Davis. Some mules and pack-ponies were sent from the Remount Depot.

In May 1915 the C.O. was ordered to proceed to France to take command of the 1/7th Royal Warwickshire Regiment, and the battalion was handed over to Major Wheeler, the second-in-command.

DEPARTURE FOR FRANCE. LAVENTIE. TRENCH RAIDS AND ATTACKS. VARENNES.

1916

On the 25th May 1916 the 2/4th Battalion left Parkhouse Camp and entrained at Tidworth in the afternoon for Southampton. Its strength, excluding about 60 left behind in hospital or for other reasons, was 35 officers and 850 other ranks, with four Lewis guns.

The officers who embarked at Southampton were :

Lieut.-Colonel M. Wheeler, commanding.
Majors : J. H. Simonds, T. Shields.
Captains : I. M. M. Anderson, R. Whitaker, C. J. D. Cave, E. P. Lucas,
    F. L. Hadden, A. N. Palmer, J. A. Reeves, G. H. Hawkes.
Lieutenants : O. J. Dowson, R. V. C. Freeth, G. W. Davies, R. G.
    Imray, R. Holland.

Second-Lieutenants : J. H. Skene, C. E. Brooke, E. O. C. Lambart, G. S. R. Webb, H. J. Gale, G. A. Brooke, G. L. Warlock, C. Cecil, G. S. Abbott, D. R. Gibson, A. T. Heathorn, D. A. Hutchings, D. C. Baker, R. D. H. Bowles, E. C. Aylett.

Adjutant : Lieut. F. W. Dilke.

Quartermaster : Lieut. W. H. Morris.

Medical Officer : Lieut. J. Nissen Deacon, R.A.M.C.

On the 26th May the battalion, less six officers and one hundred and ninety-two other ranks left to load transport, sailed from Southampton, and reached Havre at 7 a.m. on the 27th. Thence they proceeded, in two trains in the afternoon, to the neighbourhood of Merville, where they went into billets at Berguette on the 28th.

The battalion was a unit of the 184th Infantry Brigade of the 61st Division. The other battalions of the brigade were the 2/4th Oxfordshire and Buckinghamshire Light Infantry, the 2/5th Gloucestershire, and the 2/1st Buckinghamshire. The other brigades of the division were the 182nd and 183rd.

The battalion remained training at Berguette till the 8th June, when it was sent, less transport and sick men, to be attached to other battalions for practical instruction in the mysteries of trench-warfare in trenches near Laventie. Here it met with its first casualties. Second-Lieutenant C. E. Brooke was slightly wounded on the 8th, and three men were killed and as many wounded on the 9th.

By the 10th the whole battalion was in charge of trenches S.E. of Laventie, where it remained, taking its turn with other battalions in front trenches or in support or reserve, and carrying out the usual patrols.

On the 24th June a patrol, under Second-Lieutenant Skene, had found a gap in the enemy's wire where it was fired on at close range. Second-Lieutenant Skene carried in the only man who was wounded, and was himself slightly wounded, but remained on duty.

On the 26th Second-Lieutenant Baker was hit in both arms when on patrol, and Second-Lieutenant Haddington (2/6th Gloucestershire, attached 2/4th Royal Berkshire) lost his way and was never seen again. He was believed to have been killed. Besides these two officers, one man was wounded.

The rest of June was spent in billets at Laventie. On the 27th command of the battalion was taken over from Lieut.-Colonel Wheeler by Lieut.-Colonel J. H. Beer, 2/8th Royal Warwickshire Regiment.

Billets at Laventie and La Gorgue continued till the 6th July, when the battalion relieved the 1/1st Cambridgeshire in the left front sub-sector at Ferme du Bois. The 2/1st Buckinghamshire were on their right, 2/7th Royal Warwickshire on their left, with the 2/5th Gloucestershire supporting the 2/1st Buckinghamshire at Richebourg St. Vaast.

On the 13th, when the battalion was in trenches at Croix Barbée, a raid on the enemy trenches was carried out by Captain E. P. Lucas, Lieutenant O. J. Dowson, and Second-Lieutenants J. H. Skene and G. A. Brooke, with one hundred other ranks of " A " Company.

The raid, as planned, was rather an elaborate one, the raiders being divided up into no less than ten parties. The objective was the capture of prisoners, identification of enemy units, and the killing of Germans.

A start was to be made between midnight and 12.30 a.m., forming up seventy yards in front of the British wire, with intervals of five yards between the lines.

On reaching the enemy's front it was found difficult to locate a gap in the wire, and it was decided to use the Bangalore torpedo which had been brought for the purpose of blowing a gap. Unfortunately, however, some of the carriers had been wounded and had dropped the fuse, so that the torpedo was useless. Second-Lieutenant Skene, with the first wave, then found a partial gap in the wire to the right, and managed to cut a way through. Whilst he was doing so, the others lay down to wait. At this time Captain Lucas and Lieutenant Dowson were both wounded by shrapnel. Lucas was in rear with the 7th party. Touch with Skene and the first wave was lost. The report by the commanding-officer on the raid continues as follows :

" Owing to the heavy casualties amongst officers, it would appear that at this period a lack of leadership was apparent amongst N.C.O's, and consequently the first wave was not supported by the succeeding waves. Gallant attempts, however, were undoubtedly made to force a way through the wire under a galling fire from four or five machine guns.

" Second-Lieutenant Skene and 11 other ranks, forming the first wave, very gallantly penetrated the enemy's first line under severe opposition. It is greatly to be regretted that the fine efforts of the party were not more substantially supported, in which case I consider the raid would have proved successful."

All behaved well and held on until the signal for recall was given. Lieutenant R. V. C. Freeth superintended the firing of one hundred and eighty-five grenades to support the raiders, and was afterwards killed in No-Man's Land when bringing in the wounded. Captain Lucas's arrangements are considered to have been good, and he continued encouraging his men despite his wounds.

Second-Lieutenant Skene, who had behaved with great gallantry, was found to be missing, and was believed to have been wounded. The conduct of Sergeant A. E. Tallant, who led the way over the enemy's parapet, and that of C.-S.-M. A. Graham and Sergeant H. Pocock, is also commended. Much gallantry was also displayed by several men in bringing in the wounded.

The casualties in this rather unfortunate raid were specially heavy among officers, every one of whom was either killed or wounded. They were :

Officers. Killed : Lieut. R. V. C. Freeth.
           Wounded : Capt. E. P. Lucas, Lieut. O. J. Dowson, 2nd-Lieut.
               G. A. Brooke.
           Missing (believed wounded) : 2nd-Lieut. J. H. Skene.[*]
Other Ranks : Killed 6, Wounded 15, Missing 11.

After this affair the battalion was again in billets at La Gorgue and Laventie. On the 16th the battalion was preparing for an attack next day. Some casualties were suffered in moving into trenches ready for it.

Second-Lieutenant C. E. Cecil was killed and Second-Lieutenant H. J. Gale wounded, whilst of other ranks three were killed and seven wounded.

Eight more men were wounded on the 17th as " B " Company was returning to its position of the night of the 15th-16th in the afternoon. The projected attack in the morning had been cancelled, owing to the mist which prevented artillery registration.

Preparations were again made on the 18th for an attack on the evening of the 19th on the German front and support trenches. The assaulting battalions of the 184th Brigade were the 2/4th Royal Berkshire on the

* Afterwards recorded as killed.

right, the 2/1st Buckinghamshire on the left. On the right of the 184th Brigade was the 183rd with the 182nd beyond. On the left of the 2/1st Buckinghamshire was the Australian Division.

To the 2/4th Royal Berkshire was assigned a front from Sutherland Avenue on the right to Piccadilly Avenue on the left, whilst the 2/1st Buckinghamshire continued the line as far as Bond Street.

The artillery preparation began at 11 a.m., though the attack was not to commence till 6 p.m. The front assembly trenches were much crowded, with the consequence that by 5.30 p.m. the Royal Berkshire had already lost about forty killed and wounded from the German artillery fire. This necessitated reorganization of the assaulting and consolidating companies.

At 5.45 p.m. the battalion filed out from two sally ports, and at once came under machine-gun fire which caused heavy casualties. A certain proportion of the right company succeeded in getting out, but only in scattered parties. Some of them were reported to have reached the German wire, but finding themselves unsupported and suffering severely from machine-gun fire, they were compelled to fall back. They reported that the enemy wire was uncut.

Of the left company only a few succeeded in getting out by their sally port, and they were at once forced to retire by the enemy's machine guns. It was whilst directing these men from the parapet that Lieut.-Colonel J. H. Beer was killed. Several other officers were killed or wounded whilst endeavouring to organize a forward movement. The attack had failed, as had those of the 2/1st Buckinghamshire and of the Australians on their left.

The casualties in this affair were:

Officers : *Killed* : Lieut.-Colonel J. H. Beer (commanding the battalion).
2nd-Lieuts. F. C. D. Williams, G. S. Abbott.
Wounded : Major T. Shields, 2nd-Lieut. D. R. Gibson.
Other Ranks : Killed 22, Wounded 123, Missing 9.

That night the battalion was relieved and went back to billets at the Rue de la Lys, where, on the 22nd, Major R. E. Salkeld took over command.

Here, and at the Rue du Puits and Riez Bailleul, the battalions remained till, on the 27th July, it again moved up to the front line in relief of the 2/4th Oxfordshire and Buckinghamshire Light Infantry, in the left sub-sector of the Moated Grange sector.

From this position it returned to billets at La Gorgue on the 1st August, and on the 5th another seven miles to the rear near Le Sart. Its next front-line service was from the 15th to the 21st August, in the left sub-sector at Fauquissart. It was back at Laventie from the 21st to the 27th, when it again went up to Fauquissart. On the 24th an unfortunate explosion during bombing practice had wounded Lieutenant O. J. Dowson and Second-Lieutenant Greenwood.

All September and the first half of October were spent in and out of trenches in this neighbourhood with little to note.

On the 7th October a patrol, under Second-Lieutenant C. C. Hedges, was heavily bombed in the German wire. Hedges was wounded, and of other ranks one died of wounds, three were wounded, and five missing. A raid was to be attempted on the 9th, but, the Bangalore torpedo having failed to explode, it was countermanded. This raid, which had been twice post-poned, was finally carried out in the night of the 14th-15th October. Besides the party with the Bangalore torpedo, there were five parties of from ten to twenty men each (total 5 officers and 60 other ranks) to which tasks, on reaching the German trench, were assigned as follows :

    I.   Second-Lieutenant Hutchings to turn to the left along the trench and make a block in it.

    II.   Second-Lieutenant Daniels to act similarly towards the right and to deal with dugouts.

    III.   Second-Lieutenant Watson to the right and certain named points.

    IV.   Second-Lieutenant Hinchcliffe to search the trench for identification.

    V.   Second-Lieutenant Worlock, in command of the whole raid, to remain at the point of entry of the trench.

Everything went smoothly till zero hour—1.56 a.m. The 18-pdr. barrage then commenced, and ten minutes later the raiders moved out from the assembly trench under its protection. The enemy wire had been well cut by two Bangalore torpedoes fired as the barrage opened.

No. I party, moving to the left, found the German trench almost completely destroyed by the barrage, and had much difficulty in following it.

No. II found the trench they were ordered to follow, and pushed along it to within a few yards of their objective.   Here Second-Lieutenant Daniels shot a German officer and three men with his revolver.   Then he looked into a dugout and saw five men.   Several bombs were thrown into it, but Daniels and two of his men were wounded by a bomb.

No. III met with no opposition, but found the trench badly damaged, and only one dugout, which was empty.

No. IV, searching for identifications of the opposing units, missed the trench taken by Second-Lieutenant Daniels, in which were all the dead Germans.

No. V remained on the parapet in support as ordered.

They were fired on by a number of Germans who appeared above-ground at a distance of about seventy yards.   A good deal of miscellaneous information regarding the enemy and his trenches was acquired.   It was known for certain that eleven Germans had been killed, besides another twenty estimated to have been killed by the bombardment.

The casualties of the Royal Berkshire were :

Second-Lieutenant Daniels wounded, and of other ranks three wounded and one missing, quite a small number for so considerable a raid.

On the 15th the battalion was at Moated Grange, and on the 21st went back ten miles to Robecq for training till the end of the month.

There was nothing noteworthy in November till the 19th, when the battalion had gone south to Bouzincourt viâ Albert.   In trenches here on the 26th it had an extra heavy day of shelling by which Second-Lieutenant Daniels was again wounded, four other ranks were killed, and three wounded.

Next day the battalion was at Aveluy, whence it went, on the 1st December, to Varennes, where it remained till it proceeded, on the 12th, viâ Bouzincourt to huts in the Martinsart Woods.   Second-Lieutenant Keys was wounded in trenches on the 21st.   On the 4th December Major G. P. R. Beaman took over command of the battalion from Lieut.-Colonel Salkeld, who had been ill since the 23rd November, and was struck off the strength of the Regiment from the 23rd December.   In the interval between the 23rd November and the 4th December Captain H. S. Bennett had commanded temporarily.

There was nothing notable during the last days of 1916.

The battalion was at Varennes on the 31st December, 1916.

The Advance to the Hindenburg Line. Arras.
The Third Battle of Ypres. Cambrai.

1917

During January and February of this year there was nothing of note in the battalion, which spent a large part of the time in the back areas, far from the front line.

On the 16th February the battalion took over trenches at Deniecourt, S.W. of Péronne, from the French 124th Infantry, and was in billets at Rainecourt in rear on the 24th February.

During a relief on the 2nd March, when the battalion again went into front line at Deniecourt, Second-Lieutenant C. W. Thornton was wounded.

On the 17th March, owing to the sudden evacuation by the enemy, who were now falling back on the Hindenburg Line, and the forward movement of the British, the battalion was billeted at Rainecourt and on the 19th advanced to Pertain, which had recently been evacuated by the enemy who had destroyed everything as he went. The battalion was hard at work repairing roads till it crossed the Somme on the 25th to Ennemain, east of the river where it flows from the south towards the bend at Péronne. Caulaincourt, where the battalion arrived on the 30th, was utterly destroyed, not a wall nor a cellar was intact.

In the evening of the 30th a patrol of twenty men, under Captain Whitaker and Second-Lieutenant Brain, was sent to reconnoitre as far as Vermand Cemetery, a mile and a half farther on, and to hold on there. " A " Company, following close behind, was to occupy Vermand as soon as the cemetery was secured. This was accomplished without opposition at 4 a.m. on the 31st, when " C " Company came up to consolidate the new position. Battalion Head-quarters were in Vermand by 6 a.m.

During the 1st April, when working at the Vermand defences, five men were killed and fifteen wounded by shell fire. On that day orders were received for an attack next day on the line Bihécourt-Ponne Copse.

In this attack " A " Company of the 2/5th Gloucestershire, acting under the 2/4th Royal Berkshire, was on the right, with Bihécourt as its objective. On its left were the Royal Berkshire with the 2/1st Buckinghamshire on their left. The bombardment began at 5 a.m. on the 2nd April, and by 5.45 the whole of the objective had been carried.   The enemy made some opposition with rifles and machine guns, but it was not very determined.   His position was defended only by one-man posts thirty yards apart, and was at once consolidated on a line just east of the Bihécourt-Vendelles Road.   The Gloucestershire and Royal Berkshire took two machine guns, twelve unwounded, and ten wounded prisoners.

Patrols pushed out to the château at Vadencourt, N.E. of Bihécourt, reported that it was unoccupied, but the enemy was still in Maissenay just south of it.   In this affair the Royal Berkshire lost eleven other ranks wounded, of whom three died of their wounds.   That night the battalion was relieved by the 2/5th Gloucestershire and next day received the congratulations of the Brigadier on its success.   For the next day or two it was very busy in the neighbourhood repairing the damage done by the enemy as he retreated in order to hinder the British advance.

At 8 p.m. on the 6th an attack was made by the 2/5th Gloucestershire, and two platoons of " D " Company were sent up to take their place as they advanced.   The other two platoons were lent to them for carrying.   The Gloucestershire was supported in the attack by " C " of the 2/4th Royal Berkshire under Captain Whitaker, acting under orders of the O.C. 2/5th Gloucestershire Regiment.

The attack was held up by uncut wire, and the Gloucestershire returned to the starting point, now held by the two platoons of " D."   The 2/4th Royal Berkshire was ordered to relieve them before dawn.   " C " had one killed and one wounded.

This relief began at 2.30 a.m. on the 7th on the line east of Vadencourt Château.   " C " (Capt. Whitaker) took over the posts south of the Vernand-Bellenglise Road from the 13th Platoon of " D," whilst " D " (Capt. Reeves) occupied those north of the road.   " A " (Capt. Willink) was in support at Bihécourt, and " B " (Capt. Allen) in reserve in the railway cutting.   After a quiet day, two patrols went out at night to see if the trench which had been attacked unsuccessfully was still held by the enemy.   One patrol of ten men of " D," under Second-Lieutenant Wilmot, went out south of the Bihécourt-Bellenglise Road and found that the wire, though badly damaged, was still a serious obstacle in front of the enemy, who still occupied the trench.   Second-Lieutenant Robinson, with ten men of " C " north of the road, found the wire uncut and the trench occupied like that on the right. There was a bright moon which made reconnaissance difficult.

The artillery was busy trying to cut the wire during the 8th, but was unsuccessful, as was discovered by patrols in the ensuing night, which found matters in the same condition as the night before. At 2 a.m. on the 9th, Second-Lieutenant Robinson, with twenty men of " C," went out again to try and enter the enemy's trench. They succeeded in entering it south of the road, and found it now unoccupied. One platoon of " C " and two of " A " were sent forward to consolidate. Second-Lieutenant Wilmot, with twenty men of " D," acted similarly north of the road, and got into touch with the 2/1st Buckinghamshire.

Yet another patrol of " C," under Captain Preston, reconnoitred as far as the " tumulus," which they found unoccupied at 7.30 a.m. By 10 o'clock they were forced to leave it, owing to the manœuvres of about two hundred Germans endeavouring to surround it.

Second-Lieutenant Robinson, with his patrol of " C," found the Mareval Copse unoccupied, and one platoon was sent up to hold it.

The village of Pontru having been reconnoitred by Second-Lieutenant Brain and found empty, Sergeant Shephard endeavoured to obtain touch with the brigade on the right. Crossing the Omignon stream, he found Berthancourt unoccupied, but could not find any troops on the right south of the stream.

" A " Company moved up to the Vadencourt Château, and " B " to Bihécourt, whilst " C " and " D " were entering the enemy trenches east of these places.

At 8 p.m. Second-Lieutenant Mullins and one platoon of " A " established themselves in Pontru, whilst the rest of the company helped " C " and " D " in wiring the old German trenches, which now became the British main line.

Early on the 10th Second-Lieutenant Carter and a patrol of " C " again found Berthancourt empty, but were still unable to gain touch with troops on the right.

Another patrol, under Second-Lieutenant Mullins, occupied the " tumulus " at 6 a.m. Pontru was now in charge of two platoons of " B," under Second-Lieutenant Worlock, who were busy filling in a crater east of Bihécourt.

That evening the battalion was relieved by the 19th Durham Light Infantry and marched back S.W., viâ Monchy Lagache, to Voyennes and Offoy on the Somme. After being there from the 11th till the 17th April, it went into Divisional reserve at Beauvois on the 18th, and on the 19th to Brigade reserve at the Wood of Holnon. On the 23rd the battalion, less " B " Company, took over from the 2/1st Buckinghamshire at Holnon as right support battalion. " B " Company was lent to the 2/4th Oxfordshire and Buckinghamshire Light Infantry, the outpost battalion, and was employed on the construction of the " Brown Line " east of Holnon, where, on the 25th, Second-Lieutenant D. A. Hutchings was wounded whilst working on the line.

On the night of the 29th-30th the 2/4th Royal Berkshire relieved the 2/4th Oxfordshire and Buckinghamshire in front line, and a patrol, under Second-Lieutenant Hinchcliffe, went to ascertain if Cépy Farm, which had been shelled, was clear of the enemy. A patrol had reported it empty, but had been driven out later. The British guns were then again turned on to it, and it was after this that Hinchcliffe's patrol went out. He was fired on from the farm buildings into which he saw twelve Germans go. He again went out at 7 a.m. on the 30th, and returned at 9.30, reporting that he had seen or heard no movement from the farm.

At 9.30 p.m. on the 30th Lieutenant Willink of " A," with Second-Lieutenants Hinchcliffe and Watson, fifty other ranks, five Lewis guns, and two Vickers guns, went out again to Cépy Farm. They moved forward as soon as the barrage on Cépy and the valley beyond it stopped. At 10.50 p.m. they were back again, reporting that the enemy had fled as they approached the trenches north and east of the farm. They had searched the buildings and bombed the cellars without finding any trace of the Germans. They had left a standing patrol there, but, as soon as the main party retired, this standing patrol was attacked by about fifty Germans and compelled to retire to a point about one hundred yards west of the farm. Two strong listening posts were pushed forward to look out for any attempt by the enemy to occupy in strength the farm, or the valley beyond it. At 4.30 a.m. on the 1st May, Sergeant Denton and ten men again worked forward to the farm, where no sign of the enemy was seen. The casualties in these operations were only one man wounded and one shell-shocked.

The battalion was relieved by the 2/6th Gloucestershire on the 2nd May, and for the next ten days was training and working at Germaine.

On the 13th May it began to leave this neighbourhood and on the 15th went by train from Nesle to Longveau, near Amiens. After being in various places behind the line, the battalion found itself on the 31st May in trenches near the Bois des Bœufs, east of Tilloy, on the Arras-Cambrai Road.

On the 1st June it relieved the 13th Rifle Brigade in front line about Monchy le Preux. These trenches, including Tool Trench and others, were improved and wired by a special party of one hundred men till, on the 6th, the 2/4th Royal Berkshire went into reserve on the Wancourt-Feuchy line.

After this there ensued a period in which there is little to notice. The battalion was again moving gradually northwards, and doing a deal of training in the back areas during June and July. On the 15th August it was in billets near Poperinghe, on the 18th was at Goldfish Château, and on the 20th relieved the 2/4th Oxfordshire and Buckinghamshire in the left support trenches at Wieltje, N.E. of Ypres.

The Third Battle of Ypres was now in progress.

On the evening of the 21st, the battalion moved into assembly trenches for the attack on the following day. This attack, in so far as it concerned the Royal Berkshire Battalion, was that of the 184th Brigade on the enemy defences S.E. of St. Julien. On the right of the brigade was the 44th Brigade (15th Division), on the left the 3rd Brigade. The direction of the attack was north-eastwards and the front-line troops of the 184th Brigade were the 2/1st Buckinghamshire on the right, and the 2/4th Oxford and Bucks on the left. The function of the 2/4th Royal Berkshire was to supply thirteen platoons for dealing with the numerous strong points which were known to exist in the area to be attacked. The Berkshire platoons were to follow close up behind the leading battalions, and, as each strong point was approached, were to dash through the leading waves and assault it, leaving the leading battalions to pursue their way without having to consider the risk of leaving the strong points in rear. These would be either taken by the Berkshire men, or so surrounded and blockaded as to be unable to harass the assaulting battalions in flank or rear.

The Berkshire platoons were thus detailed to deal with the several strong points.

No. of Platoon.	Officer Commanding.	Strong point to be attacked.
1	2nd-Lieut. A. C. L. Hill	Somme
4	2nd-Lieut. G. W. de St. Legier	Do.
2	2nd-Lieut. A. K. Glover	Cross Cottages
3	2nd-Lieut. C. L. B. Kirkland	Aisne House
5	2nd-Lieut. H. W. Jewell	Schuler
6	2nd-Lieut. G. A. F. Gilmor	Pond Farm
13	2nd-Lieut. F. A. N. Wilmot	Do.
7	2nd-Lieut. A. E. Saw	To act as left flank guard for 2/4 Oxford and Bucks
8	2nd-Lieut. F. Exler	Hindu Cottage
9	2nd-Lieut. W. H. Stevens	Martha House
12	2nd-Lieut. A. H. Robinson	Do.
10	2nd-Lieut. D. Mackinnon	Green House
11	2nd-Lieut. H. S. Griffin	Gun positions about centre

The first strong point encountered was Pond Farm towards the left. This was attacked from the right flank by Second-Lieutenant Wilmot with No. 13 Platoon, and from the left by Second-Lieutenant Gilmor and No. 6. Both these officers were wounded at the commencement. Owing to the strong machine-gun fire, Sergeant Shackleton (in charge of Wilmot's platoon after the latter was wounded) was unable to get into the farm, but the fire of the platoons from the positions they had attained so occupied the attention of the garrison as to completely prevent their interference with the assaulting troops.

Sergeant Shackleford, who afterwards received the D.C.M. for his conduct on this day, having reorganized his platoon, made a second attempt to take the farm, but was held up twenty yards from it. He succeeded in surrounding it and keeping the garrison fully occupied till the afternoon, when he was joined by two platoons of the 2/5th Gloucestershire whom he helped in the storm of the farm, where thirty-five prisoners were taken.

The next strong point on the left was Hindu Cottage.

Here Second-Lieutenant Exler was wounded as soon as the advance began, but the platoon went on. Marshy ground prevented it from entering from the front, but it got beyond the strong point and surrounded it, thus enabling the assaulting waves to go on without hindrance from it. In connexion with

this point the Battalion Diary tells a most extraordinary story to the following effect :

Private Pike, of " A " Company, who had lost his own platoon, happened
to get into the strong point, apparently unobserved.   In it he found nineteen
Germans, of whom thirteen were unwounded.   He took the whole lot
prisoners and remained there alone guarding them for two days, till he was
relieved by an officer of the 2/6th Gloucestershire.   How he managed to
bluff these nineteen men into surrender to a single private, and to avoid being
overpowered by them during the two days, is almost inconceivable.   The
only possible explanation seems to be that they knew they were surrounded
and could not escape.   That the story was substantiated is clear from the
fact that Pike was awarded the Military Medal for his exploit.   There are
other points which are mysterious, such as why the strong point was not
entered by the attacking platoon.

Private Pike has kindly furnished us with his own account of his exploit,
of which the following is the substance : About 5 a.m. his platoon was lying
out in No-Man's Land, waiting for the barrage, with orders to make a right
incline towards its objective.   Pike, however, made a mistake and went
straight forward.   He only discovered his error when he found himself alone.
Presently, he found himself with some of the Oxfordshire and Buckinghamshire, and was with them at the clearing of several strong points.   He was
then asked by a sergeant of the Oxfordshire and Buckinghamshire Light
Infantry to carry back a message.   He started with it, hoping to get back
to his own regiment after delivering it.   He had gone some six hundred
yards when the fire was so hot that he got into a shell-hole for shelter and had
a shot or two at a German sniper whom he saw.   He then worked his way
over to the strong point, hoping to get his direction from it.   Arriving there
he found himself in an awkward position, as it was in German hands.   One
of the Germans came out and attacked him, but was wounded and got back
into the strong point.   He apparently told his friends inside that they were
surrounded, and, when summoned by Pike, they held up their hands and he
was able to remove all their arms and bombs.   After this they began to
show symptoms of resistance, but there was only one entrance to the strong
point, and Pike outside that was able to overawe them, as he was armed and
they were not.   There he remained for two days on guard, unable to eat and

not daring to sleep, for a moment's unconsciousness meant that he would be done for.

About 2 a.m. on the second day, when he was utterly exhausted, he heard footsteps coming round the strong point and, supposing them to be the enemy, believed he was lost and prepared for a fight. Fortunately, the footsteps turned out to be those of an officer of the Gloucestershire Regiment and his party, and Pike's troubles were at an end.

The Germans were duly fetched out as prisoners. It was only when they were counted that Pike knew how many prisoners he had.

The Gloucestershire officer was wounded and Pike accompanied him as he retired. He then thought of delivering the Oxford and Bucks sergeant's message, which was probably not of much value after two days' delay. It is hardly surprising that Pike found he had lost it. He was told, with what truth we do not know, that he had been recommended for the V.C.*

The remaining strong point on the left was Schuler, which fell to the lot of Second-Lieutenant Jewell and No. 5 Platoon. Despite the fact that the division on the left was held up, and his left flank was consequently exposed, Jewell pushed gallantly on and stormed the galleries constituting the strong point. In it were taken two officers and seventy-four Germans of other ranks. After despatching these to the rear, Jewell set to work to consolidate his position which, owing to a retirement on his right, and a failure to get up on his left, was almost isolated. In this post he held on for two days, breaking up three local counter-attacks of the enemy. After two days he, like Private Pike in Hindu Cottage, was relieved by the 2/6th Gloucestershire. For his exploit Jewell received a well-earned Military Cross.

We must now turn to the strong points on the right of the attack. The first of these was Somme. As Second-Lieutenant St. Legier approached this, he and two men rushed ahead through the leading waves and the British barrage in front of them. This enabled them to enter the strong point from the rear and to kill the whole garrison. St. Legier also consolidated his position like Jewell, and held it till relieved two days later. He repulsed several counter-attacks during this period, and also received the Military Cross.

Owing to the 15th Division being held up on the right, there was such a

* We have examined the diary of the 2/6th Gloucestershire Regiment, but found it was very brief and made no mention of this incident.

heavy machine-gun fire from that direction that the attacks on Green House, Cross Cottage and Martha House were impracticable; but the platoons detailed for them were able to give valuable assistance to the 2/1st Buckinghamshire in forming a curved line which ran from in front of Somme post on the right, north-eastwards in front of Hindu Cottage and Schuler posts on the left. On this line three counter-attacks were repulsed. The attack had on the whole not been too successful. Tanks had been unable to give the assistance intended, owing to the marshy ground.

In the night of the 23rd-24th the line was taken over by the 183rd Brigade and the 2/4th Royal Berkshire returned to Goldfish Château. Its heavy casualties in the operations were:

Officers. Wounded: 2nd-Lieuts. F. A. N. Wilmot, G. A. F. Gilmor, F. Exler, C. L. B. Kirkland, A. K. Glover, A. H. Robinson, A. E. Saw.
Wounded and Missing: 2nd-Lieuts. H. S. Griffin,* D. Mackinnon.
Other Ranks: Killed 32, Wounded 111, Missing 79 (25 of them known to be wounded).

The battalion remained refitting at Goldfish Château, Brandhoek, and in the neighbourhood till the 11th September, when it was again sent up into support trenches at Wieltje, where it found the artillery of both sides particularly active.

Being relieved by the 55th Division on the 14th September, the battalion was back in the Wormhoudt area on the 17th, and here the honours awarded for the action of the 22nd August were distributed. In addition to these, Captain G. O. W. Willink received the Military Cross for his conduct on the 21st August under the following circumstances.

A gun of " A " Battery, 307th Brigade R.F.A., had been blown up by a shell and several men buried. Captain Willink, with a sergeant and three men, volunteered to go forward under heavy shell fire, and by their gallant exertions several buried men were dug out and saved. This action would in any previous war probably have been rewarded with the V.C.

On the 19th September the battalion went back by train to Agnez-les-Duisans, in the back area of the Arras front, where it remained training for

* Afterwards recorded as killed.

the rest of the month and into October. On the 6th October command of the battalion was assumed by Captain (A/Lieut.-Colonel) J. H. S. Dimmer, V.C., M.C., when the battalion was in the Gavrelle Switch trenches N.E. of Arras. On the 11th it was in trenches on Greenland Hill, on the 17th at Gavrelle Switch, and again on Greenland Hill on the 22nd. On the 28th it was in barracks in Arras, where it remained till the 8th November, when it went into support trenches in the Chemical Works sector south of Gavrelle, and on the 15th into front line.

At 3 p.m. on the 18th there was a discharge of smoke along the front of the division, which led the enemy to expect an attack, and to put down a heavy barrage all over the British trenches. There was a good deal of this sort of thing during this tour of front-line service, and there were several raids by troops on either side of the 2/4th Royal Berkshire, but none by the battalion itself. This worried the enemy and caused him to expend much ammunition, but was somewhat costly to the battalion, which lost seven killed and fourteen wounded between the 18th and the 21st, when it returned to support trenches.

At this time the first part of the Battle of Cambrai had taken place, and it was to divert attention from that attack that the various operations in the neighbourhood of the battalion had been carried out.

On the 27th the battalion was warned to be ready to go to the Cambrai area. Next day it entrained at Arras for Bapaume, whence it marched south-east, by le Transloy and Rocquigny, to Léchelle.

On the 1st December the 2/4th Royal Berkshire started, at 3.45 a.m., to march through mud and water to Fins, where were Brigade Head-quarters. The cold was so great that sleep was impossible, before or after the march.

At 2 a.m. on the 2nd December a Staff Officer of the Guards Division arrived to explain the situation as it now stood since the commencement of the German general counter-attack on the newly acquired Cambrai Salient.

The Guards had retaken Gouzeaucourt, which had been lost to the Germans at the commencement of the counter-attack. It had been learned from prisoners that a big attack in this neighbourhood was about to be made. The 2/4th Royal Berkshire and 2/5th Gloucestershire were sent to support the Guards at Gouzeaucourt, moving off at 1.25 a.m. The rest of the 184th Brigade went to Metz-en-Coûture. Colonel Dimmer went back with the

G.S.O. to the Guards Head-quarters whilst the battalion marched to Gouzeau-court, where it was ordered to take up a position on the railway east of the village. Here it dug in and made all preparations and reconnaissances for the expected attack. Later, however, orders were received for the battalion to rejoin its own brigade, which was under orders to support the Secundera-bad Cavalry Brigade. It rejoined the brigade at 8 p.m. with the Gloucester-shire. The two battalions were ordered to Villers Plouich to take up support positions north of the village.

At 8.30 a.m. on the 3rd December the enemy attacked La Vacquerie and the line north and south of it after a heavy bombardment.

About 10 a.m. the 2/5th Gloucestershire were placed at the disposal of the 183rd Brigade with a view to counter-attack, while the 2/4th Royal Berkshire, also under the 183rd Brigade, were ordered to occupy the old British line in front of Villers Plouich, that is the line held before the battle of the 20th November.

At 1 p.m. " C " Company was sent to Welsh Trench, facing the enemy towards the east, whilst " D " was placed in support of the left of " C," and the rest of the battalion was posted in Corner Work.

Heavy attacks continued all day, and the enemy succeeded in taking La Vacquerie and the line north and south of it, but were held up there. During the night of the 3rd-4th December the Royal Berkshire took over Corner Support and the trenches west of it. Corner Work was a short way north-west of La Vacquerie, with Corner Support just west of it again.

At 4 a.m. on the 4th December, after a fairly quiet night, the enemy bom-barded for an hour. Orders were received for the 184th Brigade to relieve the 183rd in the night of the 5th-6th. Eight tanks also came up in order to help in a counter-attack, in the event of Welsh Ridge (between La Vacquerie and Villers Plouich) being taken by the Germans. The day, however, passed uneventfully. During the night of the 4th-5th the 2/4th Royal Berkshire bombed the enemy out of the trenches leading to La Vacquerie, but were counter-attacked and forced back to their starting point. About 4 p.m. on the 5th, after an intense bombardment lasting half an hour, the enemy made three assaults in succession on Corner Support Trench, which were all repulsed. It appears from the Battalion Diary that, previous to this, " C " and " D " Companies had been driven from Corner Work. Orders to retake it were received, but it is not clear whether any serious attempt to do so was made. In any case, it was not successful ; for the three attacks at 4 p.m. started from the west side of Corner Work against the trenches to the west, that is Corner Support.

The casualties of " C " Company are shown in the diary as Second-Lieutenant Janaway very seriously wounded, three other ranks killed, and six wounded. Those of " D " were not yet known at the time of making the entry, and are not subsequently recorded.

During the night of the 5th-6th the 184th Brigade relieved the 183rd as ordered. The Royal Berkshire were then still attached to the 183rd Brigade, but appear to have been returned to the 184th at the time of the relief, so remained in front line. The disposition of the 184th Brigade after the relief was thus—2/4th Oxfordshire and Buckinghamshire Light Infantry on the right, 2/1st Buckinghamshire in the centre, and 2/4th Royal Berkshire in their old position on the left.

The 2/5th Gloucestershire were in support in the Villers Plouich quarry.

In the morning of the 6th December the Royal Berkshire were ordered to extend their holding to the left, and, in order to enable them to garrison this extra piece of trench, two hundred and thirty-five other ranks of the 2/8th Royal Warwickshire (182nd Brigade) were placed under the orders of the O.C. 2/4th Royal Berkshire. There was no infantry action during the 6th in this part.

During the night of the 6th-7th the battalion, and the detachment of the 2/8th Royal Warwickshire, were relieved, and sent back into support in Villers Plouich quarry.

The casualties of the battalion during the period from the 1st to the 7th December are shown by companies thus :

Officers. Wounded : 2nd-Lieut. H. R. Leggett, A. E. Janaway.
Other Ranks :

	Killed.	Wounded.
" A " Company	4	15
" B " Company	2	12
" C " Company	6	16
" D " Company	9	24
Total	21	67

On the whole, looking to these losses, it seems clear the battalion was not very seriously engaged in the second part of the Battle of Cambrai.

The battalion remained on this front in front line, support, or reserve till the 23rd December, when it went back to Léchelle, and thence south-westwards, viâ Cappy, to Rosières en Santerre, where it arrived on the 31st.

THE GERMAN OFFENSIVE. RETREAT FROM ST. QUENTIN. NIEPPE FOREST. THE FINAL ADVANCE

1918

The 2/4th Royal Berkshire remained at Rosières, far behind the front, till the 6th January, when it again moved forward to Curchy, and on viâ Nesle, on the 9th, to Ugny l'Equipée.

By the 14th it was again in front line facing Pontruet, rather in advance of the position it had occupied about the 10th April 1917. Here, on the 16th soon after 3 a.m., the enemy rushed the small post known as the "International" held by a corporal and two men of the battalion, and two of the 11th Hussars. The rush was made when the post was occupied by only one Berkshire man and two Hussars. The corporal and the other Berkshire man were on patrol towards the post on the left.

At 2.45 a.m. on the 18th, Second-Lieutenant W. H. Smith and Sergeant Austin were passing along a sunken road in the support line when they were attacked by about fifteen Germans, who had cut through the wire and hidden under the bank of the road. Smith at once opened fire with his revolver which drove off some of the enemy, but the rest came on, and Smith and the sergeant had to retire, each supporting the other alternately with his fire. When they were approaching the nearest post, Smith shouted " Stand to," which had the effect of frightening the Germans and driving them off.

On the 20th a party of " C " Company in Maissemy suffered severely from three German shells, which killed four and wounded seventeen.

From the 23rd the battalion was in the Pontruet-Gricourt section till the 27th when it went back south-westwards to Germaine, and stayed there till the 7th February. On the 8th it went into the right sub-sector opposite St. Quentin, on the 20th was back at Holnon Wood, and on the 23rd at Ugny, in the back area, till the 3rd March, when it moved into the " battle zone " in front of St. Quentin. On the 11th it went into the " forward zone." On the 13th a patrol was examining the German wire when an enemy post close to them opened rapid fire, which wounded Second-Lieutenant J. C. Mullin and two men. One man was missing.

In the night of the 17th raiders went out to try and procure identifications. At 9 p.m. the intended place of entry of the German trenches was bombarded for three minutes, after which the raiders, under Captain Knott, entered the trench. They found, however, that the part of it enclosed by the " box barrage " had been evacuated and cleared of all means of identification. On the 18th the raid of the previous night was repeated, but on this occasion the enemy replied at once to the barrage, and the flanks of the point of entry of the trench were so strongly protected by machine guns and rifles that no entry was effected and the raiders were forced to retire. The diary does not mention any casualties in either of these raids, but it seems difficult to believe that there were none, at any rate in the second raid.

The battalion was relieved on the 19th, and on the 21st when the storm of the great German offensive broke upon the 5th Army, it was back in the rear zone at Ugny.

At 5 a.m. on the 21st, when the German offensive was sweeping on with all its vigour, battle stations were ordered to be manned. At 8.30 a.m. the Berkshire Battalion was at Marteville, the 2/4th Oxfordshire and Buckinghamshire Light Infantry being in the forward area, and the 2/5th Gloucestershire in the battle zone. The Oxfordshire and Buckinghamshire held on in the forward area till 4.20 p.m., when the Enghien Redoubt which they were holding had been surrounded. Under sanction conveyed to them by a buried cable, they then endeavoured to cut their way back, but only a very few succeeded in doing so.

Meanwhile, the 2/4th Royal Berkshire, on arrival at Marteville, had been put under the orders of the 183rd Brigade. The O.C. that brigade ordered them to counter-attack on the high ground about Maissemy where the enemy had succeeded in penetrating into the battle area. In this counter-attack, which was partially successful, Lieut.-Colonel Dimmer, gallantly leading it, was killed. The ground which had been recovered was again lost. In addition to Colonel Dimmer, V.C., M.C., killed, there were wounded Second-Lieutenants H. G. Champion, E. H. Shelford, W. L. Haile, and W. H. Smith. Of the casualties in other ranks the Battalion Diary merely says that they were " heavy," without giving details, or even totals.

On Colonel Dimmer's death command was assumed by Captain and Adjutant J. S. Darby. The 22nd March dawned in thick mist, and a heavy German barrage was followed by an attack by infantry in great strength. " B " and " C " Companies were in position between Ellis Redoubt and Villecholes. The Gloucestershire were farther to the right, holding the Holnon Wood defences. The Royal Berkshire maintained their positions and inflicted heavy losses on the attacking Germans up till 12.30 p.m., when they were ordered to retire to the line Vaux-Villevêque, about half-way between Vermand and Beauvois, to which the Gloucestershire also retired when the flanks of the position at Holnon Wood were turned.

The Royal Berkshire reached the new line in good order, and without suffering much loss in the retirement. The battalion was then reorganized and distributed in depth. But this line was scarcely defensible, with its trenches only eighteen inches deep.

At 6.30 p.m. a terrific barrage fell upon it, and overwhelming forces of German infantry attacked with great determination. The attack was heaviest on the right of the line, which was broken through at Vaux, and the Royal Berkshire, with their right flank thus exposed, had to retire another six hundred yards. Here, at 7 p.m., they were again reorganized and held on till midnight, when they were ordered back to Voyennes on the Somme, and on to Longuevoisin, just S.E. of Nesle, where the rest of the night and the whole of the 23rd were spent unmolested.

The casualties on the 22nd were :

Officers. Killed : Capt. E. Knott.
　　　　　　Wounded : Lieuts. H. F. F. Coggin, K. P. Smith.
　　　　　　　　　　　2nd-Lieuts. W. A. Cozens, J. Tullett.
　　　　　　Missing : Capt. G. Hinchcliffe.
　　　　　　　　　　　2nd-Lieuts. G. W. de St. Legier, M.C.,
　　　　　　　　　　　J. Lawrence.

The casualties for other ranks are not stated.

During the attack east of Beauvois the Brigadier, the Hon. R. White, C.M.G., D.S.O., was wounded and was succeeded on the 23rd by Lieut.-

Colonel Weatherall, D.S.O., M.C., of the 2/4th Oxfordshire and Buckingham-shire Light Infantry.

On the 23rd command of the 2/4th Royal Berkshire was assumed by Captain G. O. W. Willink, M.C.

On the 24th the battalion moved out to take up a defensive position at the bridgehead where the Voyennes Road crosses the canal. Eventually it took post on the line of the railway and dug itself in. The enemy opened intense machine-gun fire at 11 p.m., but no infantry attack followed. In the morning of the 25th nothing particular happened beyond activity by British snipers, who accounted for a good many of the enemy.

During the day the Germans gradually worked round the flanks of the bridgehead position, rendering it untenable by 6 p.m. and necessitating a further retirement. The battalion fought a delaying action, and got back with slight loss to a quarry behind Breuil, which is on the west bank of the canal south-east of Longuevoisin, not far from the line which then divided the French and British Armies.

Eventually they dug in on the line Cressy-Billancourt which was astride of the dividing line, with Cressy actually in the French area. The Berk-shire and Oxfordshire Battalions held Billancourt, with the Gloucestershire on the right at Cressy. French troops were assisting in the defence.

On this day Captain G. L. Worlock, M.C., and Second-Lieutenant J. W. Barber were wounded, but the casualties in other ranks are not stated.

At 1 a.m. on the 26th came orders to withdraw to Roye, which was reached without loss by 5 a.m. Here rations were issued, and the units of the brigade were reorganized. It had been placed under the orders of the 20th Division since the 24th. At 7 a.m. the retirement in the direction of Amiens continued, and towards 2 p.m. the brigade concentrated in the neighbourhood of Mezières, which village the 2/4th Royal Berkshire com-menced putting in a state of defence.

At 8 p.m. the brigade received orders to retrace its steps and defend Le Quesnel on the Amiens-Roye Road. Here the 2/5th Gloucestershire took post south of the road as far as Hangest. The Royal Berkshire were on their left, east of Le Quesnel Wood, where they improved the defences during the 27th. They were acting here again with the French. The enemy did not attack during this day, and at 2 a.m. on the 28th omnibuses carried the

battalion to Marcelcave on the Amiens-La Fère railway, reaching it at
3.30 a.m. Here, however, it appeared that the enemy had during the
night crossed the Somme at Sailly Laurette, thus endangering the position of all troops holding the line south of the Somme. The omnibuses
had been intended to take the troops to Villers Bretonneux, but this German movement necessitated their stopping at Marcelcave, in order that
an attack might be made northwards on the enemy at Warfusée.

The British troops collected at Marcelcave were a very mixed lot of
different regiments from several brigades.

At 11 a.m. the 184th Brigade, with the 183rd on its left, received orders
to attack Warfusée and Lamotte-en-Santerre. As it moved forward it
encountered very severe machine-gun fire from Warfusée and Lamotte in
front, and from Bayonvillers on its right flank. Before this it was forced to
retire, after reaching a point within two hundred yards of its objective.
At 6 p.m. the enemy attacked and succeeded in securing a footing on the
Amiens-La Fère railway, on the right of the 184th Brigade, which entailed a
general withdrawal to a line running north and south five hundred yards to
the west of Marcelcave. Here the Gloucestershire were north of the railway, the 2/4th Royal Berkshire astride of it facing east, and the Oxfordshire
and Buckinghamshire Light Infantry south of it. At this time Brigadier-
General Pagan assumed command of the brigade.

During the 29th the enemy were endeavouring to push down the valley
of the Luce River towards Aubercourt, on the right of the brigade. In the
afternoon the battalion was moved to a position east of Villers Bretonneux.

At 8 a.m. on the 30th the Germans drove in the right flank northwards
from Aubercourt, and the British line south of the railway also gave way
temporarily, but recovered its line later.

In the afternoon the Germans attacked the brigade front. They were
driven off, but succeeded in capturing Marcelcave, where they consolidated
a line four hundred yards in front of the British. An Australian Brigade
counter-attacked towards Aubercourt, and recovered part of the lost ground.
At 10 p.m. this brigade was ordered to relieve the 184th, which was withdrawn
to Gentelles, about four miles S.W. of Villers Bretonneux.

There is no list of casualties in these operations either in the Battalion or
the Brigade Diary.

Gentelles was shelled on the 1st April, and on the 2nd the battalion moved, partly by omnibus and partly by march, to Méricourt, on the Ancre five or six miles below Albert.   It appears to have received reinforcements, as it was reorganized on a basis of four companies of four platoons each.   Whilst it was training there, on the 6th April, command was taken over temporarily by Major G. F. Waterworth, D.S.O.

On the 11th the battalion was back at Amiens, and entrained for the northern area again.   Detraining at Berguette, north-west of Béthune, it marched to St. Venant in the early morning of the 12th.   At 8 a.m. it was ordered to occupy a defensive position in front of Robecq.

On the previous day command of the battalion had passed to Lieut.-Colonel W. G. Oates of the 2/8th Sherwood Foresters.   It was in this position till the 23rd, when it went into billets in rear.   It had had a specially heavy shelling on the 18th, when the casualties of the day rose to six killed and thirty-two wounded.

On the 25th the 2/4th Royal Berkshire were sent into the forward area to relieve the 2/5th Gloucestershire, who had just gained and held some ground.

From this date the battalion took its turn in front line, in support or in reserve, in the Robecq neighbourhood for some time.   The events of note during this period are the following:

On the 9th May a patrol under Lieutenant Thorne bombed a German machine-gun post and forced it to withdraw.   At least two casualties occurred on the German side, but no identifications were secured.

In the following night, which was very dark, Second-Lieutenant W. H. Fry and two men of the right listening patrol failed to return, and were believed to have lost their way and walked into the enemy lines.   On the 15th Lieut.-Colonel Oates was wounded by a shell, and Major Waterworth again took command on Colonel Oates being sent to hospital.

Major Waterworth, in turn, was sent to hospital on the 17th, and command was taken over by Major Christie-Miller of the Oxfordshire and Buckinghamshire Light Infantry.

The latter part of May was marked by a great deal of aerial activity and some heavy shelling.   On the 3rd June, the battalion being still in the same area, command was taken over by Lieut.-Colonel C. R. C. Boyle, D.S.O., of the Oxfordshire and Buckinghamshire Light Infantry.

On the 13th, when a garrison for a forward post was going to occupy it, the Germans were found in possession.   They were driven out and the post was reoccupied.   Nothing is said about casualties.

On the 24th one platoon of " D " Company raided a German post in an orchard.   The enemy put down a barrage in reply to that of the British, but it fell mainly on the reserve line.   The post was found by the raiders to be strongly held, and in the attack many casualties were inflicted on the enemy, with small loss on the British side.   Second-Lieutenant Tarrant was wounded and missing, and of other ranks one was killed and two were missing.

After this the Royal Berkshire marched, at 1 a.m. on the 25th, to Busnes Château and proceeded by omnibus to Linghem Camp, where they remained in the back area at training, diversified by sports, etc., till the 22nd July, when a move was made to a camp N.W. of Pont Asquin.   The battalion moved to Bourecq on the 31st July, and on the 5th August relieved the 1st Duke of Cornwall's Light Infantry of the 5th Division in support line in the Nieppe Forest left sub-sector.

On the 7th, Second-Lieutenant Thorne was killed by a shell.   On the 9th the Royal Berkshire relieved the Oxfordshire Battalion in the right front line of the brigade, and next day Captain H. B. Goater was killed by a German sniper.

The final British offensive had commenced on the 8th August on the Somme, and the 11th was fixed for an attack by the 184th Brigade, with the object of crossing the Platte Becque stream and establishing a bridgehead beyond it.   One battalion from the 182nd was to co-operate on the right.

The 184th Brigade was disposed for attack with the 2/4th Royal Berkshire on the right and the Gloucestershire on the left in front line.   The Oxfordshire and Buckinghamshire Light Infantry were in support.*

Zero hour was fixed for 4.15 a.m. and at that hour " D " Company of the Royal Berkshire advanced, supported by " C."   By 2 p.m. part of two platoons of " D " had passed over the Platte Becque at a broken foot-bridge, whilst the other two had crossed farther up on the left, where bridges had been placed in position during the previous night.   The crossing here was

* It will be remembered that British Brigades had been reduced, early in 1918, from four to three battalions. The 2/1st Bucks had disappeared from the 184th Brigade.

attended with great difficulty, as the plank bridges had been destroyed by shell fire, and their position was exposed to enemy machine-gun fire.

These platoons lost their leader, and only a very few of them succeeded in rushing the passage.

The two platoons on the right were more successful in getting across. Beyond the stream they had a stubborn fight, in which the Germans lost heavily.

The German position beyond was very strong, being on a slight rise, and consisting of concrete buildings held with machine guns.

Casualties being numerous in the " D " Platoons, a platoon of " C " was sent up to reinforce them. On the flanks of the Royal Berkshire the other battalions had failed to get across the stream, and consequently by 9.30 a.m., the remains of the three platoons found themselves isolated, and also very short of ammunition. A farm on a slight elevation to the left had not been taken by the adjoining battalion, and the enemy machine guns had not been silenced by the barrage. There was nothing left, in the circumstances, but to retire again across the brook.

In this unsuccessful attack Captain Bowles and Lieutenants Moilliet and Schroder, all of " D " Company, were wounded, and there were forty-one casualties (details not given) in the ranks. The battalion was relieved on the 13th August, and the casualties during this period of front-line service are stated in the diary to have been—Officers (not named) : 2 killed and 3 wounded. Other ranks : 11 killed, 3 wounded and missing, 66 wounded (32 of these gassed), and 2 missing. From the Brigade Diary it appears that the officers were :

Lieut. Thorne (5th Suffolk, attached 2/4th R. Berks), killed 7th August.
Capt. Goater, killed 10th August.
Capt. R. H. D. Bowles, wounded 11th August.
2nd-Lieuts. Moilliet and Schroder, wounded 11th August.

The same diary gives the August casualties in other ranks thus :

On the 11th, Wounded 18.
       12th, Killed 11, Wounded 6, Wounded and Missing 3, Missing 2.
       14th, Gassed 21.

Apparently the casualties of the 11th are entered partly on the 11th and

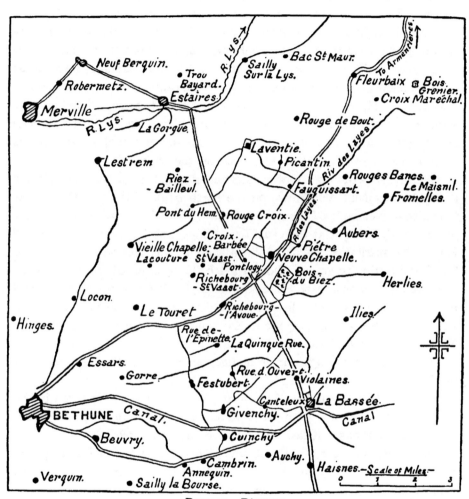

ESTAIRES—BÉTHUNE.

201

partly on the 12th. The Battalion Diary makes no mention of fighting on the 12th ; nor does it mention the gassing of 21 men on the 14th.

From the 14th to the 22nd the Royal Berkshire were in billets at Steenbecque. They were sent up on that date into the support line, and on the 25th into the right of the brigade front line. The battalion diary is extremely meagre, and that of the brigade is not much more illuminating. The former states that by the 31st August the battalion had moved slowly forwards as far as Chapelle Duvelle, and adds " progress still rather sticky, owing to bitter resistance." However, the battalion does not seem to have had any fighting worth mention ; for no casualties in other ranks are given in the Brigade Diary later than the 14th August, and the only officer casualty mentioned is Second-Lieutenant T. J. Hooper gassed on the 28th.

On the 1st September it was ascertained at Chapelle Duvelle that the enemy had evacuated Estaires, on the north bank of the Lys Canal. At 6 p.m. that evening " C " Company, followed by " D," moved forward to a position with its right at the canal drawbridge, and its left at the Bretigné Farm. No resistance, beyond a little sniping, was met with. " A " and " B " had farther to go, and did not reach the position till 2 a.m. On the 2nd, attempts to push patrols across the canal failed, and the battalion was relieved and fell back to a line about Robermetz. On the 11th the 2/4th Royal Berkshire were in Brigade reserve, and on the 17th moved to a mile N.N.W. of Trou Bayard, just N.E. of Estaires.

On the 28th it was again in front line, on the left of the right sector of the brigade.

The casualties in the battalion during September are only given in the Brigade Diary, without specification of dates. They were Lieut. A. J. Fox, killed ; Other ranks : Killed 10, wounded 21, and gassed 1.

On the 2nd October, an attack was made on Bartlette's Farm by two platoons of " A," one from the south and the other from the north. An artillery and trench-mortar barrage played on the farm for forty minutes, and then swept back behind it. Very slight resistance was encountered and the farm was taken with four prisoners. On information of this being sent back, " B " came up on the left of " A " and the advance continued with " A " and " B " in front line and " C " and " D " in support.

It was again continued at 6.30 a.m. on the 3rd with " B " and " C " leading, followed by " A " and " D." By 11.45 the first objective had been gained on the old British line running N.E. At 9 p.m. the position was in front of the distillery, where the battalion was relieved and withdrew to Rouge de Bout, which lies almost midway between Neuve Chapelle and Armentières. The battalion now moved, with the brigade, farther south, partly by omnibus, partly by rail and partly by march. On the 9th October it marched into Doullens, having been attached on the previous day to the XVIIth Corps of the 3rd Army. From Doullens it went by train to Hermies, on the road from Bapaume to Cambrai, arriving there on the 10th, and halted till the 19th, when it marched by Noyelles and the southern part of Cambrai to Cugnolles, whence it marched, on the 23rd, to St. Aubert. That place was left at 7 a.m. on the 24th, and at 2 p.m. the battalion was resting on the railway embankment at Montrecourt. It then moved up into support of the 183rd Brigade, " D " taking post a mile north of Bernerain, " A " in the quarry near the River Harpies, S.W. of St. Martin, " B " and " C " in the quarry a quarter of a mile south of Les Furrières.

On the 25th " A " and " C " captured, without resistance, the high ground north of La Justice, and took one prisoner. Moving forward to the line of the Valenciennes-Avesnes railway, the battalion consolidated, with " A " and " C " in front, and " B " and " D " in support line.

At 4 p.m. a smoke barrage was put down, under cover of which the battalion advanced with the object of ascertaining whether it was possible to cross the Rhonelle stream and effect a lodgment on the high ground beyond it. The enemy was found to be holding the heights so strongly with machine guns that advance was out of the question, and the companies were compelled to fall back to the position from which they had started.

On the 26th " A " Company on the left occupied a château near Artres, and at 10 a.m. the 4th Division on the left attacked and occupied Artres, where a bridgehead was established on the right bank of the Rhonelle. The slope of the hill beyond was also gained. " A " and " D " Companies then attempted the passage of the stream. " D " succeeded in crossing, and gained touch with the 4th Division on the slope on its left. " A " was less fortunate, being caught in a gas-shell barrage and suffering some casualties. It could not get beyond its original front line, in which it was presently relieved by " B."

Later, the battalion was relieved in front line, and withdrawn to billets in reserve at Bernerain, where it remained training till the end of October.

The casualties in these actions are not given in the Battalion Diary, but that of the brigade states them for the 2/4th Royal Berkshire during October as follows :

Officers : No casualties.
Other Ranks : From 1st to 23rd, Killed 1, Wounded 8.
               24th–31st, Killed 6, Wounded 39.
               Missing 1, Gassed 27.

It seems safe to assume that practically all the casualties in the latter period occurred on the 25th and 26th, and that most of the gas cases were in " A " when it was in the gas barrage on the latter date.

On the 1st November the battalion relieved the Gloucestershire in the main line of resistance on the high ground on the left (south) bank of the Rhonelle. The line here had remained stationary since the 26th October. At 2 p.m. the 2/4th Royal Berkshire moved up into front line as the 183rd Brigade attacked. They appear to have had no fighting on this day, and there is no casualty list from which to judge either in the Battalion or the Brigade Diary. The fighting career of the 2/4th Royal Berkshire had ended ; for on the 2nd November they returned to their billets at Bernerain. They went still farther back, viâ Montrecourt and St. Aubert, to Avesnes-lez-St. Aubert on the 3rd, returning to Bernerain on the 4th.

On the 8th they were at Sepmeries, where they remained till the Armistice at 11 a.m. on the 11th November 1918. A thanksgiving-service was held on the next day. On the 14th the battalion was at Montrecourt, and on the 16th at Cambrai, on their way back from the front, as they were not destined to advance into Germany. Between the 27th and 29th they were on their way by train viâ Lourches, Douai, Arras, St. Pol and Frevent, arriving at Coutreville early on the 29th and marching thence to Fransu, where they remained till the end of 1918.

5th BATTALION.
February 1915.

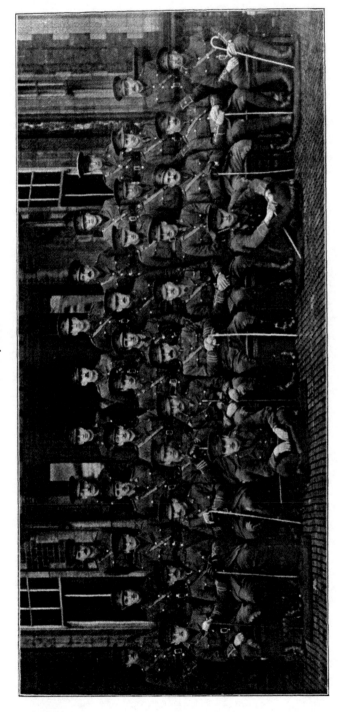

(*Back Row*) Lt. S. L. Reiss. Lt. P. B. Wace. Lt. A. H. Gold. Lt. T. H. Hudson. Lt. A. N. Scott. Lt. S. Sharp. Lt. M. S. V. Raby. Lt. H. C. Horsford.
(*Second Row*) Lt. H. Stewart. Lt. R. T. Pollard. Lt. S. G. Spencer. Lt. J. E. Warner. Lt. A. R. Trehern. Lt. D. H. Avory. Lt. D. V. T. James. Lt. P. H. Gold.
Lt. L. D. Cotteville. Lt. C. A. Gold. Lt. A. P. J. Hibbert. Lt. D. Causton.
(*Sitting*) Capt. O. N. Chadwyck-Healey. Capt. F. B. Elliot. Capt. F. Mount. Major W. R. Bayley. Major W. R. Betty. Lt.-Col. F. W. Foley, D.S.O. Major G. H.
Arbuthnot. Capt. G. W. Hopton. Capt. and Adjt. M. L. Slaughter. Lt. and Q.M. F. Tuttle. Capt. A. P. W. Rickman.
(*On Ground*) Lt. D. H. Stacey, R.A.M.C. Lt. J. E. W. Bath.

CHAPTER XXXI

THE 5th (SERVICE) BATTALION

Formation. The Battle of Loos. Givenchy

1914-1915

ON the 19th August 1914 Major F. W. Foley, D.S.O., then commanding the Royal Berkshire Depot, at Reading, received a telegram from the War Office appointing him to the command of what was then to be known as the 1st Reserve Battalion of the Regiment, afterwards the 5th (Service) Battalion. He, with Lieutenant Allfrey and Lieutenant and Quartermaster F. Tuttle, arrived at Shorncliffe on the 24th August and took over half the Risborough Hutments, the other half being assigned to the Essex Regiment. On the 26th the first draft under Captain G. W. Hopton arrived, and training began at once with a daily eight hours on parade and squad drill. Another draft arrived on the 28th, and two more, of four hundred and two hundred respectively, on the 4th and 5th September, which raised the strength of the battalion to nine hundred and ninety. Half of it was accommodated in huts, the rest in tents. Fortunately the early autumn was fine. In giving a brief account of the formation of the battalion we shall quote freely from notes kindly supplied by Colonel Foley, C.B.E. He writes :

"The initial difficulties to contend with were—

"1. The lack of clothing, arms, and equipment—these had to be bought locally.

"2. The lack of knives, forks, and plates—dishes and washing-up material had to be bought locally.

"3. The lack of towels and soap, and a shortage of bedding and blankets.

"4. The lack of non-commissioned officers.

205

" This last was a great difficulty.   The method adopted in the battalion was for the company-commander to pick out likely looking men and appoint them as lance-corporals. All these were examined by the commanding-officer and approved or rejected. All these lance-corporals were then formed into squads, with a regular N.C.O. in charge. The whole were under the care and sole charge of the Regimental-Sergeant-Major, and were under his instruction for weeks before joining their companies. From these lance-corporals were picked all the N.C.O.s for the battalion, and it tells well for the company-commander's discretion that in very few cases was the judgment wrong. The keenness and enthusiasm of the men was perfectly wonderful. No hours were too long for them : they were a most intelligent lot of men, drawn from all grades of society—from an artist to a valet. We had one platoon of butlers and footmen. The footman was often promoted before the butler, and the butlers seemed perfectly contented to be commanded by the footmen. Another platoon was almost exclusively composed of a peer's gardeners, or men on his estate.

" The battalion was inspected on the 20th September by Lord Kitchener, who expressed himself as well pleased with its appearance and steadiness. Training went on at high pressure for the next two months, being chiefly confined to squad and platoon drill, with plenty of night work and frequent route-marches.

" A recruits' course of musketry was fired on Hythe Ranges, and digging and entrenching were practised at Beachborough, and in the neighbourhood of the camp.

" The battalion was given a week's leave from the 7th December, at the conclusion of which it was moved to a new hutment camp on St. Martin's Plain ; but, owing to the unfinished state of the huts and the bad condition of the ground, there was a great deal of sickness amongst the men, and the medical authorities recommended that the battalion should be moved into billets in Folkestone—which move was effected on the 2nd January 1915.

" Battalion training began on the 1st February 1915, and on the 5th February the battalion took part in its first Brigade field day. Orders were received for the whole of the 12th Division (commanded by Major-General Spens) to be concentrated at Aldershot.

" On the 23rd February the battalion, forming part of the 35th Brigade commanded by Brig.-General Van Stranbenzee, marched to Ashford, then viâ Maidstone, Croydon, Leatherhead, Woking, to Aldershot, arriving there on the 1st March.

" Snow fell during the first part of the march and it was bitterly cold.

" The battalion at Aldershot shared Malplaquet Barracks with the 7th Norfolk Regiment.

" On the 10th March a trained soldiers' course was fired on Ash Range, which was visited by H.M. the King. Battalion training was continued till the 20th March, when Brigade training commenced, the battalion being billeted in Wokingham, and also under canvas at Eversley, and being inspected by Lord Kitchener.

" The rest of the period at Aldershot was a succession of Brigade and Divisional exercises under Major-General F. Wing, C.B., who had been appointed to command the 12th Division, vice General Spens."

The other units of the brigade were the 7th Norfolk, 7th Suffolk, and 9th Essex Regiments.

The officers present with the 5th Royal Berkshire Regiment on the 30th May 1915 were :

Lieut.-Colonel F. W. Foley, D.S.O., in command (severely wounded).
Major W. R. Kemiss Betty (second-in-command).
Major G. H. Arbuthnot.
Major W. R. Bayley (killed).
Capt. G. W. Hopton (killed).
Capt. O. N. Chadwyk Healey.
Capt. F. B. Elliot (severely wounded).
Capt. F. Mount (killed).
Capt. A. P. W. Rickman.
Capt. and Adjutant M. L. Slaughter.
Lieuts. and 2nd-Lieuts. C. A. Gold (killed).
                      P. H. Gold (wounded).
                      A. H. Gold.
                      H. Stewart (killed).
                      R. T. Pollard (killed).
                      S. L. Reiss (killed).
                      P. B. Wace (killed).
                      T. H. Hudson (killed).
                      A. N. Scott (severely wounded).

Lieuts. and 2nd-Lieuts.   S. Sharp (killed).
    contd.   H. C. Horsford (killed).
                         D. Causton.
                         D. H. Avory.
                         D. V. T. James (killed).
                         S. G. Spencer (killed).
                         L. D. Cotterill.
                         J. E. Warner (wounded).
                         A. R. Treherne (killed).
Lieut. and Qr.-Mr. F. Tuttle, D.C.M.
Medical Officer : Lieut. D. H. Stacey, R.A.M.C. (severely wounded).

The battalion was extremely fortunate in having no less than six Regular officers, four of whom were then serving : the other two had only recently left the Army.

The majority of the officers came from the O.T.C. and were of a very high standard of intelligence and character.

The 5th Battalion left Aldershot on the 30th May 1915 in two trains for Folkestone, where it embarked, and reached Boulogne at 2 a.m. on the 31st. From the rest camps at Boulogne it entrained, at Pont de Briques, in the night of the 1st-2nd June, for Lumbres, where it remained till it marched fourteen miles on the 5th to Renesence. Next day it reached Strazeele in very hot weather which was trying for marching.

On the 7th it was billeted at Armentières, the men in the ground floor of a large cotton factory, and the officers in private houses. After remaining here for a week it marched to bivouac in Ploegsteert Wood, where it formed a unit of the 145th Brigade, 48th Division, for instruction in the mysteries of trench warfare.

In this brigade it found itself in company with the 1/4th Royal Berkshire, and under the command of Brigadier-General W. K. McClintock, an officer of the Royal Berkshire Regiment.

This course of practical instruction lasted till the 20th June, the several companies taking their turn in trenches with various battalions of the 145th Brigade.

On the 20th June the battalion returned to its own brigade, and was in billets at Armentières.

On the 4th July it began its first turn of trenches on its own account, and on the 11th suffered its first officer casualties when Lieutenant A. L. Scott was severely wounded by a stray bullet, and Captain P. B. Wace by a H.E. shell.

On the 27th July the battalion lost Captain G. W. Hopton and Second-Lieutenant A. Treherne, both mortally wounded by rifle fire.

The rest of July and the whole of August were spent in the usual routine of trench warfare about Ploegsteert Wood, and this continued till the 26th September when, on relief by a Canadian Battalion, the 5th Royal Berkshire went to billets at Westhof. On the 27th it was at Merris, on the 28th it went by motor-'buses to Mt. Bernenchon, and on the 29th joined the brigade at Gonnenhem and marched with it to Sailly la Bourse.

The 12th Division was now ordered to relieve the Guards Division in the line east and north-east of Loos, which was done in the night of the 30th September-1st October. The 35th Brigade was on the right, touching the 12th French Division on its right. Here the 5th Royal Berkshire were in support trenches twelve hundred yards north of Loos till they relieved the 7th Norfolk Regiment in front trenches on the slopes of Hill 70, thirty-six hours later. These trenches were only two or three feet deep when the 5th Royal Berkshire took them over.

On the 1st October the battalion was in support trenches twelve hundred yards north of Loos. Hill 70 bore two thousand seven hundred yards S.E. of these trenches, and Hulluch two thousand yards N.E. The whole position was overlooked by the enemy, and work was only possible at night.

General Wing, the commander of the 12th Division, was killed by a shell on the 2nd October and was succeeded by Major-General A. B. Scott, C.B., D.S.O.

Nothing special happened till the 12th October, when the battalion relieved the Coldstream Guards in support trenches for the attack next day on the Hulluch Quarries.

At 10 a.m. on the 13th smoke helmets were donned during the earlier stages of the attack.

About 2.30 p.m. the Officer-Commanding the 7th Norfolk Regiment asked to be reinforced, as most of his three companies which had been in the attack were casualties, though a few had reached their objective.

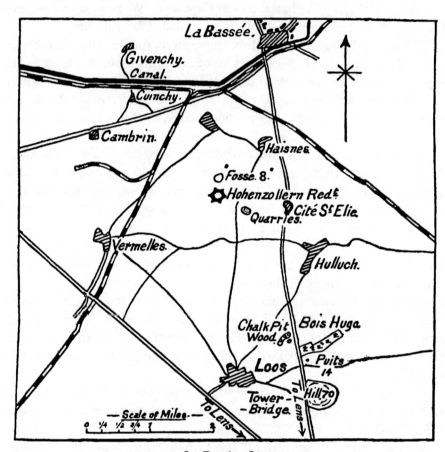

La Bassée—Loos.

When Colonel Foley at once sent up " A " Company under Major Bayley, it encountered heavy machine-gun fire from the trenches which the O.C. 7th Norfolk Regiment believed to be held by his men. Hardly any of them went more than half-way to the trenches, which were strongly held by the enemy.

The story of the four bombing parties of the 5th Royal Berkshire on this day is quite independent of that of the rest of the battalion ; for all the bombers of the brigade were given a special mission under the Brigade Bombing Officer.

They were not under the control of regimental officers, who were ignorant of their instructions or whereabouts, and were in no way responsible for the supply of bombs or in a position to control it.

The 5th Royal Berkshire contribution to these Brigade Bombers consisted of four parties, one from each company, " B " party leading, followed by " D," " A " and " C " in the order named. Lieutenant Pollard, in command of " B " party, had stationed himself in the centre of it, but finding that the way had not been cleared by trench-mortar fire, placed himself at the head of it behind the barricade of seven feet of sand-bags. The bayonet men of " B " went over first, followed closely by Lieutenant Pollard carrying bombs. Pollard had already been wounded in the face whilst still behind the barricade, and there two men had also been wounded.

On the farther side of the barricade was some wire, and the only protection for those passing through it was a bank of earth eighteen inches high. The passage of the wire therefore had to be made by crawling on the stomach. Two men who ventured to raise themselves on hands and knees were instantly hit. Discarding their equipment, Pollard and his men crawled forward, pushing their bombs in front of them.

Arrived at the German barricade, which was loopholed and surmounted by wire, Pollard's party, followed by that of " D," scrambled over and into the German trench and bombed several traverses. " A " and " C " parties were busy passing up bombs to " B " and " D," whom they were following over the German barricade, when Lance-Corporal Radford of " C," observing that no one was following him, and hearing repeated calls from the front for more bombs, returned with three men and shouted for bombs which they passed along as they were handed over the British barricade

By this time the leading parties had been checked for want of bombs. One of them, Private Mansell, who had been wounded, still held on, firing his rifle at any German who ventured to appear round a traverse. Lieutenant Pollard, too, had been wounded for the second time, but continued throwing bombs and directing operations. The German parapet here was only four feet high, so the bombers were exposed to rifle and machine-gun fire whenever they stood up to throw a bomb.

Some Germans, under an officer, attempting a counter-attack from the right, were beaten off with bombs. The bombers of " B," being now exhausted, were compelled to fall back. Their place was taken by men of " D," notably Private Branch and Lance-Corporal Day, the latter already twice wounded, as was Private Lamball who ran up and continued fighting to the end. Lieutenant Pollard was now exhausted by his wounds, but, leaning against the parapet, continued to give orders until he met his heroic death in this position.

The bomb supply continued to be unsatisfactory, and the pins of many were bent in the operation of passing them over the two barricades. During the periods when there were none, the men had to defend themselves with their rifles. The party in the German trench held stubbornly to their ground until ordered to withdraw, which they did in good order, Lance-Corporal Goddard coolly staying behind to bring in the dead Lieutenant Pollard's wrist-watch.

All the survivors were loud in their praises of the conduct of Lieutenant Pollard, and of Private Lamball (wounded), Lance-Corporal Day (died of wounds) and Private Mansell (wounded). The casualties of this day were:

Officers. *Killed :* Capt. Spencer (Machine-gun officer).
Lieut. R. Pollard.
Wounded : Capt. P. H. Gold (" B " Company).
Missing : Major W. K. Bayley, Capt. F. A. Mount,
Capt. and Adjutant T. N. Hondren.
Lieuts. L. Reiss, Trewartha-Davies, H. C. Horsford (shell-shock).
Capt. E. S. Stacey, R.A.M.C., was badly crushed by the fall of the roof of his dressing-station.
Other Ranks. Killed : Sergeant-Major Farmer and 36 others ;
Wounded 91 ; Missing 22.

Most of the night was occupied in clearing the dead from the trenches, and collecting the wounded.

On the 17th there was a bombing attack by the Guards on the left, supported by fire from the 35th Brigade. The German retaliation on this occasion caused losses to the battalion above the daily average of trench warfare. One man was killed and twenty-four were wounded or shell-shocked. The recent conduct of the brigade elicited congratulations from the Corps-Commander, and a message from the Guards Division on the 18th ran: " Well done, neighbours. Stick to it! Sincere thanks for co-operation yesterday and to-day."

During November the battalion was in and out of trenches, which were often knee deep in mud, in the same neighbourhood.

On the 22nd Captain Elliot of " D " Company was wounded whilst taking over trenches from the 7th Norfolk Regiment.

On the 26th the battalion moved by train from Fonquereuil to Thieunes by train, and on the 1st December was at Essars, just north of Béthune. On the 15th it was at Le Quesnoy and on the 17th in trenches at Windy Corner, near Givenchy, with the 9th Royal Fusiliers (38th Brigade) on its left, and the Essex on its right.

The 22nd December was an unfortunate day; for Lieutenant J. E. W. Bath was killed and Lieut.-Colonel Foley was severely wounded. On the same day eight men were gassed, owing it is believed to a leakage in the cylinders from which gas was released by the British at 9 p.m. There was also an extra heavy German bombardment at night, which was renewed next morning. The casualties of the 23rd were five killed and twenty-six wounded or gassed, besides Second-Lieutenant Hughes suffering from shell-shock. That day the battalion went back to Béthune, where Christmas Day was celebrated with plum pudding, cigars, and cigarettes for the men.

On the 27th the 5th Royal Berkshire were at the Rue de l'Epinette near Festubert. The brigade was here on the left of the division and, when the Germans made an attack, " B " Company was sent up to fill a gap in the support line between the right and the left battalions in the old British line between Rue des Cailloux and La Quinque Rue.

This was a particularly miserable part of the line. There was so much water about that regular trenches were out of the question and the defence was a line of island outposts.   Troops in these generally had to be relieved every night, though they sometimes had to do forty-eight hours at a stretch. Gum-boots were supplied for these front companies.   Reliefs were only possible at night, and during the day movement of any sort was out of the question.

THE SOMME. OVILLERS. POSIÈRES. ARRAS

1916

The first notable event of the year was on the 14th January, when there was an attack, at 2 p.m., with three " West spring guns " throwing rifle-grenades.   One of them was put out of action from the first by a German shell which knocked down the parapet and exposed it to fire.

On the 17th, in a similar attack, Second-Lieutenant Digmore Brown was wounded.   The battalion went that night to Béthune, on the 18th moved by train to Lillers, and for the rest of the month was training in back areas.   February was spent half at Lillers, and half at Noyelles, and in March there was nothing more interesting than an inspection by Sir C. Monro, the Army-Commander, on the 18th, when he presented the Military Cross to Lieutenant L. D. Cotterill.

On the last day of March the explosion of a German mine had disastrous effects, as three men were killed and twenty were injured by falling debris from it.

On the 13th April Second-Lieutenant H. M. Cook, on the 14th Second-Lieutenant Mallam were wounded, and on the 20th Second-Lieutenant H. A. Birkby died of wounds.

On the 24th the battalion went into a rest area near Lillers.   In May again there is little to record.   On the 26th the battalion was temporarily attached to the 49th Brigade.   On the 27th it was in billets at Philosophe, with one platoon of " C " Company sent as reinforcement in front of Lens.

On the 29th the battalion relieved the 7th Royal Inniskilling Fusiliers in the Loos sector.

On the 6th June, it was relieved in the 49th Brigade by the 7th Suffolk and was placed under the orders of the C.R.E., 16th Division, for work.

It was back with the 35th Brigade at Lapugny on the 8th.

Preparations were now in active progress for the great Franco-British offensive on the Somme, which eventually began on the 1st July.

On the 16th June the 5th Royal Berkshire, with the rest of the 12th Division, entrained at 9 p.m. at Lillers for the Amiens neighbourhood. It detrained next day at Longueau and marched to Vignacourt, which was reached at 6 p.m.

After ten days here, it marched to Mollien aux Bois on the 27th, and to Franvillers on the 30th.

On the 1st July, when the first great attacks of the Somme Battle were already in full swing, the battalion was on the march from Franvillers to Henencourt Wood with the battle raging far on their right and rear. Extra bandoliers and two bombs each were issued to all ranks, and two hundred entrenching tools to the battalion.

At 5 p.m. a sudden order arrived for the 12th Division to relieve the 8th near Albert, a relief which was not complete till the morning of the 2nd.

On that day the battalion found itself in front-line trenches facing Ovillers la Boisselle, with orders to take the village at dawn next day. Lieut.-Colonel Willan was in command of the battalion, which had " B " and " C " Companies in the front trench, and " A " and " D " in support.

The 12th Division engaged on the 3rd July with the 35th Brigade on the right, the 37th on the left, and the 36th as Divisional reserve.

The frontage allotted to the 5th Royal Berkshire was about one hundred and twenty yards from south to north, from Argyll Street on the extreme right to Vincent Street on the left, touching the 7th Suffolk at the latter. The attack was to be in eight waves on a front of two companies. Each company to attack on a front of one platoon, with thirty-yard intervals between the successive waves. That allowed a frontage of sixty yards for the platoon.

" B " supported by " A " were the right companies, " C " supported by " D " the left. The first objective was the enemy's support trench at the western entrance of the village. The first two waves were to go through to the first objective, the third to stop at Shrapnel Trench, the fourth at the enemy's front line. A defensive flank was to be formed on the right as the advance progressed, and special bombing parties were told off for the defence of that flank.

For ten minutes before zero an intense bombardment was to drive the enemy into his dugouts. From zero the barrage would fall for 30 minutes on a line through Ovillers Church. At zero plus 30 minutes the barrage was to lift again whilst the supporting companies attacked the second-line trenches.

Unfortunately these and further arrangements did not work out.

The artillery arrangements were altered at the last moment. There was a bombardment of an hour before zero (3.15 a.m.) on the German trenches. This drew a heavy fire upon the British line, which caused many casualties whilst the men were waiting, and subsequently as they crossed No-Man's Land.

Before they were observed by the enemy, and before the British guns lifted, the leading companies had crawled through gaps in their own wire and almost reached the German front trenches. There they encountered obstacles in the shape of large shell-holes. All four companies of the 5th Royal Berkshire kept the general direction, except " B," on the right, which went too far to the right. This was rectified before the German trench was entered. This front trench was unoccupied, and it was only after passing it that the leading waves came under serious rifle and machine-gun fire.

After crossing the front trench these waves pushed over the second, and, through some wire, into Shrapnel Trench. Here the enemy were met and a hand-to-hand combat ensued. Many dugouts were bombed, and it became clear that retention of the position was contingent on a plentiful supply of bombs. It was still so dark that it was difficult to distinguish friend from foe, or even to recognize clearly the trenches, which had been knocked out of shape by the British artillery.

Orders were inaudible in the din of the artillery, which had now lifted to the northern outskirts of Ovillers. Some men in the village were either cut off or killed. The German dugouts had not been damaged by the bombardment, and, whilst they were being bombed in one place, the enemy, like rabbits in a warren, would slip along, evidently by underground passages, and appear at other unstopped bolt-holes farther along.

There were many acts of gallantry performed by the bombing parties, but the supply of bombs ran short. The C.O. and adjutant had gone forward to close behind the first wave. They found that about one hundred of the enemy were in the space between the first and second trenches, having apparently been passed over as they lay hidden in dugouts.

Germans were also seen advancing from the left.

There was much confusion in the darkness, and elements of the Suffolk and Essex Battalions were intermingled with the Royal Berkshire.

The greater part of the men fell back to the German front line ; but only one officer (Captain Wace) was with them trying to rally and get them forward again.

The C.O. decided that it was impossible to hold on to the German front trench, which had been almost obliterated, and was exposed to attack in front and on both flanks.

There was no time to consolidate, and to stop there would have meant staying all day unsupported and short of bombs and S.A.A. Already a deadly cross-fire was sweeping No-Man's Land. All the men who had been collected on the German front line were now withdrawn and ordered to dig in on the Albert-Ovillers sunken road, facing south. This road afforded complete protection from the north and was defiladed from the south. Here from eighty to one hundred men remained unmolested the whole day, till they were withdrawn, under Brigade orders, at dusk.

Lieut. and Adjutant C. A. Gold was killed close to Lieut.-Colonel Willan, but his is the only name of an officer mentioned as a casualty. The list gives the numbers as follows :

Officers : Killed 2 ; Died of Wounds 2 ; Wounded 3 ; Missing 7.
Other Ranks : Killed 2 ; Wounded 212 ; Missing 104.
Total : 14 Officers and 318 Other Ranks.

The small number of other ranks killed seems remarkable. From the official list of officers killed it appears that the officers killed or died of wounds were Captain H. Stewart, Captain P. B. Wace, Lieutenant C. A. Gold, and Second-Lieutenant A. E. W. Butler.

When the battalion was sent back to Albert that night, there were only about seventy men left with Colonel Willan. Later, Second-Lieutenants Breach and May turned up with about sixty men who had dug in in No-Man's Land.

On the 6th the battalion relieved the 7th Suffolk in front to the right of the position from which the attack of the 3rd was made. It could only muster about three hundred and forty of all ranks.

On the 7th Ovillers was again attacked in front by the 36th Brigade, and from La Boisselle on the left by the 74th. The 5th Royal Berkshire assisted, as far as they could, with Lewis-gun fire; but, as they only had three wounded, they evidently played no serious part in this attack.

On the 8th the battalion went into billets at Bouzincourt, the rest of the brigade being at Albert. They were training and refitting in back areas till the end of the month, with the exception of a turn in trenches at Auchonvillers, west of Beaumont Hamel, from the 21st to the 26th. They were not in the front line there.

On the 7th August the 35th relieved the 36th Brigade in trenches N.W. of Pozières. The battalion held the trenches known as 3rd, 4th, and 5th Avenues when, on the 8th, the enemy counter-attacked on 5th Avenue.

The first attack was at 3 a.m. with bombs, on the left. The enemy succeeded in getting into the trench at first, but was promptly driven out again.

A second attack, at 7.30 a.m. at the same place, was easily repulsed. Simultaneously with the 3 a.m. attack on the left, a determined attack was made on the barricade in 5th Avenue on the right flank. Using " flammenwerfer " and covered by smoke, the enemy got into the trench here, but was driven out again by hand-to-hand fighting. This attack on the right was renewed at 5.30 a.m., when the Germans succeeded in getting into the trench and driving the defenders along it for about fifty yards. There they were checked and a new barricade was constructed.

The attacks were preceded by a bombardment which wounded Second-Lieutenants H. M. Thurston, A. Budmead and A. S. Shipton.

Second-Lieutenant F. A. L. Edwards was wounded mortally whilst very gallantly conducting the defence on the right flank. Second-Lieutenant G. M. Hughes was wounded and missing,* and Second-Lieutenant H. Crowhurst was wounded by a bomb. No details are given of the 128 casualties in other ranks.

German artillery fire, during an attack by the Anzacs and 7th Suffolk on the right on the 9th August, killed Second-Lieutenant R. A. Bance and

* Afterwards recorded as killed.

wounded Lieutenant C. de V. Hinde, M.C. and Second-Lieutenants A. G. C. Rice and H. C. Toogood. There were thirty-nine casualties (no details given) in other ranks.

When they were relieved in front, on the 10th, the 5th Royal Berkshire spent three days at Ovillers, working and carrying, and then went to Bouzincourt, whence the brigade moved to an area farther north. On the 21st August the battalion marched through Arras to relieve the 6th Lincoln (33rd Brigade) in trenches beyond it.

On the 27th there was a bombardment of the battalion by aerial torpedoes, followed by a small enemy raid which completely failed. On the following night another attempt was made by a party of about thirty Germans who succeeded in cutting two lanes through the wire, but were driven off without being able to reach the trench. The first three weeks of September were passed at Arras, or in the trenches in front. In the night of the 23rd-24th two officers and thirty-six other ranks under Lieutenant A. W. Taylor attempted a raid on the German trenches. The plan was to cut the enemy wire with a 36-foot Bangalore torpedo, so as to let the raiders through. The torpedo was fired, but failed to completely cut the wire. Efforts to cut a way by hand having failed also, the party returned with the loss of only one man wounded.

Another raid was made at the same place on the night of the 25th-26th. The partial gap made by the torpedo in the recent attack had been kept open and a second torpedo now destroyed the rest of the wire. The party broke through, only to find themselves in a crater beyond which was the enemy's parapet surmounted by wire. Finding no signs of the enemy in the crater, the raiders lay up there, hoping to catch a patrol. When the wire had first been passed it was believed that the near lip of the crater was the enemy parapet, whereas the whole width of the crater really lay between this supposed parapet and the real parapet beyond it. Eventually, the party was fired on and compelled to withdraw. Second-Lieutenant A. W. Taylor, who had led it with great gallantry, was killed, besides four other ranks killed and four missing. Second-Lieutenant Cobb, the other officer with the raid, had fired the torpedo on both occasions and given much assistance. When the retirement was made on the second occasion, he made a gallant but unsuccessful attempt to bring in Taylor's body.

On the last day of September the brigade began to leave Arras, and returned by stages to the southern area, reaching Bernafay Wood, E. of Montauban, on the 2nd of October.

Here the 35th Brigade was in Divisional reserve a long way behind the front line acquired by the Battle of the Somme. It was still in reserve during the unsuccessful attack by the 36th and 37th Brigades on Bayonet Trench on the 7th.

On the 8th October the 5th Royal Berkshire was temporarily attached to the 36th Brigade, and moved by Longueval to take over Flers trenches from the 9th Royal Fusiliers. On the 12th there was a fresh attack on Bayonet Trench, and the 5th Royal Berkshire were ordered, at 8.30 p.m., to support the 9th Essex.

From the casualty list of the day (two killed and six wounded) it is clear they were not very seriously engaged on this day. Next day they had Second-Lieutenant R. Cobb and C.-S.-M. T. Perkins killed by a shell. On the 17th the 9th Essex were again attacking Bayonet Trench at 3.40 a.m., and, as they advanced, the 5th Royal Berkshire were to take over their trenches.

Here again the battalion was not seriously engaged, as the attack failed.

The 88th Brigade on the right had been more successful in getting forward, and yet another attack on Bayonet Trench was ordered to be made, at 3 a.m. on the 18th, by one company Royal Berkshire from the right and one of the 7th Royal Sussex (attached for this operation) from the left. Each attacking company was to be preceded by bombs. The enemy, however, put down such a heavy barrage on the area, and the situation was so unfavourably reported on by patrols, that even the bombers never started. Nevertheless, the battalion suffered losses of Second-Lieutenant H. K. May wounded ; other ranks 3 killed, 22 wounded, and 3 missing—a curiously long list for an attack which never started !

Again, on the 19th, when the battalion was relieved and went back to its own brigade at Mametz Wood, the losses were large. Probably they occurred during the relief. They were, in other ranks, 9 killed, 23 wounded and 2 missing.

Once more the brigade returned, in the last days of October, to its old position in and east of Arras, where it spent the rest of 1916 without anything out of the usual winter routine of trench warfare.

The last ten days were in rest area.

ARRAS. CAMBRAI. BÉTHUNE

1917

January and February 1917 show nothing to be recorded.

January was all spent in rest area, where work was relieved by a good amount of sports, football, and other diversions.

During the second half of February Lieut.-Colonel Willan held temporary command of the 35th Brigade, but returned to the battalion at Arras on the 3rd March.

From the 9th March ten officers and two hundred and twenty men were under special training for a projected raid which took place on the 17th.

It was carried out at 7 a.m. on that day by nine officers and two hundred men under the orders of Major Sharp, with Lieutenant W. C. Adams as his second-in-command.

The raiders were divided into six sections, one each for the right, centre, and left fronts, each of them being supported by one of the other three. The sections were commanded by Lieutenants G. G. Debono, J. H. Ready ; Second-Lieutenants H. B. Beattie, L. P. Bartlett, B. H. A. Fellowes, T. Rowell, and A. Hanbury.

Three good gaps had been cut in the enemy wire and the right section alone had to use a Bangalore torpedo. All reached the German trench, their objective. The left party was held up for a short time by a machine gun, but that was put out of action by the centre section. Very little opposition was met with before reaching, or in, the trench where all the Germans in the sector were taken or killed.

All the dugouts were destroyed with Stokes bombs. At 25 minutes after zero the raiders were ready to return home. So far their losses had only been Second-Lieutenant Fellowes, wounded in going over, and one man wounded close to the German trench. But it was a different matter returning through the barrage put down by the enemy. Here the casualties were much heavier. Major J. S. Sharp was killed by a shell when only ten yards from home. The other casualties (all but two in the retirement) were Second-Lieutenant B. H. A. Fellowes wounded, and of other ranks one believed killed, twenty-eight wounded, and one missing.

The results of the raid were two machine-guns and six prisoners captured, and about one hundred and twenty Germans killed. On the whole, the raid was very successful, and well merited the congratulations received from Divisional and Corps-Commanders.

A period of training and preparation for the forthcoming Battle of Arras followed, and on the 6th April the battalion was again at Arras, with two days to wait for the battle to begin.

In this attack by the 3rd Army the objective of the VIth Corps was Monchy le Preux, and that of the 12th Division, as part of it, was the capture in succession of three lines east of Arras known as the black, blue, and brown. The first phases of the battle were to be the capture of the black line by the 37th Brigade, and that of the blue line by the 36th Brigade passing through the 37th on the black line. During these two phases the 35th Brigade was to be in Divisional reserve.

In the third phase the 35th Brigade would pass through the 36th and 37th, the 5th Royal Berkshire on the left, advancing south of Houdain Lane into Battery Valley, whilst the 7th Norfolk, on the right, took Maison Rouge.

There the battalions in support would pass, the 9th Essex through the Royal Berkshire, and the 7th Suffolk through the 7th Norfolk, to the capture of the brown line.

In this the 5th Royal Berkshire would act as support to the 9th Essex.

The 12th Division was between the 3rd on its right, and the 15th on the left. Zero was to be at 5.30 a.m. On the day preceding the battle, the 5th Royal Berkshire were quartered in the vast cellars and underground passages which honeycomb the ground under Arras. From these they started at 4.45 a.m. on the 9th April and entered the great sewer at the Porte de Fer half an hour later. Emerging from it in what was known as the Broad Walk at 7.15, they were in position at 8 a.m., with " B " on the right, and " A " on the left in the Reserve and Duplicate Reserve lines. " D " on the right and " C " on the left were in support in the Broad Walk.

At 10.30 a.m. orders were received to advance to a position in rear of the blue line. The movement was made in lines of platoons in single file. On the right " B," followed by " D "—on the left " A " plus one platoon of " C," followed by " C " less one platoon.

The advance was unopposed at first.   Then " B " came under machine-gun fire from a German work on its right (Heron Work).   The advance was delayed for three-quarters of an hour whilst the situation in this direction was being cleared up.

It was resumed at 11.45, one platoon of " B " having worked round the German work and captured its garrison of thirty-five officers and men with one machine gun.

Houdain Lane was reached with slight opposition and few casualties.

At 12.45 p.m. the two leading companies extended and passed over the ridge into Battery Valley.   Here they had four enemy batteries firing point-blank on them at a range of two hundred yards.   By means of concentrated rifle fire, combined with short rushes, all these batteries, and two more isolated guns were captured.   One battery consisted of four 4·2″ howitzers, the other guns being 77 m.m. field guns.   With them about forty prisoners were taken.

It was 2.30 p.m. when the Royal Berkshire reached the assembly positions for the attack on the brown line.   The delay caused by Heron Work in the early part of the advance had been unfortunate, for the battalion was now too late to take advantage of the barrage on the brown line.   As it advanced it was met by such heavy rifle and machine-gun fire that it was soon apparent that a frontal attack could not be carried through, especially as it was reported that the troops on both flanks had failed to gain the brown line.

It was not till 7.30 p.m. that information was received that the 15th Division, on the left, had taken the line, and a tank was seen moving down from the north.   An attack in co-operation with this tank was proposed, but not considered feasible.

At this time there arrived, as reinforcements to act under the orders of the O.C. 5th Royal Berkshire, three companies each of the 11th Middlesex and the 7th Royal Sussex.

An hour later orders were received that no further advance was to be made that night, but that the Royal Berkshire and the six reinforcing companies would move next day through the part of the brown line captured by the 15th Division, and descend from the north on Orange Hill. Simultaneously, the 7th Suffolk, with two extra companies attached, would attack the brown line south of the Cambrai Road.

At noon on the 10th April the British barrage lifted off the brown line. By 12.45 the line had been taken on the whole front of the 12th Division, and the Royal Berkshire had outposts on the farther slope of Orange Hill.

These were withdrawn when, a quarter of an hour later, the 37th Division passed through the 12th to attack Monchy le Preux. The battalion then re-formed in Chapel Wood. On the 11th the brigade was ordered back to dugouts in rear, but almost immediately the 12th Division was again sent forward to relieve the 37th.

The 35th Brigade was placed in Divisional reserve about Chapel Wood, and the 5th Royal Berkshire occupied two strong points on Orange Hill.

On the 12th the division was relieved and returned to Arras.

The Berkshire casualties in the operations from the 9th to the 13th April were :

Officers. *Killed :* 2nd-Lieuts. K. C. B. Storey, L. P. Bartlett.
        Wounded : Capts. H. C. Horsford, H. Wykes.
                2nd-Lieuts. A. H. Hamel Smith, L. G. Howard.
Other Ranks : Killed 5 ; Wounded 92.

After this the battalion was at various places in rear of Arras till, on the 24th, it was moved to Arras from Gouy by 'bus.

On the 25th the brigade marched by the railway to near Feuchy, and at 8.30 p.m. relieved part of the 17th Division in the line. It occupied a front with its left on the Scarpe and right on the sunken road running east from Monchy le Preux. The 7th Norfolk Regiment was on the right of the brigade front, with the 5th Royal Berkshire on the left near the Scarpe.

This line was much shelled on the 26th and 27th, but casualties were not heavy.

Orders were issued on the latter day for the capture of Bayonet Trench (which had so far defied all efforts), and that part of Rifle Trench which was still in the enemy's possession. Outposts were to be pushed in advance when these objectives were attained. The attack was to be with the 7th Norfolk on the right, the 5th Royal Berkshire on the left. When the first objectives should be taken, the 7th Suffolk were to pass through to the second, the Essex acting as Brigade reserve.

The Royal Berkshire advanced at 4.25 a.m. on a three-company front—
" C " on the right, " D " centre and " A " left, with " B " in reserve.

The companies, close behind the barrage, captured the first objectives in
Bayonet and the left of Rifle Trench without difficulty, and started to
consolidate them.

The 7th Norfolk on the right had been less successful, and the 7th
Suffolk, going through the Royal Berkshire at 50 minutes after zero, were
unable to get forward against the machine-gun fire meeting them.

The Royal Berkshire now held Bayonet Trench and Rifle Trench as far
as a block which had been made. Beyond that the Germans were still in
Rifle Trench as far as Harness Lane. The 7th Norfolk and 7th Suffolk were
still in their original positions. One company of the Essex was attached
to the Royal Berkshire as a reinforcement. These positions were maintained during the 29th and 30th, despite a rain of enemy shells. The
proximity of the Germans in Scabbard Trench prohibited attempts to bomb
them out of the right of Rifle Trench.

On the 1st May the 9th Essex attacked the enemy portion of Rifle Trench,
but failed to take it.

That night, on relief of the 35th Brigade, the Royal Berkshire went back
to Railway Triangle, between Arras and Feuchy.

Their casualties in the period 25th April to 1st May had been :

Officers. Killed : 2nd-Lieut. J. C. Orr.
              Wounded : Major D. H. Avory.
                              2nd-Lieuts. A. J. Jones, E. A. Sutton, E. Beale.
Other Ranks : Killed 31 ; Wounded 143 ; Missing 22.

On the 3rd May the battalion again went forward to the brown line to act
as support to the 36th and 37th Brigades attacking N.E. of Feuchy, in
conjunction with the divisions on the right and left. Though the battalion
had orders to support the 37th Brigade on the right, no further orders or
news were received, and it was not engaged on this or the two following days.
On the 6th the 35th Brigade relieved the 37th N.E. of Monchy in the line
which had now been straightened out south of the Scarpe, though there was
still a salient E. of Monchy. When they were relieved here they spent the
rest of May and the whole of June in Arras or other places in the rear, with
the usual turns in the brown line, or in the front. This continued till the

19th July, on which day the battalion had just relieved the 9th Essex in the front east of Monchy le Preux, in the neighbourhood of Infantry Lane leading to Boisy Notre Dame.

At 3 p.m. on this day a small attack was carried out by " D " Company, with the object of joining up certain trenches in front. A barrage was put down for ten minutes on the rear of the objective (Long Trench). Then the first wave, of two platoons on a front of two hundred and forty yards, went forward lightly equipped, the second wave following with entrenching tools. The space to be crossed was about one hundred and twenty yards, and it had been assumed that the enemy trench was only lightly held. The assumption was not justified ; for the assailants were met by a shower of bombs and a most obstinate resistance. Some of them got into the trench and remained there about a quarter of an hour, but, finding themselves greatly out-numbered and their bombs exhausted, they were compelled to retire. They were back by 3.30, but had suffered considerable casualties—Second-Lieu-tenants A. Hanbury and B. Lyons were missing, believed killed.

Of other ranks 3 were killed, 24 wounded, and 14 missing.

Owing to the disclosure of the great strength of the enemy here, the Divisional Commander decided on a defensive policy. The battalion was ordered to concentrate on wiring Hook and Hill Trenches, the linking up of which had been the object of the attack. This was carried out in the ensuing nights under great difficulties. The successful accomplishment of the task elicited congratulations from the Brigadier.

On the 21st July Lieut.-Colonel F. G. Willan was recalled to the command of his own battalion, the 2nd King's Royal Rifle Corps. He had commanded the 5th Royal Berkshire with conspicuous success for seventeen months in the field.

He was succeeded by Major T. V. Bartley-Denniss, with Captain J. L. Carr as second-in-command.

The battalion was relieved, on the 24th, by the 7th East Surrey and went into billets at Achicourt. They were again in front line on the 4th August, this time just north of the Cambrai Road.

On the 8th August command of the battalion was assumed by Lieut.-Colonel E. H. J. Nicolls of the East Surrey Regiment, during Major Bartley-Denniss' detention in hospital. Next day there was a great deal of raiding on the front of the division, in which however the battalion does not appear to have taken a hand.   Lieutenant F. J. Okey was wounded on the 11th.

The same routine continued through the rest of August, September, October, and the first half of November.   Lieut.-Colonel Bartley-Denniss returned to the command from hospital on the 14th October, and on the same day Lieutenant M. B. Beattie died of wounds, received on patrol.

On the 5th November the battalion, then at Rougefay, was ordered to move next day by rail to Péronne.   Arriving there at 3 p.m. on the 16th, it marched at 8 p.m. to Haut Allaines.

On the 18th it was at Sorel le Grand, and on the 19th at Peizières, ready for the great attack by General Byng towards Cambrai, which had been prepared, with the utmost precautions as to secrecy, for the 20th.

Here the 12th Division was the right of the IIIrd Corps, opposite which the enemy was believed to have only a weak force of fifteen battalions.   The great attack was not to be heralded by a long preliminary bombardment like that before the Somme ; there was to be practically no wire cutting by artillery ; surprise, and the rolling out of wire by tanks were the main ideas of the offensive.

The 12th Division was to attack up to the objective called the blue line on a two-brigade front—35th Brigade on the right, 36th on the left.

There was an intermediate objective, described as the black line, between the starting point and the blue line.   When the first waves of the leading brigades had reached this, the second waves would pass through to the blue line.

From the blue line the advance would be continued by the 36th and 37th Brigades moving on the farther brown line, under cover of a smoke barrage laid down during a pause on the blue line.   Co-operation of infantry and tanks was all important.   By 3 a.m. on the 20th, the 5th Royal Berkshire Battalion had moved N.E. to Villers Guislain with the tanks assigned to it, and one section of machine guns and two trench-mortar guns.   They formed up behind the tanks ten hundred yards behind the front line.   Lieut.-Colonel Nicolls, M.C., was in command of the battalion.

The British opened the attack with a tremendous barrage at zero (6.20 a.m.).   Ten minutes later the tanks started, moving only at the rate of about fifty yards per minute.   It was not till two minutes later that the German barrage opened, and then it was weak and directed on areas selected before-hand which were quickly recognized and avoided by the British infantry. The machine-gun barrage was more destructive, and " C " Company on the right suffered heavily from it.   Of the three tanks assigned to " D " two broke down, as well as three out of the four in front of " B."   The companies were disposed in line from right to left in the order " C," " B," " A," " D."

They followed closely in rear of the tanks, which, however, bore too much to the right, thereby causing a certain amount of change of objectives.

Forty-five minutes after zero the tanks were in the German front line, which was only lightly held.   The main resistance was encountered in the support trenches of the Hindenburg Line.   Here there was a very stiff fight.

By 7.45 a.m., when Battalion Head-quarters had moved up to the first objective, the disposition of the 5th Royal Berkshire was as follows :

" D " occupied the enemy's support line from the brigade boundary on the left, with " A " on the right holding Quarry support.   " B " was estab-lished in Adams and Quarry Trenches.   " C " had reached the final objective with only thirty men divided into two parties of fourteen each, under Sergeants Stokes and Seymour.   Stokes' party had pushed forward with great dash along Quarry Trench, as far as the communication trench leading to Quarry Post.   Here they established a bombing post, which was eventu-ally withdrawn to a crater on the Banteux Road.   Sergeant Seymour's party established a strong point at the junction of Quarry support with the communication trench leading to Quarry Post.   All the battalion's objectives had thus been attained, and by 1 p.m. news came in that the 12th Division had reached all its objectives.   In this attack the battalion had captured about sixty prisoners, two machine guns, one heavy, two medium, and three light trench-mortars.

Before nightfall the whole new position was consolidated, and a defensive flank on the right had been established, covering the Banteux Valley and the St. Quentin Canal.   The battalion had gone into action with seventeen officers and five hundred and ninety other ranks, and had lost

Officers.   Killed :   2nd-Lieut. H. K. De Vries.
Died of Wounds :   2nd-Lieut. T. P. Nickett.
Wounded :   Major J. L. Carr ;   Capt. W. C. Adams.
2nd-Lieuts. T. S. Tester, J. T. Ross.

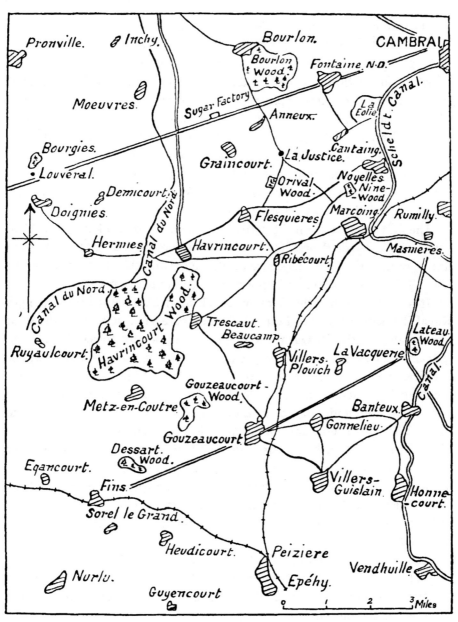

CAMBRAI.

229

Other Ranks : Killed 24 ; Wounded 121 ; Missing 16.
Total : 6 Officers and 161 Other Ranks.

The 21st and 22nd November were employed in completing consolidation.

At 8 a.m. on the 24th the battalion, in conjunction with the 7th Suffolk on the left, was ordered to capture and consolidate Quarry Post and join it up with the line on the right and left. " D," led by Captain J. R. West, took all its objectives without any loss, a feat on which congratulations were received from the Brigade and Division Commanders.

The days from the 25th to the 29th were quiet, with no casualties. The Germans were preparing their counter-attack which opened on the morning of the 30th with a heavy barrage at 7 a.m.

The first attack was on the 55th Division on the right of the 12th. The 35th Brigade was on the right of the 12th Division and the battalions in front line were the 5th Royal Berkshire on the right, and the 7th Norfolk on the left. The 9th Essex were in support, the 7th Suffolk in reserve.

It was at 7.30 that the German attack in great force fell upon the 5th Royal Berkshire at Quarry Post, where they were so far back from the slope of the valley of the St. Quentin Canal as not to be able to see the German concentration in it. From Quarry Post the battalion was forced back by the overwhelming attack some two hundred yards to Adam Trench. A fierce bombing fight ensued in which the Royal Berkshire succeeded in getting back the lost ground, but, being short of bombs, were again driven back to Adam Trench. The enemy had gained their first success by the aid of a heavy barrage of trench-mortars, and a flank attack from the south up New Trench. The battalion was still holding on at Adam Trench at 9.30 a.m., but both its flanks had been turned by the driving back of the troops of the 55th Division on the right, and of the 12th on their left. The Germans had reached Gonnelieu on the right rear, and Newton Post nearer on the same side.

The battalion was now gradually withdrawn to Bleak Trench and Bleak support trenches north of Newton Post. It was still short of bombs.

Battalion Head-quarters had moved northwards about five hundred yards along the old German line.

The enemy, who had broken through the 7th Norfolk on the left, were held up by the 9th Essex.

At 10.45 orders were received to withdraw fighting towards Villers Plouich. The enemy was supported by low-flying aeroplanes, and by noon was in possession of Villers Guislain, Gonnelieu, and Gouzeaucourt. The 9th Essex also retired by La Vacquerie. The enemy pressure was severe till the Cambrai Road had been passed, when a new position was taken up on Cemetery Ridge and in La Vacquerie. Immediately north of the latter place the 5th Royal Berkshire and the 9th Essex lined a sunken road, but found themselves out of touch with any British troops on either flank. They were then ordered to man the old British line (held before the first phase of the Battle of Cambrai) in front of Villers Plouich.

The withdrawal to this position was completed by 3.30 p.m., when " A " Company, under Captain J. M. Ready, M.C., was dug in on the right flank of the Royal Berkshire facing Gonnelieu. The remainder of the 35th Brigade, now only about three hundred strong, was holding the old British line in front, with a defensive flank west of the Cambrai Road. Here the retirement ceased for the night.

At 4.30 a.m. on the 1st December the battalion was expecting a fresh attack at dawn. But the barrage did not commence till 9.30 a.m., after which a German attack was repulsed by the Guards. There was no fighting for the 5th Royal Berkshire, and they passed the rest of the day quietly. They had now attached themselves to the 20th Division, which had been on the left of the 12th on the previous day, and had likewise been forced back. The 20th Division was relieved in the evening of the 1st December by the 61st. The 12th Division was all collected in positions assigned to it by 4 a.m. on the 2nd December. A fresh German attack was expected, but did not come off. That evening the battalion, with the rest of the 35th Brigade, now commanded by Colonel Nicolls, was withdrawn to Hendecourt.

The casualties of the 5th Royal Berkshire in the fighting from the 30th November to the 2nd December were :

Officers. *Killed :* 2nd-Lieuts. E. A. I. Wykes, F. K. Judd.
   Wounded : Lieut. H. K. Hay ; 2nd-Lieut. C. N. Adcock.
   Missing : Lieut. F. C. R. Hill ;
     2nd-Lieuts. H. Schofield, E. Jones.
Other Ranks (approximately) : Killed 55 ; Wounded 120 ; Missing 120.

The remains of the battalion were reorganized on the 3rd December in two companies, viz. " D," and a composite company made up of what was left of " A," " B," and " C." The total strength was 16 officers and 341 other ranks.

After its rough handling in the second part of the Battle of Cambrai, the battalion required a good rest out of line, and by the 8th December was at Aveluy, north of Albert, whence it moved by rail northwards to the Béthune area, where, on the 11th, it was reinforced by several officers from the 4th (Reserve) Battalion.

From the 21st December to the end of 1917 it was at Merville.

AVELUY. THE GERMAN OFFENSIVE. BEAUMONT HAMEL. THE FINAL ADVANCE BY EPÉHY. THE RETURN HOME

1918–1919

The early days of 1918 call for little regarding the 5th Royal Berkshire.

On the 5th January there was a distribution of awards for the Battles of Cambrai—the D.S.O. for Lieut.-Colonel Nicolls and Capt. Ready ; the M.C. for Capt. J. R. West, Capt. C. A. Mallam, Lieut. H. K. Hay, and Honry. Lieut.-and-Quartermaster J. R. Oxley, and several other decorations. At the end of the month and the beginning of February the battalion was in Brigade reserve behind Fleurbaix.

It was at this period that brigades were being reduced from four to three battalions, and the 12th Division, from the 6th February, was to consist of three brigades of three battalions. In the rearrangements consequent on this the 5th Royal Berkshire were transferred from the 35th to the 36th Brigade, comprising, besides them, the 9th Royal Fusiliers and the 7th Royal Sussex. They passed into their new brigade at Fleurbaix on the 6th February, and remained in that neighbourhood doing nothing requiring record till the breaking of the storm of the German offensive on the front of the 5th Army, on the 21st March, necessitated their moving rapidly southwards.

The night of the 24th-25th was spent in omnibuses travelling from Rely to Warloy, west of Albert.

At 1 p.m. they marched, from the field in which they had halted at Warloy, to Millencourt, and were informed that they were to be in the vanguard of the brigade marching at 5.30 p.m. to Montauban viâ Mametz. When they reached Albert they received orders to march through Carnoy and Mametz to Montauban. At Fricourt they were halted from 11 p.m. to 3.30 a.m., as orders were again to be changed. The cold was so great that the men had to walk about to keep warm. Then they were marched back to Brigade reserve at Martinsart, where they held the railway embankment west of Aveluy Wood.

The whole day of the 26th was spent in reconnoitring positions east and south of Martinsart, and siting trenches.

At 12.30 a.m. on the 27th an attack appeared to be developing from the north from Mesnil. One platoon was sent out to cover the Mesnil Road. The rest stood to arms, and at 2 a.m. two companies were sent to help the 37th Brigade which was being attacked. Germans were now seen marching in a column of fours by the Mesnil-Martinsart Road. The platoon on the road let them come within two hundred yards before opening on them with rifles and Lewis guns. Several were seen to fall, and the rest hastily deployed on either side of the road.

At this moment there arrived on the scene a battalion of the 63rd (Naval) Division which chased the Germans back towards Mesnil.

At 3 a.m. one of the two companies supporting the 37th Brigade was sent through Aveluy Wood to mop up any Germans in it, and generally clear up the situation. They met none of the enemy. At 11 a.m., as a heavy barrage was seen to be falling on Aveluy Ridge, the battalion stood to, the two right companies occupying battle positions S.E. of Martinsart. The 35th Brigade was reported to be counter-attacking.

At noon the right battalion of the 36th Brigade was attacked. The two Berkshire Companies S.E. of Martinsart were reinforced by the other two, and the O.C. 5th Royal Berkshire decided not to return to Martinsart. Between 3 and 4 p.m. the battalion was ordered to face south, as an attack was expected from that direction. " A " Company was sent forward to clear up the situation in a gap between the 9th Royal Fusiliers and the 7th Royal Sussex. It advanced till held up by machine-gun fire from the direction of Aveluy, in front of which the enemy now was. The company commander was killed, and there were a score of other casualties in the company.

The battalion commander now placed the other companies with " D " on the right front in touch with the Northamptonshire Pioneers, " C " on the left, and " B " in reserve in Martinsart Wood south of the village.

At 5 p.m. came a strong attack from the direction of Aveluy, which forced the left battalion of the brigade to retire, " A " Company conforming to its movement. Two platoons of " C," on the left, being outflanked, also had to fall back, whilst the other two platoons and " D " held on and inflicted severe losses on the enemy by their fire on his flank.

The retirement ceased on the line of the ridge one hundred or two hundred yards S. of Martinsart, where a strong line was formed and dug in.

After dark strong patrols were sent out to reconnoitre, and by 9 p.m. the position occupied before the retirement had been re-established.

The O.C. 5th Royal Berkshire now, after consulting the O.C. 9th Royal Fusiliers, posted his battalion thus :

The right company was in touch with the left of the Northamptonshire Pioneers and the right of the left company, which in turn joined up with the right of the 9th Royal Fusiliers. The other two companies were in support in Martinsart.

At 9 a.m. on the 28th the left company reported an attack in force from Aveluy, with the enemy massing in the sunken roads. The British artillery, being warned of this, put down a heavy barrage on Aveluy Ridge, and the enemy were met by the fire of both the Royal Berkshire front companies. By 10 a.m. the attack had been repulsed, and the enemy were seen carrying back their wounded over Aveluy Ridge. The artillery duel lasted till half an hour after noon. In this fight " C " Company lost its commander and about twenty others.

Immediately after dark strong patrols went out to clear up the situation. All of them reported the enemy north of Aveluy Ridge, but one patrol, of a N.C.O. and eight men, managed after a short fight to establish a post on the Aveluy-Bouzincourt Road.

In the early hours of the 29th the two front companies of the 5th Royal Berkshire were relieved by the 6th Royal West Kent, and the battalion went into Brigade reserve, with two companies in Martinsart and two in the defences west of it.

At 8 a.m. the battalion was moved to a position N.E. of Martinsart, where, at 7 p.m., it stood to on account of patrol encounters with the enemy. The disposition of the battalion during this day was, two companies in an orchard ready to man the line towards Mesnil, one in the defences N.E. of Martinsart, and one in support.

At 12.30 a.m. on the 30th March the battalion was relieved by the 23rd London and sent back to Warloy, where it arrived between 3 and 4 a.m.

The losses of the 5th Royal Berkshire in these days had been :

Officers. *Killed :* 2nd-Lieut. J. H. Mathews.
    Died of Wounds : Capt. G. G. Paine, M.C.
    Wounded : Capt. E. H. Lloyd, Lieut. J. S. Noble.
Other Ranks : Killed 10 ; Wounded 65.

On the 2nd April the Royal Berkshire, from Warloy, took over front-line trenches in front of Albert from the 7th Border Regiment.

The 3rd was a quiet day, but the German shelling increased on the 4th and Captain L. Fenton was wounded. At 4 a.m. on the 5th warning was received of an impending attack, and at 7 a.m. the enemy put down a barrage on the front-line trenches, and on the British batteries about Bouzincourt.

The attack commenced in the south behind an intense barrage working up from that direction. By 9.30 the artillery fire of every description was tremendous on the whole British system. Infantry attacks were launched on the whole length of the 36th Brigade front, but were everywhere repulsed. The enemy, advancing in close formation, made three several attacks on the left and centre companies of the 5th Royal Berkshire, but each was repulsed with the assistance of the 9th Royal Fusiliers on the left.

By 10 a.m. the situation was normal, but at noon the barrage again opened, and the attacking German infantry succeeded in entering the trenches held by the left and centre companies of the Royal Berkshire. The right company and one platoon of " D " held firm.

At 2.30 p.m. the C.O. sent up the three reserve platoons of " D " to restore the situation.

As they advanced up a slope, they were exposed to intense machine-gun fire, from which they lost 50 per cent. of their numbers, including Captain J. R. West and Lieutenant A. C. Punnett. When they had reached the line of the support trench they dug in.

The front of the 9th Royal Fusiliers, on the left, was still intact, and the

C.O. of that battalion reported that he was gradually regaining the trench lost by the left Berkshire company. By 6 p.m. he had extended his right by three hundred yards, which still left a gap of six hundred yards from which the enemy had not been ejected.

Colonel Nicolls now decided to counter-attack, with the help of two companies of the 7th Royal Sussex placed at his disposal. The counter-attack was delivered behind a barrage at 8.15 p.m., but was only partially successful, owing to machine-gun fire on a ridge which had to be crossed.

At 4 a.m. on the 6th the other two companies took over from the 9th Royal Fusiliers the reconquered part of the left of the Berkshire trench, and also relieved the right company. There were very few survivors of the left and centre companies, and the remains of the battalion had to be reorganized in two companies.

One, about one hundred strong, composed of " A " and " B," was placed at the disposal of the O.C. 9th Royal Fusiliers ; the other, ninety strong of " C " and " D," was made over to the 7th Royal Sussex.

The 6th was quiet till 5.30 p.m. when the outposts of the 35th Brigade were driven in by a barrage and an infantry attack. At 11 p.m. the 37th Brigade took the place of the 36th, and the 5th Royal Berkshire was attached to the 35th Brigade. Its trench strength was then two hundred and thirty-one.

The casualties in these early days of April were :

Officers. (*Killed :* none.)
>> *Wounded :* Capts. L. Fenton, D. E. Ward, M.C., J. R. West, M.C.
>> Lieut. A. C. Punnett.
>> 2nd-Lieuts. C. A. Nott, H. S. Handley, J. F. M. Shedell.
> *Missing :* 2nd-Lieuts. H. E. Palmer, A. Waite, W. Barker, B. Miles, C. Wilmshurst.
Other Ranks : Killed 243 ; Wounded, and Missing (no details given).

The battalion was returned to the 36th Brigade on the 7th April, and for the next fortnight was recuperating in rear.

On the 23rd it was again in front line in the Beaumont Hamel sector, in relief of a New Zealand Brigade.

In the night of the 29th-30th an enemy raid on the right of the Royal Berkshire was driven off, one dead German being left behind.

On the 1st May the 12th Division was rearranged on a three-brigade front, 36th on the right, 37th centre, 35th left. Each had one battalion in front, one in support, and one in reserve at Acheux. The 5th Royal Berkshire was at first in the support line of the 36th Brigade.

In the night of the 11-12th, when the battalion was in front line, an enemy patrol got into the trench, but was very roughly handled there and driven out, leaving one wounded officer behind. For their conduct on this occasion Sergeant Varney received the D.C.M. and Private Bushell the M.M. Both of them proceeded, after the repulse of the enemy, into No-Man's Land and brought back a wounded German officer, whose capture was useful for identification. Varney had led the bombers who ejected the Germans from the trench.

On the 24th an important raid was carried out. Assembly posts were beyond what was known as the purple line. The battalion was divided into a right ("A" and "B" Companies) and a left ("C" and "D") column. The leading company of each was to go as far forward as the German front trench. The rear company would then leap-frog it and get as far as the Amiens-Arras railway.

The advance progressed satisfactorily for the first stage, and then the left supporting company passed through, but only with a weak party.

On the right the supporting company, with a number of men of the Anson Battalion, lost direction, and never succeeded in getting beyond the German front line.

An enemy barrage on No-Man's Land two minutes after zero caused heavy losses and more or less disorganized the raiders early in the attack.

On the whole, however, the raid was very successful. It resulted in the capture by the battalion of twenty-four prisoners and six machine guns. Some of the prisoners appear to have escaped after passing the advanced collecting station. There were originally twenty-four, but only ten were eventually counted at Battalion Head-quarters. It was estimated that fifty casualties had been inflicted on the enemy.

The losses in this raid were unduly heavy, and the Battalion Diary attributes the comparative failure to want of training for the young recruits who now formed so large a proportion of the men.

Officers. Wounded : 2nd-Lieuts. T. H. Eayrs, D. H. Betts, T. A. Baird, M.C., E. G. Joseph.

Other Ranks : Killed 12 ; Died of Wounds 2 ; Wounded 73 ; Missing 19.

The captures of the battalion were twenty-one prisoners and six machine guns.

On the 25th May the battalion moved by 'bus to Beauquesne, and remained there till the 17th June, when it marched into front line in the Bouzincourt sector. There it spent the rest of the month working on trenches, etc. On the 24th Second-Lieutenant L. G. Howard was lost when out on patrol.

There was a bad epidemic of influenza at the end of the month.

There is nothing special to record after this till the battalion moved to Vignacourt on the 30th June, its trench strength then being seven hundred and nineteen.

On the 1st August the 12th Division relieved the 58th in the Dernancourt sector, south of Albert.

Sir H. Rawlinson's new offensive in conjunction with the IIIrd Army was timed to commence on the 8th August. On his extreme left the 18th Division was to operate along the ridge on the north bank of the Somme by the Corbie-Bray Road. But a German attack on the 6th had hit the 54th Brigade of the 18th Division so heavily, that it had to be replaced on the 8th by the 36th Brigade, lent for the purpose by the 12th to the 18th Division. On the 7th, the 36th Brigade was placed under the orders of the 53rd for the operations commencing next day. The function of the 36th Brigade on that day was the defence of the left flank of the 53rd as it advanced. The attack had been six hours in progress when, at 10.30 a.m., the brigade was called up to form a defensive flank for the 53rd.

Two companies (" C " and " D ") of the 5th Royal Berkshire moved off under Captain A. G. Revill in artillery formation at 11.15. The fighting on this day appears to have fallen to the lot of the other two battalions of the brigade, and the Royal Berkshire diary mentions no casualties.

It consolidated the road constituting the second objective with two companies in front.   It was relieved at 7 p.m. by the 7th Royal Sussex.

On the 9th again it seems to have been confined to forming a defensive flank facing south for the 175th Brigade of the 54th Division, to which it was attached, in case the troops on the right should fail.

On the 10th again there is no record of fighting, and the battalion only took over the trenches taken by the 9th Essex on the right.

On the 12th the battalion went into Brigade reserve, returning to the front from the 14th to the 16th, a quiet period.   After three days in rear from the 17th to the 20th, the 5th Royal Berkshire again went into line north of Morlancourt on the 21st in preparation for an attack in conjunction with the 6th Northamptonshire Regiment (18th Division) on the left.   That night forming up was much hampered by a gas-shell bombardment, and Lieutenant Engelbach was wounded.

At 4.55 a.m. on the 22nd the British barrage opened and the battalion advanced to the attack with " A," " B," and " C " Companies, " D " being in reserve.   With it and the 9th Royal Fusiliers went three tanks, and the advance was covered by a creeping barrage.   The objective of the 5th Royal Berkshire was the village of Méaulte.   Here they were assisted by the tanks, one of them moving up and down the main street, and the other two on either side of the village.   The village was successfully cleared and a position was consolidated.   The casualties were :

Officers.   Wounded : Capt. J. N. Gregory, M.C.
                          Lieut. E. A. Engelbach ; 2nd-Lieuts. L. Chapman,
                          S. M. Eccles, C. A. Farebrother, L. C. Oakes.
Other Ranks : Killed 3 ; Wounded 72.

At 4.45 p.m. on the 24th August the battalion again attacked, with the object of gaining touch with the 18th Division beyond Bécordel.   Two attacks earlier had failed.   The 5th Royal Berkshire, advancing under a good barrage to the left of the village, outflanked the German position, which was evacuated and occupied by the 37th Brigade.

On the 26th the battalion had orders to attack between 4 and 4.30 a.m. to the east of Carnoy.   It marched at 3.30 a.m., by compass, but only reached its forming-up position at 4.45 when the barrage had ceased.   The attack was made on both sides of Carnoy, with " B " followed by " D " on the right, and " A " followed by " C " on the left.

As the advance passed Carnoy, it was met by heavy artillery and machine-gun fire which caused many casualties. Only a few men reached the German trenches on the forward slope. Touch was gained with the 10th London Regiment on the right, but not with the 7th Royal Sussex who had been held up on the left. There was heavy fighting on the left of the battalion and after two attempts the Germans counter-attacking succeeded in rushing that flank and capturing a number of men. In trying to get away, Second-Lieutenant Stapleton was killed and Second-Lieutenant Tutton was mortally wounded.

The casualties of this day were :

Officers. Killed or Died of Wounds : 2nd-Lieuts. W. H. Stapleton, F. J. Tutton, M.M.
    Wounded : 2nd-Lieut. G. W. W. Page.
Other Ranks : Killed 43 ; Wounded 97 ; Missing 31.

The Medical Officer, Captain W. M. Lansdale, had been killed by a shell on the previous evening.

In the morning of the 27th the 9th Royal Fusiliers passed through and captured Maltz Horn Farm, and the 5th Royal Berkshire followed.

On the 28th the battalion moved back to Carnoy to allow the 19th London Regiment to pass. At Carnoy the battalion stayed till the end of August.

On the 1st September the 5th Royal Berkshire were at Maricourt. At 8 a.m. on the 2nd, they were occupying dugouts and a bank to the north of Le Forest, the assembly position for the next advance. Here they suffered a considerable long-range shelling.

At 7.30 p.m. on the 3rd they moved forward to trenches round St. Pierre Vaast Wood, which they reached at midnight, to find there was no accommodation or shelter, whilst much gas shelling was going on.

The 4th was a very wet day. At 4 p.m. orders were received to move into trenches just north of Moislains, which entailed passing through a gas-shelled area. At midnight the battalion was sharing Head-quarters with the 7th Royal Sussex, with whom they were to attack Nurlu next morning.

The attack started at 6.45 a.m. on the 5th under a creeping barrage. The Canal du Nord was passed at Moislains, with " C " Company leading on the left and " D " on the right—" A " and " B " in support.

During the forming up some casualties had occurred from shells. The battalion was acting as reserve to the 7th Royal Sussex and 9th Royal Fusiliers, who led the attack. These battalions captured Nurlu, and the 5th Royal Berkshire dug in three hundred yards east of it. Here they were in touch on the right with the supporting companies of the 10th London Regiment (58th Division), and the Cambridgeshire (35th Brigade) on the left.

At 10 a.m. the companies were rearranged and the line was extended to the right.

At 11 a.m. the 10th London had advanced towards Lieramont and the 5th Royal Berkshire moved forward on their left and dug in on a line extending from Sorel Wood on the left to the northern edge of Lieramont on the right.

The casualties of this day were :

Officers.   Killed : Capt. B. W. Hougham (commanding " C " Company).
              Wounded : 2nd-Lieut. Ralph.
Other Ranks : Wounded 12.

This line was held till the 7th, when the battalion was withdrawn to Nurlu, where it suffered from shelling at intervals. Here it was refitting till noon on the 17th, when it was attached to the 37th Brigade, and at 8 p.m. moved to assembly positions for the attack on Epéhy next day. The 18th was on the right of the 12th Division and the 58th on the left towards Peizières.

The attack commenced at 5.20 a.m. on the 18th, the rôle of the Berkshire Battalion (less " B " Company) being to move south of Epéhy and mop up between the first objective, marked on the map by a red line, and the second marked by a green line, as soon as the former should be taken by the 6th Queen's, in support of whom three companies were acting.

" B " was attached to the 6th Royal West Kent, moving north of Peizières, which itself lay north of Epéhy.

At 6.45 a.m. the three other companies moved from assembly positions in artillery formation, but, the attack on Epéhy having failed, the 6th Queen's were unable to advance with their left flank exposed to the village. It was decided, therefore, about 8.15, to withdraw to a ridge where further orders were awaited. At 1 p.m. the battalion was attached to the 35th Brigade which had now taken Epéhy. Two companies (" C " and " D ") were ordered to mop up the village, and, after clearing it, to take position in Princes Reserve to the east of it. " C " and " D " reached this position by 2.30 p.m., " A " being in reserve.

The attack was continued at 3 p.m. by the 36th and 37th Brigades on the right and left respectively, but they failed to reach the second objective, and at 7 p.m. " A," " C," and " D " Companies of the 5th Royal Berkshire, with two companies of the Northants, were ordered to hold Princes Reserve, capture some trenches beyond it, and gain touch with the 9th Essex at Chestnut Avenue on their left. This was done by 2 a.m. on the 19th, and the line was established in advance of Tétard Wood east of Princes Reserve. The trenches between Tétard Wood on the right and Chestnut Avenue on the left had been taken by the 5th Royal Berkshire at 6.15 p.m.

On the 19th, orders issued for an attack on Room and Ockenden Trenches east of Tétard Wood. The advance was commenced at 11 a.m., but was at first held up by strong opposition, and it was not till 10 p.m. that all objectives were captured. These trenches appear to have been taken by the 1st Cambridgeshire and 5th Northamptonshire without the aid of the 5th Royal Berkshire. At 10 p.m. on the 20th the battalion was relieved by the 7th Norfolk and returned to the 36th Brigade, with which it took position at Vaughan Bank.

At dawn on the 21st the 35th and 37th Brigades continued the attack with partial success towards the east. The fighting continued all day, but the Royal Berkshire do not appear to have been engaged before 7 p.m. when they received orders to form up in Mule and Bird Trenches and attack the line in front, which ran south to north from Heythrop Post on the right, through Little Priel Farm, to Cruciform Post on the left.

The battalion formed up at 11 p.m. and attacked at midnight. " D " Company on the right was immediately successful, but " B " on the left was for a time held up by machine guns on its left flank. However, by 2 a.m. all objectives had been taken and consolidated, with " B " and " D " in front, " A " in support and " C " in reserve in Mule Trench. Here they were heavily shelled all day on the 22nd, and were enfiladed by machine-gun fire from Kildare Post on the left, until that position was carried by the 58th Division. During the 23rd the divisional front was reorganized on a line from Kildare Post on the left to Fleece All Post on the right. The Berkshire Battalion was relieved and went into reserve of the 36th Brigade, with one company in Kildare Avenue on the left, and three in Poplar and Room Trenches.

On the 24th at 11 a.m. the enemy made a strong attack on the front of the 12th Division.   It was repulsed on the right, but the enemy on the front of the 36th Brigade succeeded in getting into Dados Lane and the Loop in front of Kildare Post.   A counter-attack by the 9th Royal Fusiliers, with " A " Company of the Royal Berkshire attached, failed to eject the Germans from the captured trenches.   A second attempt by the Berkshire Battalion at 10 p.m. also failed.

At 10 p.m. on the 25th the 5th Royal Berkshire relieved the 9th Royal Fusiliers at Kildare Post, and at 3 a.m. on the 26th another attempt was made to recover Dados Trench and the Loop by attacking with two platoons on each flank.   The right platoons were successful at first, but, as no progress could be made by those on the left, all were eventually forced to retire. Bomb fighting went on all day.

On the 27th the battalion was in line on the left of the brigade, and at 5.20 a.m. on the 28th yet another attack, by the 6th Queen's, failed to recover the lost trenches.

On the 29th the troops on the right attacked over the tunnel through which the St. Quentin Canal passes.   For this attack the 37th Brigade passed through the 36th, which was not engaged.   The attack on the right succeeded, but the 33rd Division on the left and the 37th Brigade failed. Next day (30th) the enemy had left the canal, and the 37th Brigade pushed on, whilst the 36th was sent back at night to the Guyencourt concentration camp.

The battalion's casualties in this period of fighting, from the 18th to the 30th September, were :

Officers.   Killed : 2nd-Lieut. E. F. Bond.
            Wounded : 2nd-Lieuts. F. S. Hawkins, W. A. Buckingham,
                  T. C. Enever, A. V. Saunders.
Other Ranks : 250 (details not specified).

On the 1st October the battalion left the Epéhy front by 'bus for the Proyart area, whence they were conveyed by rail to Acq in the Arras area, arriving there on the 4th and going to Niagara Camp.

On the 5th they proceeded by 'bus to the Vimy Ridge area, where they relieved the 12th Rifle Brigade of the 26th Division, and were in reserve behind the 9th Royal Fusiliers and 7th Royal Sussex. The line held by the 12th Division was extended from Oppy on the right and Lelen dit Leauville on the left, a distance of eleven thousand yards. All three brigades were in line, the 36th being in the centre, with the 35th on its right and 37th on the left. The 5th Royal Berkshire were in reserve to the 9th Royal Fusiliers and 7th Royal Sussex in front line. Immediately after the relief the 36th Brigade, finding that the enemy was falling back, advanced to Méricourt, and on the 7th a further advance was made to the line Fresnoy-Rouvroy.

On the 9th October, the enemy was found to be retreating, but he succeeded in holding up the British advance on the 10th. On the 11th the advance was resumed unopposed, and at 5 p.m. the Drocourt-Quéant line was occupied.

On the 12th "A" and "C" Companies of the 5th Royal Berkshire were employed to clear Henin Liétard and pass beyond it. This operation encountered considerable resistance, as did the clearing of Dourges next day.

On the 14th the enemy was still on the east bank of the canal, the bridge over which he had blown up. "D" and "B" now relieved "A" and "C" in front line and were heavily shelled at night. On the 15th no advance across the Haute Deule Canal was possible; but on the 16th the east bank was reported clear of Germans and "B" Company forced a passage at Pont à Sault on the left.

The advance continued on the 17th, and at 3 p.m. "A" and "C" again passed through "B" and "D" to clear the village of Le Forest. By 5 p.m. Cordela had been occupied, and "C" had outposts beyond it. During these last operations the 36th Brigade had been on the left of the division.

On the 18th the 37th Brigade passed through the 36th, which moved on the 19th to Baches, on the 20th to Orchies, and from the 23rd to the 26th was at Ramegies. On the 27th it relieved the 7th Royal Sussex in the front line of the whole division.

On the 28th an attempt was made to pass the Canal de l'Escau which encountered some resistance and was not at first successful. In the evening the retreat of the enemy enabled a bridge to be thrown. In this action the

5th Royal Berkshire had some fighting but apparently nothing very serious, as their casualties were only five men wounded.

Fighting for the 5th Royal Berkshire was now at an end. On the 30th October the battalion was in billets at Flines where next day it furnished a guard-of-honour for General Horne, the Army Commander, and was inspected by H.R.H. the Prince of Wales.

There are no separate statements of casualties for October, but it appears they were as follows:

Officers. Died on 29th of Wounds received on 28th : Captain and Adjutant L. M. Hallam.
　　　　　Wounded : (on 14th) 2nd-Lieut. Humphries.
Other Ranks : Killed 11 ; Wounded 55 ; Missing 3.
The days of heaviest loss were:

Date.	Killed.	Wounded.	Missing.
14	5	25	—
15	3	8	—
16	1	7	3
28	—	5	—

At the commencement of the Armistice the battalion was near Vieux Condé on the Condé-Mons Canal. From that neighbourhood it marched to winter quarters at Erre, nor far from Valenciennes. The battalion stayed in this village until May, when it moved to Somain, a larger town near Douai. There is nothing of importance to record during this period. A certain amount of training was indulged in, in order to keep the men fit, and salvage operations were carried out near Cambrai. During this work, two men were seriously wounded in picking up live ammunition.

From the 1st January 1919, demobilization proceeded rapidly, and every week saw a diminution of the ranks of the battalion caused by men being sent back to England to be absorbed in " key industries." One of the outstanding features of the battalion's history during this period was the acquisition of a cinema, purchased by subscriptions by the officers. It was housed in a building constructed by battalion labour from material salvaged from German dumps, no Government money being expended. The building was first used for the Christmas dinner of the battalion, which was followed by the first entertainment. This was the only cinema available for the division, and was very popular. The profits from it enabled the whole of the battalion's debts incurred since its raising to be paid off, and left a surplus which was given to the Regimental Memorial and the Old Comrades' Association.

During the early spring months the Battalion Football Team played several matches with the other teams of the division.

On the 14th February the battalion was presented with its King's Colour by H.R.H. the Prince of Wales at Erre, the ceremony taking place in a driving snowstorm.

By the end of May demobilization had been so rapid that the battalion was reduced practically to its cadre. About the middle of June, the 36th Brigade, including the 5th Royal Berkshire, entrained at Somain for Dunkirk, taking with them their full equipment of transport, cookers, Lewis guns, tools, and battalion equipment, but without horses. Every individual article of equipment had been thoroughly cleaned and properly checked and packed. All transport had been repainted and cleaned to the last degree of perfection.

After a week at Dunkirk, all wagons, etc., fully loaded, were put no board a transport, and about the 15th June the cadre, comprising four officers and forty other ranks, sailed for Southampton. On arrival there, the equipment (wagons, etc.) was ordered to be handed over to the Ordnance Officer at Southampton, and from there was sent to Georgetown unaccompanied, whilst the battalion was ordered to proceed to Reading, arriving there at 5 p.m. on the 18th June 1919. There it was met by Colonel Foley who had raised it, and received a magnificent welcome from the Mayor and Corporation, and also from the inhabitants of the town, who had heard it was coming. After having been formally received by the Mayor and Corporation and entertained to tea at the Town Hall, the battalion marched to the barracks, headed by the band of the 1st Battalion, and the following day the remainder of the men were disbanded and given warrants to their homes. Previous to marching back to the barracks, after the Town Hall reception, the King's Colour was deposited in the Parish Church adjoining the Town Hall, and was received by the vicar.

The names of the officers who remained with the battalion to the last were the following :

Lieut.-Col. H. T. Goodland, D.S.O.
Capt. Ashby, M.C.
Lieut. Ellis, M.C.
Lieut. Bateman, Quartermaster.

About sixteen of the men composing the cadre were original members of the 5th Battalion, having joined the battalion at Reading in August 1914.

CHAPTER XXXII

THE 6th (SERVICE) BATTALION

FORMATION. THE SOMME FRONT

1914–1915

THE raising of the 6th (Service) Battalion of the Royal Berkshire Regiment was commenced at Shorncliffe on the 12th September 1914 by Lieut.-Colonel Foley, D.S.O., who was then also in charge of the 5th Battalion.

Lieut.-Colonel A. J. W. Dowell was appointed to the command, which he held till he was promoted to a brigade in the 19th Division in March 1916.

The battalion was composed chiefly of recruits from Berkshire, Birmingham, and South Wales.

In October 1914 the newly formed battalion was moved from Shorncliffe to Colchester, where it joined the 53rd Brigade of the 18th Division, commanded by Major-General Ivor Maxse, C.B., C.V.O.

As with other Service Battalions, there was great difficulty at first in obtaining clothing and equipment, the Ordnance Department being at that time quite unable to cope with the enormous demand on it. Captain R. M. Guthrie, who joined the battalion as Quartermaster on the 18th September 1914, says that he found some eleven hundred men, of whom a very large percentage were in want of clothing and boots. The difficulty was partially solved by the sensible abolition of red-tape restrictions in allowing battalions to purchase immediate necessaries privately and locally. This enabled many of the men to be fitted out, but it was a long time before regulation clothing and equipment were supplied to all. During the whole period of its training the battalion was either under canvas or in barracks and was never billeted.

In its early days much assistance in the matter of messing was received

6th BATTALION.

(*Back Row*) 2nd Lt. G. M. Courage. 2nd Lt. Prout. 2nd Lt. A. H. Hudson. 2nd Lt. N. B. Hudson. Lt. R. E. Kemble.

(*Second Row*) Lt. E. C. Nicholson. 2nd Lt. G. H. F. Knight. 2nd Lt. H. R. Traill. Lt. F. C. Heffer. Lt. Kingsley Burns. Lt. V. G. McArthur. Lt. H. G. F. Long-hurst. Lt. A. F. G. Everitt. 2nd Lt. G. C. Freeman.

(*Sitting*) Capt. T. C. Hincks. Capt. E. G. Lees. Capt. and Adjt. W. P. Hewetson. Col. A. J. W. Dowell. Major R. Winstanley. Lt. and Q.M. R. M. Guthrie. Capt. C. D. Horne.

(*In Front*) 2nd Lt. St. J. B. Matthews. 2nd Lt. J. N. Richardson. 2nd Lt. R. Litten. 2nd Lt. W. Nicholson. 2nd Lt. R. J. F. Remnant.

from the 5th Battalion at Shorncliffe. The 6th was particularly fortunate in having Lieut.-Colonel Dowell as its commander, and also in having a nucleus of N.C.O.s in several pensioned men of that rank who joined up at once in response to Lord Kitchener's call.

Training continued at Colchester till May 1915, when the division moved to Codford St. Mary, on the western border of Salisbury Plain, where it continued and completed its training till July 1915 when it went to France.

The officers who left Codford with the battalion for France were:

Lieut.-Colonel	A. J. W. Dowell.
Majors:	R. L. Winstanley.
	E. G. Lees.
Captains:	T. C. Hincks.
	Kingsley Burns.
	C. D. Horne.
	S. Fenner.
	C. W. Hemp.
	H. G. F. Longhurst.
	V. G. McArthur.
	W. P. Hewetson (Adjutant).
Lieutenants and Second-Lieutenants:	E. C. Nicholson.
	G. C. Freeman.
	K. R. Traill.
	R. J. F. Remnant.
	J. N. H. Pleming.
	L. H. Saye.
	R. E. Kemble.
	G. W. Courage.
	G. C. Hollis.
	N. B. Hudson.
	A. H. Hudson.
	H. P. S. Wise.
	G. W. H. Nicholson.
	R. Litten.
	St. J. B. Matthews.
	J. N. Richardson.
	N. B. Souper.

Lieut. and Qr.-Mr. R. M. Guthrie.
Lieut. H. Ackroyd (Medical Officer).

The officers-commanding the battalion were:

Lieut.-Colonel Dowell till March 1916.

Major Hincks (temporarily) from March till May 1916.

Lieut.-Colonel B. G. Clay, 7th Dragoon Guards, from May 1916 till his promotion to a brigade in August 1917.

Lieut.-Colonel H. G. F. Longhurst, in succession to Colonel Clay, till his death at Poelcappelle in October 1917.

The remaining days of the battalion's existence were under Major McArthur and Lieut.-Colonel FitzHugh.

The first adjutant was Captain H. P. Hewetson, till March 1916, when he was succeeded by Captain R. A. Rochfort, who held the post practically throughout the fighting career of the battalion, till he was badly wounded at Poelcappelle in October 1917.

The transport of the battalion was sent to France, viâ Southampton and Havre, on the 24th July 1915.

On the 25th the rest of the battalion proceeded by train from Codford to Folkestone, reaching Boulogne in the early hours of the 26th and marching to the Ostrohove Rest Camp. The battalion was in the 53rd Infantry Brigade, 18th Division, the other units of the Brigade being the 8th Norfolk, 8th Suffolk, and 10th Essex. The Brigade was commanded by Brigadier-General MacAndrew ; the Division by Major-General I. Maxse.

The battalion left again by train the same night for Bertangles, whence it went into billets at Rubempré, north of Amiens. Here, the transport having come up from Havre, it was complete on the 30th July. On the 2nd August, after being inspected by Sir C. Monro, the Army Commander, it marched to Bouzincourt, N.W. of Albert, where for the next week it was in trenches, attached to the 154th Brigade for the purpose of receiving instruction in the practice of trench warfare. It had its first few casualties in these trenches. Going back to Daours on the 13th, it was at Bray sur Somme on the 21st, and next day in trenches three miles to the north, opposite Mametz, with the 54th Brigade on the left. Here it sustained several casualties from snipers.

The Battalion Diary has a curious entry as to the effect of the gases from the explosion of mines. They affected men just as alcohol does, making them violent at first, and then sleepy.

The 6th Royal Berkshire continued the ordinary routine of trench warfare in this neighbourhood till the 16th September, when they marched to Albert and took over trenches opposite La Boisselle, with a battalion of the 53rd

Brigade on the left, and one of the 55th Brigade on the right.   Here there was a great deal of mining on both sides and many craters were formed by the explosion of mines.   Mining fatigues were very heavy, and the battalion had one hundred and twelve men working day and night in four six-hour shifts of twenty-eight each.   Over three thousand bags of chalk were taken out daily, and its disposal, so as not to attract the notice of the enemy, was always a difficulty.   The rest of the month up to the 29th, when the battalion returned to Albert, was spent in and out of these trenches.

A plaintive remark is recorded in the diary of the 8th October : " Our trench-mortar ammunition, besides being very scarce, fails to explode on most occasions."

On the 15th October the battalion went into billets at Buire, and here began to enjoy some of the diversions provided for the distraction of the hard-worked soldier, in the shape of a " cinema," opened at Maricourt by the 18th Division, which was visited by one hundred and fifty of the men daily.   From the 23rd to the end of October, and on through November, the 6th Royal Berkshire were back at Albert, and in front of La Boisselle.

There is nothing to note in November, except the death of Second-Lieutenant St. J. B. Matthews, who was wounded by a rifle-grenade on the 25th, and died after an operation.

December was equally uneventful up till the 19th, on which day a patrol of a sergeant and two men who had gone out at 4.30 a.m. was believed to have been lost.   As a matter of fact, they were in a shell-hole close under the enemy's parapet when day broke.   There was nothing for it but to lie tight till nightfall enabled them to get back safely at 7.30 p.m., bringing a good deal of useful information regarding the enemy's loopholes and the condition of his wire.

The trenches, even in this neighbourhood, were very muddy, though probably the inhabitants of those in Flanders would have considered them comparatively luxurious.

THE BATTLE OF THE SOMME.   MONTAUBAN.
LONGUEVAL AND DELVILLE WOOD.   THIEPVAL.

1916

January and February passed for the battalion in the Albert and La Boisselle neighbourhood as uneventfully as the latter days of 1915.

By the 13th March it had again moved to the southern area, and was billeted in Corbie, the most considerable town it had yet been in since reaching the front. From the 21st March till the end of April there is still nothing of importance to record, whilst the battalion was in trenches or in the defensive lines about Maricourt.

On the 1st May the 6th Royal Berkshire again moved north to La Houssoye, and on to Voux en Amienois, and on the 22nd back to Corbie. From the 24th May till the 3rd June they were at Carnoy, where, or in neighbouring back areas, the whole month was spent, largely in careful training for the coming Battle of the Somme.

This training had started in March on a reproduction of the German trenches to be attacked, which had been set up at Picquigny near Amiens. It was begun under Captain T. C. Hincks, who temporarily commanded the battalion in the interval between the promotion of Colonel Dowell to a brigade, and the assumption of command by Lieut.-Colonel B. G. Clay.

So far the battalion, like the rest of the 18th Division, had not been used for any major operations, and was now to be thrown into the great battle practically intact. Its further history, like that of the 8th Norfolk and 8th Suffolk, is compressed into a brief space compared with that of other battalions which were involved in great battles almost from the beginning of their service at the front. At the other end it was cut short by its disbandment, along with many other battalions, in February 1918, before the great German offensives of that year, and before the final allied offensive and triumph. From the point of view of individuals, the history was more prolonged ; for on disbandment of battalions their constituents were distributed to others and served to the end of the war, or of their own lives or capacity, in their new units.

The prolonged artillery preparation for the Battle of the Somme had, as was the practice at that stage, begun long before the 30th June, on which day the 6th Royal Berkshire suffered their heaviest casualties, so far, on any one day. Five other ranks were killed and forty-two wounded, evidently by the German reply to the British bombardment. The losses during the artillery duel of the 27th June to the 1st July are attributed by the Battalion Diary largely to the inadequacy of the dugouts.

At 3 a.m. on the 1st July the battalion moved into its assembly positions for attack. They were much crowded in these trenches, but, owing to a fortunate fact, the losses from the enemy's shells there were much less than might have been expected under the circumstances. It so happened that the German artillery concentrated on the third trench, and, when this was observed, it was carefully left empty. The men who were to have been in it were put into the fourth trench, whilst those who should have occupied the latter lay out in the open fifty yards in rear of it.

The 18th Division was disposed with the 55th Brigade on the right, 53rd centre, 54th left. The attack was due north, with the right-hand boundary line of the 18th Division separating it from the 30th, and ultimately passing through the west corner of Montauban.

On the left of the 18th was the 7th Division, and the front covered by the 18th was about two thousand yards. Of the 53rd Brigade, the 8th Norfolk Regiment was on the right, the 6th Royal Berkshire on the left, with the 10th Essex in support, and 8th Suffolk in reserve. The 6th Royal Berkshire were immediately in front of Mine Trench, the most advanced of the enemy defences. At the west end of this trench was Casino Point, under which a British mine was exploded at 7.27 a.m. with disastrous effects on the enemy. A machine gun firing right atop of the mine was blown up and found some forty yards away. The falling debris caused slight loss among the 6th Royal Berkshire, but, on the other hand, as they advanced three minutes after the explosion, Germans came forward with hands up to surrender.

Mine Trench was captured by the Berkshire and Norfolk men at the first rush. By 7.50 a.m., twenty minutes after the assault began, the Royal Berkshire had taken Bund Support Trench and were forward to Pommiers Trench. But " B " Company, leading on the left, had suffered severely in officers, all of whom were *hors de combat,* and Captain Litten, the commander of it, had been killed. Second-Lieutenant Courage was sent to command this company.

" A," too, on the right, had lost Lieutenant K. R. Traill and Second-Lieutenant T. A. Collot killed, though Captain Fenner was believed to be still with it. From Bund Support the bombers of " B " started up the communication trench known as Popoff Lane, leading to Pommiers Trench, and Vickers guns were established at the junction of Popoff Lane and

Pommiers Trench. In this movement the Royal Berkshire had co-operated closely with the 7th Bedfordshire on the right of the 54th Brigade.

In Pommiers Trench there was a halt previous to the assault of the strong Pommiers redoubt by the 54th Brigade. By 9.30 the redoubt had been taken by the 11th Royal Fusiliers and the 7th Bedfordshire, the latter again receiving assistance from the co-operation of the Berkshire men on their right.

At 10 a.m. Captain and Adjutant R. A. Rochfort, reconnoitring from Battalion Head-quarters in Pommiers Trench, reported that the 8th Norfolk on the right were unable to get forward, and that " A " Company had established posts to cover the Berkshire right flank thus exposed.

At 10.40 the 8th Norfolk were reported to have taken the Loop, but this turned out to be incorrect. They were still held up at Back Trench.

By 12.50 p.m. the bombing attack up Montauban Alley had made good progress, and Loop Trench, leading northwards from the Loop, had been cleared from the Loop as far as its junction with the Mametz-Montauban Road.

At 1.30 the 8th Norfolk were still not up on the right, where Captain Fenner and fifty men were holding Loop Trench against fierce attacks from the right.

At 3.15 the Berkshire right was held up and had to be reinforced by Essex bombers. It was not till 6.30 p.m. that the final objective, on a line running east and west in front of Caterpillar Valley, was reached. The Loop had been handed over to the 8th Norfolk when they came up.

The enemy had been driven back from a depth of about two thousand yards of trenches on this day, but at very heavy cost in officers and men.

Officers. Killed (7) : Capt. R. Litten.
Lieut. K. R. Traill.
2nd-Lieuts. N. B. Souper.
C. K. Howe.
T. A. Collot.
G. M. Courage.
E. Bayley.
Wounded (5) : Capts. V. G. McArthur.
H. G. F. Longhurst.

2nd-Lieuts. G. W. H. Nicholson.
J. V. McLean.
L. H. Saye.*

Other Ranks : Killed 56 ; Wounded 237 ; Missing 46.
Total : 12 Officers and 339 Other Ranks.

Of this day it is recorded in the Battalion Diary that " The success of this operation was due to the thorough grounding every one had in his work. The whole scheme had been explained to the men, and, even when the majority of the officers had been knocked out, N.C.O.s and men carried on according to programme."

The following account of his personal experiences before and during the battle of the 1st July has been contributed by Captain R. A. Rochfort, D.S.O., M.C., then Adjutant of the 6th Battalion : " The key position of the German Line was considered to be Casino Point, a machine-gun nest in the front German trench—Mine Trench. The battalion went up to hold the line, and to get acquainted with the various important points on the front, early in May. It was arranged that Casino Point should be mined and blown up at zero hour. This information never went beyond Battalion Headquarters until the morning of the battle itself, when the troops were informed that this point would be wiped out. The men of the battalion actually assisted in carrying away the earth from the tunnel, but were informed that this tunnel was only a means of communication, which would be employed on the day to prevent casualties.

" A week before the attack was to take place, that is the 22nd June (as the original date for the battle was fixed for the 29th June), some men of the Tunnelling Company bored through the woodwork of the German dugouts below Casino Point, and could hear the men talking, and even smell them. The place was filled up with earth, sand-bagged, and then the charge was laid. A sentry was kept at the entrance to the tunnel, in case the Germans should have been alarmed and have discovered the mine.

" An examination was made every twelve hours, but the Germans were quite unsuspecting, and the mine remained a surprise up to the moment it was exploded. The battalion went into the line for the big attack on the 28th June, and spent the day of the 28th in the line, expecting to attack

* Died of wounds.

on the morning of the 29th. The weather, however, was so bad that the attack was postponed for forty-eight hours.

" This period of holding the line before the attack was the most extraordinary one imaginable. Throughout the day it was quite safe to walk about the front line, sit up on the trenches, look over at the German line, and watch the shelling, without any fear of being sniped at. The country in front of our barbed wire appeared absolutely devoid of German life; the German guns only replied by night, and then replied to very good effect. Rifle-shot in the daytime was an unheard-of thing. The attack on the 1st July was delivered at 7.30 a.m. The mine at Casino Point was exploded at 7.29 a.m. So eager were the men for the attack that it was difficult to keep them back once the light barrage started.

" At 7.28 a.m., when the Germans saw our men climb up on to the tops of the trenches, the machine guns at Casino Point opened fire, and were doing quite a bit of damage, when suddenly, there was a blinding flash; the whole of the earth seemed to shake, and the mine went up. The air was filled with huge lumps of earth, Germans, machine guns, baulks of wood, concrete emplacements, and all the debris of the strong point itself. One man was killed by a sphere of earth five feet in diameter which fell on him. The troops advanced after the explosion, without any fire of any sort, from Mine Trench, and within five minutes of the opening of the attack, the first two trenches were in our hands.

" I walked over and inspected the crater of Casino Point immediately the attack started. It was the biggest one I had seen. It was about forty feet deep and quite thirty yards across. Around it were all sorts of remnants of Casino Point and its garrison.

" The first serious stop that the battalion had in its victorious advance that day was at the point where the Fricourt-Montauban Road crossed the German communication trench from Pommiers Redoubt to Montauban. Here a small strong point had been made, and was garrisoned by a German officer with an automatic rifle and two or three daring and excellent bombers. ' A ' Company, under Captain Fenner, was attacking, but they were unable to take this point, and so the troops on either side of them were unable to advance owing to the enfilade fire from this point. Fenner sent a runner back to me at Head-quarters and asked for bombers. Lieutenant G. M. Courage went with four bombers. When these failed to take the strong point, Courage attacked it himself with his automatic revolver, in a forlorn hope that he or one of his bombers might reach the point and take it. He was killed in front of the barbed wire, which had not been completely cut.

" A Stokes gun was then sent up and attacked the strong point from Pommiers Redoubt. A Lewis gun, working in conjunction with the Stokes gun, accounted for three of the German bombers, but still the strong point hung on, and was hindering the advance all along the line. It was then that Second-Lieutenant Saye attempted to get into a position to enfilade the communication trench, and in doing so was badly hit. He was brought back into the trench, but never recovered from his wound, and died some hours later.

" Company-Sergeant-Major Sayer then said that he would have a try to snipe the German officer. He fired several shots, and on one occasion actually hit the officer's steel helmet, but failed to stop his fire. Then, before we realized what he intended to do, he jumped up on to the parapet, fired a round at the German officer, and succeeded in shooting him through the forehead ; but, at the moment he fired, the officer also fired and caught Sayer through the shoulder. Immediately the officer was killed, the advance was resumed.

" The 8th Norfolk, on our right, were able to continue their advance, and by the late afternoon all the objectives that we had been ordered to take were in our hands, consolidated, and garrisoned. Sayer's act was one of the bravest that I have seen, and he well deserved the Distinguished Conduct Medal which he received for it. The strong point, before it fell, cost the battalion over fifty casualties, including five officers who were killed.

" Lieutenant Souper had tried to do the same as Sergeant-Major Sayer, but had failed, and was shot through the head himself. Colonel Clay and I visited the line while the battle for this strong point was going on. The German officer had a shot at us and his bullet went through the right-hand pocket of Colonel Clay's jacket. It annoyed him very much, as it was a new ' Fielding ' jacket which he had just brought back with him from England.

" Later that day, Colonel Clay accused me of treading on his heels when I was about five yards away from him, but later discovered that a bullet had gone clean through the leather block of his heel.

" The night of 1st July was spent in Montauban Alley, preparing for the counter-attack which we felt sure would come in the morning. However, no attack was delivered and during the day we were able to wire our line and secure it against almost any attack without strong artillery preparation.

" The sight which the men most enjoyed on this day was some German gunners rushing up with their teams to the ground immediately beyond Caterpillar Wood to get their guns away, and so interested were they in this sight that they forgot to open fire on them until cursed for it by Sergeant Lynch. He managed to get the Lewis gun to open fire on them, and, as a result of his action, two guns were captured next morning, the Germans being unable to get them away."

At 3 a.m. on the 2nd July the 6th Royal Berkshire went back to Pommiers Trench, and, on relief by the 8th Suffolk, to Carnoy, where they remained resting and clearing the battlefield till the 7th, when they had a period of refitment and recuperation which carried them past the recapture of Trônes Wood on the 13th by the 54th and 55th Brigades. In this the 53rd Brigade took no part. Its turn of heavy fighting was again to come on the 19th at Longueval and Delville Wood.

At 9 p.m. on the 18th July the battalion moved from its position at Trigger Wood, south of Carnoy, to a bivouac at Talus Boisé, and, with the rest of the 53rd Brigade, was placed under the orders of the 9th Division, which had been driven from the northern part of Longueval, and all but the S.W. corner of Delville Wood adjoining it on the east. These losses it was the task of the 53rd Brigade to recover.

The bivouac was on the northern slope of the valley in which ran the light railway passing through the northern portion of Trônes Wood and by the north side of Guillemont. The strength of the 6th Royal Berkshire at this time was only nineteen officers and four hundred and one others.

The attack was to begin on the 19th, as soon as it was possible to bring up the whole of the brigade. The barrage was to be provided by the 9th Division.

The general plan of attack was for the 8th Norfolk to lead and clear the southern portion of Delville Wood from its west edge. When this had been done, the Essex on the right, and the 6th Royal Berkshire on the left, would form up in the southern portion of the wood and proceed to the clearance of the northern half. At the same time the 8th Suffolk, on the left of the Berkshire, would clear the northern portion of Longueval Village. Zero was fixed for 6.15 and the order of advance of the battalions was to be 8th Norfolk, 9th Essex, 6th Royal Berkshire, 8th Suffolk.

At 7.5 the Royal Berkshire moved off, one hundred yards in rear of the Head-quarters of the Essex. The enemy was now shelling the roads leading to the village and the wood, and, owing to the long delay which had occurred in the 8th Norfolk getting into the wood, the three battalions following them suffered severely. One 5·9″ shell, falling in No. 16 Platoon of the Royal Berkshire, killed five and wounded eleven men. Altogether there were thirty-four men killed before the village was reached at 9 a.m., after being subjected during one and a half hours to this destructive bombardment.

At 11.25 the 8th Norfolk reported the southern half of the wood practically clear. So far, the Royal Berkshire had been following the Essex through the southern part of Longueval, still suffering from German shells. At 11.55 the Royal Berkshire entered the southern part of the wood, which they found had been far from completely cleared. The leading company (" D ") at once began to lose men from the fire of a strong point south of Princes Street, the main ride which passed from the village eastwards through the wood, marking the division between its southern and northern portions. The commanding-officer now arranged for a fresh bombardment to last from 1 p.m. to 1.30, and to be followed by the infantry attack.

At 1.30 the field-gun barrage began to lift towards the northern edge of Delville Wood at the rate of fifty yards per minute, but at first "heavies" were still falling short, and some of the field-gun shrapnel also burst short. The battalion had casualties from both. The attack started, as arranged, at 1.30, but failed under the stress of German artillery fire, and of that of machine guns still south of Princes Street as the troops endeavoured to advance on that line.

The fighting in the wood was confused and scarcely possible to describe ; for three battalions of the 53rd Brigade were engaged, besides many others of the South African Brigade, from whom the greater part of the wood had been wrested before.

At 2.15 orders were given for the battalion to dig in deep and narrow on the line it then held, which was south of Princes Street on a curving line at varying distances from the ride. The digging in was completed by 5 p.m. It was eighty yards in rear of the farthest line reached, as it was found impossible to dig nearer up, on account of the machine guns. Great difficulty was found in holding the line, owing to the intermixture of elements of disorganized units on the left—South Africans, Duke of Cornwall's Light Infantry, and Royal Scots Fusiliers—without proper commanders.

The portion of the line held by the Royal Berkshire at night was manned by about two hundred and forty rifles, six Lewis guns, and four Vickers guns, all that remained of the weak battalion of the night before. On the morning of the 20th the same line was held, and continued to be held and further consolidated up to 3 p.m. The Royal Welch Fusiliers were to have attacked the northern part of the wood, but were anticipated by a German counter-attack on the southern part of Longueval, beyond which the 8th Suffolk had made practically no progress on the 19th. Here the Germans were repulsed with heavy loss, as they found themselves between the Fusiliers on their right and the South Africans in the village.

At 3 p.m. on the 20th one of the many German bombing counter-attacks fell upon the Royal Berkshire, but was repulsed by them. The position in the southern half of the wood was stubbornly held all day on the 20th, and at one time arrangements are said to have been made to recover the eighty yards over which the line had retired on the 19th. Whether anything was actually done towards this seems doubtful.

The night of the 20th-21st saw no change in the position, which was again held firmly all day on the 21st, till the 53rd Brigade was relieved in the night of the 21st-22nd. The attack had certainly failed; for at the end of it, not the whole of Delville Wood had been regained, but only the southern portion, scarcely up to Princes Street, was held. However, what the brigade had regained they held. It was long after their departure that Delville Wood was finally cleared.

The losses of the Royal Berkshire had been heaviest (about forty per cent. of the total) on the 19th, up till the time when they had dug themselves in in the afternoon.

The total casualties were:

Officers. Killed : 2nd-Lieuts. H. P. Sadler, W. V. Burgess.

Wounded : Capt. A. H. Hudson, 2nd-Lieuts. C. H. Hunt, A. J. Fox, J. N. Richardson, C. J. Fuller.

Missing : 2nd-Lieut. S. R. Collier.

Other Ranks : Killed 21 ; Wounded 126 ; Missing 29.

Captain Ackroyd, the Medical Officer, was conspicuous by his exertions in attending to the wounded in the wood, which was a real shambles strewn with dead and wounded British, South Africans, and Germans. Later in the war he gained the V.C., and he was eventually killed in the noble execution of his duties on the battlefield.

For this action, as for that of the 1st July, we are again able to quote Captain Rochfort's personal experiences in the following narrative written by him :

" The attack, as planned, was the worst show the brigade ever took part in. The four battalions were sent up through a defile (the sunken road into Longueval) in broad daylight, with German observation balloons up, and most of the battalion had to halt for quite a considerable period in the sunken road, where they were exposed to shelling from three sides. Every gun that the Germans could get turned on to the road opened fire, and I have never seen a short stretch of road with so many casualties on it as the piece leading into Longueval Village.

" Major Marks, our own Brigade-Major, who had come up to see how things were going, was killed here. On arrival in the village, there was nowhere for the troops to go, because the portion of the wood in which they were to form up was still held by the Germans.

" The general plan was that the Norfolks were to attack the southern half of the wood in an eastern direction from Longueval Village. While they were doing this, the other battalions were left to stew in the sunken road. While the Norfolks were endeavouring to clear the southern half of the wood, the other battalions were losing heavily from the well-observed German artillery fire. The attack was doomed to failure from the start, as it was based on the mistaken idea that the southern portion of the wood was only held by two or three snipers. Not only did the Norfolks have to fight hard to take any part of the southern portion of the wood, but eventually had to be reinforced by two battalions before the southern portion was cleared.

" By the time this had been done, the attacking barrage, which worked northwards, had passed over the wood about three times without any troops being able to follow it, as there was no place clear of the enemy for them to form up in.

" The South Africans were supposed to have been holding the south edge of the wood when our battalion entered it, but we only saw one South African, and he refused to leave the wood, and eventually had to be sent out under escort. Personally, I was only too glad to leave the place.

" We had more casualties in the first two hours in the sunken road than we had in the whole of the remaining forty-six hours that we were in the wood. It was the battalion's first experience of wood fighting, and it was extraordinary how well the Germans concealed themselves and maintained a continual sniping fire on our troops. They had snipers in trees, behind trees, and in positions made behind fallen trunks. The dugout which we used in Longueval Village as Battalion Head-quarters was twenty yards south of the cross-roads in Longueval. The village was held by the Suffolks, and the first morning after our arrival there I went out to visit the line and found that the Suffolk platoon, which was supposed to be holding the cross-roads, had, in mistake, held the junction roads at the south entrance to the village, so that really there had been nothing between us and the Germans except the sentry I had put at the dugout entrance."

There was very little left now of the battalion as it existed before it was first thrown into the furnace of the Battle of the Somme, and it was necessarily sent into the far-back areas to recoup throughout the rest of July.

When it came back it reappeared in quite a different part, in the neighbourhood of Godewaerswalde. August, too, was passed in a quiet neighbourhood in Flanders, in the latitude of Bailleul, and it was only on the 11th September that the battalion found itself again approaching the blood-stained battlefields of the Somme.

They were at Léalvillers from the 11th to the 16th, after which they were at Bouzincourt and Forceville till, on the 25th, they were at Aveluy Wood, north of Albert. Next day was fixed for the attack on Thiepval from the south. It had defied attack from the west in July.

The 18th Division was now attached to the IInd Corps. In the attack and capture, on the 26th, of Thiepval or the ruins which were all that now remained of that unfortunate village and its château, the 6th Battalion played only a minor part. The assaulting battalions of the 53rd Brigade were the 8th Suffolk and the 10th Essex, the latter then commanded by Lieut.-Colonel C. W. Frizell, M.C., an officer who started in the war as an officer of the 1st Battalion, Royal Berkshire.

The 8th Norfolk Regiment was in support, the 6th Royal Berkshire in reserve at Crucifix Corner. As the assault advanced, the assembly and support trenches were not occupied by the supports and reserves, and consequently the Royal Berkshire escaped casualties from the barrage put down by the enemy on those trenches.

During this day of strenuous fighting the battalion was not called up into the struggle, but " D " Company was employed in carrying up rations and ammunition for the rest of the brigade. When the action came to a standstill, after the clearing of Thiepval, the whole battalion was turned on to carrying for the others. Its casualties on this day, in the carrying parties, were only one man killed and two wounded.

Again on the 27th the battalion was held in readiness all day to counter-attack, if necessary, as the 8th Suffolk stormed the powerful Schwaben Redoubt, and again they were not required in front. Their casualties were one man killed and five wounded. At dawn on the 28th, the 6th Royal Berkshire moved up to relieve the Suffolk and Essex Battalions in front line. " B " Company was in front, " D " in Bulgar Trench, ready for the counter-attack, " C " in support in Bulgar Support Trench, and " A " in reserve in Schwaben Trench. The battalion was heavily shelled all day, and the men were suffering badly from want of sleep or rest. The casualties were again not heavy. Second-Lieutenant W. B. Chapman was wounded, and of other ranks six were wounded and two missing.

There was no change of position on the 29th, but the battalion came temporarily under the orders of the 55th Brigade, which was to complete the conquest of the Schwaben Redoubt which, so far, had only been partially effected. The casualties on this day were much heavier—6 men Killed, 49 Wounded, and 5 Missing.

Of this an explanation has been furnished by the Revd. (then Lieutenant) N. B. Hudson, who says that " The 6th R. Berks shared two trenches with the Germans and in this part there were sudden bombing attacks. Moreover, the enemy concentrated their artillery on the battalion's trenches, as a farther advance of fifty yards in that part would have been disastrous for him."

The 30th September was signalized by a German counter-attack, at 4.45 a.m. on Point 27, which was in the rear face of the redoubt towards its eastern end. This was beyond the area of the 6th Royal Berkshire.

The point was taken, and the assailants penetrated one hundred and eighty yards to the south of it. The Berkshire battalion bombers were sent forward to help the 8th East Surrey, who had held this point, and did good service in stopping and partially driving back the Germans.

An attack in the afternoon, by the 8th East Surrey and 7th Buffs, failed to completely recover the lost ground. In this the Royal Berkshire took no part. The enemy shelling continued as heavily as on the previous day, and the battalion casualties were Second-Lieutenants A. D. Bebee and G. P. Ravenor killed, Major Crookenden, D.S.O., wounded, and of other ranks 8 killed, 53 wounded and 4 missing.

On the 1st October the battalion, in the same position, lost by shells, Captain G. C. Freeman killed, and Second-Lieutenant W. J. Dymoke mortally wounded.

On the 2nd, at 7 a.m., a bombing attack was made, chiefly on the battalion on the left of the Royal Berkshire. The battalion bombers were again sent up and took part in the ejectment of the enemy from the ground which they had temporarily occupied. Second-Lieutenant G. C. Welch was wounded.

After suffering the usual bombardment during the 3rd, the battalion was attacked on its left by a strong party of German bombers, with " flammenwerfer " co-operating. They again broke through Point 27 and occupied one hundred yards of the trench south of it. Strong bombing parties of the Royal Berkshire counter-attacked from three directions, recovered the ground which had been lost, and inflicted heavy losses on the enemy.

Second-Lieutenant Lewis, with the battalion bombers, is mentioned as having done especially good work in this affair.

At 7.30 a.m. on the 5th October a bombing attack was made by the 8th Norfolk Regiment, to assist in which there were sent the battalion bombers under Second-Lieutenant Lewis, and the bombing squads of " A " and " D " Companies. The Germans, armed with the lighter " egg " bombs, were able to outthrow the British with their Mills grenades, and there ensued several hours of hard fighting, at the end of which such ground as had been lost was recovered.

The following is Captain Rochfort's account of the operations about Thiepval :

" For this engagement the battalion acted as a carrying battalion to the brigade, and took over the line immediately after the attack.

" At this time the battalion was very weak indeed, as we had received no reinforcements since the Delville Wood Battle. Companies were about thirty strong, and it was for this reason that we were not put in as one of the attacking battalions. The attack had been fairly successful, and Thiepval itself had been taken, and a line established immediately in front of a German strong point called Schwaben Redoubt.

" The general line here faced north, and the communication trenches were Bulgar Trench and Martin Way, which were really two old German communication trenches between Thiepval and Schwaben. There were no traverses in either of these trenches, and both were in view from Schwaben Redoubt. As a consequence, a visit to the front line was a most unpleasant affair. Add to this the fact that the Germans attempted to bomb down these trenches three or four times every day, and that they were well supplied with egg bombs, while our supply of Mills No. 23's, which were the only reply to an egg bomb, was very limited, and it will be realized that the six days we spent holding Thiepval were somewhat exciting.

" Probably one of the greatest efforts that a staff officer ever did was when five thousand undetonated bombs were sent up to the front line to repel the German bombing attacks. It was during one of these attacks that ' Birdie ' Freeman was killed. He was in Bulgar Alley and had just put his head over the top of the parapet when he was sniped at, and he turned round to me and said ' I'll run into a shell-hole and have a look from there.' He moved about twenty yards up the trench, got out and ran across into a shell-hole, but the moment he put his head up from the hole to have a look round, was sniped.   We got his body in at night, and found that the German had shot him clean through the head.   He was acting as a company commander at this time, and doing very well indeed.   He was a sad loss to us, as, however hot a time we were having, Freeman always made fun of it.

"Capt. Ackroyd, our usual M.O., was not with us in this action, as he had had to leave soon after Delville Wood with a breakdown.   We missed him sadly.   He meant so much to the battalion.   It can be imagined what a wonderful M.O. he was when it is realized that, on the 1st July 1916, eleven reports from officers outside the battalion were sent in with reference to his gallantry.   He was recommended for the V.C., but was only awarded the M.C.   He was exactly the same at Delville Wood, and there went out into the wood and brought in some German wounded, although sniped at by Germans in the trees."

At 4.30 p.m. on the 5th October the battalion was relieved by the 17th Sherwood Foresters, and went by lorry to Hedanville.   During the period at and beyond Thiepval, from the 27th September to the 5th October, the battalion had been engaged in no definite great assault, but had nevertheless suffered heavily from constant bombardment and minor affairs. Its casualties during the period are stated, without details, at two hundred and one.

Next day the battalion was moved by rail from Acheux to Candas, where it remained in billets till the 14th, when it returned by 'bus to Albert.

Thence "B" and "D" Companies were sent to the 8th Suffolk in front line, the rest of the battalion being in support of them in the trenches N.W. of Courcelette.

On the 21st October, Regina Trench was taken by the Norfolk and Essex Battalions, the former being assisted by one company, and the latter by two platoons of the Royal Berkshire.

After a week at Albert from the 22nd October, the battalion was in Regina Trench on the 29th, and on the 31st in Brigade reserve.   Second-Lieutenant A. Jackson was wounded on that day.

The casualties for the month of October in other ranks are given thus in the Battalion Diary:

	Killed.	Wounded.	Missing.
1st to 5th .	31	165	5
15th to 22nd .	13	38	3
29th to 31st	2	17	1
	—	—	
Total .	46	220	

There is little to be told of the month of November.

On the 7th, at Warloy, General Maxse presented medals, including the Military Cross gained by Second-Lieutenant Lewis for his conduct with the battalion bombers at Thiepval. The 18th Division was taken out of the line and spent the whole of December in rest billets in the Abbeville area, the Royal Berkshire being at Le Titre.

Their November casualties were :

Other Ranks : Killed 5 ; Wounded 42 ; Missing 4.

BOOM RAVINE. IRLES. THE THIRD BATTLE OF YPRES. GLENCORSE WOOD. POELCAPPELLE. HOUTHULST FOREST. DISBANDMENT

1917–1918

By the 15th January 1917 the battalion was back with the division at Martinsart and Aveluy, whence, on the 27th, it relieved the 7th Bedfordshire in the front line, facing north opposite Grandcourt on the south bank of the Ancre. During this relief a German shell landed right in the entrance of the dugout of " B " Company, killing two and wounding thirteen men. Between the 17th and the 31st eight men were killed and fifteen wounded, most of them by this unlucky shell.

The early part of February was spent in and out of trenches in this neighbourhood, where was Desire Trench, about one thousand yards south of Grandcourt. It had been taken by other units on the 18th November 1916.

In front of Desire Trench was the long Grandcourt Trench, still held, except at its western end, by the Germans on the southern flank of their salient projecting across the upper Ancre. On the 16th February preparations were being made for the attack next day which, in the History of the 18th Division, is called the Battle of Boom Ravine. The ravine so called was on the boundary between the 54th Brigade on the right and the 53rd on the left. It was shaped like a Y, with the stem running from the N.W.

and the branches spreading out south and east from a point within the 54th Brigade area. Grandcourt was to the left of the left boundary of the 53rd, Miraumont to the right of the right boundary of the 54th Brigade's sphere of operations.

The unfortunate and disgraceful part of this battle was that two British deserters of another division gave away the hour of the attack, and, as far as they knew it, the plan.* Another misfortune was that in the night of the 16th-17th the weather suddenly changed from an intense frost to a rapid thaw which, in a very few hours, transformed a surface of metallic hardness into a quagmire.

The disposition of the 53rd Brigade placed the 8th Suffolk on the right, reinforced by one company of the 8th Norfolk. On the left was the 6th Royal Berkshire, with another Norfolk company on their extreme left. Through the position of the Royal Berkshire, the sunken " Sixteen Road " led nearly north to join the N.W. end of Boom Ravine. It crossed Grandcourt Trench, then passed the E. end of Rum Trench, and through the centre of Coffee Trench.

The orders required the troops to begin assembling at 4.45 in preparation for the advance an hour later. As we know, the Germans had been treacherously warned, and, as the assembly began, the enemy opened the ball with a tremendous bombardment of the points of assembly which caused grievous losses. Amongst the cases of much more serious damage inflicted, one shell blew in the Head-quarters of the 6th Royal Berkshire, and Colonel Clay, who was commanding, had to move elsewhere. Besides this, the difficulties of forming up in the darkness and mist were immense. Still, it was successfully accomplished, and the brigade went over up to time.

The ground was already a sea of mud which, combined with the darkness, had rendered it impossible to get up rations, and the men went over on empty stomachs.

We shall follow the movements of individual companies as they are given in a narrative attached to the diary.

" C," the company leading on the right, pushed quickly forward and captured, without serious resistance, the enemy strong point where Grand-

* This statement is taken from the History of the 18th Division, p. 140.

court Trench crossed Sixteen Road. Here they were in close touch with the left of the 8th Suffolk. Sixteen Road was mopped up with the help of a platoon of the 8th Norfolk attached for the purpose. The advance continued past Rum Trench, which was found to be unoccupied.

When the wire in front of Coffee Trench was reached, it was found to have been only indifferently cut, but three gaps were found through which the company penetrated and pushed on to their first objective with their leading wave, after knocking out the crew of a machine gun in rear of the trench. There were many dugouts in Sixteen Road, and a fair number of prisoners were taken in them by the Royal Berkshire and the Suffolk.

After a halt of thirty-seven minutes, the British barrage lifted, and " C," which had been reorganized meanwhile, pushed on to its final objective on the Grandcourt-Miraumont Road.

When this point was reached, it was found that the troops on the right were not so far forward, and the right of " C " was attacked by Germans retiring from the ground immediately north of Boom Ravine.

As a consequence, it was necessary to withdraw the company temporarily over three hundred yards, back to the junction of Coffee Trench and Sixteen Road. Here touch was gained with " B," on the left in Tea Trench, and consolidation was commenced. The time was about 7.30 when Captain V. G. McArthur was wounded whilst siting a strong point. Second-Lieutenant A. Birch had received, at Coffee Trench, wounds from which he died later. Command of the company fell to Second-Lieutenant G. H. Tigar.

" B " was the centre company. At the beginning of the attack it crossed Grandcourt Trench unopposed, and passed Rum Trench under a shrapnel barrage. As it moved up Coffee Trench, Captain N. B. Hudson was wounded. In Coffee Trench the company was reorganized, whilst waiting for the barrage to reopen. In the fighting in this trench Second-Lieutenants Fox and Smeeton were wounded. The company was now commanded by C.-S.-M. Hine. It was this N.C.O. who, as related in the History of the 18th Division, sent to Head-quarters by pigeon the laconic message " Second objective taken. C.-S.-M. Hine." When that objective (the Grandcourt-Miraumont Road) was reached, " C " had, as we know, been withdrawn to conform to the movement of the troops on the right. To keep in touch with " C " the right of " B " had to be refused. " D," the left assaulting company, met with no resistance till it reached the enemy trench immediately east of the Grandcourt Orchards. Here the wire was not well cut, but the company forced a way through and captured the trench, which was not strongly occupied, without difficulty. Second-Lieutenant Tarrant at once pushed on to the sunken road from Grandcourt to Miraumont, and in the dugouts on its southern side took about seventy German prisoners. He advanced a patrol beyond the road, as far as the railway, and obtained touch with " B " on his right, and the Norfolk company on his left. From the latter he had received assistance in the attack. " A " was in reserve, and, as the assaulting troops went forward, it moved into Grandcourt Trench. When they again advanced to the final objective, " A " left two platoons and Company Head-quarters in Grand-court Trench, and in Folly Trench behind the starting point. The other two platoons were employed to garrison Coffee Trench.

As for Battalion Head-quarters, it will be remembered that they had been forced, by the blowing in of their dugout, to abandon their original position in the gunpits. A new position was then taken up at the junction of Sixteen Road and Regina Trench, fourteen hundred yards south of Grandcourt.

In the positions so successfully gained the battalion set about con-solidating, an operation which was facilitated by the concealment afforded by the mist arising from the thaw in the Ancre Valley. The success was great, but not so costly as it might have been. The losses were less in the actual advance than in the time preceding it, when the German barrage fell on the assembly trenches.

Officers. Wounded (none killed) : Capts. V. G. McArthur.
N. B. Hudson.
2nd-Lieuts. A. Birch (mortally).
A. J. Fox, F. J. Smeeton,
S. J. Kydd.
Other Ranks : Killed 19 ; Wounded 121 ; Missing 48.

Of this action Captain Rochfort writes :
" The long frost, which lasted from November 1916 to February 1917, broke on the morning of 16th February. The tape line laid out for this attack was actually nailed into the ground, and so hard was it to drive the

nails in that it took us five hours to lay it. Major Hoare was the Brigade-Major who accompanied us on this little exploit, and while we were laying the line we were all wondering how it would be possible to dig in in any way until the frost broke.

" The troops usually termed this ' Grocery Battle,' as the trenches we were attacking were Tea, Coffee, and Rum Trenches. Coffee Trench was a mystery trench. It came out in the aeroplane photos, was strongly wired, but no movement was ever seen in it. On the morning of the 16th, Lewis and I approached Coffee Trench from the orchard above Grandcourt. We found that Coffee Trench was only a trace 6 inches deep, but that the wire in front of it had not been cut and would be a serious obstacle to our advance. General Higginson got our artillery on to this all day, and succeeded in having the whole of it destroyed.

" The night of the attack was the darkest I have ever known. A thaw had set in, and a mist rose about 8 or 9 feet from the ground. Once in this mist it was impossible to see a yard. We had all roads blocked and guarded, and guides out with tape and wire leading up to the forming-up place. Some of the —— Division had deserted that afternoon into the Boche line, and had given away the hour of the attack. As a result we were shelled all night on our forming-up line.

" Head-quarters was in some gunpits, but so heavy was the shelling of these that Colonel Clay decided to evacuate them and use a shell-hole. As we were leaving the gunpits, a shell burst in the entrance, knocked Colonel Clay and me into a shell-hole full of water, and wiped out the two runners who were carrying our papers, namely Whitehouse and Mabson. Whitehouse was carrying a leather attaché case with the orders and maps for the battle. We never found a trace of him or the attaché case.

" The attack was a great success, but we had to withdraw our line owing to the failure of the division on our right to get their objective.

" We had some unusual adventures in this attack. Lieutenant Tarrant captured thirty Boches single-handed from the entrance of a dugout. One platoon of ours lost itself in the darkness coming up, and found itself in the Boche line. They refused to surrender, and were found in a shell-hole which they had taken up, all killed. But they were surrounded by many Boche dead, showing what a good fight they had put up."

The 18th was employed in completing the consolidation of the new positions, and on the 19th the battalion was relieved by the 10th Essex, and was in rear for the rest of the month.

On the 1st and 2nd March it was at Aveluy, and from the 6th to the 9th back again at Boom Ravine.

During the attack and capture of Irles on the 10th, by the Essex and Norfolk Battalions, the part taken by the 6th Royal Berkshire was confined to the employment of " A " Company to carry for those battalions, in which operation it lost two men killed.

Next day the battalion took over Irles and the neighbouring posts from the Essex and Norfolk Battalions.

This was the period of the German retreat to the Hindenburg Line and the 6th Royal Berkshire had little open fighting during the rest of March, though its casualties in trenches for the month amounted, for other ranks, to 10 killed, 21 wounded and 1 missing.

At the end of the month the 18th Division was moved by rail to another part, and from the 26th March till the 18th April the battalion was training at Lumbres.   The division was out of the line, forming part of the G.H.Q. Reserve of the 1st Army.

From Lumbres the battalion went for the 19th and 20th April to Béthune, and from the 21st to the 26th was at Nœux les Mines.   Thence it went by march and rail to bivouac at Beaurains, south of Arras.

On the 2nd May the 53rd Brigade was in Divisional reserve in the old German trenches between Neuville Vitasse and Wancourt.   The 18th Division was now part of the VIIth Corps in the 3rd Army, and was to attack next day at Chérisy.

The story of the ill-fated attack of the 3rd May is fully recorded, as regards the 54th and 55th Brigades, in the History of the 18th Division. With it we are little concerned, for the 53rd Brigade was on that day in reserve, and probably the 6th Royal Berkshire never fired a shot, though they lost 15 men killed, 23 wounded, and 2 missing from the barrage through which they had to move during the day.

The attack began at 3.45 a.m. (summer time).

At 1 a.m. the 6th Royal Berkshire was moved forward from the reserve trenches in which it had been so far to the sunken road west of the Cojeul

River between Heinel and Wancourt. They were still three thousand yards behind the front, separated from it by two ridges. At 4 p.m. they were again moved forward about a mile, this time through a heavy enemy barrage which probably caused most of their losses. Here they were in close support of the 55th Brigade, whose attack on Chérisy had been repulsed, and who had been forced to retire to the line from which they had started in the early morning. At 9 p.m. the 53rd Brigade relieved the troops in front line.

The relief was no easy matter. A heavy mist had descended on the field when Captain Rochfort was sent up at 8 p.m. to arrange it and he had great difficulty in finding his way through the crowded trenches. Eventually he had to mark off the front into two halves with an old door which he had whitewashed, so as to make it visible. Then he moved up one of his weak companies on each side of the door above ground, as it was impossible to get them into the trenches till the men to be relieved had come out. " A " was on the right, " D " on the left, " B " was in support four hundred yards behind the front line, Head-quarters another two hundred yards in rear, and " C " in reserve.

The 6th Royal Berkshire held this position for five days. On the 5th May Second-Lieutenant A. V. Peel was killed by a shell outside Battalion Head-quarters, and during this period Sergt.-Major Bartholomew was blown to pieces by another shell in the same place. Captain Rochfort says : " He was a splendid fellow, popular with officers and men and an example to all ranks."

The front held was about ten hundred yards west of the northern end of Chérisy on the extreme left of the divisional front. Patrols sent out on the 4th and 5th May to recover British wounded met with no success.

" A " was on the right front, "D" on the left, "B" and "C" respectively in right and left support trenches.

In this position, alternately with other battalions, the Royal Berkshire remained till the 18th May. The enemy bombardment varied in intensity from day to day.

During an attack by the division on the right, on the 20th May, the battalion was saved from severe loss from the German bombardment by the judicious thinning out of the line.

The rest of the month was spent in Divisional reserve, and from the 27th in Brigade reserve at St. Martin-sur-Cojeul.   The casualties during these operations near Chérisy were by no means small.

On the 3rd 2nd-Lieut. H. A. Mossman was wounded ; on the 5th 2nd-Lieut. A. V. Peel was killed, and 2nd-Lieuts. L. A. Kingham and C. H. Naylor were wounded.

For the whole period there were, of other ranks, killed 35, wounded 56, missing 5.   The high proportion of killed to wounded is noticeable.

The month of June was spent in the support area in training, and from the 16th June till the 2nd July in the rest area at St. Amand.

The battalion was now about to play its part in the Third Battle of Ypres. On the 3rd July it went by train to Cassel, and marched to billets at Steenworde, where it remained till the 28th, training specially for the attack which was eventually fixed for the 31st.   After a day at Reninghelst, and another at the Canal Reserve Camp at Ouderdom, it marched fully equipped for action, at 9 p.m. on the 30th July, to Dickebusch Camp, from which it moved by platoons the same night to its assembly positions for battle on the 31st.

The 18th Division was now in the IInd Corps of the 5th Army.   The attack of the 31st July was to be led by the 53rd Brigade, which had only been moved up at the last moment from its training station at Steenworde.   There it had been carefully practised on a model of the area of the coming battle. Preparations in the front line had been carried out by the 54th and 55th Brigades, who had suffered severely from the increasing shell fire.   So heavy had their losses been that the historian of the 18th Division reckons that 95 per cent. of the eight hundred and sixty-four casualties of the two brigades in eighteen days were due to shell fire.   What this means may be better realized when we remember that of the German casualties in 1870–1871 only 4 per cent. were attributed to artillery action.

On the 31st July the 30th Division was in front of the 18th, with orders to capture the " black line " running east of Shrewsbury Forest, Dumbarton Lakes, and Inverness Copse, and passing through the centre of Glencorse Wood.   On that line it was to be " leap-frogged " by the 53rd Brigade, the ultimate objective being Polygon Wood, eight hundred yards beyond Glencorse Wood.

Immediately before the attack the 53rd Brigade was in trenches just east of the Zillebeke tank. Thence the 6th Royal Berkshire and the 8th Suffolk marched to their assembly points on the west of Sanctuary Wood.

Even this march up was fruitful in casualties, which numbered two officers and seventeen other ranks.

The British barrage opened at 3.50 a.m., and the German followed quickly, being directed mostly on No-Man's Land. A few heavy shells fell in the assembly area, but did no damage.

At 5 a.m. a message was received from the Brigade saying the " blue line " had been taken. It ran generally south, in a curve convex towards the east, from the northern divisional boundary, through Surbiton Villas and Clapham Junction, to the southern boundary five hundred yards west of Dumbarton Lakes. The " black line " was on an average seven hundred yards farther on.

At 5.50 a.m. two patrols, under Second-Lieutenants G. H. Tigar and H. R. Hooper, went out to try and get into touch with the 17th Manchester of the 30th Division, who were reported to be attacking the " black line." Hooper was wounded and sent no report. Tigar reported that he had been told that the attack was held up by machine-gun fire from Surbiton Villas and Stirling Castle. He could hear nothing of the 17th Manchester, and could get very little reliable information of any sort.

At 7.15 the Royal Berkshire moved forward in artillery formation. The enemy's shelling was patchy, and fell mainly towards the left of the battalion. Very little harm was done by it till Sanctuary Wood was entered when a machine gun and 77 m.m. field-gun barrage caused a few losses. By the time the eastern edge of Sanctuary Wood was reached, the barrage had become really heavy. Still nothing was seen or heard of the 17th Manchester till it was reported that they had taken Glencorse Wood. This was known to the 8th Suffolk to be incorrect, but the 6th Royal Berkshire had received no contradiction of it.

What had really happened was that the 30th Division had missed its direction and gone away to its left. It had taken Château Wood, away to the north beyond the northern boundary of its area, in the belief apparently, that it was Glencorse Wood. The consequence of this was that the " blue line " was so far untouched, and the 53rd Brigade was left with the task of

taking this almost unshaken line, which they had expected to find in possession of the 30th Division when they formed up for their attack beyond the
" black line."

The forming-up position for the Berkshire attack was Jargon Trench, on
the western border of Glencorse Wood, and the battalion, still ignorant of the
falsity of the report about the capture of Glencorse Wood, determined to push
on, though there were disturbing reports from isolated men of continued
German machine-gun activity from Inverness Copse on the right, and the
Ypres-Menin Road in front, and no traces of the 30th Division had yet been
found.

The advance was continued through the marshy land south of the Menin
Road, in which the tanks were bogged and put out of action.   As the road
was reached, heavy machine-gun fire was met, especially from Surbiton
Villas in front and Clapham Junction on the right.   It was 8.30 a.m. and
the battalion was timed to be formed up behind the " black line " at 10.10.
The artillery, ignorant of what had happened to the 30th Division, had lifted
their barrage beyond the " blue line," which, as we know, was intact.   The
Berkshire men had now to rely on their own rifle and Lewis-gun fire.   They
received some support from the trench-mortar battery attached to the 8th
Suffolk, but neither the machine-gun section nor the trench-mortars attached
to the Royal Berkshire were up.

In extended order, and under destructive machine-gun fire, the junction
of the road and the brigade boundary had been reached, still short of the
" blue line."   The machine-gun fire came mainly from the German strong
points about Clapham Junction and in Glencorse Wood.   It was clear now
that the " black line " had not been taken.

British troops could be seen towards Jabber Drive and Westhoek on the
left.

No troops of the 30th Division had been met with.   A determined effort
was then made to reach Jargon Trench.   Two platoons of " D " were sent
out to try and get touch with the British troops seen at Jabber Drive.
These turned out to be the 2nd Royal Berkshire, of the 8th Division on the
left, who were forming a defensive flank on the right of that division, the
centre of which had got forward to the northern part of Glencorse Wood
within its boundary.   Jargon Switch, on the left front beyond the " blue

line," and the cross-roads beyond it, were taken by these two platoons in
extended order.

By 9.50 Surbiton Villas and the neighbouring cross-roads had been taken,
but the casualties had been heavy.   The dash of the attack, and the extension northwards to fill up gaps on the battalion's left, had caused some
disorganization.   The whole advance made had only been possible by the
individual exertions of small parties of men creeping forward from one shell-
hole to the next.

Under the circumstances, it was impossible to form up and attack behind
the barrage which was to open at 10.10 a.m. on a line considerably east of the
enemy who were now checking the advance of the 6th Royal Berkshire.
Orders were, however, issued to gain as much ground as possible eastwards
when the barrage came down.

It came down punctually, but of course was in rear of the enemy who were
in the space between it and the front of the 6th Royal Berkshire.   The
attempt to advance was duly made, but, as soon as the men stood up for
the purpose, they encountered machine-gun fire from Glencorse Wood and
Jargon Trench, by which the attempt was nipped in the bud.

Captain Arthur Hudson was killed on the eastern edge of Glencorse Wood
whilst making a gallant attempt to capture a German field gun which was
acting as an anti-tank gun.   The tanks had a bad time on this day.   Captain
Rochfort says seventeen of them were either knocked out or stuck in the
mud in the area between the Ypres-Menin Road and Glencorse Wood.
Some of them were nose deep in mud.   He also states that some of the
Berkshire bombers got into a strong point at the south-west corner of
Glencorse Wood which was the highest point in the neighbourhood.   They
were, however, driven out again by a German counter-attack from Inverness
Copse.

The 2nd Lincolnshire were now on the left, but separated from the left
of the battalion by a gap in filling which one company of the 8th Norfolk
took part.   Consolidation of the line attained was begun, the left flank of the
battalion being thrown forward.   A support line was commenced in shell-
holes in rear.   Battalion Head-quarters were on the Ypres-Menin Road.
When the barrage in front ceased at noon, three German aeroplanes drove off
the single British 'plane present, and proceeded to fly up and down, firing on

the troops south of the Menin Road till 4 p.m. when the setting in of mist forced them to desist.

Captain Rochfort says that one of the Berkshire bombers fired a " No. 23 " at one of these aeroplanes after actually taking out the pin and releasing the lever before firing it. It burst within a few feet of the aeroplane which, with its companions, then cleared off.

The line consolidated by the 6th Royal Berkshire met the left of the 8th Suffolk east of Surbiton Villas, and was held in front by " A " on the right and " B " and " D " and a mopping-up company of the 10th Essex on the left.

Here too was the company of the 8th Norfolk which did much work in digging a strong point, and in filling the gap between the left of " D " and the right of the 2nd Lincolnshire. Captain Patten of this company had taken command, in addition to his own men, of the twenty-one men of the Berkshire " D " Company, who had no officer left.

The rest of the gap on the left of the Norfolk Company was filled, about 4 p.m., by a party of the missing 17th Manchester.

" C " of the 6th Royal Berkshire was in support, in shell-holes one hundred yards behind the front line.

The enemy was reported to be massing for a counter-attack, but it did not come off.

The losses on this day were :

Officers. Killed : Capt. A. H. Hudson, Lieut. H. S. Tindall, 2nd-Lieut. H. G. N. Tarrant, M.C.
Wounded : 2nd-Lieuts. H. R. Hooper, W. D. Rees, E. H. G. Worden, W. H. Wood, A. A. Barrett.
Other Ranks : Killed or Died of Wounds 41 ; Wounded and Missing 1 ; Wounded 177 ; Missing 27.
Total : 8 Officers and 246 Other Ranks.

The battalion being relieved, at 2.30 a.m. on the 1st August, by the 17th Liverpool, went back to Ouderdom.

It was on this day that the Medical Officer of the 6th Royal Berkshire, Captain H. Ackroyd, who had already so highly distinguished himself at Delville Wood, gained his Victoria Cross. A man of mature years, no young surgeon fresh from the medical schools, he behaved throughout with the utmost courage and coolness, attending to the wounded in the hottest fire, and attending to them without hurry and with the greatest care and skill.

It is said that his recommendations for the Cross came from no less than twenty-three different sources. He died without knowing that he had gained it, for he was killed on the 10th August.

From the 1st to the 3rd August the battalion was reorganizing and resting at Ouderdom, and from the 4th to the 9th was at New Dickebusch Camp.

It left that camp at 6 a.m. on the 10th, and at 7.20 a message was received that the 7th Bedfordshire, now holding Jargon Trench, were being strongly counter-attacked. The battalion moved out of the Ritz Street area by platoons, encountering a heavy German barrage in Sanctuary Wood and on the Ypres-Menin Road.

No mention is made in the diary, or in the History of the 18th Division, of any fighting for the 6th Royal Berkshire on the 10th August, and the next thing in the diary after the statement as to the barrage in Sanctuary Wood is that their leading platoons reached Head-quarters of the 7th Bedfordshire on the Ypres-Menin Road at 8.10 p.m., and were sent up to reinforce the line about Clapham Junction. The counter-attack on the Bedfordshire had been beaten off, and that regiment was relieved by the 8th Norfolk at 1 a.m. on the 11th.

At 4.30 a.m. on the 11th, when the 8th Norfolk were relieving the Bedfordshire Regiment in the strong point in the south-west corner of Glencorse Wood, it was rushed by a German counter-attack. The 6th Royal Berkshire were ordered to support the Norfolk Battalion in the recapture of the strong point. Captain Rochfort says that he was sent up to arrange covering fire for this attack. Two companies of the 8th Norfolk, at the bend of the Ypres-Menin Road, attacked the strong point, and at the same time " A " Company of the 6th Royal Berkshire, under Captain G. C. Hollis, bombed southwards from the west edge of Glencorse Wood. The strong point was recovered, though not without considerable losses.

At 10.15 the 8th Norfolk, 10th Essex, and 6th Royal Berkshire were ordered to make an attack from the edge of Glencorse Wood, which had been gained by the 54th Brigade. But, in addition to the fact that the 8th Norfolk had lost heavily in the operations about the strong point, the 8th Suffolk did not turn up, and the attack was in consequence cancelled.

In the night of the 12th-13th the battalion was relieved by the Queen's Westminsters, and went to Railway Dugouts, west of Zillebeke, where they underwent some gas shelling, but had only one casualty.

In the afternoon of the 14th two companies were sent to the shelter of Crab Crawl, and the other two into the line on the Ypres-Menin Road.

For the 15th the History of the 18th Division says :

" On the 15th the Germans counter-attacked from Polygon Wood. For at least two hours there was no artillery fire, and the infantry fought it out with rifle and bayonet. The Berks and Norfolks displayed remarkable resilience, and took heavy toll with the bayonet, four men claiming ten victims each."

Curiously, there is no mention of this fight in the Berkshire diary. All that it says is that of the two companies sent up on the 14th one was in support in the tunnel under the Ypres-Menin Road. The 15th was spent in arranging for an attack by the 1/4th London Regiment, which was made on the 16th and failed.

The battalion's casualties in the period 10th–16th August were two officers (2nd-Lieut. L. A. Kingham and Capt. H. Ackroyd, M.C., R.A.M.C.) killed ; 10 other ranks killed, and 67 wounded.

On the night of the 16th-17th the 6th Royal Berkshire were relieved by the 12th Middlesex, and, after concentrating at Crab Crawl, went back to Rubrouck, where they were till the end of the month, and on till the 22nd September. On the 23rd September, they went, viâ Poperinghe, to Road Camp, and were there till the 8th October.

From the 9th to the 13th October the 6th Royal Berkshire were engaged in their last great battle of the war before their disbandment. It was fought in a neighbourhood considerably north of Sanctuary and Glencorse Woods, about Poelcappelle.

On the 9th October the battalion moved from Road Camp to Canal Bank. It was temporarily attached to the 55th Brigade, in support of which it was to act in the attack on Poelcappelle. On the 10th the battalion was, from 2.30 to 4 p.m., on the march from Canal Bank to Hurst Park. Finding no accommodation there, it went to Cane Trench, which it shared with the 8th Suffolk.

On the 11th orders were received for the forthcoming operations, and small parties from each company were employed in reconnoitring. That morning a single enemy shell, supposed to have been meant for the main line, fell short and caused eight casualties among the Berkshire men. Later in the day Second-Lieutenant G. F. Austin, the signalling-officer, who had gone out with a party to put down tapes on the forming-up position, was killed by a shell.

At 1 a.m. on the 12th the leading platoon left Cane Trench for the forward area. At first there were intervals of two hundred yards between platoons, but it was so dark, and the going was so bad through shell-holes and marsh, that it was soon found imperative to close up, in order to maintain touch and direction. It had poured the whole of the 11th and was still raining hard, rendering the country, bad at the best, almost unpassable.

The objectives were Poelcappelle and Meunier House, where the ground had already begun to rise very gradually on the way to the Westroosebeke Ridge.

The last company of the Royal Berkshire only reached the forming-up line at 5.30 a.m., five minutes after the British barrage had started, and been followed almost immediately by the German reply.

The battalion was disposed with " C " on the right, " B " in the centre, " A " on the left," and " D " in rear. The advance was not hindered till the line of the Steenbeek was reached. Here gas shells began to be encountered and masks had to be donned. At 6.10 a.m. there was no news of the troops in front, and it was decided to push on, so as to reach the final forming-up line at the prescribed hour. It was becoming clear that the first phase of the operations had failed, and that the line on which the battalions in rear were to leap-frog those in front was not likely to be taken.

Two hundred yards before even the first forming-up position was reached, machine guns and snipers at the Brewery, Meunier House, and Beek House had reaped a heavy harvest of casualties. The ground was everywhere torn up by shells, greasy, and sodden. Every movement was difficult and slow. At 6.30 a.m. Lieut.-Colonel H. G. F. Longhurst was killed at Battalion Head-quarters, and command was taken over by Captain and Adjutant R. A. Rochfort, M.C.

Still there was no news of progress in front, and Captain Rochfort, going forward to investigate the position on the left, was badly wounded and forced to make over command to Lieutenant J. W. K. Wernham, the only officer left with Battalion Head-quarters.

Towards 9 a.m. a message came in from " A " on the left, saying that the troops were disorganized by the terrible state of the ground, and that officer casualties in the advance had been very heavy. Only at noon was any definite news received, and that was that some of the Buffs on the left of the leading troops had been taken. A platoon of " D " (in rear) was at once sent up to fill the gap, but found that this had already been done by a company of the 7th Queen's.

At 12.30 p.m. " A," " B," " C " Companies were in line, " D " in rear and in touch with the 9th Division on the right and the Buffs on the left. There appeared to be no British troops in front of the battalion.

Orders were then received to consolidate the positions occupied in artillery formation.

Half an hour later came warning of an expected counter-attack on the left, but it did not materialize, and the battalion held on till 7 p.m., when the O.C. 7th Queen's came with a message from the Brigade that the battalion was to be relieved. In the darkness and difficulty of moving about, it was found impossible to reach company-commanders, and the withdrawal had to be postponed.

At 5.30 on the morning of the 13th October all companies were informed that the 7th Queen's were forming a line of posts in rear of the battalion's position. When this was complete, the Berkshire men were to get back through it, in parties of two or three, to Cane Trench, from which they had started on the previous day.

This operation was completed by " A " by 8 a.m. The other companies thought withdrawal by daylight would be too costly, and were inclined to wait for darkness. However, in the end, all had filtered back by 4.30 p.m., and, after a short rest, were sent back to Murat Camp.

The whole operation had been a failure, and scarcely any ground had been gained, notwithstanding the heavy casualties suffered. In the 6th Royal Berkshire they were :

Officers. *Killed :* Lieut.-Colonel H. G. F. Longhurst.
Capt. W. R. Wacher.
Lieut. J. W. J. Jeakes (Died of Wounds).

2nd-Lieuts. G. F. Austin (on the 11th).
     G. H. Tigar (on the 13th).
     C. H. Todd, A. T. H. Tunbridge.
Wounded : Capts. R. A. Rochfort, M.C., E. C. J. Spencer,
   G. C. Hollis.
   2nd-Lieuts. W. Angel, F. C. Morgan.
Other Ranks : Killed 33 ; Wounded 155 ; Missing 10.
   Total : 12 Officers and 198 Other Ranks.

For the failure on the 12th October the 6th Royal Berkshire can bear no blame, as is shown by the following extract from a letter from General Higginson, received by Captain Rochfort when he was in hospital :

> " The 12th was a very unfortunate day for the brigade. Neither your battalion nor the Suffolk ever had a chance. It was cruel luck, two such splendid battalions being wasted."

From the 15th to the 30th October the battalion was at Tunnelling Camp, where, on the 22nd, Major V. G. McArthur, M.C., took command.

From the 30th October the 6th Royal Berkshire was at Plumstead Camp till the 4th November, when it marched to Proven and thence went by train to Boesinghe, north of Ypres, whence it moved into front line in the afternoon.

On this day Second-Lieutenant R. E. Cripps was killed, and Major McArthur went to the base to appear before a medical board. Command of the battalion was assumed by Major FitzHugh of the Royal West Kent Regiment. During the rest of the month it was backwards and forwards between the front, now beyond Poelcappelle, and support or reserve trenches or camps. During a relief on the 16th, as the Royal Berkshire were about to leave the front line, there was a very bad gas shelling, which accounted for a large proportion of the following casualties in the month.

Officers. Killed : 2nd-Lieut. R. E. Cripps.
   Wounded : Capt. V. R. Price, 2nd-Lieut. F. G. Hazard (also
     Gassed).
   Gassed : 2nd-Lieuts. F. C. Greenfield.
     H. J. Lord.
     W. C. Molland.
Other Ranks : Killed or Died of Wounds 22 ; Wounded 27 ; Missing 9 ;
   Gassed 118 ; Died of Gas 5.

During part of November, and all December, the battalion was on the front towards the Houthulst Forest which was perhaps the worst of all the many uncomfortable fronts on which the 6th Royal Berkshire were stationed in Belgium or France. For a description of it we cannot do better than quote the following passage from Captain G. H. F. Nichols' *The 18th Division in the Great War* :

" There was nothing sylvan about Houthulst, whatever imagination may have conjured up from the name. It was a flat, low-lying six hundred acres of broken stumps and wreckage, a swamp with many a deep and treacherous hole to trap the unwary walker and let him in up to the neck. There are stories that the Germans, in as much draggled misery as ourselves, came at times to pull out with ropes men of ours who had got engulfed in the slime. It was mud that stank ; when the rain ceased the nostrils had to accept a faded musty smell that hung in the air five miles behind the line—a smell that told of desolation and decay, of gas shells, of dead men. Trenches were impossible. The men in the line garrisoned a few shell-holes, protected here and there with breastworks that were constantly becoming submerged ; company and battalion head-quarters were in old pill-boxes, where the concrete was cracked and no longer water-tight ; the line was reached by duck-board tracks from six thousand or seven thousand yards in rear. It was inadvisable to attempt to cross the intervening area in the daytime, and it was a difficult adventure in the darkness, because the nightly shell fire constantly introduced new pitfalls. . . . At first it was customary for battalions to spend four days in line and four days out, at the well-named Dirty Bucket Camp. Put in other words, it meant that men were four days wet through and four days dry. Experience showed that the reliefs were not sufficiently frequent, and casualties from trench feet rose to one hundred per battalion."

January 1918 was again spent in these horrible conditions, the misery of which was increased by the knowledge, towards the end of the month, that the battalion, as well as the 8th Suffolk and 8th Norfolk, was soon to cease to exist as a unit. Their fate was due to no fault of their own, but to the inexorable demands of the new reorganization, which reduced brigades from four to three battalions. For the men of the disbanded battalions the meaning was not that their war service was ended, but merely that it was to continue in other units, mostly other battalions of their own county regiment, whose depleted ranks they would help to fill.   There they would still be men of the Berkshire, or Norfolk, or Suffolk Regiments, but they would have to change their regimental allegiance from one battalion which no longer existed, but with which they had served through years of war, to another whose history had been different, though no less glorious.

On the 29th January the battalion listened to the farewell of its own commander, and next day was addressed, for the last time, by Brigadier-General Higginson, under whom it had so long and splendidly served.

The actual disbandment began on the 6th February 1918, and the officers and men were distributed as follows to other battalions :

1st Battalion : 2 Lieutenants, 2 Second-Lieutenants and about 150 Other Ranks.
2nd Battalion : 1 Captain (Mossman, M.C.), 2 Lieutenants, 14 Second-Lieutenants and about 330 Other Ranks.
5th Battalion : 2 Lieutenants, 2 Second-Lieutenants and about 80 Other Ranks.

About 60 other ranks went to the 18th Entrenching Battalion, and the transport to the 2nd Brigade of the 1st Division.

Colonel FitzHugh and the few men left went to Noyon, where they were finally disbanded on the 22nd February, and Colonel FitzHugh went to the 8th Royal Berkshire, which had replaced the 6th Battalion in the 18th Division.

CHAPTER XXXIII

THE 7th (SERVICE) BATTALION

FORMATION. FRANCE. SALONIKA

1914–1915

THE 7th Battalion Royal Berkshire Regiment was formed at Reading in August 1914 as a unit of Lord Kitchener's 3rd Army. Into its many initial difficulties it is not necessary to enter ; for they did not differ materially from those of other battalions formed under similar conditions. The men were drawn from all parts of England, chiefly the Midlands, with a large proportion of Berkshire men. No. 16 Platoon was almost entirely Welsh—chiefly miners.

After a short time at Reading, the battalion went to Codford and Sutton Veney in the Salisbury district, returning to Reading about November 1914. There it remained training and organizing till early in May 1915. It then moved to huts at Fovant near Salisbury. At Reading it had been gradually equipped, except for rifles. It used " Drill Purposes " rifles till four or five weeks before it went abroad. At Fovant, khaki uniform was issued, and there was much hard drilling and training, including more advanced training than had been possible at Reading.

About the 21st July 1915 the battalion moved to Sandhill Camp No. 14 at Longbridge Deverill, near Warminster, where it found the rest of the 26th Division commanded by Major-General Mackenzie Kennedy. At Fovant it had been with the 78th Brigade, commanded by Brigadier-General D'Arcy Thomas. With the division a more advanced course of training was undertaken, and, rifles having now been issued, a musketry course was fired. The battalion now proceeded to France with the rest of the division.

On the 15th September 1915 it embarked at Southampton for Havre,

7th BATTALION.

Forbury Gardens, Reading, December 1914.

(*Back Row*) Lt. H. D. Mosley. Lt. A. E. W. Butler. Lt. F. P. Cobden. Lt. G. J. H. Walls. Lt. H. J. C. Neobard. Lt. C. N. C. Field. Lt. J. L. Killick. Lt. Hanney. Lt. A. D. Breach.

(*Third Row*) Lt. V. H. Watney. Lt. G. F. Bate. Capt. Dodd (Padre). Lt. W. G. S. Curpley. Lt. R. N. Treadwell. Lt. R. A. B. Chancellor. Lt. H. E. Fletcher. Capt. and Q.M. G. Casey. Lt. H. H. Grundtvig. Lt. J. Butler. Lt. G. G. C. Piggott. Lt. H. A. R. Donkin. Lt. P. H. Williams. Lt. A. K. Barrett. Medical Officer.

(*Second Row*) Lt. F. Collins. Lt. F. W. C. Baker. Lt. J. B. Marks. and Lt. A. N. Other. Lt. C. E. Brown. Lt. S. H. Troup. Lt. H. C. Elphick. Lt. G. T. Hale. Lt. E. B. Matthews. Lt. S. A. Pike. Lt. Hon. A. Stuart. Capt. W. P. Collins.

(*First Row*) Lt. G. W. R. Bray. Lt. G. A. Cunnew. Capt. T. Close. Capt. R. B. Gillespie. Major C. E. Birch. Lt.-Col. R. E. T. Bray. Capt. J. M. Eldridge. Capt. L. Marton. Capt. H. B. Morony. Capt. F. Gill. Lt. T. V. Booth-Jones.

(*Not included in photo*) Lt. E. W. Ravenshear. Major J. J. O. B. Sexton. Lt. J. O. Hilling. Lt. L. G. B. Rogers. Lt. C. E. B. Rogers. Lt. Bray.

which was reached on the 20th. The officers who were with it at this time were the following :

Lieut.-Colonel R. E. T. Bray (Commanding).
Majors : J. J. O. B. Sexton (Second-in-command).
　　　　　H. B. Morony.
Captains : L. Marton.
　　　　　T. Close.
　　　　　R. B. Gillespie.
　　　　　J. M. Eldridge (Adjutant).
　　　　　T. H. Gill.
　　　　　W. P. Collins.
　　　　　J. O. Hilling.
　　　　　S. A. Pike.
Lieutenants : T. V. Booth-Jones (Transport Officer).
　　　　　S. H. Troup.
　　　　　R. A. B. Chancellor.
　　　　　C. E. B. Rogers.
　　　　　E. B. Matthews.
　　　　　H. J. C. Neobard.
　　　　　G. W. R. Bray.
　　　　　E. W. Ravenshear (Machine-gun Officer).
Second-Lieutenants : H. A. L. Donkin.
　　　　　H. C. Elphick.
　　　　　J. Butler.
　　　　　C. E. Brown.
　　　　　G. F. Bate.
　　　　　P. H. Williams (Signalling Officer).
　　　　　J. B. Marks.
　　　　　A. K. Barrett.
　　　　　H. D. Mosley.
Medical Officer : Lieut. M. Bryce.
Quartermaster : Honry.-Lieut. G. Casey.

Of the history of the battalion in France there is practically nothing to be said ; for its activities were almost entirely on the Salonika Front, and beyond learning trench-warfare work, it did no service on the Western Front.

From Havre it proceeded to the front at Ailly-sur-Somme on the 22nd September, and began learning its work attached to other units at Aubigny on the 26th. It was employed on this front without any incidents worth notice till the 9th November when it entrained, at 1.30 p.m. at Longueau, near Amiens, for Marseilles.   Lieut.-Colonel A. P. Dene (D.C.L.I.) had taken command of the battalion in October.   It formed a unit of the 78th Infantry Brigade of the 26th Division.   The other battalions of the brigade were the 9th Gloucestershire Regiment, 11th Worcestershire Regiment, and the 7th Oxfordshire and Buckinghamshire Light Infantry.   From Marseilles the battalion sailed, on the 11th November, on the *Arcadian*, with a strength of 25 officers and 906 other ranks.   Alexandria was reached, after an uneventful voyage, on the 18th, and the battalion sailed again on the 20th, under escort of H.M.S. *Magnificent*, for Salonika, which was reached safely on the 24th.

At Salonika itself the 7th Royal Berkshire remained for the rest of November, refitting and route-marching.   The weather was very cold and snowy.   On the 1st December the battalion went into the camp at Lembet, about four miles north of Salonika, preparatory to proceeding to the line of defence known as the Birdcage Line which was then being fortified with the view of making about Salonika an immense entrenched camp.   On the 12th they marched to Laina, another four miles to the north-east of Lembet, to dig trenches on the line Laina-Tumba, returning to camp the same day. Tumba marked the right of this part of the line ending at the western end of the Langaza Lake.   Beyond this lake was that of Beshik, and eastward again of that the sea.   On the 14th the whole brigade moved to a hill N.W. of Laina, and on the 26th moved again to the foot of the hills three-quarters of a mile east of Laina.   The front line of the brigade consisted of the Gloucestershire, Worcestershire, and Royal Berkshire Battalions, with the Oxfordshire and Buckinghamshire in reserve at Yailajik.   The Royal Berkshire occupied section C including twelve trenches.

SALONIKA AND THE DOIRAN-VARDAR FRONT
1916

From this time till the 4th June 1916 there is absolutely nothing to record.   The entry in the Battalion Diary on almost every day mentions nothing but the fact that the battalion was at work on the trenches.   Occasionally enemy aeroplanes were seen flying over to drop bombs on Salonika, and a change of position from front line to reserve is recorded on the 23rd March.   All these months were spent in road-making and trench-digging, without any appearance of the Bulgar enemy. It was weary work, and men and officers must have begun to wonder whether they were to be considered as a battalion of soldiers or a labour battalion. By the end of May the entrenched camp was completed.

On the 5th June a move was made to Redan Camp, where the defended area was taken over from the 8th South Wales Borderers at Akbunar. Here, too, there is nothing to record till the 21st, when the battalion went into the camp at Dremiglava some six miles north of Laina and the ultimate line of defence of Salonika on which so much labour had been expended.

The brigade was now, at last, about to advance to the real front line in contact with the enemy, which at that time was held by French troops in the line between Lake Doiran on the right and the Vardar River on the left. A month, however, was spent at Dremiglava, and it must be remembered that all this country was very unhealthy and a hot-bed of malaria, from which the troops throughout this campaign suffered more severely than from the enemy. Dysentery, too, was rife.

On the 22nd July Lieut.-Colonel Dene rejoined from England and took over command of the battalion from Major Morony, who had acted in his absence.

The northward march commenced on the 25th July, when Amberkoj was reached. The succeeding stages were Sarageul on the 26th, Malovci on the 27th, and the front on the 29th.

The French at this time were holding a line of which the right rested on the southern shore of Lake Doiran, the left on the River Vardar. Its length was some thirteen miles, winding along a line of hills, quite bare except for a clothing of prickly scrub growing with difficulty on the foot or so of soil which was all that covered the rock below—obviously a bad country for entrenching. These hills descended sharply on their northern edge, which was cut through by many ravines leading down to the valley. Beyond this were gradual slopes leading up to the Bulgarian positions, which generally overlooked and commanded those of the Allies.

The most conspicuous points on the Bulgarian side were Grand Couronné in the background N.W. of Doiran, and the long Pip Ridge running north and south a mile west of it. Each of these rose from ten hundred to twelve hundred feet above the hills held by the Allies, and formed admirable observation posts for the enemy.   The position is thus generally described by Major Pike :

" We were placed on small bare rocky hills looking up all the time (and at very close proximity : often only one hundred to three hundred yards of ' No-Man's Land ') at a fine, almost impregnable, series of mountain peaks. It was terrific country to fight over, consisting of a series of precipitous ravines and very steep bare slopes."

The French trenches, owing to the scanty soil, were poor, only some eighteen inches deep, whilst the enemy had been able to entrench himself more effectually, and was screened from view by a more ample scrub.

On the 29th July the brigade relieved the French troops in part of their trenches.   Those occupied by the 7th Royal Berkshire extended from Hill 420 on the right to Asagi Mahala on the left.   The 7th Oxfordshire and Buckinghamshire Light Infantry were on their left from Asagi Mahala inclusive.   Hill 420 was severely shelled on the 1st August, but no damage was done.

On the night of the 7th-8th Captain Gillespie carried out a reconnaissance of Castle Hill, which apparently met with no opposition.   An advanced post of twenty-five men under Second-Lieutenant West was established there.

The next operation was the establishment of a position on Kidney Hill by the capture of a Bulgarian outpost there.   This was a necessary preliminary to the projected attack on Horseshoe Hill farther to the north, in combination with an attack by the French on the right of the hill known from its shape as La Tortue.   The operation, which is scarcely noted in the diary, was apparently carried out by night on the 13th August.   It was entrusted to " B " Company of the 7th Royal Berkshire.

Captain Pike, who was commanding " B," has furnished an account of this affair.   The advance had to be made by the company, with a party of Royal Engineers following, over some two and a half miles of almost unreconnoitred country, up and down small nullahs where it was impossible to avoid much noise among the rocks.   When the Bulgar outpost which was the objective was reached, the opposition was not great, though a hot but erratic fire was kept up by the enemy for fifteen or twenty minutes.   Finally the post was charged and rushed, apparently without loss.   By dawn a rough trench one foot and a half deep had been made in the rocky soil and a barbed-wire fence erected.   One-fourth of the company was left in this trench, the remaining three-fourths being in reserve one hundred yards in rear. The enemy bombardment was almost continuous.   In the ensuing night a rather feeble counter-attack was repulsed, a few prisoners were taken, and the dead body of an Austrian soldier was found.   The succeeding days were "jumpy," and some valuable reconnaissances were carried out by the company towards Horseshoe Hill.

For his services on this occasion Captain Pike received the Order of the White Eagle, Serbia.

In the heavy bombardment of the 14th Second-Lieutenant Butcher and three men were wounded.

Of the attack on Horseshoe Hill, on the morning of the 18th August, little need be said, for it was carried out by the 7th Oxfordshire and Buckinghamshire Light Infantry, the History of which Battalion acknowledges the value of the occupation by the 7th Royal Berkshire of the trench on Kidney Hill.

The French had taken La Tortue, after several days' fighting to gain most of their objectives.

The Berkshire Battalion on Castle Hill had suffered on the 16th from the enemy's artillery, which had been switched on to that hill, apparently in the belief that the French were about to be supported from it.

By this bombardment Lieutenant G. W. R. Bray, Second-Lieutenant H. D. Mosley, and two other ranks were killed, and seven men were wounded.

From the 19th August the battalion was at Gugunci in the rear till the 27th, when it moved to Horseshoe Hill, in relief of the Gloucestershire, who had replaced the 7th Oxfordshire after their capture of the position.   On the 30th, Second-Lieutenant J. Butler was wounded there.

September was an uneventful month spent at Horseshoe Hill, Table Hill, and the Ravin de Senelle, with a long turn of road-making at Gugunci from the 7th to the 24th.   From the 25th the battalion was at the Ravin de Senelle, below the east side of Berks Hill, and some eight hundred yards east of Doldzeli.   Here they were constantly patrolling and being shelled at times.

On the 30th Second-Lieutenant Cuckow, with a patrol, bombed a Bulgarian post in the Ravin des Jumeaux, which ran below the Bulgar trenches on Petit Couronné.   At midnight of the 30th September-1st October two large patrols of fifty men each, under Captain Eldridge and Lieutenant Ravenshear, went out to raid the enemy trenches on the Mamelon which stood four hundred and fifty yards north-east of the village of Doldzeli in the Bulgarian lines.   Doldzeli was the point at which the French left had been held up on the 16th August, and was now in No-Man's Land between the opposing lines as they had become fixed for the winter of 1916–1917. Lieutenant Ravenshear's party on the left, after passing through Doldzeli Village, was heavily fired on in front and flank and forced to retire. Captain Eldridge's party also returned after suffering only slight casualties. Altogether the losses were twenty-one other ranks wounded, mostly in Lieutenant Ravenshear's party.

There was a heavy thunderstorm at 7.30 p.m. on the 1st October, and an hour later about sixty of the enemy attempted an attack on the left of the trenches held by the battalion, but were driven off by fire.

The attack was renewed at 9.30, this time with a stronger force of from two hundred to three hundred men, but these also were driven off.   No casualties are mentioned in the Battalion Diary, and the enemy attacks were evidently rather half-hearted affairs.

Relieved by the 9th Gloucestershire in the night of the 1st-2nd October, the 7th Royal Berkshire went back for road-making and miscellaneous work at Mihalova Ford, some seven miles behind the front, not far from the northern end of Lake Ardzan.

It is mentioned that, when attached to the 78th Trench Mortar Battery, Second-Lieutenant C. W. Halfacre was mortally injured, five men were killed, and one injured by an accident, the nature of which is not stated. Probably it was an accidental explosion.   On the 22nd October the battalion relieved the Oxfordshire and Buckinghamshire Light Infantry in the advanced line about the Ravin de Senelle.

On the 26th another raid was carried out on the Mamelon north-east of Doldzeli.

The raiders consisted of one hundred men of " A " Company, with two flanking parties from " C " and " B," each composed of twenty men with two Lewis guns.

The " C " party was posted at the N.E. corner of Doldzeli Village, that of " B " on the hill overlooking the Mamelon.   The raid failed owing to the uncut wire which was encountered, but it was ascertained that the enemy had abandoned his trench just north of the crest of the Mamelon, and had made a new one one hundred yards farther back defended by strong wire. During the raid the enemy shelled heavily, especially the left (" C ") flanking party.   The casualties were 3 other ranks killed, 17 wounded, and 1 missing.

The information as to the position of the new enemy trench was confirmed next day by a search party under Sergeant Barrett.

On the last day of October the battalion was withdrawn to Corps Reserve at Rates, and later at Mihalova.   At both places it was busy at the usual digging and road-making till the 16th, when it went into the main line in relief of the Gloucestershire Regiment at Mamelon Franc.   On the 23rd it moved into front line in relief of the Oxfordshire and Buckinghamshire Light Infantry in the " D " sub-sector, where nothing noticeable occurred till it was again withdrawn to Corps Reserve at Rates on the 1st December.   Its next turn in front, in " D " sub-sector, began on the 18th December, and on the 22nd Second-Lieutenant P. H. Williams was wounded at Battalion Head-quarters by a shell.

On the 23rd a raid was made on Hill 380, the next spur eastwards of the Mamelon in the enemy line, by Captain R. A. B. Chancellor with " D " Company, whilst a feint was made by Second-Lieutenant Eastwood with thirty other ranks and two Lewis guns to divert attention from the main body.

Captain Chancellor's party assembled at Green Ravine, at 6.38 p.m. The first wave of attack, under Lieutenant Hayter, advanced as far as the N.E. edge of Green Ravine, but was unable at first to go farther, owing to " shorts " from the British barrage.   When the barrage lifted, this wave advanced to the enemy trench which was found practically destroyed and most of its wire blown away.

The second wave, under Second-Lieutenant Thompson, then attempted to go forward beyond the trench, but suffered so severely from the fire it encountered that it had to retire.

Captain Chancellor had been wounded early in the attack. He continued to lead his men till he was again wounded, this time mortally, when command was taken by Lieutenant Troup, who now retired after the dead and wounded had been evacuated.

Before doing so a R.E. detachment laid demolition charges in the enemy's dugouts, and a Bangalore torpedo in the uncut portion of his wire. A reserve of two platoons, which had been left in Green Ravine, was not called up into action. His conduct in this affair gained the Military Cross for Second-Lieutenant H. B. Thompson.

The casualties were : Capt. R. A. B. Chancellor, died of his wounds, 2nd-Lieuts. Hayter and Thompson wounded, and of other ranks 5 killed and 29 wounded or missing.

On Christmas Day the 7th Royal Berkshire went back into the main line, where they received the congratulations of the G.O.C. 78th Brigade, and of General Kennedy commanding 26th Division, on their conduct in the raid.

THE DOIRAN FRONT. THE FIRST BATTLE OF DOIRAN. EAST OF DOIRAN LAKE, AND ON THE VARDAR

1917

The year 1917 opened with the battalion in the front line in " D " sector. On the night of the 4th January Second-Lieutenant Lambert (Worcestershire Regiment, attached 7th Royal Berkshire), with a raiding party, started from Trench " D " 10 and had gained half-way through a gap in the enemy's wire when they were fired upon and bombed. In the retirement Second-Lieutenant Lambert was found to be missing, and was believed to have been taken prisoner. Four days later a Bulgarian prisoner stated that he had died of wounds received in the raid, and he is recorded as killed in the official list for the Worcestershire Regiment.

After a turn in the main line, from the 9th to the 17th January, the battalion passed the rest of the month uneventfully in the front line, in which it remained from the 17th January to the 9th February. Such long tours of front-line service were quite exceptional on the Western Front, and their prevalence on the Salonika Front indicates the less strenuous fighting and general conditions there.

The rest of February, the whole of March, and the first three weeks of April are bare of incidents of any importance. The battalion was in various parts of the line, or in reserve. On the 20th March it was in " E " sector on Horseshoe Hill, sending out the usual patrols, regarding which there is nothing special to record. From the 1st to the 7th March it was in the main line, and on the 13th Captain Hilling was wounded by a shell when in front line in " E " sector.   On the 19th the 78th Brigade, on relief, moved into the area hitherto occupied by the 79th in front line in " C " sector.   Here it was relieved on the 24th, and went back to Pivoines and Bare Hill near Rates. During this relief Second-Lieutenant L. T. Rivett was wounded.

During the first three weeks of April front and reserve positions in " C " sector were held alternately.

After the stabilization of the line in August 1916, operations on the Doiran-Vardar front had been confined, in the words of General Milne's despatch of the 14th November 1917, to " minor operations undertaken with a view to continually harassing the enemy, entrenched in mountainous and rocky country, and to inflicting as much loss as possible, both in material and personnel."   The chief raids and patrol encounters in which the 7th Royal Berkshire were concerned have been narrated above.   Now, under instructions from the Allied Commander-in-Chief, General Sarrail, offensive operations were to be commenced.   This was not found possible till the latter end of April 1917.

On the 24th there occurred a serious attack on the enemy trenches on the right, south and south-west of Doiran, where they formed a marked salient which it was desired to reduce, especially by the capture of Pip Ridge. The front of attack extended from Doiran Lake on the east as far as the point P 5 to the west.   P 5 was the southernmost of the five peaks on Pip Ridge.   The attack was to be made in two stages.   It was to open with an advance by the 26th Division on the space between the lake on the right and the Jumeaux Ravine (inclusive) on the left.   This attack would be taken up on the left by the 22nd Division, from the Jumeaux Ravine to the point P 5. The objective of the 26th Division was the line Doiran Hill-Seton Hill-Hill 340-Hill 380 (exclusive).   The arrangements within the 26th Division were for the 79th Brigade to attack on the right, as far west as Mortar Ravine, from which point the front of the 78th Brigade would extend westwards to Jumeaux Ravine.   The leading battalions of the 78th Brigade were the 7th Royal Berkshire on the right, touching the left of the 79th Brigade at Mortar Ravine, and the right of the 11th Worcestershire of the 78th Brigade at Sabre Ravine.   The 9th Gloucestershire were in support, the 7th Oxfordshire and Buckinghamshire in reserve.

The operation had been preceded by three days of bombardment by the British artillery for the purpose of cutting the enemy's wire.   On the third day the general assault on the enemy trenches was to commence simultaneously along the whole line after dark, with the exception that the 7th Royal Berkshire was to wait till twenty minutes after zero hour before crossing the Jumeaux Ravine at point O $5\frac{1}{2}$ in the Bulgar trenches, the passage and assault on its right being made simultaneously by the left of the 79th Brigade ; in fact, the outer flanks of the two brigades were to advance twenty minutes before the two centre battalions on their inner flanks, thus breaking and turning both flanks of the enemy position before the commencement of the assault on his centre.

The barrage at these points would also lift twenty minutes later than in other places.   The positions to be attacked were those on the hill known as Petit Couronné south-west of Doiran town.   In front of these positions was a natural ditch formed by the great Jumeaux Ravine which runs in a curve round their S.W. and S. side and continues till it reaches Doiran Lake S.E. of the town.   General Milne describes it as " a deep and difficult obstacle with steep sides which separated the opposing lines."

Into this great ravine there ran from the north two ravines, " Mortar " on the east, and " Sabre " on the west, which, as already noted, formed the right and left boundaries of the Berkshire Battalion's area of attack.   Points Z 42 and 43 are on the east bank of Sabre Ravine.   Z 40 and 41 are farther east in the direction of the west bank of Mortar Ravine.   The 7th Oxfordshire and Buckinghamshire were mainly employed in carrying ammunition, etc., for the Berkshire and Worcestershire Battalions, but they appear to have sent reinforcements to the right of the Worcestershire, and they suffered considerable casualties—eighty-one in all.   None of these reinforcements appear to have joined the 7th Royal Berkshire.

The advance of the 7th Royal Berkshire began at 9.45 p.m., with " D " Company leading on the left, on points Z 42 and 43, and " C " following through it to attack points Y 15 and 16 higher up the left bank of Sabre Ravine—" A " on the right, took its direction on points Z 40 and 41.

" C " and " D " succeeded in capturing their objectives, though they encountered a heavy enemy barrage as they advanced on them.   " A " was

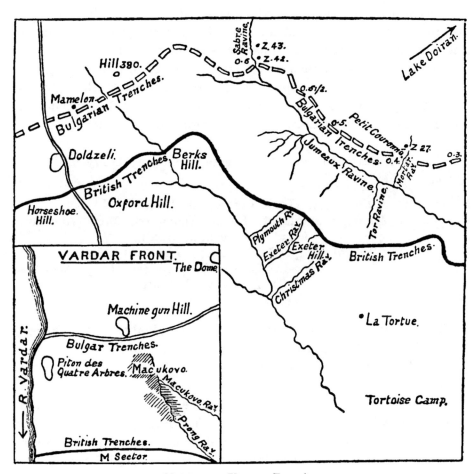

MACEDONIA (VARDAR FRONT).

297

less fortunate, for it was held up at point K on the farther slope of Jumeaux Ravine. Beyond this it was unable to progress.

Meanwhile, " C " and " D " had begun consolidating the positions they had taken when they were violently counter-attacked. By this time they had run out of bombs and had had three of their Lewis guns destroyed. In the circumstances they found themselves forced to retire.

Though the 22nd Division on the left had succeeded, with heavy loss, in taking and holding their objectives, the 79th Brigade on the right had failed to capture theirs. At 4.30 a.m. orders were received to abandon the attack and retire to the trenches, south of Jumeaux Ravine, from which it had started.

The casualties in this unfortunate action were very heavy in the battalion.

Officers. *Killed :* Capt. D. S. Currey, 2nd-Lieut. G. H. Day.
           Missing : 2nd-Lieut. H. B. Thompson, M.C. (afterwards
                 found to have been killed).
          Wounded : Capt. J. B. Marks ; Lieut. S. J. Dale.
                 2nd-Lieuts. C. W. Johnson, R. J. Williams,
                 B. D. Reilly, V. R. Watts.
Other Ranks : 245 (no details given).

The Brigade Diary shows the total casualties of other ranks in the 7th Royal Berkshire for April as :

Killed 16 ; Wounded 225 ; Missing 36.

Total 277.

As the greater part of them occurred on the 24th, the statement affords a rough indication of the distribution on that day.

The account of this affair in the Battalion and Brigade Diaries is very meagre in details. In conveying his thanks to Colonel Dene and his battalion, the Brigadier remarked that he considered the battalion had done very well in achieving all it had done with " only six platoons." Presumably, he meant that only six platoons went forward beyond the Jumeaux Ravine, the difficulty of crossing which he fully realized.

General Milne's despatch, speaking of the attack on the right, says : " This operation was carried out with the greatest gallantry and determination by representative battalions of English county regiments, among whom the Devonshire Regiment and the Berkshire Regiment deserve special credit for their dash and tenacity."

On the left the enemy's front trenches had been captured and were held against many counter-attacks on a front of nearly one mile, from Hill 380 to the point P 4½ on Pip Ridge.

The 25th was a quiet day, followed by heavy artillery bombardment of the British trenches, which probably accounted for most of the other April losses, over and above those of the 24th, as shown in the Brigade Diary quoted above.

After daybreak on the 25th the battalion was in trenches in Exeter, Plymouth, and Christmas Ravines, all south of Jumeaux Ravine and just west of La Tortue.

The first few days of May passed uneventfully in " C " sector and Vladaja Ravine. The battalion was in the latter position on the 8th, during the whole of which day the British artillery was bombarding the enemy. Orders were received to support the 7th Oxfordshire and Buckinghamshire Light Infantry in an attack on O 4, in conjunction with an attack by the 77th Brigade on O 1, 2 and 3—O 4 was at the eastern end of Petit Couronné, the others between it and the Lake.

Further orders required the 7th Royal Berkshire to send two companies to attack O 5 as soon as the Oxfordshire and Buckinghamshire Battalion had reached their objective. For this purpose " B " and " C " Companies were detailed under the command of Major Gillespie.

Before the attack the battalion was to be at La Tortue by 11 p.m., with " B " and " C " Companies at Tortoise Camp south of La Tortue, whilst " D " was on the hill itself, and " A " garrisoned the British trenches.

Of the action which followed there is fortunately a full report by Captain S. A. Pike, temporarily commanding the battalion, on which the following is based :

During the night of the 8th-9th May " B " and " C " Companies moved down Tor Ravine, leading northwards into Jumeaux Ravine opposite Point O 4.

On reaching the latter ravine some casualties were incurred from enemy shells, but the advance continued up the southern slope of Petit Couronné. Here a halt was made whilst Major Gillespie went forward to ascertain the position from the Oxfordshire and Buckinghamshire on his right front. The advance again continued to within a short distance of O 4, where the two companies were formed with " B " in 1st and " C " in 2nd line. The time was about 3.30 a.m. Both then moved to the right and formed up behind the Oxfordshire and Buckinghamshire, who at this time were holding with difficulty a line fifty yards south of Z 27, a point slightly to the N.E. of O 4. They were suffering from accurate trench-mortar fire. The point Z 27 was in the enemy line at the top of the steep ascent on the north bank of Jumeaux Ravine.

After a short time " B " Company relieved the Oxfordshire and Buckinghamshire men in this position. All the officers of " B " had been wounded, and command of the company was taken by C.-S.-M. Flood who, being himself wounded, sent back to Lieutenant Cuckow (commanding " C " Company) for help. That officer, on coming up, found " B " suffering much from trench-mortar fire, as the Oxfordshire and Buckinghamshire had previously done in the same position. Hearing now that Colonel Dene had come up to the front, Cuckow left Second-Lieutenant J. P. Harris in charge of " B " and went to see his commanding-officer. The time was 4.15 a.m. Colonel Dene ordered Lieutenant Cuckow to prepare his company for an attack on Z 27 at 5 a.m. When Cuckow got back again to " B " Company he found Second-Lieutenant Harris had been wounded during his absence. He, therefore, left C.-S.-M. Flood to organize " B " for the attack on the left, whilst he himself brought up " C " on the left of " B." " B " and " C " being now both in first line, a second line was formed by " D," which had come forward by the Colonel's orders. Cuckow then met two officers of the Oxfordshire who agreed to support the right of the Royal Berkshire attack.

At 5 a.m. " B " and " C " advanced in 1st line against Z 27. " D " was formed up in 2nd line in Jumeaux Ravine, with Lewis guns on its flanks, and bombing squads in various parts of its front. So far, it had suffered no casualties. With it were some men of the Oxfordshire and Buckinghamshire. " C " on the right, encountered but slight opposition as it broke into Z 27 and proceeded to bomb along the trench till touch was gained with " B " on the left. The latter had advanced north-westwards and rapidly proceeded in the same direction along the top of Petit Couronné. The ridge was very bare and open, with no trench on it more than two feet deep, and it was found difficult to distinguish such trenches as there were from shell-holes. An attempt was made to link up some shell-holes into a trench, and bombers were sent forward.

At this point Captain Pike says his and Major Gillespie's routes converged and the latter, apparently with " B " Company, struck off north-westwards towards where some Bulgars were seen issuing from dugouts. These were all killed by bombing. Captain Pike now sent forward a group of men, who had come up with a Lewis gun, to occupy a shell-hole N.N.W. of his position, and himself bombed forward farther north-westwards. He then saw two parties of the enemy, each about forty strong, preparing to counter-attack. To stop this he blocked the trench, and trained his Lewis gun quickly on to the enemy, whose line was only eighty yards away. The Bulgars now showed no signs of advancing; but before Captain Pike could get up reinforcements to enable him to take the offensive, the enemy had got guns on to his men. The fire was very heavy, and one 8″ shell, bursting between the opponents, caused casualties on both sides. Other shells burst right amongst the British. When the smoke cleared off, Captain Pike, finding his men without support, was compelled to retire. Meanwhile, Major Gillespie, after bombing the dugouts mentioned above, had disposed his party for bombing north-westwards along the crest of Petit Couronné. As they moved on they almost ran into the Bulgars whom Captain Pike had seen preparing to counter-attack. Eventually Major Gillespie and a sergeant struck away northwards, apparently to reconnoitre. From this expedition the sergeant alone returned. Major Gillespie was missing and believed to have been killed, as has since been recorded. As Captain Pike fell back, he found that Colonel Dene had been able to reorganize a line facing north-west in front of Point Z 27. Beyond this he did not think it advisable to attempt to advance, and therefore gave orders to retire to the original starting-point below the crest on the left bank of the Jumeaux Ravine, below Point Z 27.

Here there was some confusion, and some of the men retired by Tor Ravine, whilst others dug themselves in where they were. The enemy bombardment continued strongly till 8 a.m., when it slackened till 9.30, and then increased again. Fortunately, the steepness of the slope on which they were, saved the Royal Berkshire men from heavy loss here.

Colonel Dene being wounded and having to go to hospital, Captain Pike took over temporary command, and received orders to place himself and his men under the command of Lieut.-Colonel Robinson of the 7th Oxfordshire and Buckinghamshire Light Infantry. That officer also was wounded shortly before noon, and half an hour later Captain Pike withdrew his men by Tor Ravine, in accordance with superior orders. He succeeded in carrying off most of his bombs, etc., by means of parties of twelve men organized for the purpose.

Thanks to the energy and courage of Captain Bryce, R.A.M.C., all the wounded were removed from the slopes of Petit Couronné. Bryce and a sergeant themselves collected the wounded from the top of the hill. There was hardly a casualty in the evacuation.

The casualties in the 7th Royal Berkshire had again been severe in an attack which had failed. They were :

Officers.   *Killed :* Lieut. P. F. Bridge.
          Missing, believed killed : Major W. R. B. Gillespie.
          Wounded : Lieut.-Col. A. P. Dene ; Capt. G. F. Bate.
                    2nd-Lieuts. F. S. Eastwood, L. T. Rivett, L. A.
                         Venden, Harris, Bridgland (remained on duty).
Other Ranks : Killed 14 ; Wounded 131 ; Missing 9.

For the remainder of the day the line was held by " A " Company, the others going back to south of Valadja, where they were rejoined by " A " when relieved at night by the Worcestershire.

On the 14th an order was received saying that the Commander-in-Chief desired the communication to all ranks of "his appreciation of the magnificent gallantry and of the determination to succeed, of the 7th Oxford and Bucks L.I. and the 7th R. Berks."

Brigadier-General Duncan, in forwarding this to the 7th Royal Berkshire, wrote : " I would like you to let the battalion know how very proud I feel at the magnificent manner in which the battalion fought on the night of 8th-9th May. The way they stuck to Petit Couronné, when subjected to such a devastating fire, and after having suffered such heavy casualties, is a splendid example of how British soldiers can put a sense of duty before any selfish thought of personal safety. The fact that the battalion only evacuated the hill when ordered to do so by higher authority is a proof of the high standard of discipline.   The battalion has every reason to be proud of its action.   It is sad that the hill had to be evacuated, but that was due to circumstances beyond your control.   I am deeply grieved at the heavy losses the battalion has suffered."

In the night of the 20th-21st May the 7th Royal Berkshire left the area in front of Petit Couronné and marched eastwards viâ Kilindir to the neighbourhood of Sal Grec Avancé, whence they looked across the Doiran Lake to the town south-west of them.   On the 22nd the 78th Brigade relieved the 79th on the Salonika-Constantinople railway.   The 7th Royal Berkshire was on the left about Cakli railway station, with the 7th Oxfordshire and Buckinghamshire on their right, and the 9th Gloucestershire beyond the latter.   Cakli station was north-east of Doiran Lake, at the point where the Salonika-Constantinople railway, after running north-eastwards on the east side of the lake, again bends off towards the east.   This was a generally quiet area ; for the Bulgarian positions were so strong as to be recognized as practically impregnable.   All the fighting likely to occur consisted of encounters between the opposing outposts in the broad valley between the high Belesh Range on the north and the Lower Krusha Balkan, on the foothills of which was the main British line.

On the 3rd June the 7th Royal Berkshire prepared for a strong reconnaissance of the Cakli Wood, in conjunction with the 7th Oxfordshire and Buckinghamshire on their right.

" A " and " D " Companies were detailed for this work, and took up positions of readiness on " Clapham Common " and at Rabovo.   They started at 4.20 a.m. on the 4th June with " A " on the right and " D " on the left.   The boundary line between the 7th Royal Berkshire and the 7th Oxfordshire and Buckinghamshire ran N.E. through the Cakli railway station, past the N.E. corner of Cakli Wood, at the S.W. end of which was Cakli Village.   To the west of the town was another wood—St. Stephen's.

By 5.10 a.m. " A," pivoting on its right on the railway, had its left at a point N.W. of St. Stephen's Wood.   At this point a flanking party was left, whilst the rest of the company, after being reorganized, advanced on Cakli Village—" D " meanwhile had occupied Cakli Village without opposition, save for a few rounds of rifle fire and bombs by some Bulgars in the most northerly house of the village.

The two companies, shortly before 6 a.m., were on a line facing N.E., with their left in Cakli Village and their right (" A ") touching the 7th Oxfordshire and Buckinghamshire on the boundary line south of Cakli Wood.

" A " now advanced against the southern edge of Cakli Wood, from points in which it was " sniped." It then pushed on about fifty yards into the wood, throwing out a party to search the rest of the wood to the N.E. corner. It was still in the wood at 7.15 a.m. when orders were received to withdraw. By 9 a.m. both companies were back again well south of the railway.

The country north of the railway had been found to be very thick, with grass waist high, interspersed with bushes six feet high. Movement was difficult, and it was rarely possible to see more than thirty yards, owing to the brushwood and hedges. Moreover, owing to the extension of the front, it was difficult to keep touch along it. It rained heavily during the reconnaissance and this, as well as the straggling formation of Cakli Village, made visual signalling impossible. As the last platoon in the retirement was entering Rabovo, the village was shelled by the enemy.

During the advance the railway station had been cleared by the left of the Oxfordshire and Buckinghamshire, and the advance by its two companies northwards continued in a line of skirmishers on the right of the 7th Royal Berkshire. The Oxfordshire and Buckinghamshire encountered practically no opposition, and only had one man wounded. The losses of the Berkshire Battalion were one man killed and two wounded. Altogether, only about ten of the enemy were seen.

The 78th Brigade was now again about to move to a new area nearer the Vardar. By the 13th June, marching by night, the battalion had reached Hirsova on the metalled road running well behind the front between Lake Doiran and the Vardar. The march was difficult and fatiguing. From the 14th to the 30th the battalion was at The Crag north of Causica, and three miles or more behind " J " sector of the British line. Thence on the 2nd July, it moved up to the front line of that sector, holding trenches on the left bank of the Selimli Ravine. Here it remained till the 18th, working at trenches and carrying out the usual patrols, sometimes beyond the ravine. From the 18th till the end of July was spent uneventfully at Pyramid Camp in rear, and on the 1st August a further step leftwards was taken to Glen

Smol in Brigade reserve on the extreme left of the line. The glen was a valley reaching the left bank of the Vardar more than three miles behind the front of " M " sector. The battalion was in front line in this sector from the 15th August. There was some artillery activity on both sides, and of course the usual patrols.

After this, for several months life in the battalion was monotonous. There were the usual periods of front-line service, with turns in Brigade, Divisional, or Corps reserve. The front was generally that of " M " sector, with Glen Smol and Smol Hill in the back area. There was much malaria in the summer and autumn months in the Vardar Valley, and it was a much more dangerous enemy in those months than the Bulgar, with whom only occasional shots were exchanged. Early in November the battalion was relieved by the 1st Battalion 1re Regiment de Marche d'Afrique, and the latter part of the month was passed at Sarakli three miles from railhead. In that neighbourhood, during December 1917, the 7th Royal Berkshire were employed on railway construction, and on the 27th of that month Colonel Dene, on recovery from his wound of the 9th May, resumed command of the battalion.

When he had been wounded Lieut.-Colonel J. F. B. Morrell had taken over command. He went on leave at the end of September, and Captain Pike took command. When he had to go to hospital, the command was assumed for more than a month, before Colonel Dene rejoined, by Major Witts of the 9th Gloucestershire Regiment.

On the Vardar. Raids. The Final Advance and Occupation of Bulgaria. Izlis.

1918

During January 1918 the battalion was still in the Sarakli neighbourhood till the 25th, when it moved to Kalinova north of Lake Ardzan and on the 31st went into front line in the " F " sector of the British line till the 8th February. After five days at Tertre Vert, north of Kalinova, in Corps reserve, the battalion went for the second half of February to work in " H " sector, and was back in front line in " F " on the 1st March.

On the 2nd, Captain E. W. Ravenshear and three other officers took out " A " Company for a raid which was supported by twenty men of " D " under Second-Lieutenant G. Berry, who were left at Dautli Track Post. The plan was for the main raiding party to attack the enemy's support position N.W. of Selimli, whilst the enemy's attention and fire were diverted from them by a demonstration by Berry's party against White Scar Hill to the right.

The main party had no success ; for they lost their way in the darkness, and were unable to reach their objective. The country was difficult, and they presently found themselves facing a deep ravine over which no crossing could be found. Second-Lieutenant Berry, meanwhile, had succeeded in drawing the attention of the enemy, who fired heavily on his party, put down a barrage on Ham Ravine, and shelled Goldies Hill on his right. All the raiders eventually withdrew to their lines without any loss. The diary mentions that the battalion was at this time busy with " anti-malarial " work, an occupation in which much of the time of the troops was spent on the Salonika Front, with more or less satisfactory results. This was not the malaria season, but it was that of blizzards which blew with great fury down the valley of the Vardar, making life anything but a picnic, and adding frostbite to the many troubles the unfortunate troops on this front had to bear.

The Salonika Front has been treated too often as a " side show " of little importance and little suffering. Yet it was with the final advance on this side that the collapse of the allies of Germany began, and the sufferings of the Allied troops from malaria and heat in the summer and autumn, and cold and insufficient shelter in the winter, were very great.

There is nothing more notable till the last days of April, when the battalion was again in " M " sector on the extreme left towards the Vardar. For three days preceding the 29th the artillery had been busy cutting the enemy's wire, in preparation for a projected raid on the orchards north of Piton des Quatre Arbres, where the enemy were believed to have posts which it was proposed to destroy. This hill was on the extreme right of the enemy lines on the left bank of the Vardar. To divert the enemy's attention from the real point of attack, the artillery had been firing on the wire on the Piton des Mitrailleuses, the next hill, some twelve hundred yards to the east. The raid was fixed for the night of the 29th-30th April, and was commanded by Major J. M. Eldridge, who had under him " B " and " D " Companies.

Captain H. C. Ellis was in command of " B," with Second-Lieutenants G. W. Pearce, S. A. Banfield and E. F. Prime. " D " was under Captain H. A. L. Donkin, with Lieutenant C. R. Weaver, and Second-Lieutenants J. C. Campion, S. J. Mundy, and G. Berry.

The raiders left the trenches at 9.30 p.m. and formed up by 9.45 outside the British wire. Thence they advanced in artillery formation to a " line of slits." A white rocket then gave the signal for the commencement of the bombardment.

At 10.42 p.m. " D " moved forward, and eight minutes later entered the orchards. At the same time a flank party, of one rifle-grenade section and one Lewis-gun section, worked round the western slopes of the Piton des Quatre Arbres, and scouts moved over the top of the hill.

The orchards were found to be unoccupied, as was a hut close to the river bank. There were no dugouts in the orchard, and it was unwired, save for a few strands between the trees.

After " D " had passed through the orchard as far as the second track, Captain Donkin gave the signal to withdraw at 11.5 p.m. and " D " was back in trenches by midnight, having been molested only by a few ·77 shells fired into the orchard.

Meanwhile " B," on the right of " D," had moved off towards the Piton de l'Eglise, where the platoons were deployed west of the Smol-Macukovo track in a position S.W. of Macukovo Ravine, with their left about sixty yards north of the junction of Cardiff and Macukovo Ravines. Their flanks were covered by Lewis guns, the left guns having a good field of fire east of the orchard. Fair protection from shell fire was also afforded by the left (S.W.) bank of the Macukovo Ravine, which was higher than the right.

The other two platoons of " B " remained in reserve near Piton de l'Eglise. Gaps had been cut in the enemy's wire at three points where the attack was not to be made, and in front of each of these a party of the 11th Worcestershire was sent to demonstrate one hundred and fifty yards from the enemy trenches. Here they engaged the enemy's attention by firing and cheering, the latter magnified by the use of megaphones.

This ruse was completely successful in deceiving the Bulgars, whose barrage was put down on Cardiff, Bangor, and Macukovo Ravines, and on Macukovo Village. There was none on the Piton de l'Eglise, and only the few shells above mentioned were directed on the Piton des Quatre Arbres. The enemy appears to have at once evacuated his front trenches, as his Very lights were sent up from behind them, and the trenches themselves were shelled by him.

Two Bulgars were found in Macukovo Village, one of whom was captured. These two men, it seems, had delayed in evacuating the front line, and then found their retreat cut off by the British barrage behind it, through which they were afraid to venture. The whole raid was carried out precisely according to plan, and the casualties were slight. The 7th Royal Berkshire had only five men wounded, of whom two remained on duty.

Of the demonstrating parties of the Worcestershire Regiment six men were wounded, only one of them seriously.

The next notable event in the sector was on the 8th May, when Second-Lieutenant Shillcock, with the battalion scouts, patrolled the Piton des Quatre Arbres, with the object of clearing out an enemy post. Three parties, of about twenty Bulgars each, were met and engaged with rifles and bombs. They were driven off with losses estimated at twenty-five. The affair was very successfully handled by Second-Lieutenant Shillcock, who brought back a prisoner.

The cost to the battalion was seven men slightly wounded.

Another similar but stronger raid was made in the night of the 12th-13th May when Captain A. K. Barrett, with eighty-five men of " C " Company, met a small party of the enemy on the hill. After an exchange of rifle fire and bombs, Barrett's men charged with the bayonet. The enemy fled to the mulberry orchard north of the hill, where they were lost among the trees. The casualties on the British side are described as " very slight."

The rest of the month was spent in the Brigade reserve at Smol Hill.

The battalion returned to the front in " M " sector for the first eighteen days of June. During this period there were many small patrols of no particular note, generally lying up to try and catch enemy patrols, leaving propaganda in match-boxes for the enemy, etc. Lieutenant Shillcock took a full share in these minor operations.

After another spell at Smol Hill, the front held from the 2nd July was in " L " sector, to the right of " M." Here reconnaissance showed that the ground in front of the British trenches to the right of Grand Piton, a hill in

No-Man's Land, as far as Border Ravine was swampy. A plan for a raid in the night of the 29th-30th July was abandoned, as the enemy had filled up the gaps in his wire through which it was proposed to operate.

The next raid was in " M " sector in the night of the 24th-25th August. Three strong patrols went out to raid the enemy outpost line from the Piton des Quatre Arbres to the point of junction of Macukovo Ravine with the orchard north of Macukovo Village.

The patrol of " A " Company, under Second-Lieutenant G. I. Berry, consisted of twenty-six other ranks, with eight battalion scouts, and one Lewis gun. This pushed through Macukovo Village to the south of the orchard, keeping a flanking party under Lance-Corporal Denton to guard its right flank. This party encountered no opposition, but found it impossible to get through the uncut wire in front. After skirting the south-east edge of the orchard, it returned by the Piton de l'Eglise when the signal for the retirement of the other two patrols was given. Lance-Corporal Denton with the right flanking party, meanwhile, had heard a strong enemy patrol in Bangor Ravine. At this he threw a bomb, and his party, which was now in touch with another flanking party in Cardiff Ravine, held up the Bulgar patrol with rifle and Lewis-gun fire. They were unable to come to close quarters with the enemy, owing to a trench-mortar barrage.

Denton returned by Macukovo Church when he heard the signal for retirement of the raiders.

The patrol of " C " Company under Second-Lieutenant Worden, M.C., consisting of twenty men and a Lewis gun, moved to the sunken track south of the Piton des Quatre Arbres on Berry's left, and sent a small detachment along the bank of the Vardar, in order to get round the west side of the hill. At 9 p.m. Worden and twelve men crept up the front of the hill and charged over the crest. As they passed this point they were met by machine-gun fire and a shower of bombs, which wounded half of them at once. An attempt to get round the enemy's left flank failed, and Worden and his men were compelled to fall back, covering the removal of the wounded by throwing bombs.

The detachment near the Vardar on the left had also been driven back by bombs thrown from the slope of the hill above them on their right.

The third patrol was of " B " Company under Second-Lieutenant R. E.

Childs, and was of similar strength to Worden's. Hearing the attack on Worden's party, Childs moved north-westward to help it. As he did so, his party was heavily fired on from a sunken road one hundred and fifty yards to its right. Childs at once changed direction to the right and charged, disregarding cries of " Friend! Cease fire " which were raised by the enemy. This trick having failed, the Bulgars threw a shower of bombs and fled back into the shelter of a wood. The British party pursued as far as the road whence the fire had come, but were there forced to retire by the barrage put down on it by the enemy.

The casualties of the three patrols in this affair were one man killed and nine wounded. The report on it highly praises the conduct of Lance-Corporal Denton in getting into touch with the other flanking party and then holding up the enemy, who were endeavouring to cut off the British parties as they retired. Corporal Hiscock is also mentioned as acting with Denton. Though both were wounded, they continued firing, and eventually retired by the Piton de l'Eglise when the signal was heard.

Later in the same night, some of the enemy crawled under the outpost wire, got in rear of a post and surprised it at 7 a.m. Of the five men in it, two were wounded, and the other three taken prisoners.

As soon as information of this was received by telephone, Second-Lieutenant S. Kerman and six other ranks went out to the post, where they found the two wounded men lying unconscious. The enemy had left, apparently by the Macukovo Ravine, carrying the three prisoners with them. In the night of the 30th-31st Second-Lieutenant Shillcock and the battalion scouts went out at 9 p.m. to cover an attack by the 7th Oxfordshire and Buckinghamshire Light Infantry. They were fired on from Prong Ravine, which was a tributary of the left bank of the Macukovo Ravine, before they had even gone clear of the British wire. When they reached Prong Ravine they found it had been evacuated. They then pushed on to the Piton de l'Eglise, but were fired on from houses in Macukovo. The enemy, however, were found to have disappeared from these houses when the party arrived.

Presently, as they were advancing on the western slope of Piton de l'Eglise, they were saluted by rifle fire from the top of that hill. They charged up it, but were fired into from their rear, and had one man wounded when they had nearly reached the top. They then took position, expecting an attack which did not materialize. After ten minutes, they moved again north-westwards when they saw six Bulgars leave a small trench. They then halted about 10.30 p.m. when they began to receive machine-gun fire from the Pitons des Mitrailleuses and des Quatre Arbres. Seeing a large body of the enemy extended, Lewis-gun fire was opened on it, with the result that it melted away towards the Vardar.

As the patrol retired, it was fired on from various points, including the village. In one case a Bulgar rushed up crying, "Friend! Don't shoot," and fired at Lance-Corporal Reid who shot him down, but was himself wounded by a bomb thrown by another of the enemy. Shillcock's men again charged, and the Bulgars sought refuge in the village.

The battalion was still in " M " sector when, on the 13th September, a party of seventy men, under Lieutenant Weaver and Second-Lieutenants Shillcock and Berry, went out to raid the enemy outposts from the Piton des Quatre Arbres to Macukovo.

Lieutenant Weaver, with forty men, took up a position south of the Piton des Quatre Arbres, whilst Second-Lieutenant Shillcock with the rest formed the attacking party to the right. At 2.10 a.m. on the 3rd September, Weaver's party opened fire and moved up the slope of the Piton des Quatre Arbres. At the same time, Shillcock advanced to take the enemy outpost in rear. He was fired at from another post on the hill, but went on, and on reaching it found its garrison had evacuated it and gone up the hill behind it.

Weaver's party also found the post in front of it had been evacuated. The raiders only had one man slightly wounded. On the 15th a similar raid was carried out farther forward, over the crest of the Piton and down the northern slope. No details are given of this raid, in which six men were wounded, of whom five remained on duty. Preparations now commenced for the coming general advance on the Doiran front. From the 18th there had been desperate fighting for the possession of Grand Couronné and Pip Ridge, in which of course the 26th Division, away to the left on the Vardar, could take no part. These two great positions had defied capture, but the Bulgars had been prevented by the attacks from moving their reserves towards their right to oppose the Franco–Serbian attack which had broken through, turned the flank, and cut the communications of the enemy by the Vardar Valley. The Bulgars had no option, under the circumstances, but to let go their hold on the Doiran-Vardar line and fall back into Bulgaria. On the 21st, when the battalion was at Smol Hill, news was received that the enemy was retiring, and had evacuated the Dome and the Piton des Mitrailleuses, which had been occupied by the 7th Oxfordshire and Buckinghamshire.

On the 22nd the way was clear for the battalion to advance along the Macukovo track by the Piton des Quatre Arbres, Mulberry Hill, Frontier Hill, and Bogorodica. The outpost line was placed on that day on the line Stojekovo-Table de Bogorodica. The latter place, on the left bank of the Vardar, was four miles north of the left of the British line as it had been up till then. On the 23rd the advance continued to Gjavoto where the 7th Royal Berkshire were in Brigade reserve, covered by outposts of the 7th Oxfordshire and Buckinghamshire at Cernica.

For the events of the 24th–26th we have to guide us the report of Colonel Dene in the diary, and a very clear account kindly furnished by Captain Ravenshear, who was then acting as second-in-command of the 7th Royal Berkshire. Throughout the 24th the 7th Oxfordshire and Buckinghamshire had acted as advanced-guard of the 78th Brigade, in touch with the retreating enemy. In the evening they had occupied Valandovo at the southern foot of the high mountains on the Serbo-Bulgarian frontier.

At 8 p.m., as the rest of the brigade was about to bivouac at Cestovo in rear, Colonel Dene arrived from Brigade Head-quarters with orders placing him in command of the 7th Oxfordshire and Buckinghamshire, 7th Royal Berkshire, and 11th Worcestershire Regiments, and to push on as fast as possible. Captain Ravenshear was sent on to Valandovo with verbal orders to Major Martin, commanding the 7th Oxfordshire and Buckinghamshire, to withdraw his outposts and proceed to piquet the heights commanding the pass in front. It was quite dark when Captain Ravenshear arrived, and by the time the Oxfordshire and Buckinghamshire had discovered the route and were ready to advance, the 7th Royal Berkshire had come up, followed by the Worcestershire. The route up the mountains was a mere stony goat track pointed out by a local guide, and was quite impracticable for wheeled traffic. The Oxfordshire and Buckinghamshire Light Infantry were to lead the way, followed by the Berkshire and Worcestershire Battalions. All were to reach Izlis, the first village on the Bulgarian side of the frontier, by dawn on the 25th.

The night march was one of extreme difficulty, over a steep ascent of four thousand feet where the enemy might be met at any moment in positions of immense advantage over the British troops marching, as they generally had to, in single file. Fortunately, he did not put in an appearance, and half an hour after midnight the leading British safely reached the plateau on the top, across which passed the frontier line. It was nearly dawn when the 7th Royal Berkshire reached it. All were exhausted. On their right was the height known as Fortin Serbe, on their left Fortin Bulgare, the frontier posts on the Serbian and Bulgarian sides of the frontier respectively.

Beyond the frontier, on the left of the track leading to Izlis, were three steep bare heights known as the Pyramids. On reaching the top of the pass the Oxfordshire and Buckinghamshire had reported all clear, and the descent to Izlis was commenced by them and the 7th Royal Berkshire, the Worcestershire being left in support at the summit. As day broke the Royal Berkshire passed through the Oxfordshire, and both battalions were in close formation on some open ground near a stream, preparing to have breakfast and a short rest.

The most easterly of the three Pyramids was now some eighteen hundred yards to the left rear of the Royal Berkshire. At this moment heavy, but ill-directed, machine-gun fire was opened by a party of the enemy from this Pyramid on the Worcestershire who were cut off from the rest by the storm of bullets on the plateau. At first there were no casualties amongst the leading battalions, and the men quickly got into formation. There was, however, practically no cover, and casualties soon began to occur. Action was delayed, owing to its being believed that the fire came by mistake from a regiment of Greek cavalry, supposed to be operating on the left. This was found to be erroneous, and Colonel Dene ordered three companies of the Royal Berkshire to assault the hill. In this they were supported by the fire over their heads of the Brigade Machine Gun Company. The attack failed, owing to the steepness of the hill and its complete lack of cover, and had to be abandoned for the moment, in the hope that artillery support might be available later. The farthest point reached was two hundred yards from the enemy's position. In this attack Lieutenant R. E. Childs, commanding " C "

Company, had received wounds of which he died, two men had been killed and twelve wounded.

The Oxfordshire and Buckinghamshire, who were behind the Royal Berkshire in this affair, also had casualties, as had the Worcestershire on the top of the pass.

Till about 3 p.m. the two battalions in front lay out in great heat in the open, with very little cover to protect them against the Bulgar fire. About 3 p.m. the enemy withdrew, apparently on account of the appearance of Greek troops in their rear, and of more British troops by the main road. The Oxfordshire and Buckinghamshire and Berkshire Battalions bivouacked in peace for the night. An attempt had been made to pursue the retreating enemy with two companies of the Royal Berkshires, but the men were utterly exhausted and the pursuit had to be abandoned. The officers and men had had no sleep worth mention for forty-eight hours and no time for a proper meal. They had marched twenty miles on the 24th, and had a most exhausting climb in the night of the 24th-25th. Captain Ravenshear says the enemy force was afterwards ascertained to have consisted of only about fifty Bulgars with six machine guns. Major Marks estimates only three or four machine guns. The history of the 7th Oxfordshire and Buckinghamshire, however, says the Bulgarian prisoners gave the numbers as two hundred men and sixteen machine guns.

They would have soon been dislodged had artillery support been available, but of course the pass was impossible for guns of any sort.

It was now decided to halt for the night just south of Izlis, with outposts pushed out northwards and round the village, which had been ascertained to be clear of the enemy. It was searched for arms.

The march continued northwards without incident till the 30th September, when orders had been received by the brigade for the forcing of the Hamzali Pass. That operation never came off, for it was announced that an armistice had been concluded with the Bulgarian army, and hostilities were to cease at noon on that day. The rest of the career of the 7th Battalion can be dealt with briefly, for its fighting days were at an end.

The 26th Division was now under orders to represent the British in the Army of Occupation of Bulgaria. The march was at first in the direction of Sofia, till Slatin was reached. Since the 22nd September some one hundred and seventy miles had been marched.   Then, on the 15th October, the direction was changed, and the division was sent by rail to Mustafa Pasha on the Turkish frontier towards Adrianople, where divisional sports were held on the 9th November.

Again the direction was changed when, on the 15th November, the battalion started for Rustchuk on the Danube, which was only reached on the 10th after a miserable four days of cold in the train.

At this time the men were suffering not only from the effects of the old enemy malaria, but also from a devastating epidemic of " Spanish " influenza.   Rustchuk is a poor place, but, after Mustafa Pasha, was a haven of bliss in which the battalion remained till the 11th December, when it went by rail to Dobritch as the Bulgarians had renamed the town generally known as Bazardjik, north of Varna.   Here they were not as well off as other troops which were sent to Varna.   Dobritch is the principal place in the Dobrudja, the southern portion of which had passed from Bulgarian into Rumanian possession after the Second Balkan War of 1913.   The Bulgarians had again been in possession since the defeat of Rumania by the Germans, and it was now the turn of the Rumanians to be reinstated, and of the Bulgarians to be ejected by the Allies.   Major Marks has furnished us with details of the activities of the battalion in overawing any threat of resistance to the transfer of authority in the villages.   We cannot, however, afford space to reproduce them in full.   Generally, the functions of the battalion were the sending out of parties of about twenty-five men, under an officer, to occupy villages where there was any show of opposition to the re-entry of the Rumanian authorities.   Ordinarily, this was sufficient, but in one or two cases half a company had to be used to overawe more serious threats of disturbances.   On one of these occasions, Major Marks was in command of about one hundred men.   The resistance, if any was really contemplated, collapsed without any fighting in the face of this show of force.   On another occasion, reports of a threatened attack on Silistria by Bulgarian Bolsheviks again led to Major Marks being sent out with a composite force of Royal Berkshire, Worcestershire, and two guns.   This also came to nothing.

These instances must suffice to indicate the sort of work on which the battalion was engaged at Dobritch.   From the social point of view the place was dull in the extreme, notwithstanding dances for officers and other ranks, and sports and football.   The most characteristic feature of Dobritch seems to have been its mud.

VARNA.   THE CAUCASUS AND CONSTANTINOPLE. DEMOBILIZATION.

1919

The battalion, having been relieved at Dobritch by Italian troops, left for Varna on the 1st April 1919, being the last British troops in the Dobrudja.   They were seen off by the Mayor and other Rumanian officials, now firmly established.   During the time at Dobritch the acting R.-S.-M. disappeared one night and was never heard of again.   It was believed he had been murdered.

After remaining in camp at Varna without any special duties, the battalion was shipped, on the 4th May, across the Black Sea to Batum, where they were attached to the 27th Division.   Thence they went by rail to Tiflis to relieve the 2nd Cameron Highlanders.   Demobilization had been proceeding for some time, and the battalion's numbers were rapidly decreasing, though at times raised by additions of men from other battalions.

In June 1919 the battalion went to Kodor, the hill station of Tiflis, about twelve miles off.   Affairs were very disturbed with the operations of General Denikin's army then in progress, and severe training was recommenced.   This was varied by brigade sports and games.   The battalion again went to Batum in September.   Major Marks had already taken a detachment of one hundred men, in the middle of August, to Gagri near Soukhoum on the Black Sea, in relief of the 10th Jats.   He rejoined the battalion at Batum in the second week in September.   Exactly what the political situation was at this time seems to be still wrapped in mystery. Anyhow, the battalion had little to do till it left Batum in October. Lieut.-Colonel Dene who, except when wounded or employed temporarily in higher grades, had commanded the battalion since 1915, was left behind on duty at Batum.   Whilst with the battalion he had earned the C.M.G., D.S.O., and Legion of Honour.   The command was now taken over by Major Marks who sailed with the remains of the battalion for Constantinople where they were quartered at Haidar Pasha on the Asiatic side of the Bosphorus. Demobilization had reduced the battalion to very small numbers, with which were amalgamated, under Major Marks' command, the remains of a Gloucestershire Battalion. The unit so formed was absorbed by the beginning of November in the 8th Oxfordshire and Buckinghamshire Light Infantry and so ceased to exist. When the disbandment occurred the only two officers remaining of those who went out in 1915 were the two junior subalterns, who had now become Major J. B. Marks, commanding the battalion, and Captain A. K. Barrett, second-in-command.

CHAPTER XXXIV

THE 8th (SERVICE) BATTALION

FORMATION. FRANCE. THE BATTLE OF LOOS

1914–1915

THE 8th (Service) Battalion was raised at the Barracks, Reading, towards the end of September 1914. Besides men from Surrey, drafts were received from Birmingham and London, and a few men from Wales. Colonel W. C. Walton, Indian Army, took over command at Codford Training Camp in the first week of October 1914.

The battalion was detailed as Army Troops attached to the 26th Division.

It was some time before any uniforms were received and, owing to the absence of tent boards, the discomfort due to heavy rain was considerable. These and many other difficulties were happily overcome, and training of officers and men was pushed on. Except the Commanding-Officer and Captain C. F. N. Bartlett, none of the officers had any previous Regular Service. The latter was appointed Adjutant. Some of the young officers had received instruction in Officers' Training Corps. All worked with the utmost zeal and were keen to learn and to impart instruction.

In November 1914 the battalion was moved to billets in Reading, where steady progress was made in training with dummy rifles in the field, and with miniature rifles on the range. Owing to the patriotism and kindness of owners and farmers, the battalion was able to practise field manoeuvres and entrenching in every direction in the vicinity of the town. The Municipality placed the town swimming baths at the disposal of the battalion on certain days in the week. The battalion attended Divine service every Sunday at St. Giles' Church, Reading; and after service used to march to billets by way of the Park, where battalion drill was practised.

Whilst at Reading, Captain Bartlett was promoted Major and appointed

318

8th BATTALION.

(Back Row) 2nd Lt. Cohen. 2nd Lt. G. B. Coote. Lt. C. S. Cloake. 2nd Lt. B. D. Brigg. 2nd Lt. T. E. Allen. 2nd Lt. Dobson. 2nd Lt. F. M. Sumpster. 2nd Lt. Black. 2nd Lt. C. A. Williamson. 2nd Lt. H. C. L. Keable. 2nd Lt. H. V. Woodford. 2nd Lt. Pugh. 2nd Lt. W. H. Bissley.

(Second Row) 2nd Lt. Joseph. 2nd Lt. R. S. P. Poyntz. 2nd Lt. C. Salman. 2nd Lt. T. B. Lawrence. 2nd Lt. C. R. Watson. 2nd Lt. Thorne. Lt. D. F. Stileman. Lt. T. G. Peacock, Adjt. Lt. W. G. Hobbs. 2nd Lt. L. A. Klemantaski. 2nd Lt. F. C. Gardenner. 2nd Lt. D. E. Foot. 2nd Lt. G. F. Marsh. Lt. T. G. Robinson. 2nd Lt. Thompson.

(Third Row, Sitting) Lt. L. H. Berleiu. Rev. G. H. Hewitt. Capt. C. G. Paramore. Capt. L. H. Edwards. Major F. W. Bartlett. Col. W. C. Walton. Major R. W. Brakspear. Capt. D. Tosetti. Capt. D. M. Hanna. Capt. W. S. D. Oldman. Capt. J. Barrow, Q.M.

(Front Row, Sitting) 2nd Lt. W. L. Clarke. 2nd Lt. A. R. Rouse. Lt. B. P. Hicks. Lt. D. C. Glen. 2nd Lt. Taverner. 2nd Lt. C. Spartali. Capt. H. K. Cassells.

(Not Shown) Capt. R. H. Coote. Lt. W. G. Haynes. Lt. C. Gentry Birch.

second-in-command, and Lieutenant T. G. Peacock took over the duties of Adjutant.

The non-commissioned officers and men deservedly earned a good reputation in the town.

Early in May 1915 the battalion moved to camp in hutments at Sutton Veney, near Warminster, where Brigade and Divisional training was carried out with the 26th Division.

At the end of July 1915 orders were received to embark for France on the 7th August 1915.

New uniforms, rifles, machine guns, and field equipment were then issued, and the battalion was put through range practices for the first time with service rifles. All ranks were very proud of the parting letter from their Divisional Commander, which may conclude this account of the battalion prior to its departure for France :

> " MY DEAR WALTON,—Just a line to wish you and your battalion God-speed and every good fortune. I am exceedingly sorry that your fine battalion is not part of my Division, and that I shall not have the privilege of commanding them on service. I thank you for the splendid way you have worked ever since you have been attached to the 26th Division, and I wish you and your officers and men every good thing possible. I feel confident that you will all render a good account of yourselves and am proud of having had you under my command. God bless you all !
>
> " (Sd.) C. M. KENNEDY."

The officers who went to France with the battalion were :

Lieut.-Colonel W. C. Walton (Commanding).
Majors : C. F. N. Bartlett (Second-in-Command).
R. W. Brakspear (Company Commander).
Captains : L. H. Edwardes (Company Commander).
D. Tosetti (Company Commander).
W. S. D. Oldman (Company Commander).
R. M. Coote.
C. O. Paramore.
D. M. Hanna.
H. K. Cassels (Machine-Gun Officer).
Lieutenants : C. S. Cloake.
T. G. Peacock (Adjutant).

L. H. Berlein.
D. C. Glen.
D. F. Stileman (Signalling Officer).
C. Gentry-Birch.
B. P. Hicks (Scouts Officer).
T. G. Robinson.
W. G. Hobbs.
W. G. Haynes.
Second-Lieutenants : C. Spartali.
T. E. Allen.
G. F. Marsh.
T. B. Lawrence.
A. R. Rouse.
H. C. L. Keable.
W. H. Bissley.
C. R. Watson.
Hon.-Lieut. J. Barrow (Quartermaster).
Rev. G. H. Hewitt (Chaplain to the Forces).
Lieut. P. M. O. Gibbon (Medical Officer).

The battalion left Warminster by train for Southampton, where it embarked, on the 7th August at 6 p.m., on the R.M.S. *Viper* for Havre, arriving there at 12.45 a.m. on the 8th and marching to the concentration camp.   At 6 p.m. on the 9th it entrained for the front, reached St. Omer at 11.15 a.m. on the 10th, and marched to billets at Arques.   Thence it marched on the 15th to Ham-en-Artois.   The men had received new boots just as they left Warminster, and consequently there were about a dozen cases of footsores in this first march of any length.

On the 16th the battalion was in billets at the Orphanage in Béthune, and next day the companies were sent into trenches in front of Noyelles lez Vermelles to be initiated into the conditions of trench warfare, under the instruction of other battalions which had already learnt their lesson.

Their fighting strength at this time was 27 officers and 765 other ranks. The first officer casualty occurred just before they left the trenches on the 19th when Major R. W. Brakspear was wounded by a German sniper crawling home under cover of a screen of greenery.

For the rest of the month the battalion was in billets in the same neighbourhood.   On the 27th it was inspected at Verquin by Brigadier-

General A. J. Reddie, D.S.O., commanding the 1st Brigade 1st Division, IVth Corps, of which it was a unit. The other battalions constituting the brigade were the 10th Gloucestershire, 1st Cameron Highlanders, and 1st Black Watch.

The first twenty days of September were spent in billets, training and supplying fatigue parties for such duties as carrying up gas cylinders, etc.

On the 21st the battalion marched to a wood near Allouagne, and next day to Vaudricourt Wood where " A " and " D " Companies went into the Sailly la Bourse trenches, and " B " and " C " into those at Noyelles lez Vermelles. On the 24th it went into front-line trenches. " C " Company was half in the fire trench and half in second line, with " B " in third line and " A " and " D " in rear.

The 25th September saw the 8th Battalion engaged in its first attack directed on the German position east of Hulluch. At 5.50 a.m. the British intense bombardment of the enemy line commenced, and gas was liberated at the same time. Unfortunately, owing it is believed to leakages, the gas did some harm amongst the British troops. It was stopped at 6.20 and smoke bombs were used, which successfully concealed the advance. Ten minutes later the barrage lifted, and the battalion advanced, with the 10th Gloucestershire on its right, and the 2nd Gordon Highlanders, of the 2nd Brigade, on its left. The advance encountered heavy artillery and machine-gun fire, and when the German wire was reached it was found to have been very little damaged by the artillery. It was in cutting a way through it by hand that most of the day's casualties were incurred. To add to the difficulties, a change of wind drove back some of their own gas on the British. When, after a severe struggle with the difficulties of the wire and the machine-gun fire from which they suffered so heavily, the German front trench was entered, it was found that the garrison had consisted of little more than sufficient to man the machine guns which had caused such havoc in the assaulting ranks. The rest had been withdrawn earlier.

The advance was now continued over the second and third German trenches without meeting serious opposition. It was mostly above ground, but a communication trench was also used. From the third line the fourth was reached with equal ease, and a German field gun was captured. This fourth trench offered so little protection that Colonel Walton withdrew his men to the third, where they dug in and held on till the battalion was relieved. Colonel Walton having been sent to hospital suffering from gas, the command was held during the night by Second-Lieutenant T. B. Lawrence.

Counter-attacks were expected during the night, but were not delivered.

A separate report by Lieutenant C. Gentry-Birch refers only to the doings of about fifty of the Berkshire men who became separated from the rest during the wire cutting and attached themselves to the Gordon Highlanders of the 2nd Brigade on the left. With them they passed beyond the fourth trench, and occupied a road west of Hulluch. Here, as they suffered from British " shorts " when attempting to advance, they dug themselves in to await support. At 3.30 p.m. they were counter-attacked, both flanks were driven back, and, as there were no signs of support, they fell back one hundred yards. When supports were reported to be approaching, they again moved forward to the road and proceeded to put it in a state of defence. The small body of Royal Berkshiremen had by this time been reduced by half. At 11.30 p.m. the enemy again counter-attacked in large numbers, and drove in the right flank. The supports now opening fire, the men were caught between two fires and made their way back as best they could to the support line in the old German fourth trench. By this time only six of the fifty remained unwounded. The German counter-attack was eventually beaten off. At 10 a.m. on the 26th, when the remains of the battalion were rejoined by the commanding officer from hospital, and four other officers from the transport, it had counted only two officers and one hundred and eighty-seven men. The casualties of this day's fighting* were very heavy, altogether 17 Officers and 500 Other Ranks :

> *Officers. Killed :* Major R. W. Brakspear (Died of Wounds).
> Capts. W. S. D. Oldman, D. M. Hanna,
> C. G. Paramore, H. K. Cassels.
> Lieut. and Adjutant T. G. Peacock.
> Lieuts. L. H. Berlein, D. C. Glen, B. P. Hicks,
> W. G. Hobbs, W. G. Haynes.
> 2nd-Lieut. H. C. L. Keable.

* The casualties are really those of the 25th September to 4th October, but the majority of them were on the former date.

Wounded : Capt. D. Tosetti.
　　　　　　　Lieut. D. F. Stileman.
　　　　　　　2nd-Lieuts. G. F. Marsh, A. R. Rouse, T. E. Allen.
Other Ranks : Killed 56 ; Wounded 176 ; Missing 268.
　　　　　Total: 17 Officers and 500 Other Ranks.

Regarding the fighting in which the 8th Battalion Royal Berkshire
Regiment were concerned, Sir John French says :

" The 1st Division, attacking on the left of the 15th, was unable
at first to make any headway with its right brigade. The brigade on
its left, the 1st (including the 8th Battalion, Royal Berkshire Regiment)
was, however, able to get forward, and penetrated into the outskirts
of the village of Hulluch, capturing some gun positions on the way.
The determined advance of this brigade, with its right flank dangerously
exposed, was most praiseworthy, and, combined with the action of
divisional reserves, was instrumental in causing the surrender of a
German detachment some five hundred strong which was holding up
the advance of the right brigade in the front system of trenches. The
inability of the right of this division to get forward had, however,
caused sufficient delay to enable the enemy to collect local reserves
behind the strong second line. The arrangements, the planning, and
execution of the attack, and the conduct of the troops of the IVth Corps
were most efficient and praiseworthy."

On the 26th September an attack was made by the Guards Division
on the right of the battalion, which supported it by firing, but otherwise
took no part in the attack, which failed. At noon the men were ordered
to eat half their " iron ration," as they had had no food since the morning
of the 25th. They suffered greatly from thirst as they had had no water
except that carried in their water-bottles, and that was exhausted by this
time. The rest of the day was spent in consolidating their position.

The night of the 26th-27th was quiet, and on the latter morning the
battalion stood to arms. The ration party which had been sent to Le
Rutoire on the 26th had lost its way, so the men were again without food
or water. At 4 p.m. the Guards again attacked Hill 70 and the chalk pit.

The function of the 8th Battalion in this was only the throwing out
of smoke bombs to protect the left of the assailants from enfilade fire.

When the battalion stood to at 4.45 a.m. on the 28th, the exhaustion of the men was so great that it was difficult to keep the sentries alert.   On this day Lieut.-Colonel Walton, who had some time before been warned for service at Aden, left the battalion, to its great regret.   Command was assumed by Major C. F. N. Bartlett.   At 11 p.m. the battalion, being relieved by the Gloucestershire, returned to the old brigade front line and was in billets at Les Brebis on the 29th, and Nœux-les-Mines on the 30th.   The first four days of October were spent at Nœux-les-Mines, and on the 5th the battalion relieved the 8th Royal Fusiliers in the old German front line. Reinforcements of officers and men were rapidly coming in, and on the 12th at 11.30 p.m. the 8th Royal Berkshire again took battle positions, with the Black Watch on their left, and the London Scottish on their right.   They held two hundred yards of front, with two companies in front and two in support.   The objective was a German trench on the east side of the main Lens-La Bassée Road, separated from them by about two hundred yards of No-Man's Land.

On the 13th chlorine gas and smoke bombs were discharged at intervals from 1 p.m. till 1.50 p.m., when the artillery lifted and wire cutters went forward covered by smoke.   Ten minutes later the two front companies went over.   The enemy machine-gun fire from the chalk pit on the right was so heavy that only about half a dozen men succeeded in reaching the " estaminet " beyond the road.   These remained there till dusk, when they crawled back.   At 2.10 p.m. it was reported that the leading companies had reached the road, but were being enfiladed.   Two platoons, with the machine-gun men, were sent up from the supports.   The smoke was now getting thinner, and the machine guns were put out of action by the enemy fire, of the same description, when they had only got seventy-five yards beyond the British parapet.   Only about fifteen men of the two platoons managed to get as far as the road, which they did not pass.   They reported that there was little rifle fire, but grenades were being flung at them which fell short by ten yards.   The rest of the battalion went over, but were equally unsuccessful in getting forward.

At 2 a.m. on the 14th October the remnants of the battalion were sent to support the Black Watch, and at 8 a.m. back into the old brigade third line, whence they went, at 7 p.m., viâ Nœux-les-Mines to Lillers.   They had again suffered very heavily, especially in officers.   Their casualties were :

Officers. Killed : Capt. R. M. Coote.
2nd-Lieuts. C. Spartali, C. J. Steel (3rd Dorset, attached), C. Salman.
Wounded : Capt. L. H. Edwards.
2nd-Lieuts. T. B. Lawrence, L. Park (3rd Dorset, attached), W. C. Holland (3rd Dorset, attached).
Wounded and Missing : 2nd-Lieut. E. Frost.
Missing : 2nd-Lieuts. V. H. Woodford,* W. E. Woodthorpe (3rd Dorset, attached).
Other Ranks : Killed 18 ; Wounded 59 ; Missing 65.
Total : 11 Officers and 142 Other Ranks.

For their conduct in this or the previous action Colonel Walton received the C.M.G., Captain D. Tosetti, Lieutenant C. Gentry-Birch, and Second-Lieutenant T. B. Lawrence were awarded the M.C., and R.-S.-M. Lainsbury the D.C.M.

At Lillers the much tried battalion was training, refitting, and receiving reinforcements till the 28th, when it was sent by train to Nœux-les-Mines, but had to return at once, as the place was too full to accommodate them. They continued at Lillers till the 13th November. When he inspected the brigade, Sir H. Rawlinson thanked the troops " for the magnificent work you did on the 25th September last, especially the two battalions who led the assault, the 8th Berks and 10th Gloucester, supported by the Camerons."

On the 14th the battalion went by train to Nœux-les-Mines, marched to Mazingarbe, and proceeded to the fire trenches with the Chalk Pit on the north. Next day command of the battalion was taken over from Major Bartlett by Major T. G. Dalby, 1st King's Royal Rifle Corps, and it moved back to reserve trenches behind Loos.

On the 24th the brigade (commanded by Brig.-General A. J. Reddie) was inspected by Sir John French, the Commander-in-Chief, who paid it many compliments on its conduct in the Battle of Loos.

The rest of 1915 passed uneventfully in the usual routine of trench warfare in the same neighbourhood.

* Later recorded as killed.

TRENCH WARFARE.   THE BATTLE OF THE SOMME.   CONTALMAISON.
BAZENTIN–LE–PETIT AND MAMETZ.

1916

All January passed equally without special events between Nœux-les-Mines, Lillers, and Allouagne, as did February.   The casualties in the latter month were only six and on the 26th the effective strength of the 8th Royal Berkshire had again risen to 33 officers and 858 other ranks.

March and April again were as January and February, though casualties were somewhat heavier.

On the 2nd May the battalion marched from Les Brebis to the front-line trenches about the Double Crassier.   Next day it was decided to fire two British mines under the German sap on the south arm of the Double Crassier, and immediately after the explosion to send a raiding party to try and get prisoners for purposes of identification of the opposing enemy units.

At 8.30 a.m. the mines were blown up, and Lieutenant D. J. Footman, with two N.C.O.s and thirteen men, rushed forward, under cover of a barrage, and of a diversion made by the throwing of bombs in the direction of the northern enemy sap.   As they entered the German trench blocking parties were sent to right and left, whilst Footman and the rest threw bombs into the dugouts in the trench between the blocks.   They met a German bombing party, one of whom was killed and another, wounded and trying to crawl away, was captured.   It was, however, found impossible to bring him back through the wire, so he was left, minus his coat which was brought back. Lieutenant Footman and his party returned when their supply of bombs was exhausted.   They were certain that they had killed and wounded six of the enemy, they brought back valuable information and sketches of the enemy trenches, and an identification of the opposite unit in the wounded man's coat.

For this exploit Lieutenant Footman received the M.C., and one D.C.M., two M.M.s and certificates were given to his men.

Next day Private G. W. Yates, on patrol, found an enemy's working party busy at their end of the sap, just north of the Double Crassier.   Going quietly back, he fetched up some bombers, crawled to within four yards of the working party, and bombed them. They fled, followed by Yates alone till he had exhausted his bombs. For this exploit he received a " green ticket," which did not strike one as an over-liberal reward.

The next notable event occurred on the 20th May, when, just as the battalion " stood down " after dawn, a sentry saw something moving in the British wire. He fired at it, whereupon a German stood up with his hands up. On being called in, he came with a sigh of relief. Save for a helmet, he had no equipment or arms. He stated that he was a Pioneer, and that he had deserted because he had been struck by an officer. He seemed of a superior class, and at Head-quarters gave copious information as to positions of German batteries, etc., and stated that the enemy had brought up a Guard Division from Belgium, and were contemplating an early attempt to recover the Loos Salient. How far his information was true, we are not aware.

On the 27th May, when the battalion was in front line at Calonne, the enemy, after a short bombardment, attempted a raid at 10.30 p.m.

Unfortunately, a wiring party, under Second-Lieutenant Klementaski, was out at the time, and was surprised before it could get back. Supported by fire and bombs from the trenches, this party succeeded in breaking up the attack, but suffered heavily in doing so.

Second-Lieutenant Klementaski and eleven other ranks were killed, and sixteen other ranks wounded. Five dead Germans were brought in and two left outside the wire, and other casualties of uncertain number were inflicted on the enemy. As Klementaski had only about fifteen men with him, the British casualties are inclusive of those in the trenches.

Colonel Dalby believes that all the casualties, except Second-Lieutenant L. A. Klementaski, occurred in the trench. He adds that " the men were splendidly steady and behaved magnificently." The leading party of German raiders was about twenty in number. A Lewis gun opened upon them, and some of them seem to have run back at once. Some of the wiring party reached home, others lay down in the grass and began firing on the rest of the Germans as they advanced with fixed bayonets. From the fact that Second-Lieutenant Klementaski's body bore the marks of at least three bayonet wounds, it is clear that the fighting developed into a hand-to-hand struggle. None of the enemy reached the British trench. Only two got within bombing distance, and they were killed by rifle fire from the sap. The affair was evidently an organized raid, not merely an attempt to cut off the wiring party, and the raiders were identified as coming from all companies of the German unit. These casualties raised the total for May to one officer (Klementaski) killed, seventeen other ranks killed, and forty-eight wounded.

June was an uneventful month, passed in the Calonne neighbourhood. During it, Lieutenant and Quartermaster J. Barrow and one man were killed, and eighteen other ranks wounded, all apparently by shell fire in the trenches. A few minor operations and bombardments were carried out from the 25th onwards, evidently with the object of keeping the enemy occupied, and diverting his attention from the approaching great attack on the Somme. The casualties, as appears from the above statement of them, were not serious.

On the 6th July the battalion started for the Somme, where the great battle had been in progress since the 1st. On that day the battalion entrained at Fouquereuilles for Doullens, whence, on the 8th, it marched ten miles by the main Amiens Road to Naours, and on to the area Pierregot, Mirvaux, and Mollien-aux-Bois. The rest of the brigade had already reached Mollien-aux-Bois in advance of the 8th Royal Berkshire, which arrived there on the 8th. Next day it marched to Albert, and on the 10th took over two trenches from the 10th Gloucestershire, who had relieved the 24th Brigade there in the afternoon. Battalion Head-quarters were in a shelter on the main road from Fricourt to Contalmaison. Five officers were left behind as a reserve in Albert. The new trenches were near Lozenge Wood. On the 11th Second-Lieutenant F. S. Snell was killed whilst reconnoitring from Lozenge Wood to Contalmaison.

At 9.15 that night the battalion relieved the 8th Yorkshire, some of whose drafts had been learning their work with the 8th Royal Berkshire since the latter part of June.

The 8th Yorkshire had taken Contalmaison in the preceding night. At Contalmaison the 8th Royal Berkshire were established in two trenches in the Château grounds, with the Black Watch on their left. In the cellars of the Château there were one hundred and ten wounded Germans in charge of a German doctor, who stated that he and his wounded had been taken and retaken three times in the recent fighting since they were first in the Château on the 1st July.   The wounds were mostly septic, and the sufferings of these unfortunate men were terrible.

The battalion had orders to take, before morning, the cutting N.E. of the Château which prisoners stated was occupied by the enemy.   A fighting patrol sent out that night was forced to retire by machine-gun fire.   At 6 a.m. on the 12th another patrol was sent out and succeeded in occupying the cutting.   At 11 a.m., the commanding-officer was wounded as he returned from a visit to the cutting, and an hour later a rather feeble German counter-attack was repulsed, and the assailants took shelter in shell-holes in the woods in front of the battalion.   A patrol, sent along the sunken road to the right of the battalion position beyond the cutting, established communication with the 7th Lincolnshire occupying Mametz Wood, to which the road led.

Half an hour after noon " C " Company, which had two platoons in the sunken road, sent a bombing party along Pearl Alley, the communication trench leading to the German second line.   This party drove the occupants of Pearl Alley before them, and established a strong point three hundred yards up it in advance of the road.   The rest of the day was spent in consolidating the position.   The enemy was shelling Contalmaison heavily, especially the Château, though they must have known of the presence of their wounded there.

At midnight of the 12th-13th Second-Lieutenant F. G. Marsh took out a patrol through a severe barrage to Pearl Wood, on the right of Pearl Alley. They seized and occupied the wood, the Black Watch at the same time capturing Contalmaison Wood to the left of the Château.

A prisoner of the 122nd German Regiment, who was brought in at 9 a.m., gave a lurid account of the sufferings and losses of his regiment, which had been fighting continuously since the 1st July.   At 3 p.m., the battalion was moved from the Château to the right, so that its left was now at the cutting, its centre in the sunken road, and its right near Mametz Wood.

At 10.30 that night (13th) Second-Lieutenant G. R. Goodship, with a patrol of twenty men, seized and consolidated Lower Wood, lying to the right of Pearl Wood and in front of Mametz Wood.   He has himself furnished the following account of this operation :

" Just before dusk an urgent order was received for an officer and party to occupy ' Lower Wood' still more exposed than Pearl Wood to the right front, and the only men available were Corporal Belcher, Sergeant Woodfield, myself, and others mustering seventeen in all.   We had arrived in the front line.   I had issued my instructions, deployed, and was just going to advance when a terrific shelling from the enemy started, which, together with the darkness, disorganized the party.   However, with the aid of the Sergeant and Corporal, I got together eight or nine men, and, leaving the Sergeant to find the remainder, advanced in open order, under fire, across some four hundred yards of open ground and straight through the wood to the opposite side.   All was well, the enemy scuttling.   Leaving a sentry group of three, the remainder of us scoured the wood as best we could (we did it thoroughly at dawn) and then, to the best of our ability, consolidated the position. The Sergeant, later, arrived with four or five more men, two being missing (afterwards found killed).   I then reported through Private Vaughan to B.H.Q.   At dawn one Lewis and two machine guns were sent forward. The artillery zero was 5.20 and the infantry 9 a.m., and I have never seen land look so like a rough sea as on that occasion.   Four men were killed, four wounded and one gun completely destroyed before we were relieved at sundown.   The wood seen on the morning of the 13th was beautiful and green ;   when we left there was scarce a branch on the trunks."

It had been arranged that the 21st Division, on the right of the 1st, should attack in the early hours of the 14th July.   The preliminary bombardment which began at 3.20 a.m. had the result of drawing upon the 1st Brigade the reply of the enemy who expected the attack to be on that front.

Two parties, each of one officer and thirty other ranks, were sent up Pearl Alley, with instructions to observe the enemy from as close as possible. If he was found to have evacuated his front trench, the wire was to be cut by hand, the parties were to establish themselves in the trench, and to send up a red flare as a call for reinforcements.   As they proceeded they found that the farther part of Pearl Alley was waist deep in mud, impossible to pass.   This, and the heavy German barrage they encountered, compelled the parties to retire, after suffering several casualties.

During the morning information came in that the 21st Division on the right had taken Bazentin-le-Petit, and, at 2.30 p.m., was about to advance again from the N.W. corner of that village.   The 8th Royal Berkshire were ordered to again move by Pearl Alley, to get into the German second-line front trench, and bomb outwards along it.   The bombers towards the S.E. were, if possible, to meet those of the 21st Division coming from the S.W. corner of Bazentin-le-Petit Wood.   If they could not do this, the German trench was at least to be blocked fifty yards on either side of the point of entry.

The difficulties of getting up bombs through the mud of Pearl Alley were so great that the battalion started doing so an hour and a half before the time fixed for the attack, so as to get them as far forward as possible.   It was only possible to hope for success in this attack on condition of active co-operation by the 21st Division, and effective artillery support.

At 2.25 p.m., when it was too late to recall the Berkshire men from well up Pearl Alley, the battalion was informed that the attack of the 21st Division had been postponed.   Consequently, there was no time to stop the battalion and it went forward at the prescribed hour—2.30 p.m.

They got into the German trench, but, owing to the stoppage of the 21st Division attack, the whole of the enemy's attention was concentrated on them, and they were driven out again by a counter-attack across the open from the German second line.   There was nothing for it but to retire down Pearl Alley, an operation which was carried out with fewer casualties than might have been expected under the circumstances.   They were, for the period 11th–14th July :

Officers. Killed : 2nd-Lieuts. F. S. Snell, G. E. Maggs (Died of Wounds).
Wounded : Lieut.-Col. T. G. Dalby ; Lieut. H. C. Churchill.
2nd-Lieuts. A. C. P. Lunn, C. G. M. Morris.
Other Ranks : Killed or Died of Wounds 18 ; Wounded 123 ; Missing 2.
Total : 6 Officers and 143 Other Ranks.

From the 15th to the 18th July the battalion was at Albert refitting ; on the 19th it was at Bécourt Wood and the old German first line beyond it, and on the 20th near Lozenge Wood.   On the 21st it was in trenches W. of Mametz, in support of the Gloucestershire Regiment and Cameron Highlanders.   " B " Company was at the cutting near Contalmaison, " C " in Pearl Alley, " A " and " D " in Quadrangle Support Trench, and Head-quarters in Shelter Wood where that night they were treated to a German gas shelling.

At 9.30 p.m. the battalion moved into position to support the forthcoming attack of the 10th Gloucestershire and 1st Cameron Highlanders on the enemy's temporary switch in front of Martinpuich. " C " Company was placed at the disposal of the former, " B " at that of the latter regiment. " C " was in the old German trench, and " B " in rear of the Bazentin-le-Petit Wood, the latter with orders to fill any gap which might occur between the Cameron Highlanders and the 19th Division on their right. The 2nd Brigade was attacking on the left of the Gloucestershire. The other two companies remained in the sunken road between the Contalmaison cutting and Mametz Wood. Battalion Head-quarters in Lower Wood. The attack was started at 12.30 a.m. on the 23rd July, but the leading battalions failed to get into the German trench, largely on account of the severe fire from the Bazentin Road on the right of the Camerons, and the fact that the trench was out of sight just beyond the crest, and its wire had not been cut by the artillery. The remaining two companies (" A " and " D ") of the Royal Berkshire were now moved up in support. At 9.30 p.m. the battalion relieved the Gloucestershire and the Cameron Highlanders in front line, the Black Watch becoming support. The battalion does not seem to have had any fighting worth mentioning on this day, as no casualties are recorded.

On the 25th July the brigade was relieved by the 70th, and the battalion went back viâ Albert to Baisieux Wood, where there were sports on the 28th. When the Divisional-General inspected the new drafts on the 31st, the 8th Royal Berkshire had two hundred and sixty-eight.

The officers wounded during the month were Captain C. E. Beale, Lieutenant D. J. Footman, and Second-Lieutenant W. L. Clarke, and of other ranks 35 were killed or died of wounds, 183 were wounded, and 4 missing.

The first twelve days of August were spent at Baisieux Wood, and on the 13th the battalion went to Bécourt Wood, moving up on the next day to Brigade reserve trenches on the N. edge of Mametz Wood.

At noon on the 18th it relieved the Black Watch in front line N. of Bazentin-le-Petit. The relieved battalion had failed earlier in the day in an attempt on the German intermediate line which was now to be attacked by the Royal Berkshire. The attack was to be made on a front of three companies, "D" on the right, "B" centre, "C" left. "A" was in reserve, and after the others had started was to be distributed in strong points on the starting line. If the "intermediate line" were taken without serious losses, the companies were to proceed to a second line believed to be one hundred yards farther on. The 10th Gloucestershire were on the right of the battalion. The bombardment began at noon during the relief, and unfortunately one British gun, firing short, dropped shells in the middle of it, burying many men, and so badly damaging the trench that movement along it was impossible. This naturally caused confusion, and the companies were scarcely in position at zero.

The "intermediate line" bent back at right angles on the Martinpuich Road. South-west of this angle was Lancashire Trench, on the left of the road, and from it Lancashire Sap ran up towards the angle. The plan was for a frontal attack on the part of the German trench running E. and W. whilst a platoon of "C" moved up Lancashire Sap against the left of the angle. This attack, which might have had important results, failed to mature. The officer-commanding the platoon reports that they were blinded by smoke blowing across the line, and were unable to see their way. Lancashire Sap was within the area of the 46th Brigade which "lent" it for the purpose of this attack.

The frontal attack began at 2.45. At first there was not much resistance, but when the assailants were within one hundred yards of the "intermediate line" the German barrage and machine-gun fire was so heavy that they were held up, and what was left of them dug in about one hundred and fifty yards short of the line.

They were shelled out of this position at 4 p.m., and had to retire to the original line. The casualties were heavy :

Officers. *Killed :* 2nd-Lieuts. W. N. Conyers, C. G. B. Harrison, W. H. Bissley.
Wounded : Lieut. S. F. Stileman.
2nd-Lieuts. G. R. Goodship, S. A. G. Harvey, T. W. Prout.
Other Ranks : 160, no details given.

On the 20th August the battalion returned to support trenches on the north of Mametz Wood. The " switch " or " intermediate line " had been evacuated in the interval by the enemy and occupied by the British. During the period 20th–29th spent at Mametz Wood, Captain H. R. Fenner, Lewis-gun officer, was wounded by a shell on the 27th. When the battalion relieved the Cameron Highlanders in the night of the 29th-30th in the right sub-sector of the High Wood sector, an attack which had been proposed was postponed till the 3rd or 4th September.

At 1.15 p.m. on the 30th August the enemy made an attack, but was driven off with heavy loss by the fire of machine guns in High Wood, and that of the Berkshire Lewis guns enfilading the line from his right. At the same time as this attack was made on High Wood, an enemy party tried to enter a sap on the Berkshire front to the west of it. Here also they failed, with a loss of half a dozen killed by Lewis guns. The same evening the 1st Brigade was relieved by the 2nd, and the battalion once more returned to Mametz Wood.

Its casualties in August had been 4 officers killed or died of wounds, 7 wounded, and of other ranks 42 killed, 171 wounded and 14 missing.

On the 3rd September the 1st Brigade attacked Wood Lane and the German trenches in High Wood, with the Cameron Highlanders on the right against Wood Lane, and the Black Watch on the left. The front of attack was a line running eastwards from the western edge of High Wood. Half a company of Royal Berkshire was with the Cameron Highlanders, the rest of the battalion in close support. Zero was at midday, just after the successful explosion of a British mine in the east corner of High Wood. The Highlanders worked their way forward to beyond Wood Lane, the Black Watch were less successful. The officer-commanding the Camerons, being short of men for consolidating his new position, sought the help of the Royal Berkshire. In response two companies were sent, but " A," on the left, was held up by fire from High Wood and could not get up. At 1.15 p.m. " C," on the right, joined the Camerons, and sent men back to bring up ammunition and a Stokes mortar. The other two companies were also sent up to garrison the front line. At 1.30 the enemy counter-attacked with strong artillery support, and the British were forced back to their original line, carrying about thirty prisoners with them.

Casualties had been heavy on both sides, and at 5 p.m. the remains of the Cameron Highlanders and Royal Berkshire were reorganized under the officer commanding the former, and held the old line during the night.

In this action the 8th Royal Berkshire lost :

Officers.   *Killed :* 2nd-Lieut. L. G. Edens.
    Missing (Killed) : 2nd-Lieut. C. H. Chambers.
    Wounded and Missing : 2nd-Lieut. D. W. Prout.*
    Wounded : Capt. J. H. G. Lawrance.
      Lieuts. G. Baker, S. E. Davenport.
      2nd-Lieut. G. F. Marsh.
Other Ranks : 100, no details given.

Nothing more occurred till the Royal Berkshire and Cameron Highlanders were relieved on the 5th September and went to bivouac in Bécourt Wood, where the battalion remained till it moved, viâ Albert on the 10th, to Millencourt, and next day to billets at La Houssoye.

On the 16th, in consequence of the progress of the attack on the previous day, it was suddenly moved to billets at Bresle, on the 18th to Bécourt Wood, and on the 19th was ordered to Bazentin-le-Grand to relieve troops in the new line N.E. of High Wood. It was stopped, however, at Bazentin-le-Grand, as the New Zealanders had been driven from the trenches which the Royal Berkshire was intended to take over.

On the 20th the New Zealanders and Black Watch recovered the lost ground, and two companies of Royal Berkshire moved up to occupy trenches E. of High Wood, whilst one supported the Black Watch. Touch was established with the 50th Division on the left.

On the 22nd " D " Company was placed temporarily at the disposal of the 2nd Royal Munster Fusiliers in the Flers line, and on the 24th the whole battalion was back in Bazentin-le-Grand.

During the period 20th–26th September the companies not actually in the front line were employed carrying up ammunition and bombs from Bazentin-le-Grand to the front. Owing to the mud and the absence of communication trenches, this was very hard and dangerous work, as the men often had to carry across open ground under shell fire.

* Later recorded as killed.

The battalion also did much work in consolidating the new position and digging communication trenches.

The officer commanding the 3rd Brigade, which was holding the front line, specially thanked the carrying parties for their exertions.

From the 27th to the end of the month the battalion was out of the line at Bresle.

Its casualty list for September indicates more or less the distribution of the cases of other ranks on the 3rd:

Officers.   Killed 2 ; Wounded 4 ; Missing, Believed Killed, 1.
Other Ranks :   Killed or Died of Wounds 40 ; Wounded 124 ; Missing 20.

With the advent of October matters began to settle down into the usual weary routine of trench warfare for the winter.   From the 2nd to the end of the month the brigade was training, and when it moved to the IIIrd Corps reserve at Hennencourt on the 31st the 8th Royal Berkshire was left behind, isolated on account of an epidemic of German measles, which kept them where they were till they at last moved by train to Albert on the 27th November.

From Albert they returned, on the 28th November, to Bazentin-le-Grand, and for the first four days of December were in the new front line to the east of the Albert-Bapaume Road, with the Butte de Warlencourt away on their left.

Between these trenches and Bazentin-le-Petit they spent the first half of the month.   The weather was atrocious, and mud in places was nearly waist deep.   The left of the front line was nothing but a line of posts in shell-holes connected by a wide ditch generally full of water.

Between companies in front line there was an unoccupied interval of two hundred yards, the line being marked with tapes to prevent men losing their way and wandering into the enemy lines.

The battalion was at Bazentin-le-Petit till Christmas Eve, and, as it was under orders for the front line next day, Christmas had to be celebrated by a dinner on the 24th, when the men were served with beer, oranges, nuts, cigars and other simple comforts suitable to the season.

Christmas Day was miserable enough in front line, with communication only possible at night, and then only by means of " trench boards." Going back to Flers and Bazentin-le-Petit on the 28th, the last day of 1916 was spent in billets at Albert.

Near Péronne. Nieuport and the Coast. Poelcappelle. Houthulst Forest

1917

From the 1st to the 22nd January the battalion remained training at Albert, and then went to Warloy for the rest of the month. The weather was very cold, and there was a good deal of sickness of the ordinary kinds to be expected in such conditions. The strength of the battalion on the 31st was twenty-nine officers and seven hundred and fifty-two other ranks.

On the 4th February the brigade moved to the area about the bend of the Somme south of Péronne.

In this neighbourhood it remained throughout February and March, the only incident worth recording being on the 19th March when the battalion was unable to cross the Somme at Eterpigny owing to a bridge not being ready.

A patrol, however, was sent across and reconnoitred the enemy trenches, which had been evacuated as far east as the outskirts of Mesnil–Bruntel.

Later, the Royal Berkshire crossed and occupied trenches about Brie on the right bank.

April was passed in the same part, mainly in road-making, and it was only on the 27th May that the battalion entrained at Marcelcave to return to the north at Godewaerswelde. There it remained out of the line till the 10th June, when it began to move again, reaching the neighbourhood of Dunkirk on the 21st. Two days later it took over trenches beyond the Yser Canal east of Nieuport-les-Bains. Here it was in a country very different from what it had hitherto known. The line consisted of shallow trenches in the sand-dunes of the coast, the front and support lines having breastworks revetted with sandbags. The enemy on the larger dunes commanded the British lines, and from the Great Dune had observation of practically the whole British trench system. The trenches now occupied were taken over from the French, and the occasion was celebrated by an immediate increase in the German shelling.

The Black Watch, which was the left battalion of the brigade, had its left flank actually on the sea, whilst the 32nd Division on the right of the 8th Royal Berkshire was separated from the battalion by a large marsh.

The only casualties in June—7 other ranks killed and 7 wounded—were due to the heavy bombardment of the 25th.

On the 29th June the battalion went into support, and in the night of the 3rd-4th July, when it was again in front line, it carried out a considerable raid on the German trenches.

At 11 p.m. on the 3rd July, Lieutenant Bland and two men crept forward from the battalion's trench with the first ten-feet length of a Bangalore torpedo tube which was passed out to them. From this point it had to be moved to another place, owing to the difficulty of getting it forward. The second and third lengths (ten feet each) followed immediately.

It was 12.5 a.m. on the 4th when Lieutenant Bland and Corporal Davis (R.E.) reached the German wire, where they had great difficulty in pushing the tubes through and connecting them up. Bland then sent the corporal back to report to Captain Footman, who was commanding the raiding party, that all was ready. The latter sent up the signal rocket, but a minute and a half elapsed before the artillery commenced firing. Lieutenant Gillespie (R.E.) then fired the torpedo, at 1.20 a.m., and returned to the trench. Waiting a few minutes for the smoke to clear, the raiders rushed out ; but, just as they reached the wire, British shells exploded close to them, and they retired and lay down ten yards back, waiting for the barrage to lift. Then they advanced again and were fired on by a small party of the enemy, to whom they replied with a dozen bombs. The barrage was still in the same place, and three of the leading officers and men were knocked down by the shock of exploding percussion shells.

The party being disorganized by this, Lieutenant Bland gave the order to withdraw, and by 1.40 a.m. all were back in the trenches with only one casualty, an officer (2nd-Lieut. Johnson) slightly wounded. The Battalion Diary emphasizes the fact that every one was convinced that British shells were bursting in the German wire.

The success of the enterprise depended entirely on surprise, which was effected on this occasion ; but it was useless to expect a renewed attack would be unexpected, so none was made.

From the 4th to the 16th July the battalion was training at St. Idesbalde, and on the 17th took over part of the coast defences. On the 18th it marched to St. Pol, and on to Le Clipon Camp where the 1st Division was concentrated. On the 19th Lieut.-Colonel R. E. Dewing, D.S.O., took over command of the battalion from Lieut.-Colonel C. A. S. Carleton, who returned to his own battalion, the 1/6th Welsh Regiment.

During the whole of August, September, and the first twenty days of October the battalion was at Le Clipon, engaged chiefly in a special training called the Obstacle Course.

By the 22nd October the 8th Royal Berkshire were in billets at Rubrouck, on the 26th east of Wormhoudt, and on the 30th the division was transferred to the XVIIIth Corps commanded by Lieut.-General Sir Ivor Maxse. This Corps was in the 5th Army.

From the 1st to the 7th November the battalion was at Herzeele and Schools Camp, whence it marched on the 8th to Poperinghe, entrained there, and, after detraining at Brielen, N.W. of Ypres, marched to Dambre Camp. When it was at Irish Farm on the 11th three men were killed and eleven wounded by a bomb dropped by an enemy aeroplane. Lieutenant F. Moor's diary says that the bomb was dropped at 5.30 a.m. about thirty yards from " B " Company's marquee. It made a hole twelve feet deep and twenty in diameter, and the concussion brought down several tents.

On the 15th November, the battalion was again preparing for an attack northwards on the northern side of the Ypres Salient in the neighbourhood of Poelcappelle. On the right of the battalion were the Cameron Highlanders, on the left the 2nd Welch. Zero was fixed for 5 p.m. on the 16th. In front " B " Company under Captain Footman, and " D " under Captain T. B. Lawrence, led the advance without artillery co-operation and met with but little opposition at first. " B " reached its objective by 5.20 p.m., but " D " had more difficult swampy ground, and when at 6.40 they were as near their goal as possible, owing to the swamp, they were caught in the enemy barrage. The Camerons on the right were also in difficulties when, in response to their S.O.S., the British barrage was put down.

During the attack very few of the enemy were seen, and these could not be got at on account of unpassable ground. Communication was very difficult, and only possible by runners. The German barrage came down on the line of the Paddebeek stream, beyond which were enemy pill-boxes. The 1st Northamptonshire, on the left, crossed the stream in an endeavour to take these, in conjunction with " D " the left company of the Royal Berkshire.

After the attack the 8th Royal Berkshire were about Tournant Farm, which lies about half a mile N.W. of Goudberg, on the line between that place and Poelcappelle, and were facing north.   The casualties (6 other ranks killed and 28 wounded) were comparatively small, a fact which is attributable to the two companies getting beyond the area covered by the German barrage before it came down, except to some extent in the case of " D." Even of these casualties about one-third were due to enemy artillery in the morning before the attack began.

Lieutenant Moor's diary gives a very detailed account of his movements with Nos. 13 and 15 Platoons, but does not convey the impression that there was any severe fighting.

During the night of the 16th-17th useful patrols were carried out by Lieutenants C. F. R. Bland and W. C. A. Hanney.

In the night of the 17th-18th the battalion was relieved by the 10th Gloucestershire who, with the Black Watch, carried out a successful attack whilst the Royal Berkshire were at Hill Top Farm.   They were at Poodle Camp from the 27th November to the 3rd December, when they entrained at Proven for Boesinghe, marching thence to the French shelters at Lizerie. Here, next day, they relieved four companies of the 208th French infantry in the left battalion front of the Houthulst Forest area.   The Berkshire diary praises the French arrangements for relief, under which five officers were left behind for twenty-four hours to show the new-comers their way about.   The weather was fine and frosty.

The line here consisted of outposts without any regular trench system. During the night of the 6th-7th the 10th Belgian Infantry relieved the French 110th on the left of the Royal Berkshire.   The latter went into reserve on the 8th on relief by the Gloucestershire.   On the 12th they were at Chauny Camp where there was a presentation of medals, including the Military Cross for Lieutenant Bland.

Christmas Day was spent at Reninghof where the battalion had been billeted in farms and shelters since the 20th.

It is noted that the men had an excellent dinner of turkeys, vegetables, Christmas pudding and beer, and received presents from Queen Alexandra's Field Force Fund.

On the 27th the battalion went to the reserve position at Boche Cross Roads, where they had been on the 8th, and in the night of the 28th-29th they returned for the last days of 1917 to their old position in front line, between the Belgians on the left and the Cameron Highlanders on the right.

HOUTHULST FOREST. SOUTH OF THE SOMME. THE GERMAN OFFENSIVE. THE DEFENCE OF AMIENS. THE FINAL ADVANCE. OVILLERS. TRÔNES WOOD. ST. PIERRE VAAST. EPÉHY. MORMAL FOREST. DISBANDMENT

1918–1919

The last year of the War opened for the 8th Royal Berkshire on the Houthulst Forest front where they were at the end of December. Conditions in trenches in Flanders were generally bad, but, to judge from the History of the 18th Division,* the Houthulst Forest front was the most miserable of all. Here they remained with nothing special to record for the whole of January, taking their turn in front line, in support, or in the reserve areas.

They ended the month with a strength of 44 officers and 855 other ranks.

On the 1st February the battalion was preparing to leave the 1st Division, in consequence of the reorganization of that period. General Strickland, commanding the division, bade them farewell on the 2nd, and they received many manifestations of good feeling from the other battalions with which they had served so long in the 1st Brigade.

On the 3rd they left the 1st Division, being played out by the band of the Camerons, and marched into the area of the 18th Division, to the 53rd Brigade of which they were now to be attached. On their way to Portsmouth Camp they marched past Major-General Lee, C.B., commanding the 18th Division. The 6th Royal Berkshire was, as we know, disbanded in the early days of February 1918, and their place in the 53rd Brigade was taken by the 8th Battalion. The other battalions of the reduced brigade were the 7th Royal West Kent and the 10th Essex.

The 18th Division which, like the 1st, had spent a miserable winter in

* Cf. supra, p. 284.

the water-logged country about the Houthulst Forest, was now about to move to a more congenial country, though it was to undergo more terrible experiences of modern war than it had yet incurred in the great German offensive against the British 5th Army on the Somme Front in March 1918.

On the 7th February the battalion entrained at Proven for Noyon, S.E. of Amiens, where it arrived at 3 p.m. on the 8th and at once marched to Babœuf, whence on the 10th a fourteen-mile march carried it to Jussy on the St. Quentin Canal, and the next day saw it at Clastres, two miles farther north, working hard at the defensive lines. On the 15th the battalion was at Caillouel training and working, on the 25th at Haut Tombelle Camp, and on the 26th in the left sector of the brigade front line. Most of the 18th Division front at this time was separated from the enemy by the River Oise. flowing through a marshy plain between Alaincourt, six or seven miles S. by E. of St. Quentin, and Travecy, another six miles to the south.

There is nothing much to record in the early days of March, beyond the rather heavy loss of two men killed, fifteen wounded, and two missing, the consequence apparently of German bombardment for a raid directed on the troops to the right of the battalion.

On the 20th March warning was received of an impending enemy attack.

At this time the battalion was disposed with Battalion Head-quarters at La Guingette Farm on the high ground near Cérizy, N.W. of Moy. " B " and " D " Companies held the front line of the " forward " zone, " A " was in support, and " C," as counter-attacking company, was in a trench in rear of Battalion Head-quarters. The forward area on the right of the 8th Royal Berkshire was held by the Royal West Kent.

The great offensive opened at 4.30 a.m. on the 21st March, with a power-ful barrage and gas shells launched on the British front line, whilst the back areas were also heavily shelled. There was a thick mist, and at daybreak visibility did not exceed ten yards. All communications by telephone were broken at once by the bombardment, and the efforts of Second-Lieutenant E. Wallis and two men to restore them were in vain. Battalion Head-quarters knew nothing of what was happening in front till 10 a.m. when Lieutenant T. H. Baker, badly wounded though he was, succeeded in getting back through the barrage to report. It appeared that Lieutenant E. J. Mecey, in command of " D " Company on the left, had received a report from Second-Lieutenant W. C. A. Hanney (commanding the right platoon of " D ") that the enemy had broken through the front line. Hanney was holding out in a sunken road. The message did not state exactly where the enemy had broken in.

Of " B," the right company, and the fighting in that quarter there was no news. Two runners (Privates H. Butcher and G. Sparrow) set out to try and get into communication with the front line. They passed safely through the barrage and made for " D's " Head-quarters in Magpie Wood on the left front of Head-quarters, but, before reaching it, met the enemy and were forced to retire. From statements of N.C.O.s and men of " A " Company it appeared that the enemy had reached the support line at 10 a.m., and was temporarily checked there by " A." At 10.30 the sound of rifle fire reached Battalion Head-quarters from the main St. Quentin–Moy Road, and a few of the enemy were seen in the mist moving from that road towards Battalion Head-quarters. Colonel Dewing at once ordered Head-quarters to man the trench behind, in which was " C." Captain and Adjutant H. le G. Sarchet stayed behind to destroy papers. Whilst doing so, he was attacked by Germans, of whom he killed several with his revolver before rejoining the rest of Head-quarters. At 11 a.m. the enemy was advancing in a thick line on the trench occupied by " C " and Head-quarters. Owing to the mist, they were not discovered till they were only fifty yards away. There they were shot down almost to a man by the fire of " C." This checked the advance for a time.

Then the Germans began working round both flanks and shortly opened fire with a machine gun from in rear of the trench. From this, and snipers on all sides, heavy losses were incurred. One sniper, in a shell-hole fifty yards in front, was particularly active and deadly. This man was located by Lieutenant N. Williams, who, accompanied by his servant, Private J. E. Peters, rushed him with the bayonet, and took him prisoner. As he was returning to the trench, Williams was killed. His gallantry had probably saved many lives.

At this juncture the mist at last began to rise, and it was seen that the position was surrounded by the enemy, many of whom were already far on the way to La Fontaine, on the right rear of the battalion position. Colonel Dewing now ordered the men he still had to withdraw down Seine Alley, a trench leading from the Forward to the Battle Zone. By this time the remnants of the 8th Royal Berkshire were represented by only one hundred and eighty-two men. All the rest had either been killed or captured in the positions of the Forward Zone.

During the defence of " C's " trench, great gallantry and coolness had been shown by Lance-Corporal E. H. Noyes, and Private J. Irving, who did immense execution with their Lewis gun. The withdrawal to Seine Alley was covered by C.-S.-M. J. Orsford and several unidentified men who led the bombers forward up the trench down which the rest were pressing.

In the opposite direction, Major D. Tosetti, M.C., and Lieutenant S. A. G. Harvey led a party to clear the road for the Battalion Head-quarters and the men with them by clearing out the Germans who had gained the rear of " C " Company's trench towards La Fontaine.

Major Tosetti was shot dead under circumstances which are related in the following extract from a letter written by a private, who was evidently an eye-witness, in reply to inquiries from a relative of the dead officer.

" Major Tosetti took command of some men to fight their way through, while the C.O. took command of the men that were holding them back from the front of us. All was going well until they got a machine gun trained on us ; the Major sacrificed his life to put the gunners out of action. He was shot through the head and chest and was killed instantly, and, I can assure you, if it had not been for his bravery in locating that gun, hardly any of us would have got back. . . . It was a great loss to the battalion when he was killed, as he was undoubtedly one of the finest and bravest officers serving his country."

Writing to Major Tosetti's father, Colonel Dewing, who was himself killed a few days later, says :

" He was literally worshipped by all the men in the battalion, especially as he had been with them so long and knew so many of them personally. His loss will be felt very much by every one, and I myself feel I have lost not only a very valuable officer but one of the best friends a man could want."

Lieutenant S. A. G. Harvey, the other officer with the party, was also killed under circumstances which are narrated in the History of the 18th

Division.   He encountered a German officer face to face.   Both fired their revolvers simultaneously, and both fell dead.

The command devolved on Sergeant W. J. Spokes, who continued bombing down the trench with the utmost gallantry.   At one time he was fighting quite alone, and he succeeded in clearing Seine Alley and opening the way for those under Colonel Dewing, who themselves had constantly to turn about and check the pursuing enemy by their fire.

Continuing this running fight with an enemy on all sides, the survivors finally reached comparative safety in the Battle Zone.   There they joined with some of the 10th Essex in manning the defences.

During the afternoon and evening their positions were held against all attacks.

At midnight Colonel Dewing received orders to withdraw, which was done, without fighting or casualties, viâ Remigny and the canal bridge at Frières Faillouel.

On the morning of the 22nd the battalion went into huts between Frières Faillouel and Faillouel and was not disturbed till 4 p.m., when it was ordered to occupy a position on either side of the Frières Faillouel Road.   Attached to it were the remnants of the 7th Royal West Kent, and the 53rd French Mortar Battery.   At 8 p.m. it marched viâ Villequiers Aumont to huts in the wood at Rouez.   During this move the remains of the battalion were in rear of the front line.

On the 23rd, at 11 a.m., the 8th Royal Berkshire received a welcome reinforcement in the shape of about two hundred men of the " Battle Surplus " * under Major Morony, and it at once marched out of the wood and took position N.E. of Rouez Farm, facing the Bois de Frières, and in support of the 10th Essex.   One company was sent to a position on the high ground east of Rouez.   The 10th Essex were overwhelmed by numbers, and, according to the History of the 18th Division, " a composite battalion made up of the remnants of the West Kents and the Berkshires fell back fighting."   This fighting is not mentioned in the Battalion Diary, which says that at 3 p.m. the battalion was ordered to the high ground south of the Helut Brook, facing N.E.   From this position the French could be seen retiring from the woods of Frières, and Noreuil.   At dusk the enemy were seen

---

* Officers and men left behind to replace casualties.

taking up a position running S.S.E. from the eastern corner of Frières Wood.

At midnight orders were received to retire to the line of the road from Villequiers Aumont to Chauny. The 10th Essex were still holding out in the S. corner of Frières Wood, whence they now withdrew.

At 1 a.m. on the 24th the 8th Royal Berkshire marched by Caumont to Commenchon, but finding that place under heavy shell fire, marched back to Caillouel, which was reached at 9.30 a.m. There they had a meal of hot tea and bacon, held a muster parade, and then moved out in front of the village to a line in which they were on the right, with the 55th Brigade in the centre, and the 54th on the left. At 11 a.m. they had the 10th Essex on their left, and French infantry on their right. This position was inter-mittently shelled from 4 to 7 p.m., and at dusk, through an unfortunate misapprehension, the French on the right opened fire on the battalion with a machine gun, causing some casualties. Lieutenant Bray at once went over, found the French commander, and explained what had happened. His troops then moved up and formed a junction with the right of the Royal Berkshire. After dark the enemy moved into the valley in front, and fired on the battalion with a machine gun.

At 4 a.m. on the 25th the 8th Royal Berkshire withdrew to a position east of the Crépigny-Dampcourt Road, where they dug in. But this position, too, had to be abandoned, owing to German threats of envelopment. The withdrawal continued and the next position was reached, always under heavy shelling and machine-gun fire. The 10th Essex were now on the left of the 8th Royal Berkshire, and the two battalions alternately covered one another's retreat till a new position was reached, facing N.E. between Mondescourt and Babœuf.

It was shortly after noon when a stand was made here against artillery and machine guns in great force. Excellent service was done by four French tanks which came on the scene, inflicted heavy losses on the enemy, and are acknowledged to have given most valuable assistance in holding up the German advance for some time. About 1.15 p.m. the enemy artillery fire increased, and about one brigade of German infantry had advanced on the Grandru-Mondescourt Road, threatening the left of the brigade, and com-pelling its withdrawal to a position facing N. along the railway to the south of Babœuf. This was effected, without much loss, under cover of the

French tanks. The brigade was now close to the Oise, which here flows from east to west, with the lateral canal parallel to its north bank. At midnight of the 25th-26th the battalion marched westwards along the right bank of the river to Varesnes, crossed and reached Pontoise, where, it may be imagined, the hot soup awaiting it was more than welcome.

On the 26th the troops of the 18th Division, worn out by their long fighting retreat since the 21st, were allowed a brief breathing space in the area about Nampcel. On the 28th the remains of the Royal Berkshire and Royal West Kent were definitely constituted a composite battalion under Colonel Dewing, with the 53rd French Mortar Battery attached to it.

The composite battalion had actually with it, excluding officers and men not present :

	Officers.	Other Ranks.
8th Royal Berkshire .	17	288
7th Royal West Kent. . .	4	122
53rd French Mortar Battery	2	23
Total .	23	433

The casualties of the 8th Royal Berkshire between the 21st and the 27th March had been :

Officers. *Killed :* Major D. Tosetti, M.C.
Capt. C. A. Birch, M.C.
Lieut. S. A. G. Harvey
Lieut. N. Williams } All on the 21st.
2nd-Lieut. E. G. King
2nd-Lieut. J. C. Gordon
Wounded and Missing : Capt. H. R. Fenner. 21st March.
Wounded : Lieut. T. H. Baker. 21st March.
Lieut. H. B. F. Kenney. 25th March.
2nd-Lieut. J. W. Randall. 24th March.

Missing : Capt. D. J. Footman, M.C.
Capt. C. H. C. Byrne, R.A.M.C.
Lieut. G. R. Goodship
Lieut. N. Langston
Lieut. C. F. R. Bland, M.C.
Lieut. E. F. Mecey
2nd-Lieut. J. R. McMullen
2nd-Lieut. E. F. Johnson
2nd-Lieut. T. H. Roberts
2nd-Lieut. W. C. A. Hanney
2nd-Lieut. G. Capes
2nd-Lieut. W. V. Heale
2nd-Lieut. A. G. Williams

} All on the 21st.

Other Ranks : Killed 19 ; Wounded 37 ; Wounded and Missing 10 ;
Missing 386 ; Missing (Believed Killed) 1.
Total : 23 Officers and 453 Other Ranks.

When the division reached Boves-Gentelles, S.E. of Amiens, on the 30th, after a twenty-four-hours' 'bus journey, much of the good done by the short rest about Nampcel had been lost, and the men were still very tired.

On the afternoon of the 31st the enemy made an attack on the divisions on the right, and succeeded in taking and holding some high ground south of Hangard. This was valuable to them for observation, but still more important was the ground in front of Gentelles, which overlooked Amiens eight or ten miles in rear. There is no mention in the Battalion Diary of fighting for the Royal Berkshire on the 31st, but on that day Second-Lieutenant R. W. Crampin was wounded, four other ranks were killed and twenty-five wounded, presumably by shells.

On the 1st April the battalion was at Gentelles, which was severely shelled up till 9.30 p.m.

On the 4th, at 10 a.m., an attack appeared imminent and the battalion was sent to the north side of the Hangard Wood in readiness to counter-attack. Prior to the 4th April the 7th Royal West Kent had been reorganized as a separate battalion. The remains of the 8th Royal Berkshire had been reorganized as one company under Lieutenant C. G. M. Morris, and formed part of a composite battalion commanded by Lieut.-Colonel A. L. Ransome, but they appear to have regained their independent existence by this time.

The 3rd April had been a day of extra heavy shelling for the 53rd Brigade, which was followed by an attack before which the line threatened to break, but rallied and repulsed the Germans.

On the 4th a tremendous effort to break through was made by the enemy, after a furious bombardment from 5.30 to 7 a.m. The morning attack fell on the Australians, the 55th Brigade, and the left of the front occupied by the Royal West Kent. It failed with heavy loss to the enemy. On the left of the 18th Division it was partially successful, and the 14th Division beyond it was forced back. At 10 a.m. the 8th Royal Berkshire were brought forward from Gentelles to a post north of Hangard Wood ready to counter-attack.

On their right front were the 7th Royal West Kent, on the left troops of the 55th Brigade.

The second German onslaught began at 4.30 p.m., on the heels of a terrific bombardment which had lifted towards Cachy half an hour earlier. The German infantry, by 5 p.m., were advancing in great force in waves against Hangard, from which the French were partly ejected. The 8th Royal Berkshire opened on them with all their machine and Lewis guns, working havoc amongst them. Then the battalion went forward to the counter-attack. Colonel Dewing at this moment was wounded and obliged to leave Battalion Head-quarters. As he was being carried to the rear by Private Bailey,* his servant, a stray bullet passed through his head, killing him instantaneously. Bailey was also hit, but escaped serious injury, thanks to a tin in his haversack. The death of their gallant commander was a terrible loss to the battalion. Almost at the same time Captain and Adjutant H. le G. Sarchet was seriously wounded. Captain R. Holland was killed, and Second-Lieutenant E. Wallis, the signalling officer, was wounded. Holland had just received orders from the Colonel regarding the reserve company.

Command of the battalion devolved on Lieutenant A. M. Bray.

The machine-gun and rifle fire of superior enemy numbers necessitated a withdrawal of Head-quarters six hundred yards, to a position whence the covering fire was so effective that the enemy was presently obliged by his enormous losses to retire from the attack.

* This appears to be the man whose account of Major Tosetti's death has been quoted above.

The History of the 18th Division says : " The Berkshires did their bit, but were nearly wiped out. The battalion that night could only muster 58 men."

This is not at all in accordance with the Battalion Diary, which says that, owing to good covering fire, the casualties were comparatively few, though the large proportion amongst officers and N.C.O.s left the battalion very short of these ranks when they were most required. As the total casualties in other ranks were only 55, out of a strength of between 250 and 300, it can hardly be said the battalion was " wiped out " on this occasion. The losses were :

> *Officers. Killed :* Lieut.-Colonel R. E. Dewing, D.S.O.,
>   Capt. R. Holland.
>   *Wounded and Missing :* Capt. and Adjutant H. le G. Sar-
>   chet, M.C. (afterwards recorded as
>   Killed).
>   *Wounded :* Capt. J. M. Richardson, M.C.
>   2nd-Lieuts. E. Wallis, A. W. Morland.
> *Other Ranks :* Killed 3 ; Wounded and Missing 1 ; Wounded 39 ;
>   Missing 12.
>   Total : 6 Officers and 55 Other Ranks.

On the 5th command of the battalion was assumed by Major H. B. Morony. On the 6th the battalion, which had been acting as rearguard and had dug itself in, was relieved by the 5th Australian Brigade, and moved back to Gentelles, where matters remained quiet after the desperate attack of the 4th.

On the 10th Major T. M. Banks, M.C., 10th Essex, took over command of the 8th Royal Berkshire from Major Morony.

On the 12th the Battalion Diary says the composite battalion ceased to exist, and the Royal Berkshire portion was placed under orders of the 5th Australian Brigade.*

From the 13th to the 20th April the battalion was reorganizing at St.

---

* It is extremely difficult to make out what happened with regard to these composite battalions, formed from time to time, and again broken up when the access of reinforcements enabled components to again form separate battalions. It seems clear that on the 4th April the 8th Royal Berks were fighting as a separate battalion ; yet the composite battalion of which they are said to have been part was still in existence.

Fuscien and training the new drafts, of which during the month 16 officers and 589 other ranks joined.

They appear to have been drawn from many different units, at a time when reinforcements were being poured in from wherever they could be obtained, on other parts of the front, or at home. The IIIrd Corps, of which the 18th Division formed part, was entrusted with the guard of Amiens.

On the 21st April Captain (A/Lieut.-Col.) N. B. Hudson, M.C., took over command from Major Banks, who returned to the 10th Essex.

On the 24th the battalion moved forward to the Blangy defences, and later to relieve part of the 8th Division in those of l'Abbé. There was desperate fighting on this and the next day about Villers Bretonneux and Cachy, but the 8th Royal Berkshire do not appear to have gone into the forward area, and the only allusion to the fighting in the diary is an entry on the 25th that the Australians sent out the S.O.S. towards Cachy. The great German offensive on the Somme had come to a standstill, and the battalion now enjoyed a long period of comparative rest after the terrible weeks succeeding the 21st March.

May was passed at various places, Méricourt, Lavieville, etc. In the tour of front line between the 8th and 18th there seems to have been an unusually free use of gas shells by the Germans. From the 24th to the 31st the battalion was at Warloy, training for its next turn in front line, which began on the 8th June. In the night of the 12th-13th June a small enterprise was undertaken with the object of obtaining identifications. Second-Lieutenant C. Beche, with twenty-five men of " D " Company, went out at 12.30 a.m. covered by machine and Lewis guns. They advanced to the German trenches, into which they fired rifle-grenades, and regarding the location of which and other matters they acquired a good deal of miscellaneous information, but failed to secure any identifications. They returned without any loss.

Another raid was attempted in the night of the 14th-15th. At 10.30 p.m. an officer and two N.C.O.s crept forward and cut two gaps in the German wire without hindrance. At the same time another officer laid down forming-up tapes fifty yards short of the objective. At 1.20 a.m. the raiders, fifteen in number, formed up, covered by two Lewis guns and two trench-mortars. They were guided to the gaps by those who had cut them. Only one corporal and one man succeeded in entering the German trench, which was found to be unoccupied. The rest of the party lost their way in the darkness, came under machine-gun and trench-mortar fire, and eventually returned, bringing in the two casualties which had occurred.

When they were again in front line, in the right battalion sector of the brigade front, the 8th Royal Berkshire were much spread out to avoid loss from the retaliation expected to follow on the attack of the 54th Brigade on the left.

The June casualties were slight: Lieutenant H. J. Gale wounded on the 4th; other ranks, 3 killed and 12 wounded.

The battalion was now up to a strength of 37 officers and 906 others. In July there were only 3 killed and 5 wounded.

On the 12th the battalion went to camp near Picquigny, and remained there till the 31st, when it moved forward by 'bus and march to reserve positions at Lahoussoye on the right of the Amiens-Albert Road. Here the first five days of August were spent, and on the 6th, the battalion was in Brigade reserve. At dusk on the 7th it moved to assembly positions for the forthcoming offensive on the next day, which has been admitted by German leaders to have been the most fatal for their cause. The main advance was on a ten-mile front by the 4th Army of Sir H. Rawlinson south of the Somme, but the ridge on the north bank was a menace to the left flank of that army if held by the enemy, and the function of the 18th Division was to avert that danger by attacking the ridge along the road from Corbie to Bray-sur-Somme.

The division was astride of that road when, on the 6th August, the Germans made a sudden attack in the midst of a relief which carried them forward ten hundred yards on the road. In that day's fighting the 53rd Brigade bore no part, and it need not be described. The same may be said of a more or less successful counter-attack on the 7th, which recovered part of the lost ground, and inflicted heavy losses on the enemy.

At dusk of that day the 8th Royal Berkshire moved up into its assembly positions for the advance of the 8th.

" A " Company was on the right, " B " in the centre, " D " on the left, " C " in reserve.

The 54th Brigade had been so knocked about on the 7th that it had to be left out of the fighting on the 8th, its place being taken by the 36th Brigade of the 12th Division.   On the left, north of the Corbie-Bray Road, part of the 36th Brigade was to attack and cover the left flank of the division.

The first objective was the road from Morlancourt south to Mallard Wood, the northern tongue of which crossed the main road.

At 4.20 a.m. the British barrage opened along the whole front of the attacking army, and the 8th Royal Berkshire began its advance, in artillery formation, south of the main road.   There was a thick mist, like that which had characterized the 21st March, and the British, like the Germans on that date, had to contend with immense difficulty in maintaining direction. Touch between companies was lost, and movements had to be made by compass bearings. Progress was consequently very slow. The 36th Brigade on the left and in front of the 53rd had not succeeded in reaching the first objective when the 10th Essex leap-frogged them and, having the road to guide them, got ahead more rapidly than the Royal Berkshire on their right and the 7th Royal West Kent on their left.   The enemy barrage was largely directed on selected areas, and could therefore be avoided to a great extent.

The battalion began to run up against the enemy in his original first line, especially on the right, where one platoon was engaged by two machine guns.   This platoon lost direction, but again came into collision with these machine guns.   Battalion Head-quarters also met a machine gun.

On the left the advance was less hampered, as here the other units of the brigade were in front.

On the right the advance continued, but did not find the other troops which should have been in front.   The tanks, too, had failed to get up in the mist.

The forward movement continued slowly for some distance, encountering snipers and machine guns, especially on the flanks.   It is clear that there was much confusion in the mist, and individual platoons found themselves co-operating with other units.

Towards 8 a.m., a ravine leading to the Somme was passed, and the atmosphere began to clear somewhat.   The battalion now came under the fire of machine guns at close range, and of two field guns firing over open sights at a range of five hundred yards.   At this time the 10th Essex had gone right forward to the final objective, with the 36th Brigade consolidating the first behind them.   The Royal West Kent were bent back covering the left rear of the Essex; the 7th Queen's performed the same office for the 36th Brigade.

The Royal Berkshire were held up by the machine guns and two field guns above mentioned by the time they reached the western side of Gressaire Wood, considerably in rear of the right of the 10th Essex.   Three attempts to rush these machine-gun positions failed.   In one of these Lieut.-Colonel Hudson was wounded in five places, but escaped in a most extraordinary way, with the aid of his orderly.

The losses of other ranks are not given for each day of August separately in the Battalion Diary, but the History of the 18th Division states that when they had been forty minutes at Gressaire Wood they had lost six officers, twenty-one other ranks killed, and eighty-two wounded.   They were then withdrawn to the line of the first objective, to which the 10th Essex also made a perilous retreat with the eighty men who were all that remained of it.

The losses of the Royal Berkshire in officers were:

Killed: Lieut. E. M. Hartree, 2nd-Lieut. C. W. Moss.
Died of Wounds: Lieut. A. M. Bray, M.C.
Wounded: Lieut.-Colonel N. B. Hudson, M.C.,
          Capt. C. G. M. Morris, Lieut. A. L. Oliver,
          2nd-Lieuts. T. Starbuck, W. C. Molland.

As above stated, the losses in other ranks are only given for the whole month.

Major Warr took over command of the battalion on Colonel Hudson being wounded.

On the 9th August, at 3 a.m., the battalion went back to the original support line, and in the afternoon occupied the original enemy front line, in relief of the 5th Royal Berkshire of the 145th Brigade.

On the 10th it went back across the Ancre to Baisieux, and on the 14th was moved to shelters in Hennencourt Wood, four miles west of Albert, which town was in the possession of the Germans.

That night it replaced the 10th Essex in front line as right battalion of the brigade.

On the 17th the 8th Royal Berkshire went back to billets at Warloy till the 22nd, when they moved south-east to positions in the Bresle Valley. There they were placed temporarily at the disposal of the 54th Brigade, which was attacking.

At 11.30 the battalion was ordered, by the G.O.C. 54th Brigade, to support the 6th Northamptonshire Regiment, now holding the front line beyond the Ancre, but appears not to have been engaged.   The result of this day was the establishment of a line east of Albert, from Méaulte on the right to the flooded area of the Ancre between Albert and Aveluy.

The 8th Royal Berkshire was returned to the 53rd Brigade at 7 a.m. on the 23rd August for the attack on the commanding German positions on the so-called Usna and Tara Hills, east of Albert.   But the work had already been done by the 55th and 54th Brigades, and the opportunity of the 8th Royal Berkshire only came in the further operations timed to start at 1 a.m. on the 24th.

At 9.15 p.m. on the 23rd the battalion moved into positions for the coming attack.   It was ready by midnight, with " A " Company on the right, " C " on the left, " B " in support, and " D " in reserve.

The objective was the capture of Ovillers and La Boisselle, places famous in the Somme Battle of 1916, by the 38th Division, with which the 53rd Brigade was to co-operate.   From 1 a.m. the British barrage played upon the road in front of the objectives for twenty minutes, when it began creeping forward at the rate of one hundred yards every four minutes.   The enemy barrage began only at 1.8 a.m., when the first line was already too far forward to get much of it.   By 4.30 a.m. the battalion had reached its first objective on the road, and was busy consolidating.   All the front-line companies had passed beyond this objective, which was not easily recognized. The several reports at this period are thus summed up in the diary.   The first objective had been captured and an outpost line formed, with the exception of a gap of two hundred yards between " A " and " C," caused by the enemy's occupation of some craters, which held up our men.   The situation north of Boisselle was obscure.   The enemy was firing much from the craters.   The situation remained unchanged here all day till 8 p.m., when, under cover of Stokes mortars, an attack was launched by " A " and " C " Companies on the La Boisselle crater.   This great crater had been formed by the explosion of mines in 1916.   It was seventy yards in diameter and bristled with machine guns, and till it should be taken, no further progress was possible. The storming party consisted of sixty men, under Captain G. W. H. Nicholson and Lieutenant T. K. Pickard, M.C., commanding the contingents of " C " and " A " respectively, with Second-Lieutenants T. C. Halliburton and N. H. G. Blackburn as their subalterns. The attack was a complete success. As many as a dozen machine-gun posts were cleared out, and about two hundred prisoners captured.

The O.C. 8th Royal Berkshire highly commends the conduct of the two subalterns, and Second-Lieutenant Blackburn particularly distinguished himself. He was afterwards awarded the M.C., but was killed before it reached him. The capture of this crater was a very notable achievement, on which Lieut.-General Sir A. J. Godley, commanding the IIIrd Corps, specially congratulated the battalion.

After the crater had been taken, the O.C. " C " Company sent out a patrol which, after a short fight, established an advanced post three hundred yards in front. More prisoners were taken in this fight. The companies were then reorganized in depth. The officer casualties on this day were :

Killed : 2nd-Lieut. R. C. Guy.
Wounded : Lieut. C. J. M. Marsh, 2nd-Lieut. P. W. Rousell.

Those for other ranks are, as on the 8th, not given separately.

On the 25th the battalion was in a trench on the Amiens-Albert Road, and on the 26th, at 5 p.m., was again sent to Bécourt Château, in front of which during the day the 54th and 55th Brigades had conquered much country, as far east as Mametz Wood, which the East Surrey had traversed to its eastern edge. At 7.30 p.m. orders were received for the attack next day (27th) on Bernafay and Trônes Woods, the eastern edge of the latter being the final objective. Waterlot Farm was to be explored if possible. It will be remembered of course that, at this period, the term " Wood " was merely a convenient expression for areas which had been woods in 1916, but had long ceased to be marked by such by more than shattered tree stumps standing up in the undergrowth. The battalion formed up on the Montauban-Bazentin-le-Grand Road just north of Caterpillar Valley, with the Royal West Kent astride of that valley on the right.

The attack was to be with " D " Company, supported by " B " on the right, " C " supported by " A " on the left, the Royal West Kent extending the right through Bernafay Wood. It was assumed, wrongly as it appeared later, that Longueval on the left was in the hands of the 38th Division. If this were true, the left flank would be safe. It was known that the enemy were on the right flank, and the plan was for the Royal West Kent, after taking Bernafay Wood and reaching Trônes Wood, to turn south, facing the right flank of the enemy in that direction. Their line would be prolonged to the left by " B " of the Royal Berkshire which would turn south and reach the southern end of Trônes Wood, whilst the other companies faced east on its eastern boundary. There would thus eventually be a line facing east throughout the whole length of the east side of Trônes Wood with a continuation, of " B " of the Royal Berkshire and the Royal West Kent on their right, facing south along the southern edges of Trônes and Bernafay Woods and across the space between them. The erroneous information regarding the occupation of Longueval and Delville Wood was nearly fatal to this plan.

Lieut.-Colonel T. M. Banks, D.S.O., M.C., of the 10th Essex, was in command of the 8th Royal Berkshire at this time, having taken it over on the 25th August. On receipt of orders on the 26th, he went out to recon- noitre, whilst the battalion marched to near Mametz Wood and halted at 11.30 p.m. There was no sign of British troops at the forming-up line, and their whereabouts was uncertain. The forming-up line was reached at 2.30 a.m. on the 27th. The night was quiet with a brilliant moon. Patrols were pushed out to locate British posts, and during this time three Germans strayed into our lines and were taken prisoners by the Medical Officer of the Royal Berks. Zero was fixed for 4.55 a.m., when the barrage was to open on a line north and south through the western edge of Bernafay Wood. In order, however, to be close up to it, the front line had to advance 25 minutes earlier. The enemy, who had a few machine guns in outposts near the forming-up line, fell back on their main line, which coincided with that of the British barrage. This line being unmarked by definite features of ground, there was some difficulty with the barrage, part of which fell in the advanced infantry lines, which consequently had to fall back till it lifted.

The advance had already been detected by the enemy, and was met by machine-gun fire which was ominously heavy from the left in the direction of

Longueval, which it now appeared was in the possession of the enemy, and not of the 38th Division as had been believed. Fifteen minutes after the initial barrage commenced it began to creep forward closely, followed by the infantry who tackled the enemy with great dash, clearing the right area without serious loss. On the left the movement was delayed by the fire from Longueval. The enemy's second line of resistance was on the Bernafay Wood-Longueval Road. Here again the right was carried, but on the left the attack was held up in front of the road by the galling fire from Longueval, which made the reduction of enemy posts very difficult.

The right pushed on behind the barrage, taking prisoners in the space between the road and Trônes Wood. But the leading company on the right was by now very much reduced, and its support (" B ") Company was turning off to the right in accordance with orders.

This left very few men for the capture of the final objective—Trônes Wood.

Nevertheless, the right of the battalion succeeded in getting into the wood, where it at once came under heavy machine-gun fire from Waterlot Farm. Meanwhile, the 7th Royal West Kent had, as ordered, turned southwards through Bernafay Wood and the space between it and Trônes Wood, whilst " B " of the Royal Berkshire had taken up a position facing south on the light railway which traverses the centre of Trônes Wood from west to east.

The situation was critical. Both " A " and " C " Companies were held up well back on the left, masses of the enemy were moving out from Waterlot Farm, and Longueval and Delville Wood were also full of Germans.

These latter were apparently removing stores on limbers preparatory to evacuation, and one company could be seen in the distance forming up on its markers. This was the redeeming point in the situation which it, and the gallant conduct of the Royal Berkshire in Trônes Wood, rendered less unsatisfactory.

The attack from Waterlot Farm was checked by " D," but with the loss of many men, including Second-Lieutenant F. W. Hopwood, M.M., commanding the company, who was killed. Although it was not practicable to hold the eastern edge of Trônes Wood, enfiladed as it was, Colonel Banks thought it possible to make a stand in the trenches just west of the wood, and rallied his men for withdrawal to them.   Meanwhile, Captain Wykes of " A " Company, second-in-command of the battalion, volunteered to get back and try to bring up the left companies (" A " and " C "). In this he was successful in about half an hour, when the resistance of a strong pocket holding them up had been overcome.   This was not done without further casualties.   A number of the enemy surrendered, and the rest retreated to Longueval.

The remains of " A " and " C " were used for consolidating, and for defending the Royal Berkshire position from the threat of Longueval, whence the machine-gun fire still continued.   In this great assistance was received from Major Hopwood, D.S.O., G.S.O.2. of the Division, and also from the reserve company of the Royal West Kent sent up by Major Warr, who had taken command of that battalion when Colonel Banks took over the 8th Royal Berkshire.   While these events were taking place, " B " Company, the support of " D," had, as ordered, turned to the right in Trônes Wood to clear the southern half.   It was, however, compelled by the fire of the British " heavies," which were still firing on the southern part of the wood, to halt, and finally to conform to the withdrawal from the final objective in the northern part of the wood.   It fell back to the trench just west of the wood where it joined up with the Royal West Kent on the right.

At this juncture a counter-attack was launched by a battalion of Prussian Guards on the southern part of the wood, through which they pushed, drove in part of the Royal West Kent line, and for a moment threatened the whole position.   But the Royal West Kent and the Royal Berkshire rallied half-way down the slope and confined the enemy's gains to the upper part.   A counter-attack was now attempted, supported by fire from the left, but the enemy's position was so advantageous, and his machine guns were so numerous, that it had to be broken off whilst more complete measures were organized.   Most of the rest of the day was spent in this.   The Divisional General ordered two companies of the 10th Essex to be placed at the disposal of Colonel Banks, and Major Hopwood again did good service, in sending one of them to fill a gap which had formed between the right of the Royal Berk-shire and the left of the Royal West Kent.   By 6.30 p.m. all was ready and the British " heavies " again bombarded the southern half of Trônes Wood, whilst presently two trench mortars began firing on the western edge of it.

At 6.55 p.m. the attacking troops crept close up to the bombardment. These were " D " Company of the Essex on the right, one platoon of " C " of the Essex in the centre, and " B " of the Royal Berkshire on the left. All the enemy fire was turned to the left, but so eager were the men that they charged in amongst it before the shells had ceased to burst. The enemy was completely surprised; practically every man on the western edge of the wood was shot or bayoneted, and the victorious British, dashing into the undergrowth, surprised and demoralized the supports, and carried on to the eastern edge, where they consolidated and put out outposts. On the left flank, "D" of the Royal Berkshire formed a defensive flank facing north across the centre of the wood, whilst the Royal West Kent came up on the right of the Essex companies and continued the line from the southern end of Trônes back to that of Bernafay Wood.

The whole operation occupied less than an hour. Three German officers and seventy men, with about twenty machine guns, were captured, and about fifty of the enemy were killed.

The enemy post which was taken contained two heavy and seven light machine guns. The unit which had been defeated in this attack was identified as a battalion of the 2nd Guard Regiment (Francis Joseph).

At midnight the battalion was relieved and sent back to Caterpillar Wood at 2 a.m. On the 29th it went to Guillemont, then in British hands.

Needless to say, the brigade and its units received many congratulations, and equally needless is it to say that their losses were heavy. Of the Royal Berkshire officers there were :

Killed : 2nd-Lieuts. F. W. Hopwood, M.M., G. W. Buckley, S. M. Brown.
Wounded : 2nd-Lieuts. H. Martin, J. Buck, J. Davies, and
Capt. W. Rogerson (R.A.M.C., attached).

Again there are no details of the day's losses in other ranks, but the total of the month, which includes the battles of the 8th, 24th, and 27th was : Killed 79 ; Died of Wounds 9 ; Wounded 225 ; Wounded and Missing 8 ; Missing 10. Total 331.

On the 1st September Combles was taken by other units of the 18th Division, and that evening the 53rd Brigade was brought up from Guillemont to positions outside the village, with orders to attack, next day, the St.

Pierre Vaast Wood and the high ground north of it. The high ground in the wood was assigned as the objective of the 10th Essex, with the 8th Royal Berkshire on the right against the southern part of the wood, and the Royal West Kent on their left against the open country to the north. The Royal Berkshire were to be in echelon behind the right flank of the Essex, and to form a defensive flank facing south along the central ride running E. and W. through the wood.

At 1.5 a.m. " C " and " D " Companies, under Captain Wykes, moved to the assembly positions on the west side of the wood. " D " suffered some casualties from shells on the way, and the enemy's artillery continued active during the assembly, which was completed at 3.30 a.m. The formation for attack was " C " on the edge of the wood with one platoon south of the ride and Company Head-quarters north of it. "D" was behind in the same formation.

The barrage opened at 5.30 a.m., with the companies close behind it. At 5.50 it lifted, and Battalion Head-quarters and " D " Company established themselves facing south astride of the main ride running from north to south through the centre of the wood. " C " moved forward, leaving one platoon and Company Head-quarters on the high ground about a quarter of a mile short of the eastern edge. Patrols were sent out for five hundred yards along that edge towards the south. By 7.30 a.m. all the objectives had been attained. Some isolated German machine-gun posts were encountered, but they put up a poor fight, and no casualties had been incurred in the advance so far. As the standing barrage failed to come down on the wood, Captain Wykes proceeded to mop it up, taking over one hundred prisoners, and one motor ambulance in good order.

Attempts were made to gain touch with the 47th Division on the right, but without success. That division did not penetrate the southern portion of the wood till next day. These attempts met with resistance from scattered enemy posts in the south of the wood, and with heavy shell fire which began at 10.30 a.m. and lasted all day. It was in this period that all the casualties of the day occurred.

At 4 a.m. patrols of " C " found the trenches between St. Pierre Vaast Wood and Vaux Wood to the east unoccupied, and, an officer's patrol having verified the evacuation of St. Martin's Wood (north of Vaux Wood), the leading troops of the brigade were ordered forward, and eventually the 10th Essex occupied the high ground overlooking Manancourt and the Canal du Nord.

The 8th Royal Berkshire moved " C " and " D " north to Henois Wood to support the right of the Essex.

In this wood they were subjected to heavy machine-gun and artillery fire, which prevented "D" from debouching on its eastern side towards the canal. At 5 p.m., " A " and " B " were ordered up from their position in reserve in St. Pierre Vaast Wood—" C " was ordered to patrol Vaux Wood, south of Henois Wood, and, if possible, to make good its eastern edge and the line of the canal.

The enemy was found to be occupying the high ground east of the Tortille River, which flows parallel to the canal and beyond it. They were firing with machine guns.

At 8.30 p.m. " A " moved forward and made good the line of the canal in the dark. Later, " B " sent out patrols, to attempt to secure a passage of the Tortille, and a footing on the rising ground beyond it. They crossed the canal, but beyond it met such heavy fire from front and flanks that they could not progress, and were withdrawn at dawn.

On the 4th September, after making a personal reconnaissance, the Brigadier again ordered the patrols forward. On the left they could make no progress, but on the right they succeeded in getting a footing on the slope above Tortille, which proved of great value in the subsequent operations. During the whole day these patrols were engaged in a struggle with varying success. In the evening Captain Walls took command of them, and progress began to be more definite. By 8 p.m. they had reached the edge of River-side Wood, and the enemy retired in large numbers from his advanced posts. In this advance excellent service was rendered by Second-Lieutenant Grant, who rushed a German post which was holding out, and killed its garrison. Other patrols pushed beyond Riverside Wood, and gained contact with the enemy holding trenches on the crest of the heights to the east of the wood.

By this time it was quite dark, and relief by the 12th Division was already in progress. The line of the eastern edge of Riverside Wood was made good and handed over to the relieving troops.

The casualties of the last two days amongst officers were :

On the 3rd, *Wounded* : 2nd-Lieuts. W. G. Davies, A. E. Logsdon.
On the 4th, *Gassed* : 2nd-Lieuts. E. W. Clark and T. C. Halliburton
(Sherwood Foresters, attached).

The casualties of other ranks are again only given for the whole month.

The 5th and 6th were spent at Montauban, where Sir A. Godley, commanding the Corps, distributed parchment certificates gained by the men.

From the 7th to the 14th the battalion continued training at Montauban
where, on the former day, it received a draft of one hundred and twenty
men. It should have been one hundred and seventy-six, but the accidental
explosion of a shell at Méricourt station had unfortunately reduced it by 56,
of whom 21 were killed, 4 died subsequently in hospital, and 31 were wounded.

On the 15th orders were received to relieve part of the 74th Division in
the line, and at 8.20 a.m. on the 16th the battalion went by 'bus to Nurlu,
whence it marched to l'Epinette, and took over trenches east of Ste. Emilie.

On the next day many gas shells fell close to Head-quarters.

The 18th was quiet, and at 6 p.m. orders were received for an attack on
Lempire on the 19th.

The village is a continuation towards the N.E. of the village of Ronssoy,
which lies on the south side of the road running S.E. from Epéhy to Hargicourt.

On the left of Lempire was Yak Post, and beyond it again Zebra Post,
marking the northern boundary of the divisional area.

The plan of attack was for " C " on the left to occupy Yak Post and form
a defensive flank—" B " in the centre was to occupy Dose Trench in the
northern part, and Lempire Post at the north-east end of the village. " A,"
on the right, would take Thistle Trench running south from Lempire Post
outside the village, and join the right of " B " at the Post. One platoon of
" D " was to occupy Enfer Wood, and the other three were to be drawn up
in rear with the Royal West Kent, ready to pass through to the final objective.

At 8.15 a.m. on the 19th assembly posts were reached, " B," " C," and
" D " being in a trench south of the road running through Ronssoy and
Lempire towards the N.E. " A " was in a trench on the right. Battalion
Head-quarters, in the western edge of Ronssoy, suffered casualties from

artillery fire during the assembly, which was completed at 10.40 a.m., zero being at 11 a.m.

At 11 a.m. " A," " B," and " C " moved forward close up to the barrage as it moved on, whilst " D," less one platoon for Enfer Wood, remained at the assembly positions.

" A," which suffered few casualties in the advance, had three platoons in its objective, Thistle Trench, by 11.40. The odd platoon of " D " was in Enfer Wood by 12.15 p.m.

The situation was somewhat obscure to Head-quarters, but Captain Wykes, going foward, found " C " on the main objective and in Yak Post, which had been taken after a severe bombing fight. Proceeding to Dose Trench he found it unoccupied by either side. Returning by the Lempire-Tombois Farm Road, he found that " A " and " B " were held up by machine-gun fire from the copse on the S.E.

" B " then proceeded to occupy its objective by passing through " C " and down Dose Trench.

Reports were now received that Lempire Village was still held by the Germans. " D," when sent to mop it up, reported it quite clear of the enemy. Opposition on the right was very severe, but on the left " C " pushed some men into Zebra Post in the evening.

At 8 p.m. the line held by the battalion was, from left to right, Zebra Post—Yak Post—Dose Trench—Lempire Post—Thistle Trench—Basse Boulogne, the last named being east of Ronssoy, just north of the Epéhy-Hargicourt Road.

In the fighting of the 21st for the possession of Egg Post, Grafton Trench, and Tombois Farm, the 8th Royal Berkshire certainly did not participate, but remained in the positions occupied in the evening of the 19th. The attack on that day by the 53rd Brigade was carried out by the other two battalions, the 10th Essex and 7th Royal West Kent.

Nor does the Battalion Diary mention any fighting on the 22nd and 23rd. The History of the 18th Division, on the other hand, states that the battalion relieved the 10th Essex, which had lost two hundred and eighty men, in the evening of the 21st, that the 53rd and 54th Brigades renewed the attack by moonlight, and that the bombing attack of the Royal Berkshire on Egg and Fleeceall Posts was beaten off, after heavy fighting, in the early morning of the 22nd.   It even mentions the gallantry of Private E. J. Pocock, a stretcher bearer of the Royal Berkshire Regiment.

Again the Battalion Diary only says of the 24th that there was much sniping, by which Second-Lieutenant E. J. H. Sonnex was killed.   Finally, officer casualties are given for the 19th only.   Nothing can be gleaned from the casualties of other ranks, which are given in lump for the whole month.

The Officers' list for the 19th shows :

Killed : 2nd-Lieut. R. Cumbley.
Died of Wounds : 2nd-Lieuts. A. J. Preston and J. W. B. Palfree
        (Sherwood Foresters, attached).
Other Ranks (for the whole month) : Killed 44 ; Died of Wounds 1 ;
        Wounded 145 ; Gassed 55 ; Missing 12, besides the 56
        of the draft killed or injured by the accident at Méri
        court.

The diary at this period is generally very full, and it seems difficult to believe that any serious fighting after the 19th should have escaped mention.

On the 25th the battalion was relieved by American infantry, and went back to Curlu Wood, and on the 26th was at Priez Farm east of Combles.

On the 29th it moved up to reserve in front of Ronssoy, and on the 30th relieved the 6th Buffs, of the 12th Division, in front line.

On the 1st October the battalion was in the line between their line of the 20th September and the St. Quentin Canal, on the bank of which was posted one platoon of " C " Company.

On the 2nd they made a long journey by omnibus through Nurlu, Combles, Amiens, Albert, La Houssoye to billets at Allonville, where the whole brigade was concentrated and remained till the 17th.   On that day they went by rail to Roisel.   On the 18th they were on the Nurlu-Villers Faucon Road, and continued their journey by 'bus to Prémont.   The change here, from the ruined area of the Somme Battles to one comparatively little damaged, was very noticeable.   On the 20th they were at Reumont, and on the 22nd at Le Câteau, the scene of the battle of more than four years before.   The town had been shelled intermittently.

At 10.50 p.m. the brigade moved out to assembly posts for an attack next day directed north-eastwards, with the left of the division on the road to Bavai, and its right on a parallel line running past the north-west edge of the Bois de l'Evêque. This area ended towards the N.E. at the Mormal Forest. The 33rd Division was on the left, the 25th on the right, and the 53rd Brigade was on the right of the 18th Division, the 54th on the left, and the 55th in rear, ready to pass through to the capture of the third, fourth and fifth objectives.

Zero had been fixed for 1.20 a.m. on the 23rd, and an early move to assembly positions was fortunately made, as it was hampered by fog.

The assembly point for the 8th Royal Berkshire was in a railway cutting which had unfortunately been selected as the line for the enemy's barrage. Many shells fell in it, causing fifteen casualties, among them Captain W. H. Ferguson, M.C., R.A.M.C., the medical officer. Though wounded, he heroically carried on his duty till a second wound, as he was getting out of a blown-in dugout, compelled his withdrawal.

At 1.50, after half an hour's barrage, the companies moved out of the cutting, " D " on the right, " C " in the centre, " B " on the left, and " A " in support. In front of them, the 10th Essex and 7th Royal West Kent captured the first objective, a line crossing the divisional area from the west corner of the Bois de l'Evêque.

At 2.20 the battalion started to pass through them to the second objective, " D " to keep its right flank on the north-western ridge of the Bois de l'Evêque.

The first opposition was met at the Richemont Brook, well short of the first objective. The left of " B " was held up by a machine-gun nest which had been missed by the leading battalions. Here Second-Lieutenant J. Grant, commanding the company, was killed, and most of the Company Head-quarters became casualties. On the right some sniping by three Germans, who had resumed fighting after having surrendered, gave some trouble. The brook, too, was found to be marshy, and a more serious obstacle than aerial observations had given reason to suppose.

The battalion moved on to a line a little short of the first objective. Here they found the Essex definitely held up by machine guns in a sunken road.

Numerous attempts by the Essex, and by " C " of the Royal Berkshire, failed to rush this position, and the right of the battalion was also held up by fire from the Bois de l'Evêque. The position remained unchanged till dawn.

As soon as it was light it became clear that the attack was progressing on the left. This, and the appearance of tanks on their flank, induced the enemy to begin retiring.

Captain Wykes, appreciating the situation, went forward with the leading companies, and rushed the road, in which over thirty machine guns were taken. The advance then continued to the second objective, which was taken by 8.30 a.m.

Owing to the battalion having been held up on the Richemont Brook, it became necessary to reinforce the line on the second objective, and " A " was brought forward for the purpose. The disposition now was " C " on the left, " A " on its right and elements of " B " and " D " seeking to gain touch with the left of the 1st Worcestershire (25th Division).

The 55th Brigade now passed through the 53rd, and machine-gun fire soon began to be heard from Bousies, beyond the third objective. The 55th Brigade held a line beyond Bousies for the night.

Meanwhile, the companies of the Royal Berkshire were reorganized and held their positions during the night of the 23rd-24th. During the 23rd they had captured eleven field guns, and collected more than twenty machine guns.

Their losses had been :

Officers. Killed : 2nd-Lieuts. N. H. Blackburn, M.C., J. Grant, M.C.
　　　　　Wounded : 2nd-Lieuts. F. W. Beeny, W. Deans, W. A. McConnell.
Other Ranks : Killed 19 ; Died of Wounds 1 ; Wounded 67 ; Missing 3.

At 5 p.m. on the 24th the battalion was ordered to relieve the 6th Northamptonshire Regiment of the 54th Brigade. During the morning Lieut.-Colonel N. B. Hudson, M.C., now recovered from his wounds of the 8th August, took command of the battalion from Major A. F. S. Northcote, who returned to the West Kent Battalion.

The relief, which had been delayed by its coincidence with a minor operation being carried out by the battalion to be relieved, was not completed till 2 a.m. on the 25th, when " D " took post on the right, " C " in the centre, and " B " on the left, with " A " in reserve at Bousies Wood Farm. " A "

Company of the Cameron Highlanders was interposed between " B " and " C," and on the left of " B " a gap between it and the 10th Essex was filled by a company of the 4th King's Liverpool.   Both the Cameron and Liverpool Battalions belonged to the 33rd Division on the left, which had been forming a defensive flank before the 54th Brigade made good.   There was active patrolling till dusk.

Meanwhile, orders were received that the 53rd Brigade should co-operate with the 33rd Division in the attack on Mount Carmel, a position just beyond the Englefontaine-Robersart Road, which was only very slightly higher than the surrounding country.

The 10th Essex were to take the right, the 8th Royal Berkshire, with two companies Royal West Kent, the left, the whole being under the command of the C.O. 8th Royal Berkshire.

At midnight of the 25th-26th a move was made to the assembly positions, with " D " on the right, " C " in the centre, " B " on the left, and " A " in reserve.

The advance commenced at 1 a.m., through a difficult country in a very dark night, and in the face of machine-gun fire which rendered progress slow.   The first serious opposition was met at the Englefontaine-Robersart Road, which was strongly held by machine guns.   Here the right was held up.   On the left progress had been more rapid, and by 1.40 a.m. two platoons of " B " had reached their objective on what was known as the " red line." Heavy casualties, however, compelled them to fall back to a sunken road where " C " was held up on their right.   The right company was still no farther than the main road.

The officer commanding now adopted a policy of active patrols, and eventually made good on the sunken road, and gained touch with the 10th Essex on the right at the junction of the sunken and main roads.   " A " Company of the Royal West Kent, on the left, had kept touch with the left of " B " of the Royal Berkshire, and prolonged its line from a point slightly in advance of the main road.   The other West Kent company on the left had lost touch, had made remarkable progress, and was on the objective at some cross-roads which they had reached in advance of the 33rd Division troops on their left.   Touch was gained later, through troops of the 33rd Division on the main road.

The attack of this day appears not to have been a great success, and eventually a line was occupied, some four hundred yards short of that originally intended, at Mount Carmel.

During the fighting Lieut.-Colonel Hudson had again been wounded slightly, and command of the battalion was taken temporarily by Captain G. W. H. Nicholson. Other casualties of the day are not given.

From the 27th to the 30th October the battalion was in reserve at Bousies Wood and Epinette Farm. On the 31st it was again in the front line, which had been established on the 26th not far beyond the Englefontaine-Robersart Road.

On the 3rd November assembly positions were assumed at 9 p.m. for the final great advance through the Mormal Forest.

The Royal West Kent led the advance, in conjunction with the 54th Brigade on their right. They had first to take the villages of Hecq and Preux au Bois, the former falling to the lot of the Royal West Kent. There was strenuous fighting which we need not describe, as the Royal Berkshire were not engaged in the capture of the villages.

At 7.35 a.m. the battalion, with the 10th Essex on its right, formed up to pass through the West Kent and the troops of the 54th Brigade, who were in possession of Hecq and Preux au Bois, and to advance to their objective the " red line " passing across the forest farther on. " A " Company had orders to work along towards the right of the " red line," followed by " B," which was to form posts at the southern end of the tracks through the forest.

In a similar manner " C " was to work along the north edge of the forest on the left of the objective, with " D " following and forming posts at the northern ends of the tracks, and keeping in touch with the 38th Division operating on the left outside the forest. While this movement was in progress, a heavy barrage would be put down on the forest itself.

There was some trouble from machine-gun posts, which had not yet been mopped up by the captors of the villages.

At 9.7 a.m. the barrage began moving forward from its first line at the rate of one hundred yards in six minutes. " C " followed along the northern part of the forest. In the first four hundred yards no opposition was met ; then there was some from the left. This being overcome, " C " progressed as far as a stream running through the forest. Here the blowing up by the

Germans of a bridge wounded some men of the leading platoons. On reaching the high ground, " C " came under the point-blank fire of some guns in the wood on its left. Pushing on, it reached its final objective soon after 10.30, after rushing a strong post in a building. In the storming of this post Second-Lieutenant L. J. Field was killed, and five men were wounded.

The company was now well ahead of the line and both its flanks were exposed. Nevertheless, Lieutenant F. J. Powell, D.C.M., M.M., expressed his determination to hold on where he was with the company of which he was in command. He did so for three hours, at the end of which he had but thirty-six men left. His tenure of this position materially helped the advance of the 38th Division on his left.

Whilst " C " thus pushed forward, " D " followed as ordered, dropping posts at the northern exits from the forest. As the barrage lifted, " D " worked into the forest on its right, and killed or captured the garrisons of two German posts there. On the other flank " A," followed by " B," encountered difficulties almost at once. The 54th Brigade had not succeeded in completely clearing the assembly position, and consequently " A " came in for machine-gun fire from the banks of the stream just beyond Preux. Captain T. K. Pickard, commanding " A," halted his company and sent forward a patrol to clear up the situation. It found the 2nd Bedfordshire and 10th Essex held up in the S.W. corner of the wood where there had been a partially successful German counter-attack. Pickard determined to fight his way through to the second assembly point, and on to the final objective on the right of the " red line." For the next three hours the company was busy working round and rushing machine-gun posts. The work was most gallantly and well carried out, but naturally not without serious losses.

It was 2 p.m. before the assembly area was cleared and the company, with the 10th Essex, began working along the S.E. edge of the forest as ordered. To screen itself from the open country outside, on its right, the company kept about twenty yards inside the forest. At 2.30 p.m. it met the 7th Queen's, who had come diagonally through the forest from Preux. A few minutes after 3 p.m. the right of the " red line " was reached without much further opposition. Touch was gained with " C " on the left and the 10th Essex on the right, and consolidation was commenced, whilst the 55th Brigade passed through to the next objective.

Meanwhile, " B," following " A," had not been involved in the fighting, but had, as ordered, placed posts at the southern exits of the forest. Patrols sent to the left had come into touch with those of " D," which, as we know, had been doing for " C " what " B " had been doing for " A."

When the 55th Brigade passed through, the " red line " was held by " A " and " C " of the Royal Berkshire and the 10th Essex, with " B " in rear of " A " and " D " in rear of " C."

On the " red line," deep in the Mormal Forest, the fighting career of the 8th Battalion ended.

It spent the 5th November at Hecq, and on the 6th went back to Le Câteau, where it was when hostilities ceased at 11 a.m. on the 11th November 1918.

On the following day it moved to Prémont, where it spent the rest of the month and the first three days of December.

On the 4th December it moved to Beaurevoir, where it ended the year.

The 8th Battalion was finally reduced to cadre strength in April 1919 at Clary, and shortly after ceased to exist.

The following order of the day, by Lieut.-Colonel N. B. Hudson, was issued on the 12th April 1919. It is reproduced here as giving a good summary of the achievements of the battalion.

" On the occasion of the final reduction to cadre strength and imminent dissolution of the battalion, the Commanding-Officer wishes to place on record the magnificent work and the immortal deeds of the battalion throughout the Great War.

" In September 1914 the battalion was formed at Reading of men from Berkshire, London, and Birmingham, the majority from Berkshire. From September 1914 until August 1915 the battalion was training at Reading, Codford, and Warminster.

" On the 8th August 1915 the battalion landed in France and joined the 1st Brigade, 1st Division.

" On the 28th September 1915 and the 13th October 1915 the battalion took part in the Battles of Loos and Hulluch, and, in spite of heavy losses and against almost insuperable odds, by its gallantry and devotion to duty first gained the reputation which it was never to lose throughout the war.

" From October 1915 until July 1916 the battalion was engaged in holding the line in the Loos and Hulluch sectors.   On two occasions during this period it had the opportunity of showing of what it was made.   First, on the 3rd May 1916, when it raided the well-defended German lines on the Double Crassier with great success, and, secondly, on the 27th May 1916, when a determined raid by the enemy was met and repulsed with the greatest gallantry.

" During the months of July, August, and September 1916 the battalion was engaged in the Battle of the Somme, and further enhanced its reputation in the hard fighting at Contalmaison (12th July), Bazentin (15th August), and High Wood (3rd and 27th September).

" During the first half of 1917 the battalion spent its time in training, and in pursuing the retreating Germans on the Somme Front until June 1917, when, after being in reserve for the attack on the Messines Ridge, it moved north to the Nieuport sector.

" The battalion, with the rest of the 1st Division, was chosen to take part in special operations, which should depend on the success of the Flanders Battle.   For three months (July–October 1917) it underwent intensive train-ing at Clipon Camp, but by October 1917 it was discovered that the opera-tions for which the battalion was training would not take place, and the battalion moved forward to take its part in the Battle of Flanders.

" At Passchendaele, on the 15th November 1917, overcoming the vile conditions of mud and rain, and the violent opposition of the enemy, the battalion took a gallant and entirely successful part in the crowning victory of the battle.

" The remainder of the winter 1917–18 was spent in the mud and water of the Houthulst Forest sector.

" On the 7th February 1918 the battalion was transferred to the 53rd Brigade, 18th Division, and shortly afterwards, on the 21st March, was called upon to resist the onslaught of the Germans in the greatest offensive of the war.   The same gallantry and determination was shown in resistance as had before been shown in attack, and it was only after the enemy had penetrated deeply on either flank that the battalion, depleted and exhausted, stubbornly fought its way back.

" On the 4th April 1918, wearied and without rest, the battalion was again called upon to resist the thrust for Amiens, and after a gallant but costly resistance, at last came out to rest with but 4 Officers and 90 N.C.O.s and men left.

" After a short rest at St. Fuscien, where it was again made up to strength, and a brief spell in the line at Villers-Bretonneux at the end of April, the next three months were spent in the trenches before Albert, during which time it prepared itself once more for battle—the battle which was to win the war.

" From the 8th August 1918 until November 1918, the battalion was continually engaged, and met with nothing but success, attacking and defeating the Germans at Mallard Wood (8th August), Tara Hill (24th August), La Boisselle (24th August), Trônes Wood (27th August), where it met and broke the Prussian Guards, St. Pierre Vaast Wood (3rd September), Lempire and Ronssoy (19th September), Le Câteau (23rd October), and at the Battle of Mormal Forest (4th November). A week later the Armistice was signed and Victory was won at last.

" Although the battalion has ceased to exist, its memory can never die. The record of the battalion, from the Battle of Loos to the Battle of a Hundred Days, is a story of victories, won by devotion to duty, and by an obstinate determination which overcame all. By their steady loyalty, by their untiring self-sacrifice and by their high courage, all Officers, N.C.O.s, and men have earned the undying gratitude of their Country, and the County to which they belong."

The casualties from August 1915 to November 1918 were :

OFFICERS.

Killed in Action	57	
Wounded	68	
Missing (Exclusive of Prisoners-of-War)	2	
Prisoners-of-War	13	
	—	140

OTHER RANKS.

Killed in Action	674	
Wounded	1,805	
Missing (Exclusive of Prisoners-of-War)	359	
Prisoners-of-War . .	461	
Died, while Prisoners-of-War	13	
	——	3,312
Total		3,452

CHAPTER XXXV

THE 9th (RESERVE) BATTALION
THE 10th, 11th, 12th AND 13th LABOUR BATTALIONS
THE 1st GARRISON BATTALION

THE 9th (RESERVE) BATTALION

THE 9th (Reserve) Battalion was formed early in November 1914 at Portsmouth, under the command of Lieut.-Colonel R. Campbell from the 7th Battalion. It received comparatively few officers and recruits at first. Early in 1915 it sent four officers for service with the Hampshire Regiment at Gallipoli. Of these Lieutenants E. G. J. Humbert and L. J. Phillips-Jones were killed, and Captain A. W. Bird badly wounded.

The battalion was ordered, in May 1915, to Bovington Camp, near Wool. Very large numbers of officers and men joined it from time to time and many drafts were sent overseas. At one time the battalion had as many as 197 officers, and over 2,500 other ranks.

The battalion was originally formed as the 9th (Service) Battalion. In July 1915 it became the 9th (Reserve) Battalion. It remained at Bovington till April 1916, when it became the 37th Training Reserve Battalion.

THE LABOUR BATTALIONS

The 10th Labour Battalion was organized at Portsmouth by Colonel J. H. Balfour (Indian Army) in June 1916 from about eleven hundred men whom he found collected there. The officers of the battalion under him in August 1916 were:

Captains: H. A. Lash (Adjutant), N. E. Cobbold, E. T. Stanley, J. E. Hammond, R. J. Holton.
Second-Lieutenants: L. V. Wilson, B. H. Leigh, R. H. W. Grandin, F. Fricker.
Honry.-Lieutenant and Quartermaster: F. C. Dwight.

After considerable difficulties, due largely to an outbreak of measles among the men, it was not till the 19th June (instead of the 7th, the date originally fixed) that the battalion could embark at Southampton for Rouen, where its services were required. Disembarking at Havre, the battalion reached Rouen on the 21st. There it was marched into an uncomfortable camp in a suburb.

The battalion had hoped to be sent for employment at the front, but the hope was disappointed. It was kept busy at the miscellaneous work of a base port in time of war. Into details of this we need not enter. It included unloading and reloading on trains of wood, ammunition, and other stores. The spirits of the men were maintained by occasional entertainments and sports.

On the 12th May 1917 the battalion, as such, was dissolved, and reorganized as the 158th and 159th Companies of the Labour Corps.

The following Battalion order was issued by Colonel Balfour at this time :

B.E. Force,
France,
12-5-1917.

1. At Fort Purbrook, when about to embark for France, it was agreed that the Officers should associate themselves with the men, and that the former should do their utmost to help the men, also that the O.C. would say, later, how that compact had been observed. The time has arrived to do so. The requirements of the Service necessitate certain reorganization, but all, for the present, remain together in the same group.

2. The compact has been more than observed by Officers and other Ranks respectively. The Battalion has reached a high state of efficiency in discipline, work, and comradeship. Crime is practically non-existent. Tonnage records have been broken, and a good name earned in work and play.

It is impossible to thank individually those who have contributed to this, for it would be necessary to name one and all of the Battalion, but undoubtedly the Officers have acted up to the old Service motto " Men First," and men have without a murmur willingly undergone the hardships of hard toil in heat, cold, snow, and darkness, so as to keep their comrades supplied at the Front, and the O.C. has never for a moment wavered in his belief in the trustworthiness of the men in or out of camp, and asks them to give the same support in the future as in the past twelve months to the Captains commanding, and to quickly settle down in the new organization under their Non-Commissioned Officers.

3. Last Christmas the O.C. sent a message to the Battalion congratulating it on the progress made so far.

4. It is well to remember that results are not attained without effort on the part of all concerned. Discipline has been attained, but it has to be maintained, and Colonel Balfour will always be thankful that he has had an opportunity of assisting some twelve hundred good men to do their duty.

Regarding the other Labour Battalions, the only information forthcoming gives the names of their Commanding Officers and states that they were incorporated in the Labour Corps in May 1917, like the 10th. Though they nominally formed part of the Royal Berkshire Regiment, their connexion with it seems to have been but slight.

The Commanding Officers were :

11th (Labour) Battn.	July 1916 to May 1917	Lieut.-Colonel (temp.) W. Bodle, C.M.G. (Lieut.-Colonel late S. African Military Forces).
12th	Aug. 1916 to May 1917	Honry. Brig.-Genl. R. C. B. Lawrence, C.B. (retired pay).
13th	do.	Bt.-Colonel A. E. S. Searle, Indian Army (retired).

There was also for a short period during the War a 1st Home Service Garrison Battalion.

It was raised in October 1916, and disbanded in December 1917. It was commanded by Lieut.-Colonel (temp.) Lord P. J. Joicey-Cecil.

THE
BATTLE HONOURS

THE GREAT WAR

16 Battalions

" Mons "
" Retreat from Mons "
" Marne, 1914 "
" Aisne, 1914, '18 "
" Ypres, 1914, '17 "
" Langemarck, 1914, '17 "
" Gheluvelt "
" Nonne Bosschen "
" Neuve Chapelle "
" Aubers "
" Festubert, 1915 "
" Loos "
" Somme, 1916, '18 "
" Albert, 1916, '18 "
" Bazentin "
" Delville Wood "
" Pozières "
" Flers-Courcelette "
" Morval "

" Thiepval "
" Le Transloy "
" Ancre Heights "
" Ancre, 1916, '18 "
" Arras, 1917, '18 "
" Scarpe, 1917, '18 "
" Arleux "
" Pilckem "
" Polygon Wood "
" Broodseinde "
" Poelcappelle "
" Passchendaele "
" Cambrai, 1917, '18 "
" St. Quentin "
" Bapaume, 1918 "
" Rosières "
" Avre "
" Villers Bretonneux "
" Lys "

" Hazebrouck "
" Béthune "
" Amiens "
" Hindenburg Line "
" Havrincourt "
" Épéhy "
" Canal du Nord "
" St. Quentin Canal "
" Selle "
" Valenciennes "
" Sambre "
" France and Flanders, 1914–18 "
" Piave "
" Vittorio Veneto "
" Italy, 1917–18 "
" Doiran, 1917, '18 "
" Macedonia, 1915–18 "

The ten awards printed in Capital Letters are those selected to be borne on the Colours and appointments.

APPENDICES
I—VII

   I   SUCCESSION OF COLONELS

  II   SANCTIONED ESTABLISHMENTS

 III   UNIFORM AND EQUIPMENT

 IV   COLOURS AND BATTLE-HONOURS

   V   OLD COMRADES ASSOCIATION

 VI   BANNER FOR COMMEMORATION
       OF THE FIRST SEVEN DIVISIONS

VII   MESS PLATE AND FURNITURE

APPENDIX I

THE SUCCESSION OF COLONELS OF THE 49th FOOT, 66th FOOT, BERKSHIRE AND ROYAL BERKSHIRE REGIMENT

YEAR.	49TH.	YEAR.	66TH.
1743–1754	Col. Edward Trelawny (25th Dec. 1743)		
1754–1763	Maj.-Gen. G. Walsh.		
1763–1765	Maj.-Gen. J. Stanwix.	1758	Col. Edward Sandford.
1765–1769	Maj.-Gen. D. Graeme.	1758–1763	Col. John La Faussille.
1769–1820	Gen. Hon. Alexander Maitland.	1764–1776	Col. Lord Adam Gordon.
		1777–1793	Col. Joseph Gabbett.
1820–1830	Lieut.-Gen. Sir Miles Nightingall, K.C.B.	1794–1807	Col. John Earl of Clanricarde.
1830–1846	Gen. Sir Gordon Drummond, G.C.B.	1808–1829	Col. Oliver Nicolls.
		1830–1835	Col. Sir William Anson, K.C.B.
1846–1860	Gen. Sir Edward Bowater, K.C.H.	1836–1858	Col. Richard Blunt.
1860–1871	Gen. Sir Edmund Finucane Morris.	1859–1871	Col. Edward Wells Bell.
		1871–1881	Col. T. H. Johnston.
1871–1874	Lieut.-Gen. T. J. Galloway.		
1874–1881	Gen. Sir Charles Ellice, G.C.B.		

BERKSHIRE REGIMENT

1881–1883 (1st Battalion). General Sir Charles Ellice, G.C.B.
1881–1883 (2nd Battalion). General T. H. Johnston.
1883–1885 (Both Battalions). General T. H. Johnston.

ROYAL BERKSHIRE REGIMENT

1885–1894. General T. H. Johnston.
1894–1905. Major-General (Honry. Lieut.-General) Robert W. Lowry, C.B.
1905–1913. Major-General (Honry. Lieut.-General) Sir William Bellairs, K.C.M.G., C.B.
1913. Major-General E. T. Dickson.

SANCTIONED ESTABLISHMENT

Year.	Companies.	Lieut.-Colonels.	Majors.	Captains.	Lieutenants, including Capt.-Lt.	Ensigns or 2nd Lieutenants.	Surgeon.	Asst.-Surgeon.	Sergeants.	Corporals.	Drummers and Fifers.	Privates.
1744	10	1	1	7	30	—	4	10	40	40	20	1000
1748	10	1	1	7	30	—	4	10	40	40	20	1000
1749	10	1	1	7	20	—	1	1	30	30	20	700
1750	10	1	1	7	30	—	1	9	30	30	20	600
1757	10	1	1	7	30	—	1	9	30	30	20	1000
1758	10	1	1	7	30	—	1	9	40	40	20	1000
1761	10	1	1	7	30	—	1	9	30	30	20	700
1764	9	1	1	6	10	8	1	1	30	30	22	470
1771	—	—	—	—	—	—	—	—	—	—	—	—
1775	10	1	1	7	12	8	1	1	20	30	22	380
1777	12	1	1	9	14	10	1	1	36	36	26	672
1793	10	1	1	7	12	8	1	1	22	30	12	400
1797 {	10	2	2	7	22	8	1	2	52	50	20	950
	2	—	—	2	4	2	—	—	10	10	8	—
1800	11	2	2	8	13	9	1	1	55	55	24	605
1802	10	2	2	7	22	8	1	2	50	50	22	950
1806	10	1	2	10	12	8	1	2	40	40	22	760
1812 {	10	1	2	10	14	8	1	2	40	40	21	760
	1	—	—	1	2	1	—	—	8	8	4	—
1815	10	1	2	10	22	8	1	2	30	30	21	570
1823	8	1	2	8	10	6	1	1	24	24	11	552
1830	9	2	2	10	22	8	1	2	40	40	13	700
1839 {	9	2	2	9	20	7	1	2	40	40	18	926
	1	—	—	1	2	1	—	—	5	5	1	—
1842 {	9	2	2	9	20	7	1	3	36	45	18	1114
	1	—	—	1	2	1	—	—	6	5	1	—

THE 49TH (HERTFORDSHIRE) REGIMENT, 1744–1881

REMARKS.

1744–1803. Colonel, Lieut.-Colonel and Major each commanded a company. There was a Captain Lieutenant instead of a Lieutenant for the Colonel's Company. He is included in the numbers of Lieutenants.

1771. Light Company introduced, with two Lieutenants and no Ensign, as in Grenadier Company.

1772. Captain-Lieutenant ranked as Captain with Lieutenant's pay. He is still shown among Lieutenants.

1776. Two fifers added for Grenadier Company.

1787. Two sergeants added with an extra allowance of 6d. per diem. These were the first staff sergeants.

1797. Two recruiting companies, shown below the ten ordinary companies.

1798. Sergeant-major first appointed. He is not shown in statement. Nor are the two extra sergeants, who are now called Quartermaster- and Paymaster-sergeants.

1800. One Lieut.-Colonel and one Major had no company. One Captain, one Lieutenant, one Ensign "en second," not shown in statement.

1803. Colonel, Lieut.-Colonel and Major cease to command companies, and Captain-Lieutenant abolished. Henceforward a Captain shown for each company.

1805 Armourer-sergeant added. Not shown on statement.

1810 Drum-major first officially recognized, in addition to number of drummers shown.

1812. One recruiting company, shown below ten ordinary companies.

1815. Colour-sergeants, one for each ordinary company, shown for first time on lists of sanctioned establishment. Also Schoolmaster-sergeant not shown.

1830. One recruiting company in England.

1839. Indian establishment scale. Nine service companies and one depôt company.

SANCTIONED ESTABLISHMENT

Year.	Companies.	Lieut.-Colonels.	Majors.	Captains.	Lieutenants, including Capt.-Lt.	Ensigns or 2nd Lieutenants.	Surgeon.	Asst.-Surgeon.	Sergeants.	Corporals.	Drummers and Fifers.	Privates.
1848	10	1	2	10	12	8	1	1	40	50	20	950
1851	6	1	1	6	8	4	1	1	31	24	11	536
	4	—	1	4	4	4	—	1	26	26	10	414
1854 (May)	8	1	2	8	16	8	1	3	50	50	20	950
	8	—	1	8	8	8	—	—	50	50	20	950
1854 (June)	8	1	2	8	16	8	1	3	50	50	21	950
	4	—	1	8	8	8	—	—	50	50	8	380
1855 (March)	8	1	1	8	14	6	—	—	50	50	21	950
	4	—	1	6	8	4	—	—	25	25	10	475
	4	—	—	2	4	4	—	—	25	25	10	475
1856 (Nov.)	12	1	2	12	14	14	1	2	60	48	25	952
1857 (Aug.)	8	1	2	18	10	6	1	2	40	40	21	760
	4	—	—	4	4	4	—	—	10	10	4	190
1858 (Jan.)	10	1	2	10	12	8	1	2	46	—	21	800
	2	—	—	2	2	2	—	—	10	—	4	200
1858 (April)	10	1	2	10	12	8	1	2	46	—	21	800
	2	—	—	2	2	2	—	—	8	—	4	150
1865	10	1	2	10	12	8	—	—	48	40	21	810
	2	—	—	2	2	2	—	—	10	10	4	90
1878	8	1	1	8	8	4	—	—	42	40	16	560
1879 (Jan.)	8	1	1	8	8	4	—	—	42	40	16	540
1879 (May)	8	1	1	8	8	4	—	—	42	40	16	600
1881	8	1	2	8	8	8	—	—	50	40	16	760

THE 49TH (HERTFORDSHIRE) REGIMENT, 1744–1881 *(continued)*.

REMARKS.

1851. Lower figures represent depôt companies; upper are service companies. Staff sergeants included in figures.

1852. Establishment reduced by 10 sergeants, 10 corporals, 5 drummers and 140 privates.

1854 (Jan.). Augmentation for Crimean War. Upper figures, service; lower, depôt companies.

1854 (June). Upper figures, service; lower, depôt companies.

1855 (March). Top figures, service companies, Crimea. Middle figures, at Malta. Bottom figures, at Home.

1857. Eight service and four depôt companies.

1858. Ten service, eight depôt companies. Corporals included in privates.

1857. As above.

1865. Corporals shown separately again.

1866. Privates reduced to 860, in 750 for service and 110 for depôt companies.

SANCTIONED ESTABLISHMENT

Year.	Companies.	Lieut.-Colonels.	Majors.	Captains other than Col., Lt.-Col. and Major.	Lieutenants, including Capt.-Lt.	Ensigns or 2nd Lieutenants.	Surgeons.	Asst.-Surgeons or Mates.	Sergeants exclusive of staff but including Colour-sergeants.	Corporals.	Drummers and Fifers and Buglers.	Privates.
1758–59	9	1	1	6	19	8	1	2	36	36	20	900
1766	9	1	1	6	10	8	1	1	18	18	9	423
1771	10	1	1	7	12	8	1	1	30	30	22	620
1773	10	1	1	7	12	8	1	1	20	30	12	360
1775	10	1	1	7	12	8	1	1	30	30	22	540
1778	10	1	1	7	22	8	1	1	40	40	22	770
1787 {	10	1	1	7	23	10	1	1	54	46	34	994
	1	—	—	1	1	1	—	—	8	8	4	30
1788	10	1	1	7	12	8	1	1	20	30	12	370
1795 (April)	10	1	1	7	12	8	1	1	40	40	22	610
1795 (Oct.) {	10	2	2	9	22	8	1	2	50	50	22	750
	2	—	—	2	4	2	—	—	10	10	8	—
1796	10	2	2	9	22	8	1	2	50	50	22	950
1800	10	2	2	9	14	10	1	1	50	50	22	550
1803	10	1	2	10	12	8	1	2	50	50	22	950
1805	10	1	2	10	12	8	1	2	50	50	22	950
1812–13 {	10	2	2	10	22	8	1	2	60	50	22	950
	1	—	—	1	2	1	—	—	3	3	3	—
1816–17	10	1	2	10	22	8	1	2	60	60	22	1140
1818	10	1	2	10	12	8	1	1	40	30	22	620
1821	10	1	1	10	12	8	1	1	30	30	22	620
1822	8	1	2	8	10	6	1	1	32	24	12	552
1830	10	1	2	10	12	8	1	2	36	36	14	704
1841	10	1	2	10	12	8	1	1	40	40	14	760
1846 {	6	1	1	6	8	4	1	1	36	24	12	516
	4	—	1	4	4	4	1	—	26	26	8	434

THE 66TH (BERKSHIRE) REGIMENT, 1758–1870

REMARKS.

1771. Light Company introduced.

1773. Captain-Lieutenant ranks as Captain, but draws Lieutenant's pay and is shown under Lieutenants.

1787. One recruiting company shown in second line.

1788. Also two extra sergeants, with special allowance of 6d. per diem.

1795 (Oct.). Two recruiting companies shown in lower line. One Lieut.-Colonel and one Major without companies. Two Captains and two Lieutenants " en second." Also Sergeant-major and Quartermaster-sergeant, not shown on statement.

1796. As above.

1800. As above, with two Ensigns " en second " shown on statement. Paymaster-sergeant added, but not shown.

1803. Captain-Lieutenant abolished, and Colonel, Lieut.-Colonel and Major no longer had companies.

1805. Also Armourer-sergeant, not shown.

1812–13. One recruiting company shown in second line. In July 1813 one Colour-sergeant for each service company added, and shown in statement. There were now five staff sergeants, not shown.

1816–17. Drum-major introduced, but is included in number of drummers.

1846. Upper line, service companies ; lower, depôt.

SANCTIONED ESTABLISHMENT

Year.	Companies.	Lieut.-Colonels.	Majors.	Captains other than Col., Lt.-Col. and Major.	Lieutenants, including Capt.-Lt.	Ensigns or 2nd Lieutenants.	Surgeons.	Asst.-Surgeons or Mates.	Sergeants exclusive of staff but including Colour-sergeants.	Corporals.	Drummers and Fifers and Buglers.	Privates.
1857	10	2	2	10	12	8	1	3	60	—	21	1000
	2	—	—	2	2	2	—	—	10	—	4	200
1861	10	1	2	10	12	8	1	3	50	40	21	810
	2	—	—	2	2	2	—	—	10	10	4	90
1865	12	1	2	12	14	10	1	1	50	50	24	650
1866	10	1	2	10	10	10	1	1	50	40	21	750
1869	12	1	2	12	14	10	1	1	50	50	25	800
1870	8	1	2	8	10	6	—	—	40	40	17	780
	2	—	—	2	2	—	—	—	8	8	4	92

2ND BATTALION.

Year.	Companies.	Lieut.-Colonels.	Majors.	Captains other than Col., Lt.-Col. and Major.	Lieutenants, including Capt.-Lt.	Ensigns or 2nd Lieutenants.	Surgeons.	Asst.-Surgeons or Mates.	Sergeants exclusive of staff but including Colour-sergeants.	Corporals.	Drummers and Fifers and Buglers.	Privates.
1803	10	1	2	10	12	8	1	2	50	50	22	950
1809	10	1	2	10	12	8	1	2	40	40	22	760
1811	10	1	2	10	12	8	1	1	30	30	21	570
	1	—	—	1	2	1	—	—	3	3	3	—
1812–13	10	1	2	10	42	8	1	2	50	40	25	760
	1	—	—	1	2	1	—	—	3	3	3	—
1816–17	10	1	2	10	12	8	1	2	40	40	21	570

THE 66TH (BERKSHIRE) REGIMENT, 1758–1870 (*continued*).

REMARKS.

1857. Service companies above, depôt below. Corporals included with privates. Six staff sergeants.

1861. Service above, depôt below. Sergeant-major and six staff sergeants not shown.

1865. Sergeant-major, etc., as above.

1870. Service companies above, depôt below.

1811. One recruiting company shown in second line.

1812–13. As above.

1816–17. Disbanded.

APPENDIX III

UNIFORM AND EQUIPMENT

We do not propose in this note to attempt anything like a complete account of British Infantry uniforms, even as affecting the 49th and 66th. All that we shall try is to give a general idea of the dress of those regiments at different periods of their existence, with such particulars as we have been able to gather as to changes or differences peculiar to each of them.*

Neither regiment had been formed when the well-known " Representation of the Cloathing of His Majesty's Household, etc.," was published in 1742, forming the basis of and supplement to the dress regulation of 1743.

Nevertheless, the 49th, when it was constituted at the end of 1743, was, no doubt, uniformed in accordance with that regulation, and we may safely assume that the uniform of privates of the battalion companies closely resembled the representation in the book of a man of the 46th Foot † which also was a regiment with green facings.

The private of a battalion company would have the familiar three-cornered cocked hat of those days. His coat was red with green facings, and a green lining showing in the turn backs of the coat skirt. His breeches were red, and he had white gaiters or " spatterdashes " reaching above the knee.

The dress regulation of 1743, on which the uniform of the 49th (then 63rd) was based, is not very full ; but it lays down the colour of the drummers' coats as the same as the facings of the regiment (green), faced and lapelled with red, and laced in such a manner as the Colonel should think fit for distinction sake. The only restraint put on his discretion in this matter was the requirement that the lace was to be of the colour of that on the soldiers' coats. What that colour was is not indicated till we come to the book of 1768, when we find that it had a white ground with three coloured lines, the two outer being red and the centre one green.

The regulation of 1743 lays down some particulars for the grenadiers. The

* There is at present no complete history of British military uniforms and equipment, but anyone interested in the subject will get an excellent general idea from Appendix I to the *Records of the Royal Scots*, compiled by Mr. J. C. Leask and Capt. McCance. The first-named writer contributed notes on the uniform of the 49th and 66th to the *China Dragon* of April, July, and October 1907, which have been consulted.

† Though the position of the picture shows it as of a man of the 46th, it was really one of the 45th. The pictures and the succession of Colonels appear to have been transposed in binding. The same thing happened with the 8th and 9th.

388

front of their mitre-shaped cap was to be of the same colour as the facings (green for the 49th) with the King's cypher embroidered, and the crown over it.

The " little flap " at the bottom of the front was to be red, with the White Horse of Hanover, and the motto of the regiment over it. What was meant by the " motto of the regiment " appears not to have been the motto of the 49th (a motto which did not exist) but the general motto of all grenadiers " Nec aspera terrent."

The next dress regulation of importance was that of 1751 * when the 49th had acquired that number, instead of its former one of 63rd, but the 66th was still not formed.

The regulation also deals with Colours, a subject which is dealt with in another Appendix (IV). It also lays down the orders for drummers' and grenadiers' uniforms, but there is no important change in this, except that the grenadiers' motto is distinctly stated to be " Nec aspera terrent."

The back part of their cap was to be red, the turn-up to be the colour of the front (green for the 49th), with the number of the regiment in the middle part behind. The lace round the buttonholes of the 49th in 1751 was rather elaborate, as figured at p. 135 of the *China Dragon* for April 1907. It had a white ground with a yellow stripe in the centre, and green " twirls " above and below the stripe. Drums and bells of arms were to be painted in front with the colour of the facings of the regiment, with the King's cypher and crown, and the number of the regiment under it. At the end of the regulation there is a list of the facings of regiments, in which those of the 49th appear as " green." The regulation also distinctly recognizes the title of the regiment as the " 49th Foot," though, even after this, regiments are sometimes described, even in official correspondence, by the name of the colonel for the time being.

Neither the regulations of 1743 nor those of 1751 deal with officers' uniforms, and it is not till we come to that of the 19th December 1768 that we find a really full description of all classes of uniforms. That regulation was accompanied by a volume of illustrations, of which the only extant copy appears to be that in the Prince Consort's Library at Aldershot. All that we can say, therefore, of officers' uniforms previous to 1768 is that they were, no doubt, a glorified edition of those of privates. We do know that the sash was then worn over the right shoulder.

The only orders of importance in the interval between 1751 and 1768 were the following :

In January 1753 it was laid down that grenadiers' coats were to have " the usual little ornaments on the point of the shoulder," and drummers were to have short hanging sleeves like the Foot Guards. Sergeants' coats were to be lapelled on the breast with green (for the 49th) with white buttons.

In 1761 the colour of stockings for all regiments was ordered to be white. The 66th had now been formed, and we have a record of its uniform very soon

* In the warrant of April 1751, at Windsor Castle, the regiment is described as the " 49th Regiment of Fusiliers " of which the Colonel was Trelawny.

after its formation in an inspection report at Newcastle, dated 20th May 1759, which says :

" Officers' uniforms red, lapelled with green, laced and looped with gold. Buff waistcoat and breeches. Men's uniform—red, lapelled, faced, and lined with green. Well laced. Red breeches."

The regulation of 1768 goes into details hitherto unknown in such orders, and the book of illustrations above mentioned gives a representation of a grenadier of every infantry regiment. There is no representation of a private of a battalion company, but it is only necessary, in order to get it, to substitute the three-cornered cocked hat for the grenadier's cap, and to cut out the match case, which grenadiers still carried on their cross belts * as a relic of the older days of hand grenades.

The main changes and provisions made in 1768 were as follows :

Officers. All coats to be lined with white, thus making white turn backs at the front of the skirt. The coats might be plain red, without embroidery or lace, but the colonel might, at his discretion, require them to be embroidered or laced round the buttonholes. Number of regiment on buttons.

Epaulettes.† Grenadier officers to wear one on each shoulder. Officers of battalion companies to wear only one, on the right shoulder. They were to be of embroidery or lace, with gold or silver fringe. The 49th had gold fringe, as had the 66th at this time. The 49th had embroidery, not lace, as is shown by an inspection report at Dublin dated 27th August 1768.

The lace round the buttonholes of the 49th was in the " bastion " or " pointed " shape, whilst the 66th had " straight-laced " buttonholes. Both patterns are depicted at p. 135 of the *China Dragon* of April 1907. The buttonholes of both regiments were equidistant, not in pairs.

To continue with the terms of the 1768 regulations—

Officers' waistcoats were to be plain, without embroidery or lace. Their swords were to be uniform for each regiment, which implies that no general pattern had yet been prescribed for the infantry. The sword knot to be of crimson and gold in stripes, and the sword hilt of gilt for regiments with gold lace, which both the 49th and 66th then had. Hats laced with gold for both regiments. Sashes of crimson silk, worn round the waist. The gorget was gilt, for these regiments, engraved with the King's arms and cypher. The gorget, which was the last relic of armour, was worn suspended from the neck by a ribbon of the colour of the facings (green for both regiments). There was a rosette or tuft of the same colour at each end, where the ribbon was attached to the horseshoe-shaped gorget.

Grenadier officers now wore a black bearskin cap of a mitre shape, similar to the former grenadiers' caps. Their shoulder belts were white or buff, according to the colour of the waistcoat. Both regiments now had white waistcoats, breeches, and turn backs. Facings of the 49th " green," of the 66th " yellowish green."

* The match case was abolished in 1769 for grenadiers.
† Epaulettes replaced shoulder knots in 1763.

Grenadier officers carried a " fuzil," battalion officers an esponton, a sort of light halberd.*

Officers and men all now wore black linen gaiters with black buttons, garters, and buckles. The gaiters had stiff tops reaching above the knee.

Sergeants' coats were lapelled to the waist with green (the colour of the facings). The buttonholes of the coat were braided with white, those of the waistcoat plain. Sergeants of grenadiers carried fuzils and pouches ; those of battalion companies had halberds and no pouches.

All sergeants wore, round the waist, a sash of crimson worsted, with a stripe of green (colour of facings).

Corporals' coats had an epaulette of silk on the right shoulder.

Privates of the grenadier companies had round " wings " of red cloth on the point of the shoulder, with six loops of the same sort of lace as was round the buttonholes, and a border round the bottom. Privates of battalion companies had coats looped with worsted lace, but no border. The ground of the lace was white, with coloured stripes, buttons white. There were four loops on the sleeves, and four on the pockets, with two on each side of the slit behind. Lapels, three inches wide, to reach down to the waist. Sleeves to have a small round cuff three and a half inches wide, made so that they may be unbuttoned and let down.

Shoulder and waistbelts white, in the case of the 49th and 66th, as both had white waistcoats.

Drummers' and Fifers' Coats. To be of the colour of the facings (green), faced and lapelled with red. To be laced in such a manner as the Colonel chooses. The only restriction on his discretion was that the lace was to be of the colour of that on the soldiers' coats. Hanging sleeves behind were forbidden for drummers and fifers.

Grenadiers', Drummers' and Fifers' Caps. Grenadiers wore a black mitre-shaped bearskin like their officers. It had decorations and motto as the former coloured caps had, but had on the back a grenade with the number of the regiment in the centre of it.

Drummers and Fifers wore a bearskin cap like that of the grenadiers. On the front was the King's crest in silver-plated metal on a black ground, with trophies of colours and drums. The number of the regiment was on the back of the cap. All drummers and fifers carried a short sword with scimitar blade. Grenadiers of both regiments wore steel hilted swords. Swords for privates in other companies had been abolished in 1763. All other ranks wore black gaiters, like those of the officers.

Pioneers carried an axe and a saw, and wore an apron. Their cap had a leather crown with black bearskin front, on which was the King's crest in white plated metal on a red ground, as well as a representation of an axe and a saw. The number of the regiment was at the back. The laces for the different regiments are laid down in a schedule at the end of the regulation. That of the 49th is described as " white with two red stripes and one green stripe." The 66th had one stripe of crimson (upper half) and green, and one green stripe.

* They had previously carried a half pike.

In 1918 H.M. King George V presented to Major-General Dickson, Colonei of the Royal Berkshire Regiment, a sample of the facings and lace of the 49th as approved by King George III in 1768. These had been found amongst the archives of King George IV, and the letter accompanying them, from Mr. Fortescue, said " His Majesty trusts that this relic of old times may be thought worthy of preservation among the household gods of your regiment." It is encased in a frame presented by Colonel M. D. Graham, C.B., C.M.G., C.V.O., who commanded the 1st Battalion from September 1912 till September 1916.

The sample is now at the Officers' Mess, 1st Battalion, Royal Berkshire Regiment.

Drummers'.

The braids of 1768 were :

49th—White ground as usual, with two crimson stripes.

66th—Stripes the same as the regimental lace.

About 1771 * Light Companies were introduced as the left flank company of infantry battalions. The men of these wore, instead of a hat, a black leather skull cap, with a black leather upright front and green feather. Here we must deal with the question of special colours for feathers or tufts worn by flank companies of the 49th. We have already given one account of how the light company is said to have adopted a red instead of a green feather.† Another version is given in the information which was furnished to Mr. Cannon, about 1842, for his projected history of the 49th.‡ According to that, the flank companies of the 49th were ordered, during the American War of Independence, to be distinguished by the grenadiers wearing a black top to their white feathers, and the Light Company wearing red instead of green feathers. No one has yet succeeded in tracing any such order, and we have had no better success than others. There is also a tradition in the regiment that at one time they had black and white check bands to their forage caps, which was supposed to have some connexion with the grenadiers' black and white feathers of the American War time.

The two accounts are quite inconsistent, except as regards the Light Company's wearing red feathers in America.

The only other evidence we have come across showing the wearing of unusual coloured feathers is a coloured print, published by Ackerman in 1849. It depicts two officers of the flank companies of the 49th. The Light Company officer wears the usual green ball, the grenadier a red one, instead of the usual white. We do not know what authority there is for the accuracy of the colours. In any case, the print does not support either of the stories above given. No trace of the wearing of unusual coloured feathers or tufts has been found in inspection

---

* Some regiments, but not the 49th or 66th, had them rather earlier.

† Cf. Vol. I, p. 32.

‡ This cannot be implicitly trusted. The records were burnt at Fort George in the American War of 1812–15, and were only reconstructed from memory. Moreover, just before this statement it is alleged in the record that the Regiment was engaged at Bunker's Hill, which was certainly not the case.

reports of the 49th. One would certainly expect such deviation from general custom, if it existed, to be noticed by inspecting officers. On the whole, therefore, it seems that the matter must rest entirely on tradition, and even that not a clear one. The story of the adoption of red feathers by the Light Company in consequence of the affair with the American General Wayne seems the more probable. The 46th continued their Light Company red feathers. Whether the 49th did so, and if so till when, cannot at present be proved. Nor can that of the grenadiers' white feathers with a black top.

In 1769 the grenadiers' match cases and swords were abolished.

In 1774 an inspection report, dated Dublin 25th July, thus describes the 49th uniform :

" Officers' uniform—scarlet lapelled full green, white lining, gold embroidered buttonholes. Buttons gold, ' No. 49.' White waistcoat and breeches. One epaulette. Black silk stocks."

The gold embroidery, instead of lace, was always worn by the 49th.

In 1784 the sash was worn by officers and sergeants over the right shoulder, instead of round the waist. In 1786 officers of battalion companies ceased to carry the esponton, and a new general pattern of sword was prescribed, a straight cut and thrust blade, thirty-two inches long, broader at the shoulder.

In 1790 tufts, instead of feathers, were ordered to be worn on hats or caps. The colours were generally red and white for battalion companies, white for grenadiers, and green for light companies.

1791. Field officers ordered to wear two epaulettes ; officers of flank companies to have, embroidered on their epaulettes, a grenade for the grenadier, and a bugle for the light company.

1792. Sergeants of battalion companies to carry pikes, instead of halberds. Officers of flank companies no longer to carry fuzils. Sergeants of grenadier companies to carry pikes, those of light companies to retain their fuzils.

In this year an inspection report, dated St. Vincent 22nd February 1792, records for the 66th as follows :

" Trowsers. Officers' uniform, yellowish green facings, with *silver* lace. Buttons numbered, and in every respect according to regulation."

The trousers were correct when the regiment was on service in the West Indies.

1797. Hair powder abolished for N.C.O.s and men. The hair had previously been worn plaited, and tied up behind with a black ribbon. Men whose hair was not long enough for this had false plaits.

N.C.O.s, drummers, and privates no longer to wear lapels ; lace to be put on their coats, as previously it had been on their lapels.

1799. Officers and men to wear their hair in " queues " ten inches long.

1800. The old three-cornered hat was abolished for battalion companies, except for officers. Officers of grenadiers wore bearskins, those of light companies caps.

Other ranks wore a black lacquered cylindrical hat with a leather peak in front. These were also worn by the Light Company, and by the grenadiers when the latter were not wearing their bearskins, a matter which was left to the discretion of the colonel.

Regiments without a badge * had on the front of the hat a garter surmounted by a crown. Inside the garter was the royal cypher, below the garter was the lion, and on either side of the lion it was permissible to have the regimental number. There was also in front a black cockade with a regimental button in the centre, or, in the grenadier company, a grenade.

Out of the cockade there rose a red and white plume for battalion companies, white for grenadiers, or green for the light company.

1801. Great coats issued to all men.

1802. Epaulettes abolished for non-commissioned officers. They were to wear instead chevrons on the right arm. The first chevron was silver, the second white tape, the third regimental lace. Sergeant-Major and Quartermaster-Sergeants had four bars, other sergeants three, and corporals two.

1804. Hair queues reduced to nine inches.

1806. Lacquering of hats abolished.

1808. Grey trousers substituted for breeches and gaiters on active service. Queues and hair powder abolished for all ranks. Hair was now cut short on the neck.

1809. Hitherto there had been no distinguishing badges of rank for officers. They were now introduced for Field-Officers only. The colonel to wear, on the straps of his epaulettes, a crown and star, Lieutenant-Colonels a crown only, and majors a star only. All Field-Officers now wore two epaulettes, others only one.

The adjutant to wear a laced strap on his left shoulder, and epaulette on right.

1811. The officers' dress on active service was assimilated to that of the private, in order to render them less easily picked off by sharpshooters. They were to wear caps like the men, and a coat similar to that of the men, but with lapels to button over the breast and body. They also had a grey great-coat like the men, with a stand-up collar and cape to protect the shoulders, and regimental buttons. On foreign service they wore grey pantaloons and short boots, or shoes and gaiters, also like privates.

The coat was cut short in front, with tails behind. Unfortunately it had an upright stiff collar and a stock, which made it extremely uncomfortable. In this year was introduced the new pattern of hat which continued till after the Battle of Waterloo. The cylindrical hat of hard felt had a rounded front, on which was a plate similar to that previously worn. Across the front were festooned cap-lines, or cords, of red and gold cord for officers, and white worsted for other ranks. The cords terminated in two tassels on the right side of the hat. On the left side was a plume of the usual colours for battalion, grenadier, and light companies, and outside of this was a black cockade with a button in the centre.

---

* Neither 49th nor 66th had a badge at this date.

1814. The brass cap plate was abolished for the light company, and replaced by a bugle with the regimental number.

At this time the private had a single-breasted red coat with square headed loops (bastion shaped for 49th) four inches long put on in pairs ; lace round the high collar, showing a white frill in front. Also round shoulder-straps, terminating in a small white shoulder tuft. In the flank companies wings of red cloth were worn, trimmed with stripes of regimental lace, and edged with an overhanging fringe of white worsted. Gaiters and breeches the same as officers.

Sergeants had the same coats as privates, but of finer cloth ; chevrons on right arm which, as well as the coat lace, were of fine white tape. Crimson sash with a stripe of the facings colour. They wore a straight sword on a shoulder belt, and a brass plate like the men.

Sergeants carried a halberd which had a plain steel spear head with a cross piece, not unlike the esponton. The old halberd with a battle-axe head had been discontinued in 1792.

A report, dated Portsmouth 20th April 1815, says, for the 66th :

" Uniform according to regulation, except the officers' pantaloons, and the skirts of their jackets that turn back being laced."

In this year also the facings of the 66th are described as " gosling green." That colour was more of a dirty brown with a tinge of green in it.

1816. The passion for imitating the Prussian Army, which lasted for the greater part of a century, resulted in this year in the adoption for the British infantry of the heavy bell-topped hat worn by the Prussians. In front there was a plume twelve inches high, of the usual colours, fitted into a socket covered by a cockade as before. Below the cockade there was a brass plate with the regimental number surmounted by a crown, except in the case of the light company, which had a bugle. All other devices were prohibited. Instead of the plate, officers wore a circular disc with the regimental number, surmounted by a scaled loop passing up to the cockade. On the loop were inscribed the battle-honours of the regiment.

Officers had a brass scaled chin strap, and round the top of the hat was a border of gold lace, two inches broad, and another, three-quarters of an inch broad, round the bottom. Grenadiers had a bearskin with a brass chin strap, which was changed to leather in 1822. Cocked hats were finally abolished for officers.

1820. Short tailed coats gave place to the coatee.

After 1822 dress regulations have always been printed.

1823. In place of breeches, gaiters, and shoes, officers were to wear blue-grey trousers and half boots. They also wore a coatee and a black beaver cap. Battalion company officers wore one epaulette, field officers two, and officers of flank companies " wings," instead of epaulettes. The officers' cap feather was of the usual colours for battalion, grenadier, and light companies. Except for full dress, when breeches were worn, officers wore white kerseymere pantaloons. Their sash was crimson, with bullion fringes, and worn round the waist. In undress they had grey trousers.

1824. The facings of the 66th, which were of a dull willow green, were altered to a much brighter shade.

1828. The officer's hat was to be of black beaver, six inches deep, with a patent leather peak. The diameter of the top of the hat was eleven inches. It was ornamented in front by a gilt star plate, surmounted by a crown. The height of the feather was reduced to eight inches.

1829. The Commander-in-Chief (Lord Hill) started inquiries as to extravagances in uniforms, which imposed harsh burdens of expense on junior officers. Both the 49th and 66th were pilloried in a list of thirty regiments which were found to be disregarding regulations in such matters as wearing pantaloons laced with gold or silver. This it will be remembered had been noticed, in the case of the 66th, in the inspection report of 20th April 1815.

Eventually, the cost of outfit for officers of ordinary infantry regiments was limited to £53 16s. 6d. where the regiment (66th) wore lace, or £60 where it had embroidery (49th). Lapels for officers' coatees abolished.

1830. Light companies were given a green ball, instead of a plume. Sergeants to carry fuzil instead of pike. Gorgets abolished.

1839. Introduction of the universal brass plate for other ranks.

After 1840 the 66th were wearing a silver shako plate of the form of a cross, with " 66 " in a garter in the centre. The battle-honours were recorded thus:

" Peninsula " under " 66 " on a scroll.

" Nive," " Orthes," " Douro " and " Pyrenees " on the garter.

" Vittoria," " Talavera," " Albuhera," " Nivelle " on the extremities of the cross.

In 1842 a new pattern of black beaver was introduced for officers, but was almost immediately superseded by the " Albert " hat, of which the body was of beaver for officers, and felt for other ranks. It was bound at top and bottom with black patent leather, and had a peak behind as well as in front. Officers had a brass chin strap, other ranks one of leather.

1843. In this year the 49th, as has already been narrated, was given the badge of the China Dragon, which they carried with them when they became the 1st Battalion Berkshire Regiment in 1881.

In 1846 officers of regiments having a badge, amongst which was now the 49th, were ordered to wear it on their forage caps, instead of the regimental number.

In this year the grenadiers gave up their bearskins, and wore the same headgear as the battalion companies.

1855. Substitution of a tunic for the coatee. Epaulettes were abolished, and rank distinctions were introduced for captains, lieutenants, and ensigns, who wore respectively the same crowns and stars as colonels, lieutenant-colonels and majors, but carried them at each end of the collar, instead of on the shoulder strap. The sash was worn over the left shoulder for officers, the right for sergeants.

In this year also the French shako was adopted. It was of black felt with patent leather binding, and peaks in front and behind. Its height was five and a half inches in front, and seven and a half inches behind, and the top was sunk three-quarters of an inch. On the front it had a gilt star plate three and three-eight inches in diameter, surmounted by a red and white ball. Majors' shakos had one gold stripe round the top. Those of Colonels and Lieutenant-Colonels had two.

1860. Shako made of blue stiffened canvas. Flank companies were abolished.

1864. Badge ordered to be worn on cap plate, waist-belt, and forage cap, above the number.

1866. Adoption of the Snider rifle, the first breech loader.

1871. A new shako, lighter than the previous one. Height four inches in front, six and a half inches behind ; number on front, with or without the garter.

1874. Badge in silver to be worn on shako plate, in addition to number. Also on waist plate and forage cap. This affected the 49th, but not the 66th, which had no badge.

In May 1881 the hitherto green facings of the 49th and 66th were changed to white, the colour which was prescribed for all English and Welsh regiments. The reason for this general adoption of white seems evident. The linking of battalions was in contemplation, and was actually ordered shortly afterwards. Had old facings been left unchanged, there would certainly have been difficulties, in the case of two battalions with different-coloured facings, as to which was to prevail in the united territorial regiment. There would have been heart burnings, and still more difficulty than there actually was at first in getting the two battalions to amalgamate cordially.

Later, in some cases where the new regiment was composed of two battalions which originally had the same coloured facings, they were allowed to return to their old colour. This was not necessary in the case of the Berkshire, as it was soon afterwards made a " Royal " Regiment, and its facings were of course altered to blue, the colour distinctive of Royal regiments. During the period 1857 to 1871 patterns of drummers' lace were approved, many of which were very elaborate. In the case of the 49th there was no elaboration, and the lace was simply a white ground with two stripes of crimson and a central one of green. That of the 66th was more varied. It had two marginal stripes of green, and in the centre squares of black lines with diagonals of pink.

During the same period the approved drummers' fringe for the 49th was white, crimson, and green ; that of the 66th white, green, pink, and black.

This fringe was one and three-quarters inches deep, arranged in half-inch widths of each colour. It, like the drummers' lace, was abolished in 1871.

In concluding these notes on uniforms, a few more are required on officers' facings, and regimental lace. Officers' lace, or embroidery in the 49th, was lace, throughout gold with gilt buttons.

With the 66th it was otherwise. They had gold lace in their earlier years, and in 1768. At some date between 1768 and 1792, which we have not been able to discover, the officers' lace changed from gold to silver ; for an inspection report, of the 22nd November 1792 at St. Vincent, shows the lace and buttons as silver.

De Bosset's scheme of uniforms shows them again as silver in 1803. From 1813 to 1824 the Army Lists show silver lace, and in 1825 the regiment reverted to gold, which remained unchanged thereafter. We may, therefore, safely conclude that from some unascertained date between 1768 and 1792 till 1825 the officers' lace was silver.*

The facings of the two regiments varied in their shade of green as follows :

1755	49th, " full green."
1767	66th, " deep green."
1768	49th, " green " ; 66th, " yellowish green."
1774	49th, " full green."
1794–1800	49th, " full green " ; 66th, " yellowish green."
1813	49th, " green "; 66th, still " yellowish green."
1815	66th, " gosling green."
1825–34	66th, " emerald green."
1834–1868	66th, " green."
1868–1881	{ 49th, " Lincoln green." 66th, " grass green."

The regimental lace of both regiments always had a white ground with stripes varying at times.

The 49th had, in and before 1768, two red stripes with a central green one. The drummers' lace had two crimson stripes. These continued unchanged.

Up to 1768 the 66th had two crimson stripes. In that year they had, both for lace and drummers' braid, one crimson and green stripe, and a second green stripe.

In 1824 the 66th had two yellow stripes with a central green one, and there was a purple " worm " under the lower yellow stripe. In 1836 the stripes of the 66th were reduced to one central green " worm," or zigzag line.

MILITIA

Militia uniforms did not differ widely from those of Regular Regiments. Of course facings and lace varied from one regiment to another, as did the officers' lace and buttons. In later days nearly all Regular Regiments wore gold lace and gilt or brass buttons, and all Militia Battalions wore silver. But up to 1830 many Regular Regiments wore silver, and many Militia regiments gold.

In 1779 the Berkshire Militia had red uniforms faced with light blue. In 1800 and 1807 the colour of the facings is given as " blue " without any specification of shade.

In 1814 it was the same. The loops, like those of the 49th, were " bastion " shaped. The drummers' lace between 1859 and 1871 had blue edges and a

* One of the two officers' coats presented to the R.U.S.I. Museum is attributed to the period 1822 ; but this appears to be an error, as it has gold lace, whilst the Army List of 1822 gives silver. Its date is probably later than 1824.

blue pattern, supposed to represent fleur-de-lis, between them. The uniform of the Royal Berkshire Militia appears to have remained red or scarlet with blue facings till 1881, when it became the 3rd Battalion of the Berkshire Regiment, and had to change its facings to white. When the Regiment became " Royal " after Tofrek, the blue facings were returned to the Militia Battalion, which re-acquired its old title of " Royal."

The officers' lace and buttons appear always to have been silver.

VOLUNTEERS

Volunteer uniforms at first were made as simple as possible, as the corps themselves had to pay for them, without assistance from Government. It was only as more interest was taken in the movement, and the Volunteers were assisted to a greater extent pecuniarily, that they were able to indulge in uniforms approximating to those of the Regulars and Militia.

In 1882 the Berkshire Volunteers were wearing scarlet, with Lincoln green facings, just after the Regular and Militia Battalions of the Berkshire Regiment had shed their green facings and had to adopt white. These facings continued till June 1886, after which they are shown as blue, like the rest of the Regiment.

APPENDIX IV

COLOURS AND BATTLE-HONOURS

THE COLOURS

We have no record of when Trelawny's Regiment first received Colours and no trace of the ultimate fate of those Colours. Assuming that they were received within the first six years of its existence, they must have been as follows :

What was called in the regulation of 1743 the " First Colour " was the Great Union with, in the centre of the St. George's Cross, painted in gold Roman figures, the " number of the rank of the regiment," viz. " LXIII Regt." * within a wreath of roses and thistles on one stalk. The " Second Colour " was a sheet of green (the colour of the facings) with a small union in the top corner nearest the staff. In the centre of the Colour was the regimental number, painted as in the case of the First Colour. We have nothing to show if new Colours were received in 1749 when the regiment became the 49th. Possibly only the number in the centre may have been changed. That is all that would have been required. The regulation of 1751 styled the First and Second Colours respectively the " King's " and the " Regimental Colour," as they have been ever since.†

Regiments were still known by the names of their colonels for the time being, though their numerical rank had been decided long before, as far back as 1694. The practice of describing them by the colonel's name died hard, and even after 1758 they were often known by a combination of the number and the colonel's name. In the case of the 49th, the regiment would sometimes be called the " 49th Walsh's " during the incumbency of that colonel. The records which we have of the receipt of new Colours are in inspection reports, which state that they had been received in 1769, again in 1772, and again in 1781. The periods seem very short, especially that between 1769 and 1772. Of this we can offer no explanation. The short period 1772–1781 may perhaps be explained by hard usage in the American War of Independence, and in St. Lucia.

The next record is in 1816, when the regiment had just been through the American War of 1812–1814. The report, dated in October 1815 at Weymouth,

---

* It will be remembered that Trelawny's Regiment was so numbered till the disbandment of the 6th Marines in 1749 resulted in its becoming the 49th.

† According to official orders in 1881, the Queen's Colour was styled " Royal," which would do equally well if a King or a Queen were on the throne. This order appears to have fallen into abeyance, and War Office letters of date as recently as December 1922 speak of the " King's Colour."

says " Colours worn out from being torn from the staffs at Fort George to prevent them from falling into the hands of the enemy." This refers to the capture of Fort George by the Americans in May 1813. They were replaced, as noted in the text,* on the 17th August 1816. There is nothing to show what became of the old Colours on any of these occasions.

The next new Colours were presented on the 27th August 1844 at Winchester.† The disposal of the old Colours on this occasion is also not known. The next Colours were received at the end of 1861 or beginning of 1862, but there is no record of presentation. The next record is in 1889, when the first Royal Colours were presented by H.R.H. the Duke of Edinburgh. The next Colours were those presented at Dublin on the 14th August 1908. They are still in use.

Of the early Colours of the 66th we know more than of those of the 49th. The first set appears to have been acquired immediately on the formation of the regiment in 1758. These Colours were reported to be " bad " in 1773, and were replaced in 1774 or 1775. This new set only lasted till some date between 1785 and 1793, when the regiment was in St. Vincent. Here it received a new set of Colours, though we have been unable to trace the exact date. It was probably near the end of the period. The story of the leaving of the old ones in the Court House, St. Vincent, has already been told.‡

We have referred to the Administrator of the Colony, but regret that he has been unable to trace any record of the presentation of the old Colours, or of their existence at the present time. This is much to be regretted.

We have no further record of new Colours prior to the formation of the 2nd Battalion in August 1803. When that battalion was formed it received new Colours in 1803.

As has been told in the First Volume of this History, the Colours of the 2nd Battalion received in 1803 were lost at the Battle of Albuera. The battalion then became the left wing of the First Provisional Battalion, and the Colours carried through the rest of the Peninsular War by that composite battalion were those of the 2/31st, as the senior regiment.

New Colours were provided for the 66th, but were sent to Lisbon in 1812 and thence home, as not being required owing to the Colours of the 31st being carried by the Provisional Battalion.‖

When the 2nd Battalion of the 66th returned to England in 1814, these new Colours were sent to Plymouth to meet it. It actually landed at Portsmouth, and somehow or other the Colours appear to have gone astray, and never to have reached the battalion.§

A new set had to be made up. This had been done, and the new Colours had been taken into use, when the missing set, which had never been carried, appears to have turned up. Naturally, they would be made over to Major-General Nicolls, who, as Colonel of the 66th, must have had to pay for both sets.

---

* Vol. I, p. 112.   † Vol. I, p. 140.   ‡ Cf. ante, Vol. I, p. 167.
‖ This is stated in an Inspection Report, late in 1813, at Roncesvalles in the Pyrenees.
§ Stated in an Inspection Report, dated Portsmouth, 20th April 1815.

They eventually seem to have passed into the possession of Miss Louisa Nicolls a relative of the General, and were presented by her to the Royal United Service Institution on the 8th March 1876. They now hang in the Museum in White-hall. The ground of the Regimental Colour now looks more like a dirty brown, with only a tinge of green in it. As the facings at the time when it was made were " gosling green," the change from fading does not appear to have been so great as one would suppose at first.

There is in the Officers' Mess at the Depot at Reading a set of Colours such as the 1st Battalion would have carried whilst wearing white facings after 1881. This set was never presented to the battalion.

It was prepared in the early eighties, but could not be given to the battalion before its acquisition of the Royal title gave it the right to blue Colours.

The white ones therefore were useless. They were kept for some years by the late head of the Army Clothing Department who returned them to store in 1920. The head of the Department then offered them to Major-General Dickson, who handed them over to the Depot for safe custody.

In the same place are preserved the Colours of the 3rd (Militia) Battalion, which became in 1908 the 3rd (Special Reserve) Battalion.

SERVICE BATTALIONS

5th Battalion. King's Colour presented by H.R.H. the Prince of Wales at Erre (France) on the 14th February 1919. Deposited on disbandment in the Parish Church, Reading.

6th Battalion. King's Colour presented at the Depot, Reading, 31st August 1920 by Major-General H. B. Walker, K.C.B., and deposited in the Church of St. Giles, Reading.

7th Battalion. King's Colour presented by the same officer and at the same time as that of the 6th. Now deposited at St. George's Church, Reading.

8th Battalion. King's Colour presented at Bartry (France) in January 1919 by Lieut.-General Sir R. H. K. Butler, commanding IIIrd Corps. Deposited in St. Giles' Church, Reading.

BATTLE-HONOURS

The earliest in chronological order of the battle-honours borne on the Colours of the Royal Berkshire Regiment is " St. Lucia 1778." It was gained by what was then the 49th, under circumstances which have been detailed in the First Volume of this History. Yet it was only in 1909 that it was awarded.

The next, " Egmont-op-Zee," was also gained by the 49th in September 1799. The third honour was gained by the 49th at Copenhagen in 1801.

This honour is borne by only one other regiment—the Rifle Brigade. Neither regiment is entitled to add the naval crown which was granted to the Queen's, Worcestershire, and Welch Regiments for naval actions in which they took part. After this we come to a long series of honours gained by the 2nd Battalion of the 66th in the Peninsular Campaigns, in which neither the 1st Battalion 66th nor the 49th were engaged. They are:

Douro, gained 1809
Talavera, ,, 1809
Albuhera, ,, 1811
Vittoria, ,, 1813
Pyrenees, ,, 1813
Nivelle, ,, 1813
Nive, ,, 1813
Orthes, ,, 1814
Peninsula, ,, 1809–1814

In between Albuhera and Vittoria comes " Queenstown," gained by the 49th in the American War of 1812–1814. The only other regiment having this honour is the Welch Regiment (41st in 1812).

The Crimean Battle-Honours—" Alma "—" Inkerman," " Sevastopol "—were gained by the 49th—" Kandahar 1880 " was awarded to the 66th. In the Siege of Kandahar by the Afghans, and in the subsequent Battle of Kandahar, the part played by the small remains of the regiment was a minor one. Its real title to the honour rests on its magnificent stand at Maiwand; but Maiwand was a British defeat and, at any rate before the Great War, battle-honours were not granted for defeats however bravely regiments fought, witness Almanza, Fontenoy, and Isandhlwana. " Afghanistan 1879–80 " was also gained by the 66th for the same period of Maiwand and Kandahar.

" Egypt 1882," " Tofrek " and " Suakin 1885 " all fell to the 1st Battalion, Royal Berkshire Regiment, which had, up to 1881, been the 49th.

" South Africa 1899–1902 " was awarded for the services there of the 2nd Battalion, formerly the 66th.

After that there were no battle-honours till those for the Great War were awarded.

The rule against awarding honours for defeats appears to have been very properly abrogated; for honours have been given in this war for many actions which were distinctly defeats.

All the Battle-Honours of the Regiment are shown in the following Table:

THE BATTLE-HONOURS OF THE ROYAL BERKSHIRE REGIMENT

Honours awarded previous to the Great War, and borne on the Regimental Colour. The second column shows by which of the original Regiments, or of the two Battalions after 1881, each honour was gained.

BATTLES.	BATTALION PRESENT.
St. Lucia, 1778	49th.
Egmont-op-Zee	49th.
Copenhagen .	49th.
Douro .	2nd Bn. 66th.
Talavera	do.
Albuhera .	do.
Queenstown .	49th.

BATTLES.	BATTALION PRESENT
Vittoria	2nd Bn. 66th.
Pyrenees	do.
Nivelle	do.
Nive .	do.
Orthes .	do.
Peninsula	do.
Alma .	49th.
Inkerman	do.
Sevastopol .	do.
Kandahar, 1880 .	66th.
Afghanistan, 1879–80	do.
Egypt, 1882	1st Bn. Berkshire.
Tofrek . .	1st Bn. Royal Berkshire.
Suakin, 1885 . .	do.
South Africa, 1899–1902	2nd Bn. Royal Berkshire.

Honours awarded for the Great War, 1914–1918, with the battalions which were present when each was gained. The ten printed in capitals are to be borne on the King's Colour. The rest appear in the Army List but not on the Colours.

In some cases the honour represents a battle of the same name fought in two different years, but counts as one honour—e.g. "YPRES 1914, 1917." In the Table the two battles are shown, one below the other, so as to indicate the battalions which took part in each.

BATTLES.	BATTALIONS PRESENT.
MONS . . .	1st.
Retreat from Mons.	1st.
Marne, 1914	1st.
Aisne, 1914	1st.
,, 1918	2nd.
YPRES, 1914	1st.
,, 1917 .	2nd, 1/4th, 2/4th.
Langemarck, 1914 .	1st.
,, 1917	2nd and 1/4th.
Gheluvelt .	1st.
Nonne Boschen	1st.
NEUVE-CHAPELLE	2nd.
Aubers . .	2nd.
Festubert, 1915	1st.
Loos .	1st, 2nd, 5th and 8th.
SOMME, 1916 .	1st, 2nd, 1/4th, 2/4th, 5th, 6th, and 8th.
,, 1918 .	1st, 2/4th, 5th and 8th.
Albert, 1916	1st and 2nd.
,, 1918	1st, 5th and 8th.
Bazentin .	2/4th, 6th and 8th.
Delville Wood	1st.

BATTLES.	BATTALIONS PRESENT.
Pozières .	1/4th.
Flèrs-Courcelette	8th.
Morval .	8th.
Thiepval	8th.
Le Transloy .	8th.
Ancre Heights	4th.
Ancre, 1916	1st.
„ 1918	5th.
ARRAS, 1917	1st and 5th.
„ 1918 .	2nd.
Scarpe, 1917 .	5th.
„ 1918 .	2nd.
Arleux .	1st and 5th.
Pilckem .	2nd and 6th.
Polygon Wood	1/4th.
Broodseinde	1/4th.
Poelcappelle .	1/4th.
Passchendaele	6th.
CAMBRAI, 1917	1st, 2/4th and 5th.
„ 1918	1st.
St. Quentin .	1st and 2/4th.
Bapaume, 1918	1st and 5th.
Rosières	2nd.
Avre . . .	8th.
Villers-Bretonneux .	2nd.
Lys .	2/4th.
Hazebrouck	2/4th.
Béthune.	2/4th.
Amiens . .	8th.
Hindenburg Line	8th.
Havrincourt	1st.
Epéhy . .	5th and 8th.
Canal du Nord	1st.
St. Quentin Canal .	8th.
SELLE .	1st, 1/4th, 5th and 8th.
Valenciennes	2/4th.
Sambre	8th.
France and Flanders, 1914–18	1st, 2nd, 1/4th, 2/4th, 5th, 6th, and 8th.
Piave . .	1/4th.
VITTORIO VENETO	1/4th.
Italy, 1917–18	1/4th.
DOIRAN, 1917–18 .	7th.
Macedonia, 1915–18	7th.

TOTAL 55

APPENDIX V

ROYAL BERKSHIRE REGIMENT OLD COMRADES ASSOCIATION

ORIGIN. The idea of forming a Royal Berkshire Regiment Old Comrades Dinner Club first took practical shape early in 1908. The Commanding Officers at that time were, 1st Battalion Lieut.-Colonel W. K. McClintock, 2nd Battalion Lieut.-Colonel R. N. Gamble, D.S.O. Depot: Major H. M. Finch, D.S.O.

On the 20th March 1908, a General Meeting of this Club was convened, and assembled at the Barracks, Reading, Major H. M. Finch, D.S.O., in the Chair. At this Meeting a copy of the suggested rules was drawn up and approved.

The date of the first Annual Dinner was fixed for 25th July 1908, to be held at the Barracks, Reading.

Before this first Dinner the first Annual General Meeting was held, Lieut.-Colonel R. N. Gamble, D.S.O., in the Chair. At this Meeting the following important resolutions were passed:

1st. That the title "Old Comrades Association" should be substituted for that of "Old Comrades Dinner Club."

2nd. That the Association should be a Benevolent Society.

RULES. The original Rules have been amended from time to time. The more important rules are now:

Rule 2. "The object of the Association is to bring together Old Comrades with a view of keeping up acquaintance and relieving necessitous cases."

Rule 3. "All well-conducted N.C.O.s and men who have served or are serving in any unit of the Royal Berkshire Regiment (Special Reserve, Territorial, Service, or Labour Battalions included) are eligible for membership."

Extract from Rule 4. "The annual subscription for all ranks (except officers) is one shilling. Life membership for ranks other than Officers is optional, the payment being 10s. for such life membership."
(Officers subscribe varying sums—the amount for 1924 was £44 10s. 6d.)

Rule 13. "The credit balance of the General Fund on 31st December in each year shall be transferred to a fund which shall be called ' the Benevolent Fund.' This fund shall be administered in accordance with a Trust Deed which shall be drawn out in such a manner as shall constitute a Dividing Trust for charitable purposes only."

(*Note.* It was found necessary to place the Fund under a Trust deed, in order to obtain a remission of Income Tax.)

GENERAL. The Benevolent Fund was started with only a few pounds. On the 31st December 1924 the capital reached £3,321 13s. 9d. The income from dividends for 1924 was £139. Of this sum £95 10s. was disbursed in relieving necessitous cases.

SUBSIDIARY FUNDS. In addition to the Benevolent Fund the Committee O.C.A. are entrusted with the administration of two capital funds, to which the following conditions attach :

1st. They cannot be invested.

2nd. They are ear-marked for soldiers who served in the Great War, or their Dependents. The funds are :

(*a*) A bequest of £100 from the late Captain Ransom ; of this £16 10s. remains.

(*b*) A sum of £600 derived from the balance of the Royal Berkshire Regiment Prisoners-of-War Fund so ably administered during the War by Lady Mount, C.B.E. Of this sum, £189 7s. was expended in 1924, leaving £410 13s. to be expended.

APPENDIX VI

BANNER FOR THE COMMEMORATION OF
THE FIRST SEVEN DIVISIONS

In October 1917, Major-General Dickson, Colonel of the Regiment, organized a Committee of Ladies, headed by Mrs. Dickson, to collect subscriptions for a banner to be hung in the Albert Hall on the occasion of the great choral commemoration of the First Seven Divisions on the 15th December.

Under the supervision of the ladies and of Colonel M. D. Graham, a banner was made by the Royal School of Art Needlework. It was of royal blue silk, shield shaped. In the centre was embroidered a garter surmounted by a crown. On the garter were the words " Princess Charlotte of Wales's " and on a scroll below " Royal Berkshire Regiment."

Inside the garter was the Dragon, with the word " China " below. Below the scroll were the words :

6th Brigade   2nd Division

B.E.F.

After use at the impressive ceremony of the 15th December, the banner was made over to the Depot of the Regiment for temporary custody. It is now in the possession of the 1st Battalion.

The subscriptions amounted to £93 10s. 6d.; but, after meeting all expenses, there was a balance of £65 in hand. Of this £15 15s. was expended on five thousand coloured post cards of the banner, and the remaining £50 was equally distributed between—

(a) The " Tobacco and Newspaper Fund for Royal Berkshire Regiment."

(b) " Bread and Clothing Fund for Prisoners-of-War of the Regiment."

(c) " Old Comrades Benevolent Fund for men and dependents of the Regiment."

APPENDIX VII

MESS PLATE AND FURNITURE

1ST BATTALION

The most important piece of plate owned by the 1st Battalion is a centre-piece.

The figures represent officers and privates of the years 1744 and 1877. Embossed plates depict the Battles of Queenstown and Inkerman.

Above the figures are the Regimental Colours, the whole surmounted by a figure of Mars. At the four corners of the base are well-modelled China Dragons.

The centre-piece was made by Messrs. Smith & Sons of Covent Garden in 1877 on the return of the 49th from India. Its cost was approximately £420. It was presented and paid for by voluntary subscriptions of £5 each from officers on appointment, and by subscriptions from former officers.

The " Redan " Table.—The Battalion also has a folding card table which was taken by the 49th from the Redan, after the evacuation of that work by the Russians on the 9th September 1855. Cards hastily thrown down were found on the table.

2ND BATTALION

The Officers' Mess Table was purchased about 1878 by the officers of the 66th at Karachi. It is reputed to have previously belonged to an Indian Cavalry Regiment.

It measures sixty feet in length by six feet in breadth. It was thoroughly overhauled and repaired in 1907. It has been the subject of numerous bets, recorded in the bet book, chiefly as to its dimensions. It is recorded that in 1904 at Alexandria, Lieutenant Wighton bet Captain North a bottle of Mess wine that he would not jump over the table within the ensuing fortnight. The bet was lost by Captain North.

The Bet Book.—The Mess Rules of the Officers' Mess ordain that " All bets made at the Mess Table shall be entered in the bet book at the time by the Vice-President, under the direction of the President, who shall be responsible for the proper keeping of the book, and any Officer defacing the bet or fine book shall, in accordance with custom, be fined one bottle of Mess Wine."

409

Prior to 1841 all bets and fines were entered together, but subsequent to that date fines have been entered separately.

The first bet recorded in the bet book is dated 24th December 1815, at Camp Bullwee in the Presidency of Bengal, when Lieut.-Colonel Nicol bets with Major Carlyon one dozen of Madeira there will be no British Troops serving in France on the 1st January 1816, except those under orders for England.

The fourth bet in the book, made at the same camp on the 15th January 1816, records that Major Carlyon bets Captain Jordan three bottles of Madeira that Buonaparte will be sent to St. Helena.

The Bets may, in the main, be classified under the following headings :

  (i) Sport.
  (ii) Physical feats.
  (iii) Dimensions.
  (iv) Professional matters.
  (v) Marriage.

Many bets have been made over sporting matters, from donkey and pony races to the classics, while yacht racing, shooting, and games in general figure largely under this heading.

Physical feats are numerous, from Khud Races to races to the Cookhouse and back, and such minor matters as balancing a coin on the edge of a wineglass.

Dimensions have a peculiar charm as subjects for bets, many being made regarding the height, etc., of Mess Rooms and articles of furniture, while a more personal note can be found in respect of the dimensions of individuals.

Professional matters constantly appear and cover prospective changes of station, promotions, examinations and such like.

Marriage often appears as a subject for a bet, and much speculation has taken place from time to time as to who the next member of the mess shall be to marry.

Surgeon Henry, the author of *Events of a Military Life*, often figures as the maker of a bet.

On the 14th August 1829 he bet Mr. Ross that he would not make a million dots with a pen in seven days. Surgeon Henry won the bet, but the book does not record who counted the dots.

The largest bet recorded in the book is of a " pype " of port, and this bet has given rise to subsequent bets as to the amount contained in a " pype."

It is noted in this case that the amounts differ in various decisions.

INDEX

A

Abingdon, Col., Earl of, 119
Ackroyd, Capt. H. (R.A.M.C.), gains V.C.,
  249, 261, 266, 278–280
Aldershot, at, 1, 113, 116, 206–208
Aldworth, Maj., 157, 164
Alexandria, at, 288
Allies, decorations : 166, 167.
  Dene, Lieut.-Col. A. P., 316
  Pike, Capt. S. A., 291
Armistice, The, 61, 112, 204, 245, 371
Armistice (Austria), 170
Armistice (Bulgaria), 314
Artillery, " ration," the, 124

B

Balfour, Col. J. H., 374–376
Banks, Lieut.-Col. T. M., 350–359
Banner, Commemoration, the, 408
Barker, Lieut.-Col. F. G., 116–117
Bartlett, Maj. C. F. N., 318–325
Battalions :
1st Battalion, 1–64, 116, 127, 133, 246, 285,
  392, 396, 402
  Ablainzeville, raid at, 53
  Aisne, The, 6–7
  Aldershot, 1, 116
  Ancre, The, retirement to, 50
  Armistice, The, 61
  Boiry St. Martin, trenches, 52
  Boom Ravine, action, 31–32
  Bourlon Wood, 37–47
  Cambrai, 37
  Coats, great, lost, 5, 6
  Commissions, N.C.O.'s, to, 13, 14
  Cuinchy, trenches, 17–24
  Delville Wood, attack on, 27–28
  Distinguished Service Order, 31
  Ervillers, attack on, 54–56
  Escarmain, arrival at, 61
  Flesquières, re-organized at, 59
  Florenville, captured, 59

  1st Battalion, France, arrival in, 2
  George V., H.M. King, inspection by, 1
  Gheluvelt, evacuated, 10
  Givenchy, 14–17, 21, 37
  Hulluch, quarries, 22
  Irles, at, 32
  Longueval, 27
  Marne, The, crossed, 5
  Mary, H.M. Queen, 1
  Medals :
    Distinguished Conduct, 16
    Military, 42
  Military Cross, 31
  Mobilization, 1, 116
  Mons, near, 2
    Retreat from, 2–5
  Nord, Canal du, 57–58
  Offensive, final, begins, 53
  Officers, list of, 1–2
  Oppy Wood, 33–36
  Persia, N. (1919–21), 61–64, 113
  Rhine, The, march to, 61
  Richebourg l'Avoué, 18–20
  Rifle-fire, superiority of, 6, 46
  St. Quentin Canal, crossed, 57–58
  St. Simeon, near, 5
  Sea, Race for the, 7
  Serre, 29–31
  Somme, The, Battle of, commences, 25
  Souchez, at, 24–25
  Strength, 5, 24, 36, 37, 52, 61
  Trench warfare, beginning of, 7
  Turner, 2nd Lieut. A. B., gains V.C., 22–24
  Victoria Cross, The :
    Turner, 2nd Lieut. A. B., 22–24
    Welch, Lce.-Cpl. J., 35
  Welch, Lce.-Cpl. J., gains V.C., 35
  Ypres, First Battle of, 7–14
2nd Battalion, 2, 21, 65–115, 119, 285
  Aisne, The, 106–108
  Amiens, enemy offensive at, 98
  Armistice, The, 112
  Ath, quartered at, 113

2nd Battalion, Bacquerot, Rue, 68
　Bellewaarde Ridge, 93–94
　Béthune, at, 82
　Bois Grenier, 75–78
　Bridoux, Le, 76–78
　Castel, counter-attack, 102–103
　Casualties, percentage of, 81
　Curlu, inspection at, 86–87
　Douai, pursuit to, 112
　Enghien, reached, 113
　England, arrival in, 66
　Estaires, 67, 68, 75, 79
　Fauquissart, trenches, 67–72
　France, arrival in, 66
　Gouzeaucourt Wood, 88, 89
　Hindenburg Line, 87, 88
　India, leaves, 65
　Marne, The, 106
　Medals presented, 111
　Mobilization completed, 67
　Moreuil Wood, 102–103
　Neuve Chapelle, 67–75
　Officers, list of, 66–67
　Organization, four-company, 65
　Ovillers, attack on, 80–81
　Quéant-Drocourt Line, occupied, 112
　Rancourt, at, 85
　Reading, civic reception, 113
　Rosières, 101–102
　Russia, N., detachment in (1919), 113–115
　Scarpe, River, 112
　Sercus, at, 79
　Sights, telescopic, introduced, 75
　Somme, The, Battle of, 79–85, 99
　Strength, 66, 81, 94, 101, 108
　Vermelles, trenches, 82
　Villers Bretonneux, 104–105
　Villers-Guislains, captured, 89
　Vimy Ridge, 109
　Winchester, at, 66
　Ypres, Third Battle of, 91–97
3rd Battalion (S.R.), 116–119, 399
　Colours, The, 402
　Cosham, at, 116
　Demobilization, 118
　Disembodiment, 119
　Dublin, quartered at, 116–119
　" Pivotal men," 118
　Plate—mess, the, 119
　Portsmouth, at, 116
　Reservists called up, 116
　Statistics, 117, 119
　Strength, 116, 117
1st/4th Battalion (T.), 120–171, 173, 208
　Albert, 150–151

1st/4thBattalion(T.), Ancre,The, Battle of,150
　Arras, Battle of, 157
　Artillery, " ration," the, 124
　Bailleul, at, 127
　Beaumont Hamel, trenches, 149, 153, 156
　Cassel, arrival at, 122
　Casualties, 152, 163
　Chelmsford, at, 121–122
　Commissions, N.C.O.'s, to, 150
　Company, double, adopted, 121
　Couin, at, 138–141
　Distinguished Service Order, 150
　Doullens, 128
　Epéhy, near, 154
　Foreign-service, volunteers for, 120–121
　France, arrival in, 122
　　Italy, to, 164
　Gheer, Le, at, 123
　Gommecourt, 129–133, 140, 150
　Hardships, campaign, 134, 159
　Hearts, blue, 139, 150
　Hébuterne, 128–136, 150
　Hindenburg Line, 154–158
　Italy, The Campaign in, 164–171
　　Armistice, 170
　　Asiago Plateau, 165–171
　　Cornedo, plains at, 166
　　Croce Bigolina S., at, 165
　　Enemy, plight of, 170
　　Monte Catz, assaulted, 169–170
　　Montello, area, 165
　　Nogaro, in billets at, 165
　　Paviola, departure to, 165
　　Saletto, detrained at, 164
　　Vigalzano Village, 170
　Lapugnoy, marched to, 127
　Loos, 127, 131
　Marlow, in camp, at, 120
　Medals :
　　Distinguished Conduct, 125, 143, 147,
　　　149, 167
　　Military, 138, 147, 149, 153, 158
　Military Cross, 125, 138, 142, 144, 150, 153,
　　155, 156, 161, 166, 167
　Mobilization orders, 120
　Ovillers, 141–148
　Pozières, at, 141–143, 147
　Peronne, entered, 154
　Ploegsteert, shelled, 123–126
　Portsmouth, quartered at, 120
　Ronssoy, at, 155–157
　Second Battalion, raised, 121
　Serre Village, 129
　Somme, The, 153–159
　Strength, 120, 134, 135, 148, 152, 158, 161

1st/4th Battalion (T.), Swindon, concentration at, 120
  Thiepval, attack on, 140–149
  Trench-warfare, instruction in, 122–123
  Vimy Ridge, 163
  Ypres, Second Battle of, 124–126
    Third Battle of, begins, 157
2nd/4th Battalion (T.), 121, 147, 162, 172–204
  Armistice, The, 204
  Arras, at, 189–190
  Bapaume, detrained at, 190
  Berguette, billeted, 175
  Bernerain, at, 204
  Bihécourt, attack on, 181–183
  Bouzincourt, trenches, 180
  Brigades—three Battalions, 199
  Cambrai, Battle of, 190–193
  Chelmsford, moved to, 174
  Doullens, marched to, 203
  Equipment, dearth of, 172, 173
  Estaires, evacuated, 202
  Ferme du Bois, 176
  Fransu, marched to, 204
  Gouzeaucourt, entrenched at, 190–191
  Hindenburg Line, advance to, 181
  Hitcham, billeted at, 172–173
  Laventie, trenches, 175–179
  Maidenhead, quartered at, 173
  Maissemy, counter-attack at, 194–195
  Marcelcave, concentration at, 197
  Medals :
    Distinguished Conduct, 186
    Military, 187
    Presented, 189
  Mezières Village, 196
  Military Cross, 188, 189
  Monchy le Preux, trenches, 185
  Nieppe Forest, 199
  Northampton, billeted at, 173–174
  Offensive, the final, 199–204
  Officers, list of, 174–175
  Prisoners-of-War, guarded, 173
  Rifles, Japanese, issued, 174
  Robecq, neighbourhood of, 198
  Robermetz, 202
  Rosières, at, 193
  Rouge de Bout, withdrawal to, 203
  Roye, re-organization at, 196
  St. Quentin, retreat from, 193–195
  Strength, 173, 174
  Varennes, at, 180
  Villers Bretonneux, 197
  Ypres, Third Battle of, 185–189
5th Battalion (S.), 21, 116, 126–127, 141, 145, 205–247, 248, 285, 402

5th Battalion (S.), Aldershot, at, 206–208
  Armistice, The, 245
  Arras, 219–225
  Aveluy Wood, 233–234
  Battalion raised, 205
  Beaumont Hamel, 236–238
  Béthune, at, 213, 214, 232
  Cambrai, Battle of, 227–232
  Colours, The, 246, 402
  Demobilization, 245–247
  Difficulties, initial, 205–206
  Drocourt-Quèant Line, 244
  Distinguished Service Order, 232
  Epéhy, attack, 241–243
  Erre, quartered at, 246
    Colour, presented, 246
  Festubert, near, 213
  Flines, in billets, 245
  France, arrival in, 208
  George, H.M. King, visit by, 207
  Givenchy, trenches, 213
  Hindenburg Line, 228
  Loos, Battle of, 209–213
  Medals :
    Distinguished Conduct, 237
    Military, 237
  Military Cross, 214, 232
  Nurlu, capture of, 241
  Officers, list of, 207–208, 247
  Ovillers la Boisselle, 215–219
  Pozières, trenches, 218
  Reading, return to, 246
  Shorncliffe, at, 205
  Somme, The, Battle of, 215
  Strength, 205, 218, 232, 236, 238
  Vimy Ridge, area, 244
  Wales, H.R.H. Prince of :
    Colour, presents, 246
    Inspection by, 245
6th Battalion (S.), 248–285, 341, 402
  Ackroyd, Capt. H. (R.A.M.C.), 249, 261, 266, 278–280
    gains V.C., 278–279
  Aveluy, at, 267, 272
  Boisselle, La, trenches, 250–251
  Boom Ravine, 267–272
  Bouzincourt, instruction at, 250
  Casualties, percentage of, 274
  Chérisy, trenches, 272–274
  Clothing, shortage of, 248
  Codford, at, 249–250
  Cojeul River, 272–274
  Colchester, training at, 248–249
  Colours, The, 402
  Courcelette, trenches, 266

6th Battalion (S.), Delville Wood, 258–266
  Disbandment, 252, 284–285
  Formation, 248
  France, arrival in, 250
  Gas, effect of, 250
  Glencorse Wood, 275–280
  Hindenburg Line, 272
  Houthulst Forest, 284
  Irles, at, 272
  Longueval, at, 258–262
  Medals :
    Distinguished Conduct, 257
    Presented, 267
  Military Cross, 267
  Montauban, 253–258
  Officers, list of, 249
  Poelcappelle, attack on, 280–283
  Shorncliffe, at, 248–249
  Somme, The, Battle of, 252–262
  Strength, 258, 265
  Thiepval, capture of, 262–267
  Victoria Cross, The :
    Ackroyd, Capt. H. (R.A.M.C.), 278–279
  Ypres, Third Battle of, 274–284
7th Battalion (S.), 286–317, 374, 402
  Alexandria, at, 288
  Armistice, 314
  Batum, shipped to, 316
  Bulgaria, occupation of, 314–316
  Cakli Village, 303–304
  Colours, The, 402
  Constantinople, quartered at, 317
  Decorations, Allies, 291, 316
  Demobilization, 317
  Distinguished Service Order, 316
  Dobritch, at, 315–316
  Doiran, 289–296, 304, 312
  Formation, 286
  Fovant, at, 286
  France, in, 286–287
  Gagri, relief to, 316
  Izlis, reached, 313, 314
  Jumeaux Ravine, 291–301
  Macukovo Ravine, 307–312
  Malaria, outbreak, 289, 305
  Marseilles, at, 288
  Military Cross, 294
  Mustafa Pasha, at, 315
  Officers, list of, 287
  Petit Couronné, advance, 291, 299–303
  Raids, 306–312
  Reading, raised at, 286
  Rustchuk, reached, 315
  Salisbury area, the, 286
  Salonika, arrival at, 288

7th Battalion (S.), Selimli Ravine, 304–306
  Smol Hill, 304–312
  Strength, 288
  Tiflis, at, 316
  Vardar River, 289–294, 304–312
  Varna, encamped at, 316
  Warminster, at, 286
8th Battalion (S.), 285, 318–373, 402
  Amiens, defence of, 348
  Armistice, The, 371, 373
  Bazentin-le-Grand, 335, 336, 356
  Bazentin-le-Petit, 331, 332, 336, 337, 372
  Boisselle, La, attack on, 355, 372, 373
  Casualties, total, 373
  Cateau, Le, 365, 371, 373
  Codford, at, 318, 371
  Colours, The, 402
  Contalmaison, trenches, 328–332, 372
  Delville Wood, 357–358
  Disbandment, 371
  Draft, accident to, 363
  Epéhy, reached, 363, 364
  Formation, 318
  France, arrival in, 320
  Generosity of the public, 318
  Gentelles, shelled, 348
  Godewaerswelde, at, 337
  Houthulst Forest, 340–342, 372
  Hulluch, attack on, 321–323, 371, 372
  Lempire Village, attack on, 363–364, 372
  Lillers, at, 324–326
  Loos, 325, 327, 371, 372
  Mametz Wood, 329–334, 356–357
  Martinpuich, 332–333
  Measles, epidemic of, 336
  Medals :
    Distinguished Conduct, 325, 326
    Military, 326
    Presented, 340
  Military Cross, 325, 326, 340, 356
  Mormal Forest, 366–371, 373
  Nieuport-les-Bains, 337–338, 372
  Officers, list of, 319–320
  Ovillers, attack on, 355
  Peronne, near, 337
  Poelcappelle, 339–340
  Reading, in billets, 318, 371
  Ronssoy, at, 363–364, 373
  St. Pierre Vaast, trenches, 361–362, 372
  Sea, flank on the, 338
  Somme, The, Battle of, 328
  Strength, 320, 326, 337, 341, 344, 347, 350, 351, 352, 373
  Summary of service, 371–373
  Supplies, shortage of, 318

8th Battalion (S.), Trônes Wood, 356–360, 373
   Warminster, at, 319–320, 371
9th Battalion (R.), 117, 374
   Bovington Camp, 374
   Strength, 374
10th Battalion (L.), 374–376
   Labour Corps, incorporated in, 375
   Measles, outbreak of, 375
   Port, base, duties at, 375
   Portsmouth, organized at, 374
   Rouen, arrival at, 375
   Strength, 374
11th Battalion (L.), 376
12th Battalion (L.), 376
13th Battalion (L.), 376
1st Garrison (Home) Battalion, 376
Battle-Honours, 377, 396, 402–405
Batum, shipped to, 316
Beer, Lieut.-Col. J. H., 176–178
Bell, Rev. C., killed, 54, 56
Berkshire Regt., R., 1–410
Bet book, the, 409–410
Bland, Lieut. G. F. R., murdered, 114
Bodle, Lieut.-Col. W., 376
Bovington Camp, at, 374
Boyle, Lieut.-Col. C. R. C., 198
Bray, Lieut.-Col. R. E. T., 287
Brett, Maj. R. J., 52, 61
Brigades, three Battalions, 99, 199
Bulgaria, occupation of, 314–316

C

Campbell, Lieut.-Col. R., 374
Carleton, Lieut.-Col. C. A. S., 339
Casualties, percentage of, 81, 274
Caucasus, The, 316
Chatham, at, 61
Chelmsford, at, 121–122, 174
Children, entertainment to, 112
Clarke, Lieut.-Col. R. J., 133, 145, 146, 150,
   152, 164, 165
Clay, Lieut.-Col. B. G., 250, 252, 257, 268, 271
Clothing, shortage of, 172, 173, 205, 248, 286,
   318
Codford, at, 249, 250, 286, 318, 371
Colchester, 248–249
Colonels, Succession of, 379
Colours, The, 246, 389, 400–402, 409
   3rd Battalion, 402
   5th Battalion, King's, The :
      Deposited, 246, 402
      Presented, 246
   6th Battalion, 402
   7th Battalion, 402
   8th Battalion, 402

Commissions, N.C.O.'s to, 13, 150
Comrades, Old, Association, 246, 406–407
Conscription, in force, 144
Constantinople, quartered at, 316
Cosham, at, 116
Crowborough, training at, 113
Cruttwell, Capt. C. R. M. F., 120–171

D

Dalby, Lieut.-Col. T. G., 325–327, 331
Decorations, Allies, 166, 167, 291, 316
Dene, Lieut.-Col. A. P., 288, 289, 298–305,
   312–316
Dennis, Lieut.-Col. T. V. B., 2, 70, 226, 227
Depot, The, 113, 116, 119, 408
Dewing, Lieut.-Col. R. E., 339, 343–350
Dickson, Maj.-Gen. E. T., 18, 71, 379, 392,
   402, 408
Dimmer, Lieut.-Col. J. H. S., 190–195
Distinguished Service Order, 31, 150, 232, 316
Divisions :
   First Seven—Commemoration Banner, 408
   47th : 25, 38–40, 44, 46, 50, 122, 361
   56th : 44, 46, 135, 136, 141
   58th : 241
Dobritch, at, 315–316
Dowell, Lieut.-Col. A. J. W., 248–252
Drafts, lack of training, 144–145
Dublin, quartered at, 116–119
Dunstable, at, 121

E

Elwell, Rev. W., wounded, 84
Enemy, the :
   Deceiving, 125
   Misinformed, 43
   Well informed, 132, 152
Equipment, shortage of, 172, 173, 205, 248,
   286, 318
Equipment and uniform, 388–399
Establishments, sanctioned, 380–387

F

Facings, Regimental, 397–399
Fanshawe, Gen. Sir R., 7, 21, 126, 156, 157,
   167
Farmers, generosity of, 121
Feetham, Lieut.-Col. E., 66–71
Finch, Maj. H. M., 1, 4, 10–14, 72, 74, 406
FitzHugh, Col. E., 250, 283, 285
Foley, Lieut.-Col. F. W., 116–118, 205–213,
   246–249
Fovant, in huts, 286

France and Flanders, 2–61, 66–113, 122–164, 175–204, 208–246, 250–285, 287–288, 320–373, 375
France to Salonika, 288
Francis, Lieut.-Col. S. G., 63
French, F.-M. Sir J., 72, 323, 325
French Army, attached to, 105–108
Frizell, Lieut.-Col. C. W., 1, 13, 18, 22–24, 263

G

Gamble, Lieut.-Col. R. N., 406
Garrison Battalion :
  1st (Home), 376
Gas, effect of, 250
  mustard, casualties from, 48
George V., H.M. King :
  Inspection by, 1
  Presentation from, 392
  Visit by, 207
Godley, Lieut.-Gen. Sir A. J., congratulations from, 356
Goodland, Lieut.-Col. H. T., 247
Graham, Lieut.-Col. M. D., 1, 10, 12, 392, 408
Great War, The, 1–61, 65–113, 116–376, 402, 404–405, 408
Grenades, hand, primitive, 69
Griffin, Lieut.-Col. J. A. A., 103–108

H

Haig, F.-M. Sir D., 44–47
Haig, Lieut.-Col. R., 82–92, 101
Haking, Gen., inspection by, 165
Hanbury, Col. L. H., 172–174
Hanbury-Sparrow, Lieut.-Col. A. A. H., 1–10, 82–96
Harvey, Maj. R. P., 71–74
Hill, Maj. C. G., 16–21
Hincks, Maj. T. C., 249–252
Hitcham, billeted at, 172–173
Holdsworth, Lieut.-Col. A. M., 79–81, 116
Honours—Battle, 377, 396, 402–405
Horne, Gen. :
  Guard-of-Honour to, 245
  Praised by, 21
Hudson, Lieut.-Col. N. B., 351, 354, 367, 369, 371
Hunt, Lieut.-Col. G. P. S., 37–41, 50–52, 66, 69, 75–79

I

India to France, 65–67
Ironside, Maj.-Gen. Sir E., 63, 113–114
Isaac, Lieut.-Col. A. G. F., 110
Italy, The Campaign in, 164–171

J

Japanese rifles, issued, 174
Joicey-Cecil, Lieut.-Col. Lord P. J., 376

K

Kitchener, F.-M. Lord, inspection by, 206, 207

L

Labour Battalions :
  10th Battalion, 374–376
  11th Battalion, 376
  12th Battalion, 376
  13th Battalion, 376
Lawrence, Brig.-Gen. R.C.B., 376
Lloyd Baker, Lieut.-Col., 166
Longhurst, Lieut.-Col. H. G. F., 249, 250, 254, 281, 282

M

McArthur, Maj. V. G., 249, 250, 254, 283
McClintock, Brig.-Gen. W. K., 208, 406
Macdonald, Maj., 113
Macedonia, 288–314
Maidenhead, quartered at, 173
Marks, Maj. J. B., 287, 298, 314–317
Marlow, in camp, at, 120
Mary, H.M. Queen, 1
Maxse, Lieut.-Gen. Sir I., 248, 250, 267, 339
Medals :
  Distinguished Conduct, 16, 125, 143, 147, 149, 167, 186, 237, 257, 325, 326
  Military, 42, 138, 147, 149, 153, 158, 187, 237, 326
  Presented, 111, 267, 340
Mess :
  Furniture, 409
  Plate, 119, 409
Message, cordial, a, 213,
Military Cross, 31, 115, 125, 138, 142, 144, 150, 153, 155, 156, 161, 166, 167, 188, 189, 214, 232, 266, 267, 294, 325, 326, 340, 356
Monro, Gen. Sir C., 2, 128, 130, 214, 250
Morrell, Lieut.-Col. J. F. B., 305
Mudge, Lieut.-Col. A., 61

N

Nicolls, Lieut.-Col. E. H. J., 226–236
North, Lieut.-Col. P. W., 117–119
Northampton, billeted at, 173–174
Nugent, Capt. C., in command, 75

O

Oates, Lieut.-Col. W. G., 198
Officers, lists of, 1–2, 66–67, 174–175, 207–208, 249, 287, 319–320
Old Comrades Association, 246, 406–407
Organization, "four-company," adopted, 65, 121

P

Pearce-Serocold, Col. O., 120, 133
Pereira, Gen., congratulations by, 43
Persia, N., 1st Battalion (1919–21), 61–64, 113
　Baghdad, entrained for, 64
　Basra, reached, 61
　Ganagh, at, 63–64
　Gravesend, embarked at, 61
　Karind Village, 61–62
　Kasvin, at, 62–64
　Kuhin, move to, 63
　Quaraitu, railhead, 64
Pike, Pte., exploit of, 187–188
Portsmouth, at, 116, 120, 374
Poulton-Palmer, Lieut. R., 123–124
Plate, officers', 119, 409
Plumer, Gen., inspection by, 165
Public, generosity of, 121, 318
Pugh, Capt., in command, 50
Pulteney, Lieut.-Gen. Sir W., inspection, 76

R

Ransome, Lieut.-Col. A. L., 348
Rawlinson, Lieut.-Gen. Sir H. S., 66, 113, 115, 325, 352
Reading, 113, 116, 120, 173, 246, 286, 318, 371, 402, 406
Ready, Maj. F. F., 1
Recreations, 109, 112, 118, 135, 246
Regiments :
　7th Dragoon Guards, 250
　11th Hussars, 193
　15th Hussars, 3

　Guides Cavalry, The, 62, 63

　R.H.A., " A " Battery, 63

　Argyll and Sutherland Highlanders, 109, 123, 151
　Bedfordshire, 267, 279, 370
　Berkshire, R., 1–379, 402–410
　Black Watch, 321–338, 349
　Border, 235
　Buckinghamshire, 122, 131, 133, 143, 145, 161–170, 175–185, 192, 199

Regiments :
　Cambridgeshire, 176, 241, 242
　Cameron Highlanders, 316, 321, 325, 331–341, 368
　Cheshire, 107
　Coldstream Guards, 209
　Connaught Rangers, 10
　Cornwall L.I., 50, 199, 260, 288
　Devonshire, 68, 80, 113, 114, 299
　Dorsetshire, 325
　Dublin Fusiliers, R., 123
　Durham L.I., 105, 107, 117, 184
　Essex, 205, 207, 217–242, 250–279, 341–371
　Fusiliers, R., 27–67, 213, 220, 232–244, 254, 324
　Gloucestershire, 12, 71, 122, 128, 130, 135, 141, 144, 148, 155, 166, 175, 176, 181–199, 204, 288–295, 303, 305, 316, 321–333, 349
　Gordon Highlanders, 27, 321, 322
　Grenadier Guards, 52
　Hampshire, 113, 114, 123, 374
　Highland L.I., 10, 60, 116
　Inniskilling Fusiliers, R., 214
　Irish Fusiliers, R., 62
　Irish Rifles, R., 66, 68, 73, 80–86, 93, 96, 123
　Kent, E., 264, 282, 365
　Kent, R.W., 234, 241, 283, 341–369
　King's Royal Rifles, 2–7, 13, 16, 20–38, 50–60, 76, 226, 325
　Lancashire, E., 90, 102–110
　Lancashire, Loyal N., 92
　Lancashire, S., 107
　Leicestershire, 83, 116
　Lincolnshire, 66–99, 219, 277, 278, 329
　Liverpool, 2–9, 16, 20, 24, 30, 53, 79, 278, 368
　London, 66, 68, 74, 125, 162, 235, 240, 241, 280, 324
　Manchester, 275, 278
　Middlesex, 150, 162, 223, 280
　Munster Fusiliers, R., 335
　Norfolk, 150, 207, 209, 213, 222–225, 230, 242, 250–285
　Northamptonshire, 94, 150, 234, 242, 340, 355, 367
　Northumberland Fusiliers, 60
　Oxfordshire and Buckinghamshire L.I., 113–116, 122, 125, 128, 133, 135, 142–146, 155, 156, 162, 166, 170, 178, 184–199, 288–317
　Rifle Brigade, 65–112, 185, 244, 402
　Scots, R., 114, 133
　Scots Fusiliers, R., 27, 260
　Scottish Borderers, K.O., 27

Regiments :
  Scottish Rifles, 68, 74, 96
  Seaforth Highlanders, 123
  Sherwood Foresters, 78, 101, 105, 158, 198, 266, 363, 365
  Somerset L.I., 51
  Staffordshire, S., 2–17, 54, 57
  Suffolk, 200, 207, 214–230, 250–285
  Surrey, E., 67, 147, 148, 161, 226, 264, 356, 401
  Surrey, R.W., 165, 241, 243, 282, 354, 370, 402
  Sussex, R., 67, 70, 148, 150, 220, 223, 232–244
  Wales, S., Borderers, 15, 289
  Warwickshire, R., 113, 123, 140, 143, 148, 154, 155, 176, 192
  Welch, 339, 402
  Welch Fusiliers, R., 260
  Wiltshire, 14, 67, 163
  Worcestershire, 7, 10, 22, 85, 90, 163, 288, 294–296, 302, 308, 312–315, 367, 402
  York and Lancaster, 62, 78
  Yorkshire, 328
  Yorkshire L.I., 78
  Yorkshire, W., 109, 137

  2nd Gurkha Rifles, 63
  10th Jats, 316
Regular Battalions :
  1st Battalion, 1–64, 116, 127, 133, 246, 285, 392, 396, 402
  2nd Battalion, 2, 21, 65–115, 119, 285
Reserve, life in, 125–126
Reserve Battalion :
  9th Battalion, 117, 374
Reservists equipped, 116
Rhine, The, march to, 61
Rifle-fire, superiority of, 6, 46
Rifles :
  Japanese issued, 174
  Shortage of, 286, 318
  Telescopic sights, with, 75
Rouen, port-duties at, 375
Russia, N., 2nd Battalion (1919), 113–115
  Archangel :
    arrival at, 113
    evacuated, 115
  Beresink, advanced base, 114–115
  Crowborough, at, 113
  Koslova, at, 114
  Military Cross, 115
  Onega, near, 115
  Oust Vaga, raided, 114
  Southampton, embarked at, 113

S

Salisbury area, the, 249, 250, 286, 318, 371
Salkeld, Lieut.-Col. R. E., 178–180
Salonika Front, The, 288–314
Sarrail, Gen., 295
Sea, the :
  Flank on, 338
  Race for, 7
Searle, Bt.-Col. A. E. S., 376
Service Battalions :
  5th Battalion, 21, 116, 126–127, 141, 145, 205–247, 248, 285, 402
  6th Battalion, 248–285, 341, 402
  7th Battalion, 286–317, 374, 402
  8th Battalion, 285, 318–373, 402
Shorncliffe, 205, 248, 249
Signs, divisional, 139, 150
Smith-Dorrien, Lieut.-Gen. Sir H., 122
Smoke helmets donned, 209, 281
Special Reserve :
  3rd Battalion, 2, 116–119, 399
Statistics, 117, 119
Strength, 5, 24, 36, 37, 52, 61, 66, 81, 94, 101, 108, 116, 117, 120, 134, 135, 148, 152, 158, 173, 174, 205, 218, 232, 236, 238, 258, 265, 288, 320, 326, 337, 341, 344, 347, 350–352, 373, 374
Stirling, Lieut.-Col. C. R. H., 96–103

T

Territorial Battalions :
  1st/4th Battalion, 120–171, 173, 208
  2nd/4th Battalion, 121, 147, 162, 172–204
Thornton, Lieut.-Col. W. B., 61, 66, 70
Tiflis, at, 316
Tosetti, Maj. D., 319, 323, 344, 347
Training, lack of, 144–145
Trench warfare, beginning of, 7
Trenches, condition of, 68, 69, 79, 124, 125, 134, 213, 214, 284, 341
Truce, Christmas, informal, 69
Turner, 2nd Lieut. A. B., gains V.C., 22–24

U

Uniform, shortage of, 173, 205, 248, 286, 318
Uniform and equipment, 388–399

V

Varna, in camp at, 316
Victoria Cross, The :
  Ackroyd, Capt. H. (R.A.M.C.), 278–279
  Turner, 2nd Lieut. A. B., 22–24
  Welch, Lce.-Cpl. J., 35

W

Wales, H.R.H. Prince of :
Colour, presents, 246, 402
Inspection by, 245
Walker, Maj.-Gen. H. B., 402
Walton, Lieut.-Col. W. C., 318–324
War, The Great, 1–61, 65–113, 116–376, 402, 404–405, 408
Warminster, at, 286, 319, 320, 371
Warr, Maj., in command, 354, 359
Waterworth, Maj. G. F., 198

Welch, Lce.-Cpl. J., gains V.C., 35
Western Front, the, 2–61, 66–113, 122–164, 175–204, 208–246, 250–285, 287–288, 320–373, 375
Weston, Sir A. Hunter, complimented by, 138
Wheeler, Lieut.-Col. M., 174–176
Willan, Lieut.-Col. F. G., 215, 217, 221, 226
Willink, Capt. G. O. W., in command, 196
Winchester, at, 66
Winter, hardships of, 151
Wounded, left behind, 94, 329

1914–1918

THE GREAT WAR

THE ROYAL BERKSHIRE REGIMENT

1919–1921   1919
NORTH PERSIA   NORTH RUSSIA

CHINA

ROYAL BERKSHIRE REGIMENT

Lightning Source UK Ltd.
Milton Keynes UK
UKOW022354310113

205660UK00002B/10/P